Global Education Policy and International Development

Global Education Policy and International Development

New Agendas, Issues and Policies

EDITED BY

ANTONI VERGER,

MARIO NOVELLI AND

HÜLYA KOSAR ALTINYELKEN

B L O O M S B U R Y

LONDON • NEW DELHI • NEW YORK • SYDNEY

Bloomsbury Academic
An imprint of Bloomsbury Publishing Plc

50 Bedford Square	175 Fifth Avenue
London	New York
WC1B 3DP	NY 10010
UK	USA

www.bloomsbury.com

First published 2012

© Antoni Verger, Mario Novelli, Hülya Kosa Altinyelken and contributors, 2012

British Library Cataloguing-in-Publication Data
A catalogue record for this book is available from the British Library.

ISBN: HB: 978-1-1441-4390-7
PB: 978-1-4411-6983-9
PDF: 978-1-4411-3035-8
ePub: 978-1-4411-7090-3

Library of Congress Cataloging-in-Publication Data
Global education policy and international development : new agendas, issues, and policies / edited by Antoni Verger, Mario Novelli and Hülya Kosa Altinyelken.
p. cm.
Includes bibliographical references and index.
ISBN 978-1-4411-4390-7-- ISBN 978-1-4411-6983-9-- ISBN 978-1-4411-3035-8--
ISBN 978-1-4411-7090-3
1. Education--Economic aspects--Developing countries. 2. Education and state--Developing countries. 3. Education and globalization--Developing countries. 4. Economic development--Developing countries. I. Verger, Antoni, 1975- II. Novelli, Mario. III. Altinyelken, Hülya K.
LC67.D44G56 2012
338.4'337091724--dc23
2012005874

Typeset by Fakenham Prepress Solutions, Fakenham, Norfolk NR21 8NN
Printed and bound in India

CONTENTS

NOTES ON CONTRIBUTORS

Hülya Kosa Altinyelken is a lecturer and researcher at the Child Development and Education Department of the University of Amsterdam (UvA), the Netherlands. Her research engages with issues such as gender, migration, educational policy transfer, educational reforms, pedagogy and teachers. She has published in journals such as *Journal of Education Policy, Comparative Education* and *International Journal of Educational Development.*

Xavier Bonal is Special Professor in Education and International Development at the UvA and Associate Professor in Sociology at the Universitat Autònoma de Barcelona. He is Director of the Social Policy Research Group (Seminari d'Anàlisi de Polítiques Socials, SAPS) at the Department of Sociology of the same institution. He has published widely in national and international journals and is author of several books on the sociology of education, education policy and globalization, education and development.

Roger Dale is currently Professor of Sociology of Education at the University of Bristol and at the University of Auckland. Roger has had a distinguished career, and published widely on the state and education, processes of globalization and regionalisation, and the governance of education. Roger is also founding co-editor (with Susan Robertson) of the journal, *Globalisation, Societies and Education.*

D. Brent Edwards Jr. is a PhD candidate in International Education Policy at the University of Maryland, College Park. In addition to the Decentralisation of and participation in education governance, his research focuses on the involvement and interaction of international, national and local level actors in processes of education policy formation. His publications have appeared in journals such as *Research in Comparative and International Education; Policy Futures in Education; Education, Citizenship, and Social Justice; Comparative Education Review* and *The Urban Review.*

Anja P. Jakobi, Dr phil., is senior researcher at the Peace Research Institute, Frankfurt (PRIF/HSFK) and project co-director at the DFG Cluster of Excellence 'The Formation of Normative Orders'. She has been working on international institutions, world society and global political change. Recent publications include *International Organizations and Lifelong Learning: From Global Agendas to Policy Diffusion* (2009, Palgrave), *Mechanisms of OECD Governance. International Incentives for National Policy Making?* (2010, Oxford University Press, co-editor) and articles published e.g. in *Comparative Education Review, Compare, European Educational Research Journal* or *Zeitschrift für Pädagogik*.

Steven J. Klees is the R. W. Benjamin Professor of International and Comparative Education at the University of Maryland. Prof. Klees' work examines the political economy of education and development with specific research interests in globalization, neoliberalism, and education; the role of aid agencies; education, human rights and social justice; the education of disadvantaged populations; the role of class, gender and race in reproducing and challenging educational and social inequality; and alternative approaches to education and development.

Mieke T. A. Lopes Cardozo is a researcher and lecturer at the Amsterdam Institute for Social Science Research of the University of Amsterdam, in the framework of the 'IS-Academie' – a co-funded project of the University of Amsterdam and the Dutch Ministry of Foreign Affairs. Within the field of Education, Development and Conflict, her publications focus on the themes of social justice, international education and conflict policies, teacher training, teacher agency, progressive education reforms, critical approaches to multicultural and intercultural education and decolorisation debates.

Mario Novelli is Senior Lecturer in Education and International Development at the University of Sussex, UK. His research focuses on the intersections between globalization, education and international development, and most recently the relationship between education and conflict. He is particularly interested in the securitisation of aid and the relationship between geopolitics and international development assistance to education in conflict-affected states. He has published in journals such as the *International Journal of Educational Development; Globalisation, Societies* and *Education and Educational Review*.

Margriet Poppema is Senior Lecturer in Education and International Development at the Universiteit van Amsterdam. She teaches on Education and Development in Diverse Societies and on International Development. Her research focuses on education and decentralisation policies in post conflict societies, and on educational reforms in multicultural and plurilingual societies.

Xavier Rambla is Associate Professor in Sociology at the Universitat Autònoma de Barcelona. His research focuses on the interaction between education and social inequalities, as well as on the politics of the global educational agenda. Recently he has published his results in journals such as *Convergencia. Revista de Ciencias Sociales (Mx)* and *Journal of Education Policy (UK)*.

Susan L. Robertson is a Professor of Sociology of Education in the Graduate School of Education, University of Bristol. Her academic career has spanned four countries – Australia, Canada, New Zealand and England. She is founding Director of the Centre for Globalisation, Education and Societies (GES) at the University of Bristol as well as founding co-editor (with Roger Dale) of the journal *Globalisation, Societies and Education*. Her research is focused on the study of education and broader social, economic and political forces by analysing the complexities of globalising and regionalising projects, strategies and materialisations.

Renato Emerson dos Santos is a Professor of Human Geography in the Teachers Training College, State University of Rio de Janeiro (Brazil). His research is focused on the spatialities of social movements, cartographical activisms, Brazilian Black Movement's struggles in education, and geography teaching. He has published books in Brazil including *Diversity, Space and ethnic/race relations: blacks in Brazilian Geography* (2007) and *Social Movements and Geography: the spatialities of action (2011)*.

Yusuf Sayed is a Reader in International Education at the University of Sussex. He is also Research Associate at the Institute of Social and Economic Research, Rhodes University, South Africa. Yusuf is an education policy specialist with a career in international education and development research. Previously Yusuf was Senior Policy Analyst at the EFA Global Monitoring Report, UNESCO, Team Leader for Education and Skills, the Department for International Development UK, and Head of Department of Comparative Education at the University of the Western Cape, South Africa. He has published widely in international journals on education policy formulation and implementation as it relates to concerns of equity, social justice and transformation.

Inti Soeterik is researcher at the Amsterdam Institute for Social Sciences Research at the University of Amsterdam, the Netherlands. The focus of her work is on issues related to social justice; ethnicity/race issues and diversity; minorities; the role of social movements in education reforms; and teachers and teacher training. Currently she is undertaking a PhD research project on the inclusion of ethnicity/race issues in the contemporary Brazilian education curriculum.

Gita Steiner-Khamsi is Professor of Comparative and International Education at Teachers College, Columbia University in New York. Her most recent books are *World Yearbook of Education 2012 – Policy Borrowing and Lending in Education* (co-edited with Florian Waldow, Routledge, 2012), *South-South Cooperation in Education and Development* (co-edited with Linda Chisholm, Teachers College Press and HSRC Publisher, 2009). She has published several books and articles on globalization, transnational policy borrowing and lending, as well as school reform and teacher policy in developing countries, mostly in post-Soviet Central Asia and Mongolia. She was 2009/2010 President of the Comparative and International Education Society (CIES).

Daryl Stenvoll-Wells is an international education consultant with a focus on the arts and global citizenship. For fifteen years she has taught students of all ages, developed curricula for public and private education programmes, and spoken at international conferences on the importance of non-traditional education programming in reaching marginalized students. She completed an MA in Fine Art at Slade School of Fine Art, University College London, and an MA in International Education and Development at Sussex University. Daryl has designed and supervised education projects in India, the UK, the US and Kenya, and currently works as an education consultant in San Francisco, California.

Aina Tarabini is Lecturer in Sociology at the Universitat Autònoma de Barcelona and a member of the Interdisciplinary Group on Educational Policies (gipe-igep. org/). Her research deals with the sociology of education, educational inequalities and educational policies. Specifically, it is focused in three main topics: the effects of globalization on education policies and systems (both in northern and southern countries), the relationship between education policies and policies to fight poverty and the processes of 're-contextualization' of global agendas and national policies at the school level.

Elaine Unterhalter is Professor of Education and International Development at the Institute of Education, University of London, UK. She works on gender, education and international development, most recently co-ordinating a number of research projects in this area in South Africa, Kenya, Tanzania, Nigeria and Ghana, and selected global organisations. Her recent books include *Gender, schooling and global social justice* (2007) and the co-authored works *Towards equality? Gender in South African schools during the HIV and AIDS epidemic* (2009) and Global inequalities and higher education. Whose interests are we serving? (2010).

Sanne VanderKaaij currently works as a researcher for the ICICI Foundation for Inclusive Growth in India. Here she provides academic input to development projects aimed at improving the quality of education in government schools in India. In addition she is completing her PhD in International Development Studies at the University of Amsterdam. Her PhD research concerns private faith-based education in urban India, with a special focus on Muslim and Hindu schools.

Antoni Verger is a 'Ramon y Cajal' senior researcher at the Sociology Department of the Universitat Autònoma de Barcelona. His main areas of expertise are global education policy and international development, with a focus on the role of international organizations and transnational civil society networks, and privatisation and quasi-markets in education. He has published widely on these topics in international journals such as *Comparative Education Review, Globalization Societies and Education, British Journal of Sociology of Education, Journal of Education Policy* and *International Studies in Sociology of Education.*

ACKNOWLEDGEMENTS

This book has been possible due to the support, scholarly activity and financial assistance of a wide range of people and institutions. The idea of a book exploring the global governance of education first emerged during meetings of the IS-Academie 'Education Quality and International Development', based at the University of Amsterdam (2006–2011). The IS-Academie is a research and capacity-building partnership between the University of Amsterdam and the Dutch Ministry of Foreign Affairs, and the resources necessary for underpinning this publication were drawn from this programme. It is therefore, first and foremost, necessary to thank both of these institutions for the generous support and encouragement that they have provided. Many of the contributors to this publication were either full-time members of the team, and based at the University of Amsterdam, or scholars who have worked with us, in a variety of capacities, during the last five years.

Draft papers for this publication were presented in the workshop 'Global Education Policies and Policy Programmes' that took place in Istanbul on 13 June 2010, one day prior to the beginning of the 14th World Congress of Comparative Education Societies. We would like to thank all the participants in this workshop for a very rich day of debate and discussion. For great assistance in organising that event, the editors would like to acknowledge Joosje Hoop, our IS-Academy research assistant. Over the last year, as the book moved towards its conclusion, we would like to thank all the authors for their prompt responses to our emails, and the positive way in which they engaged with the feedback and suggestions we provided on their drafts. We would also like to congratulate them on the excellent quality of the chapters produced. We extend our appreciation to Roger Dale and Gita Steiner-Khamsi for reading the entire volume and writing a conclusion to it from their respective theoretical positions, under tight deadlines, and to Susan Robertson for her special contribution to the theoretical and methodological section of the book.

We would also like to acknowledge Claudia Talavera for copy-editing the chapters prior to them being sent to Continuum. Turning now to the Editorial Team at Continuum, we would like to thank Rosie Pattinson for her patience and understanding, and all the final copy-editing and publishing team for their excellent support and assistance. The quality of the final publication is a product of all the work and effort mentioned above, and as editors we would like to extend our gratitude to everyone for their different forms of participation. Finally, each of us, in our own way, would like to thank our families for their understanding and support. In the demanding academic environment that we operate in, this work has inevitably infringed on our free time, which should have been spent with them.

PART ONE

Introduction: Theoretical and Methodological Insights

CHAPTER ONE

Global Education Policy and International Development: An Introductory Framework

Antoni Verger, Mario Novelli and Hülya Kosa Altinyelken

About this book

Today, as we speak, similar education reforms and a common set of education policy jargon are being applied in many parts of the world, in locations that are incredibly diverse both culturally and in terms of economic development. Education policies and programmes such as child-centred pedagogies, school-based management, teachers' accountability, public-private partnerships or conditional-cash transfer schemes are being discussed and implemented everywhere, to the point that they have acquired the status of 'global education polices' (GEP). More and more researchers, coming from different disciplines and sub-disciplines such as comparative education, political sociology, anthropology and political sciences, are paying attention to the GEP phenomenon. Traditionally, scholars have used very diverse terms to refer to this phenomenon, among others policy diffusion, policy borrowing, policy transfer, policy travelling, isomorphism or convergence, among others.

However, paradoxically, existing research on GEP does not always incorporate processes of globalization into its analytical framework, at least in a comprehensive way. Quite often, research on the topic does not provide an account of how and why policies are globally constructed and settled in global agendas. They are focused on the *international* dimension of the policy process, i.e. they look at the transfer of policies 'within countries and across countries' (Stone 2004, p. 545) or as a 'boundary-crossing practice' (Peck *et al.* 2010, p. 169), but do not grasp the global dimension that education policy-making is now acquiring. Another habitual problem in the policy transfer literature is that it often implies a dichotomy between the local and the global 'levels' and represents them as separate layers of educational governance (Mukhopadhyay *et al.* 2011). When doing so, research fails to capture the complexity of global politics and the fact that different political scales are mutually constituted (Robertson *et al.* 2002). Furthermore, much research on GEP does not provide sufficiently rich empirical evidence on the interplay between processes of globalization and the re-contextualization of education policy in local places. Doing so is methodologically challenging, but if we attempt to understand education policies globally, the study of the complex relationships between global ideas, its dissemination and re-contextualization becomes a key task (Ball 1998).

This book contributes to addressing these and other challenges that globalization poses in education policy analysis. Its main objective is *to analyze the reasons, agents and factors behind the globalization of educational policy and, by doing so, reflect on the structures, processes and events through which a global education policy landscape is being constituted.* Contributions to the book provide an in-depth theoretical and empirical understanding of educational change and education reform in an increasingly globalizing world. The authors are a mix of established and up-and-coming Southern and Northern scholars with great expertise in the analysis of specific global programmatic ideas. The book also draws on the special contribution of Roger Dale and Gita Steiner-Khamsi. In their concluding remarks, these two distinguished scholars look at the GEP phenomenon and, in particular, the cases collected in the book, with the different theoretical lenses through which they look at the globalization-education relationship, and as a way to develop some crucial and original insights.

The case studies collected in the volume reflect, on the one hand, on the capacity of international organisations and other political actors to shape education agendas and disseminate education policies globally. On the other hand, they analyze the complex process of the re-contextualization of global policies at the country level, and their effects on educational governance. India, Brazil, South Africa, Turkey, Kenya, Uganda and Central America are some of the locations in which the case studies have been developed. In the different studies, authors look at the globalization-education relationship from multiple theoretical perspectives, including neo-institutionalism, constructivism, international political economy and social movements theory, and by applying different methodological approaches, mainly qualitative, such as comparative analysis, the vertical case study or discourse analysis. Despite their diversity, all chapters in this volume converge on the idea that processes of *globalization* have drastically altered the education policy landscape across the world and, more particularly, in the context of developing countries.

To a great extent, this book focuses on the **developing world** due to the particular nature and intensity of global influences in these areas. Developing countries, especially Less-Developed Countries, are often highly dependent on foreign expertise, information and financing (Rose 2007). In fact, in low-income contexts, there is a bigger presence of external actors, including international NGOs, donor agencies and international organisations (IOs) that have a great capacity – both material and ideational – to set agendas and priorities for a particular country. In this sense, these countries' policy landscapes are much more penetrated than countries in more industrialized societies (although the current financial crisis and the way it is being managed in many European countries is challenging this premise). Furthermore, from the point of view of policy transfer, developing states are not only the object of a more intense flow of external pressures, but also depend on hindered capacities to mediate supranational policy pressures (Grek *et al.* 2009).

Taking globalization 'seriously'

While notoriously slippery and expansive (Rupert 2005), globalization is today a very well-established term in the social sciences. It can be broadly defined as a constitutive process of increasing interdependence between people, territories and organisations in the economic, political and cultural domains. The dominant processes of globalization can be characterized as hyper-liberalism in the economic domain, governance without government in the political domain, and commodification and consumerism in the cultural one (Dale 2000). Globalization is a very convenient concept for social scientists due to its euphemistic character and due to all the meanings it subsumes within it. Nevertheless, on occasion referring to the *supranational* would be more accurate than to the *global*, since many of the trends we are witnessing in education policy have a regional (and not necessarily global) scope.

Taking globalization seriously implies capturing the multiple ways globalization affects education policy. In the following analysis, we detail a comprehensive, although not exhaustive, list of impact dimensions of globalization in education policy. Some of them will then be further developed in this introductory chapter.

- Globalization generates new inputs for education policy-making and *defines new problems that education policy needs to address* (Ball 1998). Among them, the transformation of the labour market and the re-organisation of work worldwide stand-out. In a global economy, most countries aim at raising their international competitiveness by offering knowledge-intense products and services, and new manpower profiles. Accordingly, they expand education and base its content and processes on skills, competences and the notion of flexibility (Carnoy 1999).

- Globalization, or the 'idea of globalisation' (see Hay 2006), *alters the capacity of welfare states* to address education and non-education problems via education policy, as well as their capacity to provide and finance education directly.

- Globalization *revitalizes the role of international agencies* in the making of educational policy. Among them, international governmental organisations (IOs) with an explicit or implicit education mandate, such as the World Bank, the OECD or UNESCO, stand out. However, globalization also brings new international players into education policy-making, most of which are non-governmental, including transnational corporations and foundations, international consultants, transnational advocacy coalitions and epistemic communities.

- The revitalized role of international players in educational politics contributes to the *deterritorialisation of the education policy process* and to the 'national' territory losing its centrality in such processes (Robertson, Chapter 2 in this volume). Deterritorialisation implies the redefinition of the scale, the space and the dynamics through which education policy is being negotiated, formulated and implemented. International players have an increasing capacity to settle education agendas and define the priorities of countries concerning education reform processes, but also to impose certain policies via funding mechanisms and aid conditionality.

- Beyond the formulation and dissemination of policies, some IOs have the capacity to *transform the legal framework* of member-countries and, by doing so, alter the rules of the game through which policies are being formulated. The most remarkable case here is that of the World Trade Organisation (WTO) that, through the General Agreement on Trade in Services (GATS), modifies a range of in-country 'regulatory barriers' to cross-border trade in education, including ownership, taxation, licensing or quality assurance rules (Verger 2009).

- The advances in *Information and Communication Technologies (ICT)*, which are, at the same time, cause and consequence of globalization, allow the intensification of the international circulation of policy ideas (Peck *et al.* 2010). ICT is also transforming education practices and the patters of education delivery for instance by reducing the costs of cross-border distance learning.

- Globalization also creates a *transnational private market of education provision* that complements and/or competes against national education providers. This emerging global market challenges some of the core functions of conventional education systems such as 'nation building' (Robertson *et al.* 2002).

- *Neoliberalism,* as the currently dominant political-economic ideology worldwide, frames many of the education policy ideas that circulate (Ball 2007). Proposals such as the introduction of market mechanisms and logics (choice, competition, decentralisation), the liberalisation and privatisation of the education sector, and the importation of management techniques coming from the corporate sector, resonate strongly in the neoliberal ideational context.

- Globalization fosters the organisation of *transnational social justice movements* that struggle for the realisation of education as a global public good and its endorsement as a human right. At the same time, these movements contest the neoliberal global education agenda sketched above. In the education for development field, the most remarkable organisation with these objectives is the Global Campaign for Education (Mundy *et al.* 2001). Importantly, it is not only civil society movements that are reacting to the expansion of neoliberal policies. Like-minded coalitions of nation-states, such as the ALBA[1] countries in Latin America, are pushing for a counter-hegemonic regional education agenda that includes aspects such as increasing state intervention in education or the so-called decolonisation of the curriculum (Muhr 2012, forthcoming).

In conclusion, globalization needs to be first and foremost understood as a new terrain, the new '*context of contexts*' (cf. Peck *et al.* 2010), of education policy. It defines the problems to be addressed and, at the same time, alters the capacity of the states to respond to these problems by themselves; it empowers international actors and makes the transnational organisation of policy networks more pressing; and it is a strategically selective and conflicting terrain for educational policy-making, which is more conducive to certain education policy ideas and political actors than others.

Global Education Policy Studies: Methodological considerations

Globalization has altered education policy, but also the way we think about and study education policy. Global Education Policy is an emerging area of research that examines *the different ways in which globalization processes, agents and events contribute to educational policy change on a range of scales, and with what consequences*. GEP studies raise important theoretical and methodological implications for education policy analysts. The shaping of this new area does not simply mean introducing globalization as a 'topic' onto the educational research agenda, but rather revising certain theoretical postulations, models of analysis and research methodologies (Green 2003). Many of these implications have to be seen in relation to the changing relationship between the state and education in a global setting.

The first and most obvious of these implications is that globalization challenges the basic unit of analysis, the nation-state, and, accordingly, the *methodological nationalism* that predominates in educational research and in comparative education in particular (Green 2003; Dale *et al.* 2007). Based on a Westphalian understanding of political authority,[2] education policies have traditionally been developed within national settings. However, national policies are today the result of a 'combination of political forces, social structures, cultural traditions and economic processes entangled in a matrix of intersecting multi-level, multi-scalar (local, national, regional and global) sites and spaces' (Yeates 2001, p. 637).

Directly related to the latter, a second challenge consists in overcoming the *global-local binary* and the understanding of the relationship between the national and the global as a zero-sum (Dale 2005). The concept of scale, instead of that of level, is helpful for this purpose because it allows an understanding of the production of space as a mutable product of social relations and struggle in which the global and the local are mutually embedded (Robertson, Chapter 2 in this volume). Transcending the global-local binary split means the problematisation of the state as a merely 'national' entity. Many state components (ministries, departments) and bureaucrats operating within the state are networked or, at the same time, part of IOs (usually identified as the 'global' level). In fact, IOs are not something external to the state; in any case, it would be more accurate to say that IOs are more external for some states than for others or, in other words, that they are more owned by some states than by others: see the unequal distribution of power and bargaining capacity in Jawara and Kwa (2004) for the case of the WTO, or in Woods (2000) for the World Bank.

Bourdieu's concept of 'field' contributes to overcoming the local-global binary split in the analysis of GEP. Thus, rather than understanding policy borrowing or transfer as the simple correspondence or influence between two institutions (like IO-state), it is more accurate to consider that a global education field, which interacts with the broader social context of international development, is being constituted (Vavrus 2004). Fields need to be understood as conflicting terrains in which different actors struggle for their transformation or reproduction (Bourdieu 1999). The increasing political dimension acquired by international standardized tests such as PISA and global targets such as the EFA goals, and the corresponding international comparisons; the growing cross-border flows in trade in education and scholars' mobility; the generation of funding mechanisms such as the Fast-Track Initiative (now called Global Partnership for Education) etc. have generated growing awareness among policy-makers, scholars and practitioners of being part of a common 'global education policy' field. In this field, an official from an IO and a teacher in a Peruvian rural school intersect in the production and reproduction of policy texts and practices (Lingard *et al.* 2005). However, not all actors are equally influential in the GEP field. Key international policy players and policy entrepreneurs, with the capacity to transcend different scales at any moment, have more chance of introducing their ideas, preferences and languages in this field.

Thirdly, globalization urges us to transcend *educationism* (Dale *et al.* 2007). Thus, when analyzing new policy trends, policy changes and/or regulatory transformations in the educational field, we have to consider that these elements may be shaped by extra-educational structures, events and processes (such as the prevailing welfare regime, the levels of poverty and social cohesion or the economic performance in a country). The comparative education mainstream is still strongly marked by a disciplinary parochialism that encourages researchers to base education policy studies on approaches that come exclusively from within the field of education (Dale 2005). To overcome this problem, educational changes should be better understood as being as embedded within interdependent local, national and global political economy complexes (Novelli *et al.* 2008).

A fourth challenge concerns *methodological statism,* i.e. assuming that the state is a rationale and cohesive entity, and that it has the monopoly over political action within the borders that delimit a territory. Overcoming statism implies, first, that the state cannot be understood as a monolithic unit of analysis, but as a range of diverse apparatuses that represent distinct material condensations of social forces (Hartmann 2007). In fact, the different (and differentiated) factions constituting the state usually push for diverging, and sometimes even contradicting, interests and agendas (Cox 1995). For instance, in education, it is quite common that, within the same country, the Minister of Education and the Minister of Finance have very different preferences about the amount of public resources needed in the education system. In some countries, this has generated interesting alliances between the EFA civil society movement and the Ministry of Education to pressure the Ministry of Finance with the objective of obtaining more funding for public education (Verger *et al.* 2012, forthcoming).

Overcoming statism implies, secondly, understanding that non-state actors are relevant political agents in the governance of education (Dale *et al.* 2007). Recognizing the political relevance of non-state actors does not necessarily mean assuming that the state is becoming less powerful. Rather, it means accepting that the role and functions of the state have been altered and redefined in the broad scenario of governance, that other players are actively participating at the levels of education policies and politics, and that the state is not as autonomous in relation to the definition of certain policy issues as it was in other periods (Hay 2006).

The concept of 'global governance' aims at capturing this increasingly complex policy landscape in which non-state actors, which operate at a range of scales, gain political authority and presence in a range of policy fields, including education. Global governance also refers to the intensification of the interactions and the embeddedness between different scales in policy processes. According to Dale (2005, p. 132) 'what we are witnessing is a developing functional, scalar and sectoral division of the labour of educational governance.' Funding, provision and ownership of education are carried out by a broad range of supra-national, national and sub-national agents, including IOs, the state, the market, the community and/or the families. To a great extent, the global governance of education means the redefinition of the relationship between education and the state. In fact the state today is less inclined towards the direct provision of education and more towards the establishment of standards and evaluation mechanisms that determine whether schools and universities are achieving standards effectively (Neave 1998).

Global governance refers to both 'formal institutions and regimes empowered to enforce compliance, as well as informal arrangements that people and institutions either have agreed to or perceive to be in their interest' (Commission on Global Governance 1995, p. 4). Indeed, currently, states' action and, in particular, their social policies are framed and conditioned by a dense web of international legal and political obligations (Yeates 2001). These obligations include, in the case of education, legally binding agreements such as the GATS agreement or UNESCO conventions, as well as non-binding declarations such as the Education for All (EFA) action framework or the Bologna Process, which have also triggered important educational transformations both in the South and in the North. As Snyder (1999) states, socio-cultural norms and soft-law are also powerful governance devices with regulatory powers.

To sum up, to incorporate processes of globalization in educational research, the different methodological and epistemological challenges described above need to be faced, and theoretical and conceptual frameworks coming from sociology, political geography or political sciences considered. However, taking globalization seriously also means the revision of the core questions that frame research agendas and projects. We identify four main sets of interlinked research questions that can contribute to putting globalization at the center of education policy studies. These questions allow us to analyze the whole global education policy process: from the structural selectivity of certain policies to its actual implementation in particular contexts. Of course, research can often only focus on one or two of these sets of questions, since going through all of them would require a huge amount of data-collection. They are:

1   What is the nature of the relationship between globalization and processes of educational change? Why is 'global education policy' happening?

2   How are global education agendas and global policy solutions

formulated and constituted, and by whom? Why do certain policies and not others become selected and privileged in global agendas?

3 To what extent are global education policies being disseminated effectively? Why do local policy-makers and practitioners adopt them?

4 What are the mediating elements and institutions affecting the translation and re-contextualization of global policies to particular education contexts? What are the specific difficulties associated with the implementation of global education policies in local contexts?

In the following sections we explore how the GEP literature has dealt with these questions and, in particular, the way the case studies included in this book address them.

Globalization's effects on education

There are two main macro-approaches that address the nature of the effects of globalization in education. We refer on the one hand to neo-institutionalist approaches, represented by the 'World Society' theory, and on the other international political economy approaches, represented by the 'Globally Structured Agenda for Education'.

World society theorists argue that a single global model of schooling has spread around the world as part of the diffusion of a more general culturally embedded model of the modern nation-state (Anderson-Levitt 2003). The need for nation-states to conform to an international ideal of the rationalized bureaucratic state has led to a process of institutional isomorphism and convergence (Drezner 2001). First and foremost, nation-states expand schooling as part of a broader process of adherence to world models of the organisation of sovereignty (the modern state) and the organisation of society as composed of individuals (the modern nation) (Meyer *et al.* 1997). In this process, education is a key area for governments to demonstrate to the international community that they are building a modern state.

World Society scholars have validated their thesis empirically by showing, for instance, that school expansion in African countries has not been so related to their level of development (industrialisation, urbanisation, racial and religious composition, etc.) and to the expected educational needs according to these variables, but to how close countries were to Colonial powers and Western influence (Meyer *et al.* 1992a).

Their research problematizes the presumption that education measures are applicable globally, independently of the needs and capacities of the countries adopting them. They observe that education policies (but also health, fiscal policies, etc.) are being adopted in a quite routine way all around the planet due to external and internal legitimation reasons. This is something especially challenging for developing countries since they command fewer resources and organisational capacity than rich countries, but feel similar pressures to comply with educational reform imperatives (Meyer *et al.* 1997).

World Society proponents have conducted extensive research on curriculum convergence (Meyer *et al.* 1992b) and, more recently, on institutional isomorphism in higher education policy (Ramirez 2006). However, they are not so focused on education policy change, or specific forms of education reform since, to them, the main point is not whether state policy is exogenously influenced, but the fact that the state itself is an exogenously constructed entity. Nevertheless, some authors follow an analogous institutionalist and culture-centered approach to analyze education reform. This is the case of Schriewer *et al.* (2004) who argue that decisions on education policy (and, more broadly speaking, the educational conceptions of decision-makers) are affected by the dissemination of a world-level developmental cultural account and education ideology. Based on Luhmann's work, they propose the concept of 'externalisation' to analyze the way policy-makers argue for the necessity of education reform based on external models. Externalisation can be subtle and does not refer to specific models, but to a web of norms and beliefs that make national constituencies more receptive to educational reform. Education reforms are thus today embedded in a universalized web of ideas about development and social problems, 'a web of reciprocal references which takes a life of its own, moving, reinforcing and dynamising the worldwide universalisation of educational ideas, models, standards, and options of reform' (Schriewer 2000a, p. 334).

Carney (2009), for his part, elaborates the concept of 'policyscape' to provide a similar argument. A policyscape is an ensemble of policy ideas and visions (managerial practices, conceptions of the role of the state in education, the functions of education, etc.) that are shared by a range of political actors operating on multiple scales and affect the way these actors think and decide about education policy. According to him, a transnational policyscape, grounded on the principles of hyperliberalism, is contributing to 'standardising the flow of educational ideas internationally and changing fundamentally what education is and can be' (p. 68). He shows very convincingly how this policyscape has effectively contributed to shaping education reform in countries as different as Denmark, Nepal and China.

For her part, Jakobi (Chapter 6) in this volume shows how different African countries are implementing notions of lifelong learning by aligning themselves to the global discourses disseminated by several IOs in the continent. As the World Society theory would predict, these countries are engaging with the worldwide discourse on lifelong learning even when it does not fit within their particular needs and when they have only scarce resources for implementing it.

International Political Economy (IPE) theories do not put so much emphasis on cultural or ideational factors, but on economic ones as the main drivers of educational change. According to the Globally Structured Agenda for Education approach (GSAE), the world capitalist economy is the driving force of globalization and the first causal source of multiple transformations manifested in different policy sectors, including education (Dale 2000).

The World Society model has an implicit theory of the state in which legitimation, both internally and externally, is the main problem to be addressed by the state. In contrast, for the GSAE, apart from providing the basis of legitimation, the core problems of the state include supporting the regime of accumulation and providing a context for its reproduction (Robertson *et al.* 2002). These problems cannot all be solved together, and solutions to them tend to be rather contradictory. These contradictions provide the dynamic of educational systems and frame the state educational agenda. Globalization has significantly altered the nature of the core problems confronting nation-states as well as the nature of their capacity to respond to them (Dale 2000). As we discuss below, economic globalization needs to be seen as a political force with a great capacity to structure a global education agenda.

IPE approaches focus on the indirect effects of globalization in education, and not exclusively on the direct influences between countries or between IOs and countries. They suggest that the most important way globalization is affecting education policy is by altering the structural conditions in which education reform happens, including the conditions in which reform is framed and perceived by policy-makers as necessary. A good example of how globalization altered the structural conditions of educational governance can be found in the World Bank/IMF sponsored Structural Adjustment Programmes (SAPS) implemented in Latin American and African countries in the 1980s and 1990s. The SAPS had serious repercussions in education, firstly by lowering the public budget necessary to fund educational expansion and second by raising the levels of poverty and, consequently, the opportunity costs of schooling (Bonal 2002). The new social structure after the SAPs period became highly conducive to the adoption and implementation of Conditional Cash Transfer policies, which contribute, via economic incentives to the families, to poor students being enrolled in schools (see Bonal *et al.*, Chapter 7 in this volume).

For IPE scholars, economic globalization, and the competitive pressures associated with this phenomenon, are provoking educational changes all around the planet. Globalization is putting governments under financial pressure to control inflation and the public deficit and, as a consequence, to reduce public spending growth and find alternative funding sources to cover educational expansion. In fact, many governments believe that, in a global economy, they have to reduce the rates of corporate taxation to avoid capital moving away from their jurisdiction. In this intensely competitive economic environment, finance-driven reforms such as privatisation and decentralisation become highly attractive (Carnoy 1999).

Furthermore, most political and economic actors, including state actors (Cerny 1997), aim to raise their competitiveness and perceive education and knowledge as key competitive assets for this purpose (Brown *et al.* 1996 and Carnoy *et al.* 2002). This is also the case of individuals who increasingly conceive education as a 'positional good' (Marginson 2004) in a highly competitive and dualized labour market. These beliefs have spread to the extent that most countries and regions in the world today aspire to become 'knowledge economies'. The knowledge economy idea works as a powerful economic imaginary (Jessop *et al.* 2008), or a 'political condensation' (cf. Ball 1998), that frames the preferences of political actors and guides the way they intervene in society. This ideal puts education at the centre of the economic strategies of governments due to its crucial contribution to the formation of knowledge-intensive manpower, applied research and knowledge transfer (Barrow *et al.* 2004). The knowledge economy ideal is often associated with an educational reform jargon based on the principles of quality, learning, accountability and standards (Carney 2009).

The emphasis given by IPE approaches to the 'knowledge economy' idea shows that there is room for reconciliation between materialist and idealist approaches when it comes to explaining educational change, although for IPE scholars ideas are usually subordinated – an 'entry point' – to material factors when it comes to understanding changes in the political economy of education. Novelli and Lopes Cardozo (Chapter 11 in this volume) demonstrate the complex interplay between discourse and material factors, when analysing the way Dutch aid to education in conflict-affected low-income countries is conditioned by the powerful influencing role of the World Bank and DFID, despite its status as a wealthy Northern donor. This reflects a global hierarchy within Northern donors as well as between them and their Southern partners.

IPE approaches problematize globalization's effects in education for two main reasons. First, they provoke neoliberal and efficiency-driven types of reforms that, among other implications, put education equity in the background (Carnoy 1999). Second, they imply the weakening of sovereignty. The main problem here is that globalization favours important education decisions being taken within transnational networks rather than by democratically elected institutions (Moutsios 2010).

Poppema (Chapter 8 in this volume) shows how School-Based Management initiatives in Central America, spearheaded by the World Bank and USAID, were powerfully promoted across the region. These policies were complicit in weakening processes of participation, leading to the 'depolitisation of socio-economic relations', and the promotion of de-facto privatisation of education. In this case, 'progressive' discourses aimed at giving poor people more 'voice' appear as mechanisms merely to support the smoother functioning of neoliberal reforms in education (see also Edwards and Klees, Chapter 3 in this volume).

Setting education policies in global agendas

The two approaches described above focus on the structural conditions that favour the selection and retention of particular policies. However, GEP studies are also attentive to the more micro-level types of analysis concerning how policies are settled in global agendas and by whom. As we show in this section, there is a range of research that looks at the structuring capacity of particular actors and focuses on decision-making dynamics in multi-scalar political systems.

The literature on global agenda setting usually refers to the key role of IOs. According to the World Society approach, IOs contribute to policy convergence in education by spreading the Western system of political organisation and state authority around the world (Meyer *et al.* 1992a). However, this approach seems to put all IOs, including international NGOs, in the same package of Western modernising agents. Certainly, IOs might represent Western modernity broadly speaking, but when we look at them in more detail we observe that they express divergent and even rivalling education agendas. For instance, Robertson (2005) analyses the different meanings of the 'Knowledge economy' label that the OECD and the World Bank are trying to fix, and shows how the latter favours the market and individualism as the means for developing knowledge economies, while the OECD favours a more institutionally embedded liberal approach to knowledge production. Edwards and Klees, in this volume, reflect on the way political actors, including IOs and international aid agencies, operating on a range of scales, compete to promote different meanings of participation policies in education. They demonstrate the way participation in educational governance is 'predominantly neoliberal–instrumentalist in purpose, limited in nature, and imbued with market ideology.' See also Mundy (1998, 1999), Chabbott (2003), Jones (2006) or King (2007) on the competition between IOs such as UNESCO, UNICEF and the World Bank to frame and dominate the education for development field.

For IPE theories, IOs are conceptualized as key transmitters of particular views of education and educational reform, basically instrumental and market-oriented, to national contexts. Roger Dale (1999) systematizes a range of policy mechanisms activated by IOs and other external actors that allows them to frame and influence national and sub-national education policies (see Box 1. 1). In recent decades, these global mechanisms have acquired more centrality than traditional mechanisms of bilateral influence such as 'policy borrowing' and 'policy learning' (Dale 1999).

Box 1. 1. Global mechanisms of influence

- *Imposition:* external actors compel some countries to take on particular education policies (the classic example being the conditionality to credit of the World Bank, the IMF and other aid agencies to borrower countries).
- *Harmonisation*: a set of countries mutually agree on the implementation of common policies in a certain policy area (e.g. the configuration of the European Space for Higher Education).
- *Dissemination*: external agents use persuasion and its technical knowledge to convince countries on the implementation of certain policies (e.g. through annual reports, best practices data-bases and technical assistance).
- *Standardisation*: the international community defines and promotes the adhesion to a set of policy principles and standards that frame the countries' behavior (e.g. international performance tests, such as PISA, contribute to the standardisation of curricular content at the global level).
- *Installing interdependence* occurs when countries agree to achieve common objectives to tackle problems that require international cooperation (e.g. climate change, 'education for all').

Source: Adapted from Dale 1999.

IOs are forums of cooperation and struggle between nations. However, they are more than the aggregate of the interests of their member states. Even if they are usually instrumentalized by the most powerful states, they are not simply the extension of particular national interests (Dale 2005). A range of scholars, often based on constructivist approaches, conceive IOs as relatively autonomous sources of power. To them, IOs and specifically their bureaucracies are not exclusively at the service of member-states. They count on sufficient autonomy to interpret and redefine the broad political mandate of the organisation, and to exercise power over members, even when they do not have formal political power. The main sources of power of IOs bureaucracies rely first on the legitimacy of the rational-legal authority that they represent, and second their control over information/ data and technical expertise (Finnemore 1996).

According to Barnett *et al.* (2004), IOs exercise power by orgainising three types of apparently apolitical and technical actions. They are, first, *classifying the world,* for instance, by stratifying countries according to their level of performance in international evaluations such as TIMMS or PISA and, according to their results, putting governments under great pressure to introduce education reforms; secondly, *fixing meanings in the social world* by, for instance, defining what educational development means, this is something that IOs can do explicitly, but also indirectly in the form of indicators and benchmarks; and thirdly, *articulating and disseminating new norms, principles and beliefs* by, for instance, spreading what they consider 'good' or 'best' practices in educational development.

Departing from the assumption of IOs as autonomous sources of power, some researchers have analysed the organisational culture and the internal divergences within IOs to understand the particular education polices they disseminate globally. Several of them focus on the role and strategies of IO officials when it comes to push for their preferences and approaches to educational development. Thus Heyneman (2003) provides us with a complete story of how and why rates of return analysis have become the most important analytical tool to guide World Bank education policy since the eighties, and about the divisions this has generated between economists and educationists within Bank staff. For their part, Mundy *et al.* (2011) have reflected on the internal division among the officials of the World Bank Group concerning the promotion of education privatisation in developing contexts. They apply the 'organised hypocrisy' concept (i.e. the disjuncture between the official discourse of IOs and their actual practices as a way to deal with external pressures, demands and expectations) to understand, in part, the reasons for this division.

Beyond IOs

International actors other than IOs, by using norms and ideas as tools of power also play an important role in global education politics. Educational scholars, among others, have focused on the role and impact of epistemic communities (Chabbott 2003), transnational civil society networks (Mundy *et al.* 2001), networks of international consultants and policy entrepreneurs (Ball 2007; Robertson *et al.* 2012, forthcoming) or international foundations (Srivastrava *et al.* 2010). These pieces of work show that under some circumstances different types of non-state actors can mould state preferences for various policy options or help states to identify their interests, above all in moments of uncertainty. At the same time, they also show how these new actors are becoming an integral part of emerging forms of global governance and count on an increasing capacity to provoke processes of policy transfer and learning, or to introduce issues into global policy agendas.

The power of non-state actors in international politics is not something new. This type of actor has traditionally influenced international forums and agreements *through* the state. However, more recently, we have witnessed how multilateralism is moving away from an exclusively state-based structure, and how private actors play an increasingly relevant role in multilateral structures. In this emerging 'complex multilateralism' (O'Brien *et al.* 2000), non-state actors have more spaces and opportunities to influence IOs directly, and without the necessary mediation of the state. Examples of 'complex multilateralism' in the educational sector can be found in the membership of the Global Campaign for Education and the World Economic Forum in the board of the *Global Partnership for Education*, or on the role of transnational corporations (TNCs) in educational assistance structures.

TNCs such as Microsoft are promoting educational programmes and establishing bilateral relations with Southern countries, as traditional donor countries would do (Bhanji 2008), or provide international organisations such as UNESCO with funds (Bull *et al.* 2007). These emerging forms of private authority in education are under suspicion due to the fact that private players are usually policy advocates and service providers at the same time (Deacon 2007). For instance, Microsoft and other ICT companies are using corporate social responsibility to open markets abroad (van Fleet 2012, forthcoming), and big consultancy firms such as CfBT are advocating for PPPs using scientific arguments, but at the same time benefiting from PPP contracts all around the world (Robertson *et al.* 2012, forthcoming).

Social movements and advocacy coalitions are also adopting pluriscalar political strategies to achieve their objectives. When their access to the state is blocked for whatever reason, it is quite common for them to try to influence national policies by activating international agreements. This is a political strategy that has been labelled as the 'boomerang effect' (Keck *et al.* 1998). Santos and Soeterik (Chapter 9 in this volume) demonstrate how the Brazilian Black Movement successfully utilized a 'politics of scale' to strengthen their national movement and made the Brazilian government comply with several policy measures, particularly through their engagement with the *World Conference Against Racism, Racial Discrimination, Xenophobia and Related Intolerance* in Durban in 2001.

New actors have very different interests and reasons to become involved in the global education arena. However, what they have in common is that they are knowledge-intensive entities, and that their main power source relies on knowledge and ideas (TNCs being an exception to this premise due to the huge material power they also count on). Thus, most of them are gaining authority in global governance structures because of the scientific knowledge they possess, their track record for problem-solving and, in the particular case of civil society networks, their principled-oriented views to the problems they deal with (Keck *et al.* 1998; Haas 2004).

However, being knowledge actors does not mean that international players are continuously innovating and/or producing new policy alternatives. Most of the time, policy entrepreneurs sitting in international foundations, think-tanks or IOs act more as brokers and framers than as pure theorizers. They usually take already existing policy practices, re-label them and sell them around. Many global education policies have started their journey in this way, being first formulated and implemented in particular countries. School-Based Management originated in the UK

(Ball 2007), OBM in New Zealand (Spreen 2004), and charter schools in the US (Bulkley *et al.* 2003). Since most global policy-entrepreneurs come from the Anglo-Saxon world, it does not come as a surprise that their policy *référentiels* come from Anglo-Saxon countries. There are some exceptions, however. For example, Conditional-Cash Transfer schemes started being implemented in different localities in Brazil and Mexico and later on they became adopted by the World Bank and other regional development banks (see Bonal *et al.*, Chapter 7 in this volume).

Adoption: why do policy-makers *buy* into GEP?

The adoption moment is the other side of the coin of the globalising policy phenomenon. For education policies to become effectively globalized, they need to be adopted in particular contexts by policy-makers. In fact, once a particular policy programme is being adopted in a critical number of locations, we can start considering that some sort of policy convergence in education would be happening. Often, countries adopt GEPs because they are externally imposed via aid conditionality (see Box 1. 1). However, from an analytical point of view, it is also relevant to understand why it is that local policy-makers voluntarily adopt GEPs.

A first type of answer to this question would say that local policy-makers implement global policies because these policies 'work'. In this case, we would be assuming that policy-makers are well-informed rational actors who choose the best and internationally tested policy solutions to improve their education systems. However, interestingly enough, it is not always clear whether many GEPs work or not, or under what conditions they do so. For instance, diverse policies such as quasi-markets or Child-Centred Pedagogies have been extensively criticized for their uneven and even negative impacts, but this has not prevented them from continuing to be disseminated around the world (Luke 2003, Altinglken, Chapter 10 in this volume).

A more nuanced answer to the GEP adoption question would say that policy-makers adopt GEP because they *perceive* that these policies work. In this case, policy-makers would perceive GEP as appropriate policy solutions in their countries for educational, but also political and economic reasons. The literature is very rich in explanations and hypotheses related to this line of argument. Different research places the emphasis on a wide range of elements, from the persuasive capacity of global agents, to the capacity of local actors to instrumentalize the global arena to advance pre-established policy preferences. We explore the most relevant of them in this section.

Framing matters. IOs and, more broadly speaking, global policy entrepreneurs are very active, and even compete among themselves, to make policy-makers perceive that their policy ideas work and have an impact

(Steiner-Khamsi 2004). In general terms, more than the internal consistency of policy ideas, the way they are framed and presented affect policy-makers' decisions on whether to buy or not to buy a certain policy (Verger 2011). IOs know this well and put a lot of resources and effort in dissemination. Global policy ideas are launched and spread through highly distributed policy briefs, papers and reports, and in public or private events (seminars, workshops, report launches, etc.) that are usually well attended by national political leaders and policy-makers (Ball *et al.* 2010). Despite IOs use of an apparently neutral and technical discourse, at the same time they strongly advocate their proposals, often with great enthusiasm. To frame GEP ideas in an appealing way, IOs need to present them in a clear and concise manner. Moreover, new policy ideas are most likely to be taken up if they are perceived as technically workable, and fit within budgetary and administrative constraints (Kingdon 2002). Not surprisingly, most education policy entrepreneurs highlight the cost-effectiveness and efficiency gains of the policies they are promoting.

However, framing strategies are often in dispute with scientific rigor. In order to sell their ideas and frame them in a more convincing way, policy entrepreneurs might on occasion need, more or less explicitly, to simplify reality (Ball 1998) and resort to different types of logical fallacy and argumentative shortcuts (Verger 2011). In fact, beyond their argumentation strengths and consistency, GEPs often maintain their credibility through repetition (Ball 2007; Fairclough 2000). Indeed, the international travelling of education policies has been strengthened by the consolidation of the evidence-based policy idea (i.e. basing policy decisions on research that shows what kind of policies 'work'). In fact, evidence-based policy has been welcomed by many policy-makers and donors as a superior way of taking decisions, even when it is well known that evidence can be easily instrumentalized to support the adoption of certain policies instead of others (see how this bias affects the international debate on quasi-markets in education in Luke 2003 or Verger 2011).[3]

Global status and deterritorialisation. As pointed out earlier, all policies have an origin, which is usually Western and, more precisely, Anglo-Saxon. For this reason, it is useful to think about GEPs as globalized localisms (cf. Santos 2005). Likewise, once a critical number of countries borrow a policy, it seems as though its particular origins vanish; it becomes *global* and is traded as a *global model* (Steiner-Khamsi 2010). The acquisition of 'global status' raises the attractiveness of policies and predisposes policy-makers to discuss educational reforms guided by them.

Apart from the global status of policy ideas, the global prestige of the actors backing them is similarly important. Usually, the most successful policy entrepreneurs are based in IOs that are located at the interstices of a range of influential social and policy networks (Campbell 2004). Indeed, in many countries, the opinion of a World Bank expert will be more considered than that of a scholar from a local university, even if they have a similar high-quality training and propose the same successful or failed policy ideas. The definitive move for a policy to become globally traded comes when a global institution that counts on high levels of exposure and good networks adopts it. On occasion, social networks are key to understanding this type of movement. For instance, Outcomes-Based Education became a global policy in part because one of the promoters in New Zealand, Maris O'Rourke became tenured at the World Bank (Steiner-Khamsi 2004).

GEP selectivity. Some scholars consider that policy-makers perceive importing new policies from elsewhere as necessary when the situation of their education systems is critical. Phillips *et al.* (2003) use the concept of 'impulses' to refer to the preconditions for borrowing. Impulses include an eclectic set of elements such as internal dissatisfaction with the education system on the part of families, teachers, etc. ; the collapse or inadequacy of educational provision; negative external evaluation; political change and the changing demands for education; and so on.

IOs play a key role in some of these aspects, especially when it comes to making countries aware of the need to implement reforms, and become more receptive toward their policy recommendations. International standardized tests such as PISA have generated a feeling of reform urgency even in powerful countries such as Germany and Switzerland (Bieber 2010). In developing countries, the EFA Actions Framework – and, in particular, the fact that many countries are still far from reaching the EFA goals – is working as a great political opportunity for many IOs and policy entrepreneurs trying to sell their policy prescriptions.

In general, those policies that resonate best within the prevailing form of the capitalist system and the prevailing development policy paradigm will have more chances of being retained in global agendas and selected in particular countries (Dale 2000). From a semiotic perspective, neoliberalism and related policy discourses have become hegemonic, and a sort of common sense. Ideas such as performance-based incentives, competitive funding, education as a competitiveness device, etc. have been interiorized by many decision-makers and practitioners (Carney 2009). As a consequence, this type of market-oriented principle is shaping the parameters of policy-making in many countries (Taylor *et al.* 2000). However, at the same time, governmental decision-makers often reject hard-privatisation policies. That is why, to make them more normatively acceptable, most IOs promoting quasi-markets in education avoid using the 'privatisation' concept and use instead more friendly concepts such as PPPs (Robertson *et al.* 2012, forthcoming).

Instrumentalising GEP. Steiner-Khamsi (2004, 2010), on the basis of intensive fieldwork in several Asian countries, concludes that local policy-makers have a double register in their education policy discourse; they speak differently to local constituents than to international donors. Policy-makers adopt the international language of reform as a way of securing international funds but, once they get them, they implement the type of reforms they consider more relevant and go ahead with business as usual. Thus, according to this scholar, more than *global policies*, what is being actually disseminated is a *global policy speak*. This is indeed a sceptical approach to globalization's effects in policy change that breaks with the usual approach that perceives developing countries as victims of IOs and passive recipients of global ideas. In this volume, Verger and Van der Kaaij (Chapter 12) shows that in India the global PPP idea, beyond an external imposition, works as a floating signifier for local actors to settle national and sub-national education agendas, and advance their pre-established preferences in the educational field.

Although following a different reasoning, Martens *et al.* (2009) also consider that countries instrumentalize the global arena to advance certain policy reforms. They consider that countries approach global institutions to reduce transaction costs for problem-solving and policy formulation purposes, but also to gain leverage at the domestic level when it comes to advancing policy changes. From this point of view, global policy recommendations would be instrumentally invoked by policy-makers for legitimatory reasons and as a way of softening internal resistance. The Bologna process has been, to some extent, manipulated in this way by a range of European countries to advance pre-established governmental policy preferences (Huisman *et al.* 2004). In her analysis of the political dimension of PISA, Grek (2007, p. 35) makes a similar point when she states that 'reference to "world situations" enables policy-makers to make the case for education reforms at home that would otherwise be contested'.

Re-contextualization and implementation

Methodologically speaking, research on the recontextualization of GEP traces the translations of policy programmes, and tries to find out about the multiple relationships that reconstitute such programmes in multiple scales (Mukhopadhyay *et al.* 2011). Experiences from the field tell us that we should question those hyperbolic arguments about globalization as a driver of absolute world convergence of policy and practice in education. Most scholars agree on the fact that globalization is not an absolute project with identical effects in all places (Appadurai 1996; Robertson *et al.* 2006). Although globalization presents common features around the world, the effects of globalization in education policy are mediated by domestic history and politics, and by the complex interplay of global and local forces, among other contingencies.

Research stresses that borrowed policy ideas are modified, indigenized or resisted as they are implemented in the recipient countries (Schriewer 2000b; Philips *et al.* 2003; Steiner-Khamsi 2004; Steiner-Khamsi *et al.* 2006). According to Peck et al. (2010, p. 170) global policies mutate during their journeys, they 'rarely travel as complete packages, they move in bits and pieces – as selective discourses, inchoate ideas, and synthesized models – and they therefore "arrive" not as replicas but as policies already-in-transformation'. Ball (1998), who focuses on the globalization of education policies that emanate from what he calls the 'new orthodoxy', considers that policies are rarely translated into policy practices in pristine form. One of the main reasons for this to happen is that policies, beyond a 'text' that is easily transferable across scales, are also part of an often-disputed technical and political debate that is highly contingent and situated.

Altinyelken (Chapter 10 in this volume) looks at how Child-Centred Pedagogy (CCP) was re-contextualized in Uganda and Turkey. Her study points to convergence at a superficial level and around new rituals that have emerged as a result of the dissemination of CCP. However, her findings indicate more strongly the persistence of divergences across countries as CCP was interpreted differently, the reform practices were embraced unevenly, and adaptations to classroom realities and student background have resulted in very distinct practices. Stenvoll-Wells and Sayed (Chapter 5 in this volume), demonstrate that in several locations of South Africa and Zimbabwe, despite policy rhetoric around decentralisation and school management reform as delivering more power to local actors, there appears little transformation on the ground. In fact, their analysis indicates that a few groups dominated decision-making within the school governing bodies and blocked the participation of many other local agents.

Overall, since imported education policies are locally mediated and re-contextualized through multiple processes, the consequences of transfer remains unpredictable (Beech 2006). By ignoring differences in contextual capacity and culture at national, regional and local levels, globalization has resulted in unintended and unexpected consequences for educational practice, such as the deterioration of education quality (Carnoy *et al.* 2002). The development of global education programmes is often questioned for not taking sufficiently into account the social context and needs (Crossley *et al.* 2003). In the literature, we find four main arguments that reflect on why the GEP re-contextualization can be so problematic, especially in developing countries. According to their different emphases, we call these explanations *material, political, cultural* and *scalar*.

Material. As Lewin (2007) notes, it is not appropriate to import models that might have worked in consolidated, well-funded, highly profession-alized and well-regulated educational systems to places whose educational conditions are far from reaching these standards. Many developing countries often do not have the appropriate material and human resources to implement very costly and technically demanding global education programmes such as quasi-markets in education or accountability policies. The World Bank faces this issue with the projects it finances. In fact, the 2011 report of the World Bank's Independent Evaluation Group finds quite 'uneven results' in the Bank's portfolio of education projects, precisely, due to 'design and implementation weaknesses' including 'overly complex designs relative to local capacities' (IEG 2011, p. 13).

However, local policy-makers are often aware of the resources available and the material needs in their countries when engaging with GEP and, accordingly, adapt global discourses to them. This is for instance the case of many African countries when embracing worldwide principles on life-long learning. Under the life-long learning discourse, African policy-makers basically emphasize adult literacy and basic education, instead of higher education or alternative qualification frameworks as more industrialized countries do (see Jakobi, Chapter 6 in this volume).

Bonal, Tarabini and Rambla (Chapter 7 in this volume) show very convincingly how technical capacities and, specifically, the final design of global policies are key mediating factors in understanding the outcomes of global policies in the terrain. They do so by comparing the effects of Conditional Cash Transfers in different Brazilian locations on the basis of the intensity of the economic transfer, the targeting criteria and the coverage of the beneficiaries, among other aspects of the policy design.

Political. Political mediations and institutions also shape the adaptation of global policies. A range of case studies emphasizes the mediating role of political factors in the re-contextualization of diverse policies such as 'education assessment' (Benveniste 2002), 'decentralisation' (Rhoten 2000), or the 'Bologna process' (Heinze *et al.* 2008).

According to Taylor *et al.* (2000), political ideology is one of the main reasons why nations do not deliver equally in the GEP field. Specifically, they show that government ideologies (market-liberal, liberal-democratic and social-democratic) represent a key filter when it comes to adopting the OECD recommendations in educational policy. Martens *et al.* (2010), for their part, focus on the potential role of national veto players in the implementation and modification of global policies. By veto players they mean political actors who have the power to block or hinder legislative initiatives, such as the senate or the national ministry of education. However, based on the cases of Bologna and PISA in several countries, they show that when there is a strong political consensus and leadership to advance a certain reform, veto players and veto points can be easily by-passed.

In the political approach, we also identify political economy accounts of education reform that show how, beyond veto players, key professional groups and constituencies are key when it comes to advancing or resisting educational change. Key actors here are teachers unions for primary and secondary education, and university associations in the case of higher education. Altinyelken's work in this volume also reflects on how teachers and other local actors 'sometimes resist and always transform' the official models they are handed (Anderson-Levitt 2003, p. 4).

Cultural. Another group of scholars highlights how a range of ideas including policy principles, public sentiments or policy paradigms can mediate effectively GEP implementation. For instance, in many Latin American countries there are strong public sentiments (cf. Campbell 2004) around the idea of education as a public good. Consequently, in this region it is more difficult to advance privatisation policies than in countries such as India where these sentiments do not prevail and, moreover, there is a historically rooted elitism in society that makes it socially acceptable not to provide the same quality education for all (Verger and Van der Kaaij, Chapter 12 in this volume). For their part, Santos and Soeterik (Chapter 9) show how the strong social belief of Brazil being a 'racial democracy' makes the implementation of racial affirmative policies in the country more challenging.

Scalar. The professionals who ultimately have to make new policies work (teachers, principals, local government officials, etc.) often perceive education reform as something imposed from above. This problem is more striking in the case of global education policies that have been designed and negotiated at supranational level. Incrementalist approaches tell us that policy changes, to work out smoothly, need to be grounded on previous practices and advance progressively. As the gap between the new policy and the previous system becomes bigger, implementation processes become more problematic (Rizvi *et al.* 2009). This 'gap' is usually accentuated in relation to policies imported from elsewhere and initially designed by officials unconnected to local realities.

Following this type of reasoning, Steiner-Khamsi (2010, p. 331) argues that very often reform failures are not due to technicalities, limited funding or similar implementation problems. Rather, such failures reflect 'the fundamental contradictions that arise when (policy) solutions are borrowed from educational systems where the problems are entirely different.' Thus the main implementation problem can be found in the decoupling between the global policy, whose programme ontology has a universalistic pretension, and the local reality, with the particular configuration of problems that predominate.

Unterhalter (Chapter 4) observes how global targets inevitably oversimplify reality, as well as the complexity of the problems that policies are intended to address. The main issue here is thinking that by achieving a specific target, the problem that the target relates to has been solved as well. She shows how this 'political relaxation' effect happens in the case of the EFA gender parity target; once countries have achieved this target, decision-makers consider that they have solved the problem of gender equity, which is much more complex and difficult to measure.

Concluding remarks

Having laid out schematically the landscape of the different methodological and theoretical approaches on globalization, education policy and international development, it is perhaps fitting now to conclude that there remains a great deal of work to be done. Many of the debates outlined above, beyond their analytical dimension, have hugely important implications for social justice and the right to education around the world. Globalization, far from producing a flat-world, has increased inequalities both within and between countries, and has altered the cartography of contemporary social relations and education politics. Power, and its unequal distribution, are reflected throughout these pages, and challenge us to think beyond the current mainstream in the education/globalization relationship and to develop more inclusive, participatory and egalitarian educational policy processes. Hopefully this book can contribute to highlighting the fault lines upon which these principles can emerge.

Notes

1 ALBA stands for *Alternativa Bolivariana de las Américas*.

2 The basic rules of the Westphalian State are: 1. Authority can only be exercised by a state over a defined geographical territory; 2. Each state is autonomous to develop its own policies; 3. No external actor can direct the state's priorities (Yeates 2001).

3 Accordingly to Pawson (2011), this way of using science and evidence to legitimate predefined policy preferences, instead of evidence-based policy, should be called 'policy-based evidence'.

References

Anderson-Levitt, K. M. (2003), *Local meanings, global schooling: anthropology and world culture theory*. Basingstoke: Palgrave Macmillan.

Appadurai, A. (1996), *Modernity at Large: Cultural Dimensions of Globalisation*. Minneapolis: University of Minnesota Press.

—(1998), 'Big Policies/Small World: An introduction to international perspectives in education policy'. *Comparative Education*, 34, (2), 119–130.

Ball, S. J. (2007), *Education Plc: Understanding Private Sector Participation in Public Sector Education*. New York: Routledge.

Ball, S. J, and Exley, S. (2010), 'Making policy with "good ideas": Policy networks and the "intellectuals" of New Labour'. *Journal of Education Policy*, 25, (2), 151–69.

Barnett, M. and Finnemore, M. (2004), *Rules for the World: International Organisations in Global Politics*. Ithaca: Cornell University Press.

Barrow, C. W., Didou-Aupetit, S. and Mallea, J. (2004), *Globalisation, Trade Liberalisation, and Higher Education in North America: The Emergence of a new market under NAFTA?* Dordrecht: Kluwer Academic Publishers.

Beech, J. (2006), 'The theme of educational transfer in comparative education: a view over time'. *Research in Comparative and International Education*, 1, (1), 2–13.

Benveniste, L. (2002), 'The Political Structuration of Assessment: Negotiating State Power and Legitimacy'. *Comparative Education Review*, 46, (1), 89–118.

Bhanji, Z. (2008), 'Transnational corporations in education: filling the governance gap through new social norms and market multilateralism?' *Globalisation, Societies and Education*, 6, (1), 55–73.

Bieber, T. (2010), 'Playing the Multilevel Game in Education-the PISA Study and the Bologna Process Triggering Swiss Harmonisation', in K. Martens, A. Nagel, M. Windzio and A. Weymann (eds), *Transformation of Education Policy*. Basingstoke: Palgrave Macmillan, pp. 105–31.

Bonal, X. (2002), 'Plus ça change ... The World Bank Global Education Policy and the Post-Washington Consensus.' *International Studies in Sociology of Educational*, 12, (1), 3–21.

Bourdieu, P. (1999), 'Rethinking the state: genesis and structure of the bureaucratic field', in G. Steinmetz ed., *State/culture: State-formation after the cultural turn*. New York: Cornell University Press, pp. 53–75.

Brown, P. and Lauder, H. (1996), 'Education, Globalisation and Economic Development', *Journal of Education Policy*, 11, (1), 1–24.

Bulkley, K. and Fisler, J. (2003), 'A decade of charter schools: From theory to practice'. *Educational Policy*, 17, (3), 317–42.

Bull, B. and McNeill, D. (2007), *Development issues in global governance: Public-private partnerships and market multilateralism*. London: Routledge.

Campbell, J. L. (2004), *Institutional Change and Globalisation*. Princeton: Princeton University Press.

Carney, S. (2009), 'Negotiating Policy in an Age of Globalisation: Exploring Educational "Policyscapes" in Denmark, Nepal, and China'. *Comparative Education Review*, 53, (1), 63–88.

Carnoy, M. (1999), *Globalisation and Educational Reform: What planners need to know*. Paris: UNESCO.

Carnoy, M. and Rhoten, D. (2002), 'What does globalisation mean for educational change? A comparative approach'. *Comparative Education Review*, 46, (1), 1–9.

Cerny, P. G. (1997), 'Paradoxes of the Competition State: The Dynamics of Political Globalisation'. *Government and Opposition*, 32, (2), 251–74.

Chabbott, C. (2003), *Constructing education for development: International organisations and education for all*. New York: Routledge.

Commission on Global Governance (1995), *Our Global Neighbourhood*. Oxford: Oxford University Press.

Cox, R. W. (1995), 'Social forces, states, and world orders: Beyond international relations theory (1981)', in R. W. Cox and T. J. Sinclair (eds), *Approaches to world order*. Cambridge: Cambridge University Press, pp. 85–123.

Crossley, M. and Watson, K. (2003), *Comparative and international research in education: Globalisation, context and difference*. London: Routledge Falmer.

Dale, R. (1999), 'Specifying globalisation effects on national policy: Focus on the mechanisms'. *Journal of Education Policy*, 14, (1), 1–17.

—(2000), 'Globalisation and Education: Demonstrating a "common world educational culture" or locating a "globally structured educational agenda"'? *Educational Theory*, 50, (4), 427–48.

—(2005), 'Globalisation, knowledge economy and comparative education'. *Comparative Education*, 41, (2), 117–149.

Dale, R. and Robertson, S. (2007), 'Beyond methodological "isms" in comparative education in an era of globalisation', in A. Kazamias and R. Cowan (eds), *Handbook on Comparative Education*. Netherlands: Springer, 19–32.

Deacon, B. (2007), *Global social policy and governance*. London: Sage.

Drezner, D. W. (2001), 'Globalisation and Policy Convergence'. *International Studies Review*, 3, (1), 53–78.

Fairclough, N. (2000), *New Labour, New Language?* New York: Routledge.

Finnemore, M. (1996), 'Constructing Norms of Humanitarian Intervention', in P. J. Katzenstein ed., *The Culture of National Security: Norms and Identity in World Politics*. New York: Columbia University Press, pp. 153–85.

Green, A. (2003), 'Education, Globalisation and the Role of Comparative Research'. *London Review of Education*, 1, (2), 84–97.

Grek, S. (2007), 'Governing by numbers: the PISA Effect'. *Journal of Education Policy*, 24, (1), 23–37.

Grek, S., Lawn, M., Lingard, B. and Varjo, J. (2009), 'North by northwest: quality assurance and evaluation processes in European education'. *Journal of Education Policy*, 24, (2), 121–33.

Haas, P. M. (2004), 'When does power listen to truth? A constructivist approach to the policy process?' *Journal of European Public Policy*, 11, (4), 569–92.

Hartmann, E. (2007), 'Towards an International Regime for the Recognition of Higher Education Qualifications – The Empowered Role of UNESCO in the Emerging Global Knowledge-based Economy', in K. Martens, A. Rusconi, and K. Leuze (eds), *New Arenas of Education Governance: The Impact of International Organisations and Markets on Educational Policy Making*. New York: Palgrave Macmillan, pp. 76–94

Hay, C. (2006), 'What's Globalisation Got to Do with It? Economic Interdependence and the Future of European Welfare States'. *Government and Opposition*, 41, (1), 1–22.

Heinze, T. and Knill, C. (2008), 'Analysing the differential impact of the Bologna Process: Theoretical considerations on national conditions for international policy convergence'. *Higher Education*, 56, (4), 493–510.

Heyneman, S. P. (2003), 'The history and problems in the making of education policy at the World Bank 1960–2000'. *International Journal of Educational Development*, 23, (3), 315–37.

Huisman, J. and Van Der Wende, M. (2004), 'The EU and Bologna: are supra- and international initiatives threatening domestic agendas?' *European Journal of Education*, 39, (3), 349–57.

IEG (2011), *IEG Annual Report 2011: Results and Performance of the World Bank Group*. Washington DC: World Bank.

Jawara, F. and Kwa, A. (2004), *Behind the scenes at the WTO: The real world of international trade negotiations. Lessons of Cancun*. London-New York: Zed Books.

Jessop, B., Fairclough, N. and Wodak, R. (2008), *Education and the Knowledge-Based Economy in Europe*. Rotterdam: Sense Publishers.

Jones, P. W. (2006), *Education, poverty and the World Bank*. Rotterdam: Sense.

Keck, M. E. and Sikkink, K. (1998), *Activists Beyond Borders. Advocacy Networks in International Politics*. New York: Cornell University Press.

King, K. (2007), 'Multilateral agencies in the construction of the global agenda on education'. *Comparative Education*, 43, (3), 377–91.

Kingdon, J. W. (2002), *Agendas, Alternatives, and Public Policies*. London: Longman Publishing Group.

Lewin, K. M. (2007), 'The Limits to Growth of Non-Government: Private Schooling in Sub Saharan Africa', in P. Srivastava and G. Walford (eds), *Private Schooling in Less Economically Developed Countries: Asian and African Perspectives*. Oxford: Symposium, pp. 41–65.

Lingard, B., Rawolle, S. and Taylor, S. (2005), 'Globalising policy sociology in education: working with Bourdieu'. *Journal of Education Policy*, 20, (6), 759–77.

Luke, A. (2003), 'After the marketplace: Evidence, social science and educational research'. *The Australian Educational Researcher*, 30, (2), 89–109.

Marginson, S. (2004), 'Competition and Markets in Higher Education: A "glonacal" Analysis'. *Policy Futures in Education*, 2,(2), 175–244.

Martens, K., Nagel, A., Windzio, M. and Weymann, A. (2010), *Transformation of Education Policy*. Basingstoke: Palgrave Macmillan.

Martens, K. and Wolf, K. D. (2009), 'Boomerangs and Trojan Horses: The Unintended Consequences of Internationalising Education Policy Through the EU and the OECD', in A. Amaral, G. Neave, C. Musselin and P. Maassen (eds), *European Integration and the Governance of Higher Education and Research*. Dordrecht: Springer Netherlands, pp. 81–107.

Meyer, J. W., Ramirez, F. O. and Soysal, Y. N. (1992a), 'World expansion of mass education, 1870–1980'. *Sociology of Education*, 65, 128–49.

Meyer, J. W., Boli, J., Thomas, G. M. and Ramirez, F. O. (1997), 'World Society and the Nation-State'. *The American Journal of Sociology*, 103, (1), 144–81.

Meyer, J. W., Kamens, D. H., Benavot, A. with Cha, Y. K. and Wong, S. Y. (eds) (1992b), *School knowledge for the masses: World models and national primary curricular categories in the twentieth century*. Washington, DC: Falmer press.

Moutsios, S. (2010), 'Power, politics and transnational policy-making in education'. *Globalisation, Societies and Education*, 8, (1), 121–41.

Muhr, T. (2012, forthcoming), *Alternativa Bolivariana para las Américas (ALBA) and Counter-Globalisation: Resistance and the Construction of 21st Century Socialism*. New York: Routledge.

Mukhopadhyay, R., and Sriprakash, A. (2011), 'Global frameworks, local contingencies: policy translations and education development in India'. *Compare*, 41, (3), 311–26.

Mundy, K. (1998), 'Educational Multilateralism and World (Dis)Order'. *Comparative Education Review*, 42, (4), 448–78.

—(1999), 'Educational multilateralism in a changing world order: UNESCO and the limits of the possible'. *Journal of Education Development*, 19, (1), 27–52.

Mundy, K. and Menashy, F. (2011), 'Varieties of Organised Hypocrisy: The Case of the World Bank and Private Provision of Education', paper presented to Workshop 'Studying International Organisations in Social Policy', Bremen, 21 October.

Mundy, K. and Murphy, L. (2001), 'Transnational Advocacy, Global Civil Society? Emerging Evidence from the Field of Education'. *Comparative Education Review*, 45, (1), 85–126.

Neave, G. (1998), 'The evaluative state reconsidered'. *European Journal of Education*, 33, (3), 265–84.

Novelli, M. and Lopes Cardozo, M. T. A. (2008), 'Conflict, education and the global south: New critical directions'. *International Journal of Educational Development*, 28, (4), 473–88.

O'Brien, R., Goetz, A. M., Scholte, J. A. and Williams, M. (2000), *Contesting Global Governance: Multilateral Economic Institutions and Global Social Movements*. Cambridge: Cambridge University Press.

Peck, J., and Theodore, N. (2010), 'Mobilizing policy: models, methods, and mutations'. *Geoforum*, 41, (2), 169–74.

Phillips, D., and Ochs, K. (2003), 'Processes of policy borrowing in education: Some explanatory and analytical devices'. *Comparative Education*, 39,(4), 451–61.

Ramirez, F. O. (2006), 'Growing Commonalities and Persistent Differences in Higher Education: Universities between Globalisation and National Tradition', in H. D. Meyer and B. Rowan (eds), *The New Institutionalism in Education: Advancing Research and Policy*. Albany, NY: SUNY University Press, pp. 123–41.

Rhoten, D. (2000), 'Education decentralisation in Argentina: A "global-local conditions of possibility" approach to state, market, and society change'. *Journal of Education Policy*, 15, (6), 593–619.

Rizvi, F. and Lingard, B. (2009), *Globalizing Education Policy*. London: Routledge.

Robertson, S. (2005), 'Re-imagining and rescripting the future of education: global knowledge economy discourses and the challenge to education systems'. *Comparative Education*, 41, (2), 151–70.

Robertson, S., Bonal, X. and Dale, R. (2002), 'GATS and the education services industry: The politics of scale and global reterritorialisation'. *Comparative Education Review*, 46, (4), 472–96.

Robertson, S. and Dale, R. (2006), 'Changing geographies of power in education: The politics of rescaling and its contradictions', in D. Kassem, E. Mufti and J. Robinson eds, *Education studies: Issues and critical perspectives*. Buckinghamshire: Open University Press, pp. 21–232.

Robertson, S. and Verger, A. (2012, forthcoming), 'Governing education through Public-Private Partnerships', in S. Robertson, A. Verger, K. Mundy and F. Menashy (eds.), *Public Private Partnerships in Education: New Actors and Modes of Governance in a Globalizing World*. London: Edward Elgar.

Rose, P. M. (2007), *Supporting Non-state Providers in Basic Education Service Delivery*, paper commissioned by DFID Policy Division. Brighton: Consortium for Research on Educational Access, Transitions and Equity (CREATE). Research Monograph 4/2007.

Rupert, M. (2005), 'Reflections on some lessons learned from a decade of globalisation studies'. *New Political Economy*, 10, (4), 457–78.

Santos, B. S. (2005), *El milenio huérfano. Ensayos para una nueva cultura política*. Madrid: Trotta.

Schriewer, J. (2000a), 'World system and interrelationship networks: The internationalisation of education and the role of comparative inquiry', in T. S. Popkewitz ed., *Educational knowledge: Changing relations between the state, civil society, and the educational community*. Albany: State University of New York Press, pp. 305–43.

—J. (2000b), 'Comparative education methodology in transition: towards a science of complexity?' in J. Schriewer ed., *Discourse formation in comparative education*. Berlin: Peter Lang, pp. 3–52.

Schriewer, J., and Martinez, C. (2004), 'Constructions of internationality in education', in G. Steiner-Khamsi ed., *The global politics of educational borrowing and lending*. New York: Teachers' College Press, pp. 29–53.

Snyder, F. (1999), 'Governing economic globalisation: global legal pluralism and European law'. *European Law Journal*, 5, (4), 334–74.

Spreen, C. A. (2004), 'Appropriating borrowed policies: Outcomes-based education in South Africa', in G. Steiner-Khamsi ed, *The global politics of educational borrowing and lending*. New York: Teachers' College Press, pp. 101–13.

Srivastava, P. and Oh, S. A. (2010), 'Private foundations, philanthropy, and partnership in education and development: mapping the terrain'. *International Journal of Educational Development*, 30, (5), 460–71.

Steiner-Khamsi, G. (2004), *The Global Politics of Educational Borrowing and Lending*. New York: Teachers' College Press.

— (2010), 'The Politics and Economics of Comparison'. *Comparative Education Review*, 54, (3), 323–42.

Steiner-Khamsi, G. and Stolpe, I. (2006), *Educational import: local encounters with global forces in Mongolia*. New York: Palgrave Macmillan.

Stone, D. (2004), 'Transfer agents and global networks in the "transnationalisation" of policy'. *Journal of European Public Policy*, 11, (3), 545–66.

Taylor, S., and Henry, M. (2000), 'Globalisation and educational policymaking: A case study'. *Educational Theory*, 50, (4), 487–503.

Van Fleet, J. (2012, forthcoming), 'A disconnect between motivations and education needs: Why American corporate philanthropy alone will not educate the most marginalized', in S. Robertson, A. Verger, K. Mundy and F. Menashy (eds), *Public Private Partnerships in Education: New Actors and Modes of Governance in a Globalizing World*. London: Edward Elgar.

Vavrus, F. (2004), 'The referential web: Externalisation beyond education in Tanzania', in G. Steiner-Khamsi (ed.) *The global politics of educational borrowing and lending*. New York: Teachers' College Press, pp. 141–53.

Verger, A. (2009), 'The merchants of education: global politics and the uneven education liberalisation process within the WTO'. *Comparative Education Review*, 53, (3), 379–401.

—(2012), 'Framing and selling global education policy: the promotion of PPPs in education in low-income countries'. *Journal of Education Policy*, 27, (1), 109–30.

Verger, A. and Novelli, M. (2012, forthcoming), 'Understanding the outcomes of advocacy coalitions in education. A comparative perspective', in A. Verger and M. Novelli (eds), *Campaigning For 'Education For All': Histories, Strategies and Outcomes of Transnational Social Movements in Education*. Rotterdam: Sense.

Woods, N. (2000), 'The challenge of good governance for the IMF and the World Bank themselves'. *World Development*, 28, (5), 823–41.

Yeates, N. (2001), *Globalisation and Social Policy*. London: Sage.

CHAPTER TWO

Researching Global Education Policy: Angles In/On/Out …

Susan L. Robertson

Introduction

This chapter is concerned with researching global education policy. This is not a straightforward task, particularly in the area of education policy studies. To begin with, it involves going beyond accounts of the global as 'outside/exogenous' that acts upon and shapes education policymaking to what is described as the 'inside/endogenous', or 'local'. This way of seeing reinforces a view of the global as abstract, homogeneous, structural, and without agents or agency, while the local is concrete, diverse, agentic and imbued with democratic notions of bottom-up legitimacy however tenuous or thin in reality.

What is increasingly clear is that to understand our changing social worlds, new epistemic paradigms are needed. For instance, researching global education policy means making visible methodological statist and nationalist assumptions of policy studies more generally, and the ways in which these assumptions continue to influence education policy analyses in particular (Robertson *et al.* 2008). It also involves us asking about the policy process itself, particularly when it is no longer only, or primarily, the nationally-located state engaged in the making (and regulating) of policy and its implementation; and if this is the case, what then are the implications for thinking about policy as political, contested and public.

Yet invoking the need for a new epistemological paradigm, as opposed to articulating the basic elements entailed, are very different things, and the challenges are huge. How best to capture the complexities of education projects, policies and programmes that are now increasingly dispersed over what were once tightly managed boundaries around units of social life? How to generate analyses of the moments and movements of education actors and policies (and their varying forms – ideationally, materially, institutionally) across time and in space, that take into account policies as '… a complex, uneven and asymmetrical set of multi-layered cross-cutting processes and nodes of interaction?' (Cerny 2001, p. 397). Or how better to understand the process of education policymaking and its implementation when it involves a range of actors who are geographically dispersed, engaged in diverse governance activities, involving different accountability communities?And if education policy continues to be the 'authoritive allocation of values' as Prunty (1984, p. 42) reminded us more than two decades ago in his political framing of policy, then questions of authority, as well as whose values are represented, how, where, when, and the relationships between competing sites of power (state, private), continue to be important ways of understanding education policy analytically, including when it invokes and involves the global in new ways.

Rather than engage in a major review of the extant literature in the education policy field, my entry point into the challenges posed above is to engage with methodological accounts of global education policy being advanced by a group of critical education scholars working in international development contexts (see, Steiner-Khamsi 2004; Vavrus et al. 2006; Sobe et al. 2009; Carney 2009; 2011; Bartlett et al. 2011). These writers challenge 'orthodox' comparative and international education approaches, and are engaged in a lively debate around different aspects of global education policy. A range of concepts has emerged to describe these processes: from 'borrowing and lending' to 'transfer', 'circulation', 'pipes' and 'mobilities'. Their challenge is to advance ways of 'seeing' and studying education policies transnationally which are theoretically and empirically sensitive to the specificities of space, time and sociality, without giving ground to what Marginson and Mollis call 'ultra-relativism' (2001, p. 588).

This chapter will therefore proceed in the following way. I will begin with some brief comments on different ways of understanding the global in education policy. I then review contributions by Steiner-Khamsi (2002, 2004), Sobe et al. (2009), Vavrus et al. (2006, 2011), and Carney (2009, 2011). These authors advance new ways of researching these global processes. My engagement with their work is intended to stimulate a dialogue with and generate notes toward a critical account which I hope is helpful for researching global education policy.

Locating the 'Global' in Education Policy

The question of how the 'global' features in education policy and how wemight come to know the global in researching global education policy is dependent on how we understand each of the constituent elements – the 'global', 'education' and 'policy', and the relationships between them. I will be arguing that the global features in education policy are somewhat different though related ways: as a 'condition of the world', 'discourse', 'project', 'scale' and 'means of identifying the reach of particular actors'. As a *condition of the world*, this signals an ontological shift – a world that has profoundly changed as a result of neoliberalism as an organising project, the advance of new technologies, the blurring of boundaries between national territorial states, and so on. As a *discourse* in education policies, the global is invoked as a particular image, often tied to ideas like a 'global knowledge economy', 'global village', 'global social justice', and so on. As a *project* in education policy, it is to propose and set into motion by extending out into 'global' space particular ways of framing 'education' problems and their desirable/preferred solutions (such as privatisation, decentralisation, 'Education for All', quality, and so on). As *scale*, it is to register the ways in which platforms for action are constructed – in this case the 'global' – from which particular actors, as global actors, claim the legitimate right to advance ideas, to represent constituencies, or to govern. And finally, the global as *reach* refers to the horizon of action of particular institutions and actors engaged in different aspects of education policy work.

These ways of understanding the global in education are not meant to be exhaustive. Rather, they are meant to indicate the rather different ways in which the global features, and from there the different method-ologies we might deploy in researching the global in education policy. For instance, the global as discourse suggests we use some form of discourse analysis, while the global as reach, or spatial extension, suggests ways of understanding education policies, such as mobility or spatial theories, to capture movements from one point of origin (local) through space to be fixed/altered/ in a new locality or place. Whatever approach to research we might use, I will be suggesting that it is important to view concepts like the global and the local as relational. In other words, we must not essentialize particular actors, such as the World Bank Group, located in Washington, USA, as *always being* global. There are many activities of the Bank as an institution that are local, such as 'in-house' organisational policies. It is when the Bank's policies are promoted in distant locations that we might view the Bank's activity as global. This leads us to suggest that rather than see the global as operating in some stratosphere – up there – that we see them as *places* made up of a range of spatial relation-ships – some global, some local and so on. This then is suggestive of place as topological, as:

> ... a 'meeting place' of a whole series of complex networks and social relations. Its boundedness is understood not as forming a simple enclosure but as being permeated by the multiple relations that stretch across the globe. The specificity of place is not linked to a place-based identity, for places are traversed by unequal relations of power and struggles to contest these relations' (Massey 1994, p. 155).

Importantly too, as Peck and Theodore (2010) and Sobe *et al.* (2009, p. 63) argue, our approaches to the global need to be attentive to the ways in which movement involves reciprocal, reversible and multiple vectors, forming dense, overlapping webs of relationships.

And what of 'education'? And policy? It is clear that education as a sector, teaching as a profession, and learning as a means of regulation/emancipation, has been radically transformed; the outcome of political projects, like neoliberalism that have cut deep into the social fabrics of societies and sought to remake them. The division of labour in education that characterized post-war societies has been subject to major efforts, or policies, to unpick deeply embedded and institutionalized relationships, and to insert new ways of doing education. Not only has the global been invoked as the reason for policy, but education policies have been advanced by actors on new scales, such as the global, the regional, or local, in order to develop very different education sectors, teachers and learners. Finally, policy is both a medium as well as a message system. It is also a process. As medium, policies may take different forms, dependent on what kind of policy arenas we are looking at. As a message system, policies are ideational. They have at their heart a set of ideas (values) about what education as a social institution and set of practices should look like, including who is taught what, how, etc. and how these practices should be governed. With new actors in the education sector (such as for-profit firms), with different kinds of aspirations (such as making a profit, realising a different kind of learner), means of accounting (such as shareholders), and scalar horizons, this demands new ways of thinking about and researching education policy. As a process, policies are never 'one off' and discrete events. Rather, policies are social practices that unfold over time and in space. Untangling these analytically and empirically, with what tools, are clearly challenges we face in doing research.

Angles In/On: Researching the Global in Education Policy and International Development

As noted earlier, my intention is not to offer an exhaustive 'review' of different research approaches to global education policy in international development. Rather, it is to use the work of a small group of critical education researchers engaged in a range of education development sites and projects, as angles in/on global education policy with the intention of looking at how they are approaching these challenges.

The global as policy movement

Gita Steiner-Khamsi's (2002, 2004) work engages explicitly with the *movement* of education policies from one locality to another – that is, 'transnational borrowing and lending' (2004, p. 1) – and in the process of becoming 'global'. As she notes, in much of the literature, what motivates the movement of education policies from one location to another is the (normative) view that we can learn from elsewhere. Stepping aside from this more lesson-learning stance, Steiner-Khamsi proposes an analytical way forward: to focus on the 'why', 'how' and 'who' in the transfer of education policies. While noting that this concern might be regarded as 'old hat' (Steiner-Khamsi 2004, p. 4), she points out that the 'global', as the 'out-there education policy trend', is now being mobilized by a new 'semantics of globalisation' (Steiner-Khamsi 2004, p. 5) to legitimate the adoption of particular education policies to 'problems in-here'. These policies are not just discourses; rather, they are real, and must be under-stood – not just as something borrowed – but as discourses that enter into local circuits that are then 'adapted, modified and resisted' (Steiner-Khamsi 2004, p. 5). In other words, these policies are discourses that have real effects, though quite what these effects are cannot be known (only imagined) in advance.

Drawing on cases that are presented in her 2004 edited book, Steiner-Khamsi offers some answers to the question of 'why' policies are moving from one location to another: for example, the 'certification' (or legiti-mation) of changes in one locality will reference an 'external' set of social practices; the export of policies and programmes as part of an emerging trade within the education sector; the territorial practices of organisations who operate trans-nationally, 'leaving their mark'; when returns to invest-ments in education are dependent on economies of scale, hence forms of going global; or as certain kinds of technologies (rankings) able to accelerate change. Why are global policies taken up in particular locations? A range of possibilities is presented: for example, referential networks operating in different locations who take up ideas because there is a shared outlook, or because they are part of a *similar* professional network, and so on.

Steiner-Khamsi's methodological move is to focus on social networks and network analysis, and these are clearly promising ideas and ways of viewing the movement of education policy. For example, from the late 1990s onward, a small network of global education policy entrepreneurs has been highly influential in advancing the World Bank's version of Public Private Partnerships in education (see Verger 2012). However, as Verger observes, there are clear limits in this network advancing their PPP agenda, limits that arise because of wider structural agendas (or what Peck *et al.* [2010, p. 174] call a 'context of contexts'), because of contestation within the Bank about proper engagement with the private sector, the suspicion of client countries about Bank agendas, and so on. The issue therefore with social network analysis is not that it is not valuable, but that it is not enough. And by underplaying the structural or purposeful intermediation, it tends by default an overly agency/actor account. In doing so, it also risks obscuring the complexity of the connections and inter-crossings that engender certain cultural forms and social patterns, and not others (Sobe et al. 2009), on the one hand, and the deeper forms of hegemony that limit ways of seeing, doing and going on in this world on the other.

Like network theory in general, with its eschewal of hierarchy (and scale theory), social network theory tends to assume a flat ontology of social sites. And in flattening out space, we also do not see the ways in which key actors concerned with education policy, the state and non-state actors (such as the World Bank Group [WB], the European Commission [EC], the Organisation for Economic Cooperation and Development [OECD]), all mobilize hierarchy as a means of legitimating rule. In other words, as Amin and Thrift observe:'... those concerned with the politics of regulation and governance associated with globalization are right to note the very real and felt contest of jurisdiction between local, national and global state and non-state organisations' (2002, p. 396). What is important, however, is not to view scales as fixed, but as mutable; they are produced and reproduced by socio-economic processes and political struggles, with education policies selectively and strategically advanced to do precisely some of this kind of work. In other words, global education policies may well move along social networks, but they are also mobilized by social networks, as well as hierarchically organized actors – such as the state and non-state actors – to advance projects of governing and rule.

The vertical case

If hierarchy can be shown to be ontologically important in social space, then to what extent does the 'vertical case' of Vavrus et al. (2006, p. 95) help us understand global education policy? Their approach is epistemological; that is, it is animated by a concern about *what* can be known about the world, and *how*. They are also particularly interested in comparison as a methodology; what can be known about specific localities which is in turn part of larger structures, forces and politics.

They argue that epistemologically, the aim of the vertical case is to '... grasp the complexity of the relationships between the knowledge claims among actors with different social locations as an attempt to situate local action and interpretation within a broader cultural, historical and political investigation.' They are particularly concerned with the importance of 'context', but unlike case studies whose context is regarded as 'local' and 'situated', their context extends to 'take account of historical trends, social structures, and national and international forces that shape local processes at this site' (Vavrus *et al.* 2006, p. 960). In other words, their extended view of context includes 'the global'.

Bartlett and Vavrus (2011) argue that the vertical case makes three important contributions. First, it insists on simultaneous attention to the micro-, meso-, and macro-levels to enable 'vertical comparison'. Second, it emphasizes the importance of historically-situating processes under consideration to enable comparing across time in what they call 'transversal comparison'. Third, it emphasizes the importance of comparing how similar processes unfold in distinct locations in space, or 'horizontal comparison' (Bartlett *et al.* 2011, pp. 1–2). In looking at Learner Centred Pedagogy (LCP) in Tanzania and Kenya using the vertical case methodology, horizontal comparison with other sites suggests there is a common semantic clustering of codes at work in the policy arena; for instance, there are strong discourses around 'secondary education for all', investments in technology, and the need for a particular kind of pedagogy in secondary education to advance a competitive knowledge-based economy.

The strength of their vertical case is to move beyond what Bartlett and Vavrus (2011) call 'policy discourse', to developing the links between the production of policy discourses and the ways in which they are appropriated and practiced, and the relationships between these newer discourses and older, more deeply embedded, ones. In the case of Tanzania and LCP, they are able to detect an older 'socialist discourse' with its focus on education for self-reliance with a newer discourse that emphasizes competition, individualism and authority. They also show that the differences between Tanzania and Kenya in terms of LCP, and between different schools in each national setting (horizontal comparisons), is mediated by different training experiences, the outcome of different levels of engagement with the global economy.

There is a great deal of value in their approach to doing global education policy research, particularly ways of undertaking 'transversal' and 'horizontal' comparisons, and what links, overlappings and asymmetries we can see as a result. By drawing attention to the multilayered and cross-cutting processes and modes of interaction – some recent and others less so – they provide us with a strong sense of both present and past, and of the complexities of what it means to refer to 'situatedness', or what Polanyi (1944) refers to as 'embeddedness'.

However, the implicit assumption in the idea of 'vertical comparison' is that the global is equated to the macro, and structural; a social force that the local (or micro) must face. Here we have an unhelpful pitting of structures (as global/macro) against agents (as local/micro). Yet I have argued earlier, following Massey (1994), places are made up of actors with local and global horizons of action. The question here for education policy analysis ought to be; whose values are allocated, how, and with what outcomes for education as a sector, teachers and learners. That we have a way of viewing the 'global' as simultaneously lived, concrete and local is important, for it emphasizes locality and place as a meeting point for complex networks and social relations that stretch out into global space.

Finally, we need a way of finessing how we talk about different things in the social worlds we are studying; for the moment they tend to be caught in a micro-meso-macro 'catch-all' when actually what we are doing is referring to rather different things, such as hierarchy and rule, or structures and agents, or the global and the local, or the abstract and the concrete, and so on. These are clearly a different order of concepts to the idea of the macro as level of abstraction and where the abstract is necessarily derived from objects, structures and mechanisms (Sayer 1984, p. 140).

Scopic systems and the global

In a rather different contribution Sobe *et al.* (2009) draw attention to the work of Knorr Cetina (2008) and her problematisation of networks for understanding currency markets. Knorr Cetina's argument is that the ideas of the network do not capture the totality of what is in play, including the significance of heightened moments of reflexivity when multiple forms of information are presented simultaneously, then aggregated, articulated and projected, and in doing so give it new meaning. She refers to these processes as 'scopic systems'; that is, '... ways of seeing the global that tend toward a single collective' (Sobe *et al.* 2009, p. 58). Sobe and Ortegon make use of this suggestive idea to think of the way in which education, both histori- cally and in the present, has been projected globally, as well as projecting globality. They point to International Expositions and World Fairs held in the late nineteenth century as an example of the ways in which objects were placed together, classified and then evaluated against a notion of an unfolding future given forward momentum by assumptions of progress and modernity. In this very moment, the world is presented as a singular world (Sobe *et al.* 2009, p. 61).

Similarly, today there is a burgeoning array of scopic systems that gather together, place in hierarchies and project globally a singular education world – from the OECD's Programme in International Student Assessment (PISA), or their Teaching and Learning International Survey (TALIS), to global university rankings (Shanghai Jiao Tong, Times Higher, U-Multi-Rank), the World Bank's Knowledge Assessment Methodology (KAM) (Robertson 2009), and the recently launched SABER system to assess and rank school and teacher performance globally (Robertson 2011). What is significant about these scopic systems, argue Sobe *et al.* (2009, p. 62) is '... the extent to which they function like an array of crystals that collects and focuses light on one surface.'

Yet what is important to note is that scopic systems in global education policy take *fragments* (partial understandings) of knowledge about complex education processes, yet present them as a *fractal* (a smaller versions of a whole). In doing so, the complexity and diversity of education systems, and their need for diverse policies for diverse issues, also disappears.

Fractals (as disguised fragments) act as a proxy, shorthand and lever for education policy problems. Their power as levers of policy reside in their capacity to project a singular solution to an imagined single problem (competition, efficiency, world class), and in doing so, diversity is produced as absent. Scopic systems in education are also forms of power in that they simultaneously *frame* education problems, offer a *desired* re/solution, project *outward* with considerable spatial extension, reinforce new social practices over time because of further rounds of data gathering and projection, and tap into *emotions* (shame, pride) that change behaviour – deep inside national territorial states (Robertson 2011). These are powerful systems, which both state and non-state actors have mobilized as a new means for governing education systems. They are key sites of global education policy, as project, projection and propagation. What is important for ongoing research into global education policymaking is discerning the different array of actors and interests involved in scopic systems, the values that are being advanced, the ways in which authority to govern is generated, and whether and how the processes are open to, and visible to, the wider public and public debate.

Policyscapes and the global as 'optique'

To study the global in international development, Steve Carney (2009, 2011) has suggested the concept of *'policyscapes'*. Using what he describes as an *optique* of globalization, Carney advances 'an experiment in method' to derive accounts of the *experiences* of different countries in the *production* of globalization. In doing so, he aims to focus attention on the constitutive moment of globalization in particular places which he argues are being deterritorialized as a result of global processes. What is central, Carney argues, is the need to theorize the dynamics of space, and bring to the fore the specificities of education, and the implementation of education policy in particular places.

Carney's experiment is to study three places in one global space, Denmark, Tibet/China and Nepal, to 'present some of the lived consequences of these entanglements' (Carney 2009, p. 6) in global education reform. As he argues: 'This interest in the entangled and co-produced experience of global education reform is lacking in many recent analyses of education policy.' Drawing from the work of Tsing (2005), Carney explores the 'friction' of global connectivity between these imagined worlds, in which '... heterogeneous and unequal encounters' share '... new arrangements of culture and power' (Carney 2011, p. 7). In a context of globally-shared visions for education, and with the advance of neoliberal political projects privileging the market, new localities are emerging as '... the embodiment of the practices that make certain de-territorialized displays of identity' (Carney 2011, p. 8). In other words, localities are being reconfigured, as global educational policies, institutional fabrics, and other social relationships move over national territorial boundaries.

However, though Carney aims for an approach that he describes as 'mutually constitutive and dialectically constructed' (Carney 2011, p. 7), he does not go far enough because of the limitations imposed by this particular conceptualisation of globalization, one that tends to privilege, and thus fetishize, flows, motion, instabilities and uncertainty, without attending to the new ways in which processes of fixity, reterritorialisation, rebordering, and reordering are at work (cf. Robertson 2011).

Given Carney's (and by implication Bartlett *et al.* 2011) debt to Appadurai, it is important we look more closely at Appadurai's anchoring ideas. In a series of works, Appadurai (1996) popularized the idea of global flows, along with his locution 'scapes' (as in ethnoscapes, technoscapes, mediascapes, ideoscapes and financescapes) as '... different streams or flows along which cultural material may be seen to be moving across national boundaries' (1996, pp. 45–6). Scapes are therefore a means of superseding standard geographical thinking advanced by the nation state. It is also a way of capturing what he saw to be the multiple, chaotic and disjunctive nature of flows, and the distributions and results of processes at any given time.

While recognising there have always been flows in the past, Appadurai insists the present is radically different. As he says: '... globalisation has shrunk the distance between elites, shifted key relations between producers and consumers, broken many links between labour and family life, obscured the lines between temporary locales and imaginary national attachments...' and '... broken the monopoly of autonomous nation states over the project of modernisation' (1996, pp. 10–11). And if the past was 'placed' and 'localistic', the present is now a 'placeless locality of flows'. These transformations are the outcome of new information technologies and the speed of transport, as well as the deep rupturing of modernity, its signs and centres of power. For Appadurai this opens the space for a new global imagination, drawing its energy, vitality and creativity from the unpredictable outcomes from 'disjunctures' between flows, and from the possibilities enabled by the faster pace of new technologies and the accelerated speed of transport.

Appadurai extends his argument for 'disjuncture' through the concept of 'deterritorialisation', as a process in the actual world *and* a conceptual break with a past constructed from the tightly bound containers of home and social life located within nation states. Processes of deterritorialisation now permit diaspora-based ethnic politics to be communicated across the globe, enabling, in turn, the diffusion of mediascapes and ideoscapes beyond their narrow places into global networks. Most importantly, deterritorialisation makes the normal functioning of nation states problematic and contingent, since their prime cultural challengers are transnational ethnic movements (Appadurai 1996, pp. 39–40).

However, there are a number of issues with Appadurai's account of globalization which also then feature in Carney's globalization *optique*. Appadurai's project is to advance a more dynamic, contingent and less static, reading of contemporary social and political life by emphasising movement, flows, disjunctures and the disappearance of borders. However, he now veers in the opposite direction, so that power is now amorphous, history is obscured, there is an under-developed conception of the present, and there are no boundaries that order difference (Heyman *et al.* 2009). And while Carney is concerned to see power as 'frictions' using the work of Anna Tsing (2005), these are only the more visible manifestations of power (as productive). A more complex view of power would lead us to search for absences (Dale *et al.* 2004) as well as to focus on those events that generate events, or as Stephen Lukes (1974) describes it, the third face of power or 'rules of the game' that determine hegemonies.

A sympathetic reading of Appadurai's work suggests that the focus on movement and radical rupture tends to typify early work on globalization. More recently, scholars (Harvey 2000, 2005; Mittelman 2004) have pointed to the duality of change and continuity making up the transformation of the world order. For example, if we look at the global education policy landscape, we can detect longer-standing claims about education as a public good, and the public sector encountering more recent claims about education as a market, a private good and a services sector.

Secondly, Appadurai's understandings of transnationalism, as the extension outward from a particular locality into global networks, and whose horizons of action are now global, broadly aligns with Santos' (2004) understanding of globalization. However, Santos goes further than this 'node on a global network' understanding by arguing that globalization can be understood as a localism that acquires for itself universal hegemonic status, so that all other contenders are deemed local. This way of thinking about globalization helps us to work with a more complex view of power, as not only positionality in a network (Sheppard 2002), but where *some* localisms secure sufficient power and reach, including through scopic systems, to enable them to determine the rules of the game.

Thirdly, Appadurai's transnational network metaphor of globalization places it *above*, and not *on*, the terrain that is also occupied by a range of actors, including the national territorial state, sub-national actors, and so on. The local and place are now dislodged by the global, as the key category in a hierarchy of categories to understand social life. In other words, he moves from the rejection of the localized and bounded to an opposite extreme. Several problems follow from this. The first is that the researcher is invited to see the world through a global optic that ontologically flattens space. Second, by viewing the world as having no boundaries: '… the global exists as a space that is neither here nor there; it has no distributed patterns, and has no internal relations reproducing convergence or differentiation. It is simply a space that is everywhere' (Heyman *et al.* 2009, p. 136). Ironically, this encourages a homogenous view of social life, despite intending the opposite. In other words, this way of seeing the world encourages us to bypass a fundamental *effect* of flows: how they constitute, reproduce and reconstitute social life.

Fourthly, Appadurai conceptualizes the present (as global) and flows, while borders as realities disappear. This leads to his adoption of deterritorialisation as a key organising concept. Deterritorialistion is the name given to the problematic wherein a territory loses its significance and power in everyday social life. The effect here, however, is to end up conceptually in the same place as Kenichi Omhae's (1990) 'borderless world', or Thomas Friedman's (2005) 'flat earth'. And as Ó Tuathail (1999, p. 140) argues, '... discourses of deterritorialisation tend to ascribe a unique transcendency to the contemporary condition, defining it as a moment of overwhelming newness. Such functionally anti-historical notions of deterritorialisation find a variety of different expressions in political, economic and techno-cultural knowledge.' The problem here of course is that these discourses have considerable ideological power and rhetorical force and '... are part of neoliberal ideology in that it strives to denaturalize and delimit the power of the state and naturalize and bolster the virtues of the market' (Ó Tuathail 1999, p. 147).

Angles Out: Notes Toward a Critical Processual Account

In the opening paragraphs of this chapter I posed a series of questions around researching global education policy; questions that have been at the heart of the different angles *in and on* global education policy that I have been exploring. In this section I want to draw these insights together, and look at what more we need to do in order to advance this research agenda. We might call this next move, *angles out*. For instance, while social networks give us new insights into how education policies move through space, we need to keep in view sites' specific experimentation, purposeful intermediation, mutations, transformations in linked sites, and hierarchical power, such as states, and the production and strategic use of scale that enables the launch of new education actors, projects, policies and practices.

Similarly, while the idea of flows as a metaphor helps us to grasp hold of the movement of education policies around the global, it is clear that we must also be attentive to the new forms of bordering that are also at work.' Flow speak' tends to '... detach global flows from the material and institutional conditions which underpin global culture' (Bude *et al.* 2010, p. 482). And while recognising that a new set of dynamics is at work reflected in distinctive developments in contemporary world history (Scholte 2005), it is not possible to imagine a world which is *only* borderless and deterritorialized in that the basic ordering of social groups and societies *requires* categories and compartments (Harvey 2006). More recently, researchers have begun to argue we need to study the other side of movement and change; for instance 'stickiness' (along with slipperiness) (Markusen 1996), 'fixity' (along with motion) (Harvey 1999), and 'borders' (along with flows), as correctives. In studies of globalising education policy-making it is critical that we see the collapsing of boundaries as accompanied by new bordering processes, giving rise to new ordering practices and subjectivities (cf. Robertson 2011). Sassen (2006) argues that new bordering practices are taking place within a context of dissolving or weakening boundaries. In his paper, 'Europe as borderland', Balibar argues that, far from being at the outer limit of territories, '... these borders are dispersed a little everywhere, wherever the movement of information, people, and things is happening and is controlled, for example in cosmopolitan cities' (Balibar 2002, p. 71). In other words, when we conceive of globalization as partly enacted at various sub-national scales and institutional domains, we can see a proliferation of borderings deep inside national territories. A focus on such bordering capabilities allows us to see a 'geopolitics of space' easily obscured in the kind of account advanced which assumes the mutual exclusivity of the national and the global by the way in which we represent them as discrete hierarchical spaces (Sassen 2006). This has led Amin to argue that:

> I have distanced myself from the territorial idea of sequestered spatial logics – local, national, continental and global – pitted against each other. Instead, I have chosen to interpret globalisation in relational terms as the interdependence and intermingling of global, distant and local layers, resulting in the greater hybridisation and perforation of social, economic and political life (Amin 1997, p. 133).

In their own ways, the different analytical approaches raise direct and indirect questions about the national state and its role in global education policy. For instance, how is national state power challenged by scopic systems, or networks? And, whose interests are advanced by these represen-tations of education, whose framings count, and with what consequences for fundamental questions that state education policy has historically been asked to account for (social justice, legitimation, issues of redistribution, the state-citizen contract, and so on)? What is entailed in the decentering of the national state? Furthermore, we need to ask about the whereabouts of state power, when education policy is dispersed over scales?

In order to bring to the fore the spatiality of state power, I have found the account of Ferguson *et al.* (2002) of the spatiality of the modern nation state particularly helpful. Ferguson *et al.* (2002, p. 982) argue modern nation states use two sources of spatial imaginary and projection: 'vertical power' and 'encompassment'. Vertical power leads to the idea of the state as an institution 'above' civil society, the community and family. It is a powerful container of social and political life that not only sits above, but also encompasses in a series of radiating circles outward, from the family to the system of nation states. As Ferguson *et al.* (2002, p. 982 remark, '... this is a profoundly consequential understanding of scale, one in which the locality is encompassed by the region, the region by the nation state, and the nation state by the international community'. Such metaphors are powerful ideas; in relation to the national state, they reinforce a view of the state as possessing higher functions (reason, control, capacity for regulation) which are productive of social and political life.

If verticality and encompassment capture the geometry of state power in the modern nation state, what is the geography of the contemporary state? Theoretical work is still in its early stages, largely because this new geography has not yet stabilized (Jessop 2002). For the moment let me point to two (somewhat different) lines of work emerging that may prove to be fruitful for the study of the globalization of education policy. The first focuses attention on the rescaling of the state (Brenner 2004, 2009) which has paralleled the rescaling of capital accumulation. Scales in this work are argued to be sites for political struggle as well as one of their key mechanisms and outcomes (MacLeod *et al.* 1999; Jessop 2002). As Brenner observes, 'the rescaling of institutions and policies is now conceptualized as a key means through which social forces may attempt to "rejig" the balance of class power and manage the contradictory social relations of capitalism' (Brenner 2009, p. 126). This leads to the question of what post-national statehood might look like, and what might be the implications of this for education policy.

While the notion of the post-national in work by Jessop (2002) and Brenner (2009) is argued to be a tendential rather than a substantive concept, both make it clear that it does not mean the national is marginalized, *but that the national itself is being redefined in relation to the other scales*. This kind of account contrasts with Appadurai's approach where, as we have seen, the national/local is absorbed into global networks. The reading of Jessop and Brenner of the transformation of state space resonates with a growing body of work on the globalization of education, where it is possible to see education policies as simultaneously constitutive of new scales that contain newer social actors and relations (such as Europe, the European citizen, the European Higher Education Area, and so on), as well as being platforms from which to advance projects of rule, and projects that concern themselves with the development of globally-competitive education systems and subjectivities.

A rather different kind of analysis of the geography of contemporary state power in modern western neoliberal economies comes from John Allen *et al.* (2010). They argue that while Brenner stretches the language of scale to take account of a new institutional complexity that views multi-scalar power relations as multiple, overlapping, tangled and so on, in their view it does not quite grasp the changing geography of state power. Advancing a topological account of state spatiality, Allen and Cochrane draw attention to the state's reconfiguration of hierarchical power (or what Ferguson and Gupta called verticality) and the ways in which a more transverse set of political interactions, or reach, holds that hierarchy in place. They stress that it is not extensivity of reach that characterizes the new geography of state power but intensivity, serving to disrupt what is near or far, in turn loosening our sense of defined times and distances. As Allen and Cochrane argue: 'what is politically at stake... is that such an approach is able to show how the state's hierarchical powers have not so much been rescaled or redistributed as reassembled in terms of spatial reach' (2010, p. 1073). 'Reach' here means those arts of governing that enable the state to permeate and penetrate those spaces that hitherto had been unreachable. They add:

> ... it is *not* that state hierarchies have transformed themselves into horizontal networking arrangements, but rather that the hierarchies of decision-making that matter are *institutional* and not scalar ones. ... In that sense, the apparatus of state authority is not so much 'up there' or indeed 'over there' as part of a spatial arrangement within which different elements of government, as well as private agencies, exercise powers of reach that enable them to be more or less present within and across ... political structures (Allen *et al.* 2010, p. 1074).

Drawing on Sassen's (2006) work, and her use of 'assemblage' to signal a new geography of state power, they suggest that different bits and pieces of institutional authority (state/private) are drawn within reach of one another. State hierarchies, together with private agencies, partnerships and supranational institutions may, in that sense, be seen as part of a geographical assemblage of distributed authority in which power is continually being renegotiated. Cerny (2001) refers to this newer kind of formation as a 'golden pentangle', contrasting it with the 'iron triangle' (state/civil society/economy) of the modern national welfare state period. Public-Private-Partnerships – dense linkages that include state, local forms, transnational organisations, venture philanthropists – are one example of this reworking of institutional boundaries, sectors and the redistribution and reassembling of authority. However, future work will need to ensure that assemblages are not simply viewed as a coincidental, contingent activity. Rather, assemblages will have their own forms of structural and strategic selectivity that produce and reproduce education sectors, forms of labour, learning and subjectivities.

My own conclusion, too, in examining the rescaling of education through globalising education policy, is that hierarchy continues to be invoked as a basis of authority and right to rule, for example, the EC's determination to advance a European higher education area in relation to national, sub-national and institutional higher education systems. These assemblages can be viewed as having particular territorial regimes, ones that need to be traced out in detail, including how modes of rule and claims to rights are navigated and negotiated. In education sectors, these include a new array of scopic systems, networks and hierarchical systems, criss-crossing, overlapping and extending out from particular meeting places. As a result, authority and sovereignty is no longer fused with the national scale but rather is unevenly spread.

Finally, in the education sector at least, both extensivity and intensivity characterize the new geography of state power, and these are not mutually exclusive categories. For example, the state's engagement with scopic systems, like league tables, both generate a singular (statistical) representation of social activity as well as a hierarchical ordering to produce a moral judgement about social life; in doing so we can see these two elements working in combination, and with considerable effect.

Concluding Remarks

This chapter set out to explore researching global education policy in ways that aim to avoid the cul-de-sacs that dog many explanations. This is a challenging and ambitious project, and the works reviewed in this chapter have made a significant contribution. However, I have argued there is more to do, and that an account that is critical, processual and relational might help advance the project further. A critical account is attentive to discursive and material power, and the new forms of uneven spatial development that are the outcome of policy mobility. In arguing for a processual approach, I want to point to the risks and political consequences of failing to historicize our accounts of transformations in the education sector, or inadvertently allowing ourselves to be seduced by arguments that everything has changed and that now nothing is fixed in either meaning, sites or sources of power and authority. Rather, our challenge must be to identify and trace out the sites, actors, institutions, scales, technologies of rule and consequences of the new assemblages of education policymaking and practice which increasingly include private forms of authority mobilized by powerful players. A processual account would be attentive to the new and different ways in which points of fixity, bordering and ordering are taking place in the education sector, as well as the changing spatiality of state power. And, like Allen and Cochrane, I do not believe that the state is *not* a presence in our everyday lives. Far from it! The state has increasingly acquired for itself a new range of scales from which to act, as well as new tools and means of governing. In combination, this new spatiality of state power strategically advances educational projects that shape the lives and subjectivities of each of us, albeit it in contested and mediated ways.

Our analytic accounts of global education policy must also be relational in three senses, first in a strategic sense, in that policy is advanced in order to secure particular projects and interests. These interests are always in relation to others' interests. Second, flows themselves or 'scapes' may be discrete, but they are not disconnected. They overlap as well as interpenetrate one other. We see this very clearly at the current time with intense financialisation of the education section, on the one hand, and the attempt to construct education as a trading sector on the other. Education finds itself caught in the swirl of other flows, and the object and target for new points of fixity. It is relational in a third sense, and that is that policies that are being globalized enter into locations that are themselves circuits of flows anchored in social relations. Global education policy interventions not only generate potential frictions but might, as Sassen (2006) argues, result in the emergence of new logics, and new tipping points, in turn altering the nature and shape of the education sector.

By way of a final conclusion, it is worth returning to Prunty's (1984) conceptualisation of education policy as the authoritative allocation of values. In asking what difference the global makes, it is clear that it does in this way. Not only have the sites and sources of authority been dispersed away from the national, but the state itself – and with it education as a public service – has been transformed. This has not been the result of a global steamroller, but rather of the complex reworking, re/bordering and re/ordering of education spaces to include a range of scales of action. What are the consequences of these developments, particularly in relation to whose interests are advanced? These are clearly empirical questions and ones that deserve urgent attention.

References

Allen, J. and Cochrane, A. (2010), 'Assemblages of state power: topological shifts in the organisation of government and politics'. *Antipode*, 42 (5), 1071–89.

Amin, A. (1997), 'Placing globalisation'. *Theory, Culture and Society*, 14, (2), 123–37.

Amin, A. and Thrift, N. (2002), *Cities*. Oxford: Polity.

Appadurai A. (1996), *Modernity at Large: Cultural Dimensions of Globalisation*, Minneapolis, MN: University of Minnesota Press.

Balibar, E. (2002), 'World Borders, Political Borders'. *PMLA*, 117, (1), 71–8.

Bartlett, L. and Vavrus, F. (2011), '*Knowing Comparatively: Vertical Case Studies as an Approach to Policy as Practice*', paper presented to CIES, Montreal, 1–5 May.

Brenner, N. (2004), *New State Spaces*, Oxford: Oxford University Press.

—(2009), 'Open questions on state rescaling'. *Cambridge J. of Regions, Economy and Society*, 2, (2), 123–39.

Bude, H. and Durrschmidt, J. (2010), 'What's wrong with globalization?

Contra-flow speak – toward an existential turn in the theory of globalisation'. *European Journal of Social Theory*, 13, (4), 481–500.

Carney, S. (2009), 'Negotiating policy in an age of globalization: exploring educational policyscapes in Denmark, Nepal and China'. *Comparative Education Review*, 53, (1), 63–88.

—(2011, forthcoming), 'Imagining globalisation: Educational policyscapes', in G. Steiner-Khamsi and F. Waldow (eds), *World Yearbook of Education 2012 'Policy Borrowing, Policy Lending'*. London and New York: Routledge.

Cerny, P. (2001), 'From "Iron Triangles" to "Golden Pentagles"? Globalising the Policy Process'. *Global Governance*, 7, (4), 397–410.

Dale, R. and Robertson, S. (2004), 'Interview with Boaventura de Sousa Santos', *Globalisation, Societies and Education*, 2, (2), 147–60.

Ferguson, J. and Gupta, A. (2002), 'Spatialising states: toward an ethnography of neoliberal governmentality'. *American Ethologist*, 29, (4), 981–1002.

Friedman, T. (2005), *The World is Flat: a Brief History of the Twenty-first Century*. New York: Farrar, Straus & Giroux.

Harvey, D. (1999), *The Limits to Capita*, new edn. London and New York: Verso.

—(2006), *Spaces of Global Capitalism: Toward a Theory of Uneven Geographical Development*. London and New York: Verso.

Heyman, J. and Campbell, H. (2009), 'The anthropology of global flows: a critical reading of Appadurai's "Disjuncture and Difference in the Global Cultural Economy"'. *Anthropological Theory*, 9, 131–47.

Jessop, B. (2002), *The Future of the Capitalist State*. London: Polity.

Knorr Cetina, K. (2008), 'Micro-globalization', in I. Rossi ed., *Frontiers of Globalization Research: Theoretical and Methodological Approaches*. New York: Springer, pp. 65–92.

Lukes, S. (1986), 'Introduction', in S. Lukes ed. *Power*. Oxford: Blackwells, pp. 1–18.

MacLeod, G. and Goodwin, M. (1999), 'Space, scale and state strategy; rethinking urban and regional governance'. *Progress in Human Geography*, 23, 503–27.

Marginson, S. and Mollis, M. (2001), 'The door opens and the tiger leaps: theories and reflexivities of comparative education for a global millennium'. *Comparative Education Review*, 45, (4), 581–615.

Markusen, A. (1996), 'Sticky places in slippery space: a typology of industrial districts'. *Economic Geography*, 72, (3), 293–313.

Massey, D. (1994), *Space, Place and Gender*. Cambridge: Polity.

Mittelman, J. (2004), *Whither Globalisation: The Vortex of Knowledge and Ideology*. London and New York: Routledge.

Ó Tuathail, G. (1999), 'Borderless worlds: problematising discourses of deterritorialisation'. *Geopolitics*, 4, (2), 139–54.

Omhae, K. (1990), *The Borderless World*. New York: HarperCollins.

Peck, J. and Theodore, N. (2010), 'Mobilising policy: models, methods and mutations'. *Geoforum*, 41, 169–74.

Polanyi, K. (1944), *The Great Transformation: the Political and Economic Origins of our Time*. Boston, MA: Beacon Press.

Prunty, J. (1984), *A Critical Reformulation of Educational Policy Analysis*. Geelong: Deakin University.

Robertson, S. (2009), '"Producing" the global knowledge economy: the World Bank, The Knowledge Assessment Methodology and Education', in M. Simons,

M. Olssen, and M. Peters (eds), *Re-reading Education Policies*, Rotterdam: Sense Publishers, pp. 235–56.

—(2011a), 'The new spatial politics of (re)bordering and (re)ordering the education-state-society relation'. *International Review of Education*, 57, 277–97.

—(2011b), *'Placing' Teachers in Global Governance Agendas*, paper presented to the CIES Annual Conference, Montreal, 1–5th May.

Robertson, S. and Dale, R. (2008), 'Researching education in a globalising era: beyond methodological nationalism, methodological statism, methodological educationism and spatial fetishism', in J. Resnik ed., *The Production of Educational Knowledge in the Global Era*. Rotterdam: Sense Publications, pp. 19–32.

Sassen, S. (2006), *Territory, Authority, Rights*. Princeton, USA: Princeton University Press.

Sayer, A. (1984), *Method in Social Science: A Realist Approach*. London and New York: Routledge.

Scholte, J-A (2005), *Globalization: A Critical Introduction*, 2nd edn. New York: Palgrave Macmillan.

Sobe, N. and Ortegon, N. (2009), 'Scopic systems, pipes, models and transfers in the global circulation of educational knowledge and practices', in T. Popkewitz and F. Rizvi (eds), *Globalization and the Study of Education*. New York: NSSE/ Teachers College Press, pp. 49–66.

Steiner-Khamsi, G. (2002), 'Re-framing educational borrowing as a policy strategy', in M. Caruso and H. E. Tenworth (eds), *Internationalisierung-Internationalisation*. Frankfurt: Lang, pp. 57–89.

—(2004), *The Global Politics of Educational Borrowing and Lending*. New York: Teachers' College Columbia.

Tsing, A. (2005), *Friction*. Princeton: Princeton University Press.

Vavrus, F. and Bartlett, L. (2006), 'Comparatively knowing: making a case for the vertical case study'. *Current Issues in Comparative Education*, 8, (2), 95–103.

Verger, A. (2012), 'Framing and selling global education policy: the promotion of PPPs in education in low-income countries'. *Journal of Education Policy*, 27, (1), 109–30.

PART TWO

Global Education Policy: Case Studies

CHAPTER THREE

Participation in International Development and Education Governance

D. Brent Edwards Jr. and Steven Klees

Participation in Development and Education Governance

The global nature of participation as a development strategy is evinced by the wide range of interests which invoke this term as an aspect of appropriate action which should be pursued (Cornwall 2006). However, while the profile of this idea – which has a long history in development (Cornwall 2006; Leal 2007) – has become increasingly prominent, its meaning is uncertain. Proponents of distinctly different perspectives which favour markedly disparate reforms all contend that participation constitutes one element of strategies to improve development generally and education governance specifically. Thus we argue that – as with any idea that has reached the status of global reform rhetoric – the concept of participation must be unpacked and discussed in concrete terms.

To do this, our chapter first presents a tripartite framework which subsumes and classifies the diversity of participation perspectives and practices currently found in the literature on development and education governance in low-income countries. We then elabourate in the second half of the chapter one case study from El Salvador for each of the three participation perspectives. Our hope is that, by offering both a framework for understanding participation's multiple meanings, as well as three case studies of how participation has taken form in practice, we can help to ground the discussion of this concept and reduce the ambiguity that shrouds it. Following the elabouration of the three case studies, we also comment on the multilevel – that is, international, national, and local – politics of participation that emerge among them.

Three Perspectives

The perspectives delineated in this chapter include: neoliberal, liberal, and progressive. In characterising these perspectives, we briefly discuss the approach to development taken by each and then flesh out the envisioned roles for participation within that. Thus, we attempt to organize and clarify the differences among these perspectives. It should be noted, however, that these three paradigms overlap are not mutually exclusive.

Neoliberal Perspective on Participation

The neoliberal perspective is inspired by the supposed efficient operation of free markets, as understood by the neoclassical school of economics. Neoliberal development centers on, among other things, privatisation, deregulation, competition, and market liberalisation. Concomitantly, in the realm of education governance, many strategies, either wholly or partially, take their cue from these policies. The result is that proponents advocate the following: school privatisation, public-private partnerships, parental choice, user fees and school management decentralisation[1] to the community level (Thobani 1984; Chubb *et al.* 1990; World Bank 2003; Chakrabarti *et al.* 2009). Justifying these reforms are the concepts of efficiency and accountability (see Klees [2008] for a critique). Generally it is thought that schools will respond to the desires and pressures of consumers and therefore use their resources more effectively and efficiently.

But where is there space for participation in this approach to education governance? Specifically, the neoliberal perspective conceives of two main forms: individual participation in the market and community participation in school councils. Market-based policies assume individuals choose among available options for where to send their child to school (Chubb *et al.* 1990; World Bank 2003); community-level decentralisation policies assume parents will apply pressure to or through the councils governing education in their locale (Di Gropello 2006). In each case, by instituting such policies, the state creates a situation in which it removes itself from the direct management of schools; shifts instead responsibility to individuals, communities and the market; and restricts itself to the role of holding teachers and communities accountable for academic results. In sum, then, participation occurs through individual consumers acting in the marketplace, or through communities acting as management and accountability mechanisms.

To neoliberal critics, market-based policies are seen as a weak and/or detrimental form of participation in governance. This is because privatisation policies presuppose the possession of sufficient resources to attend private school and see participation as an individualistic as opposed to a collective phenomenon. Decentralisation policies confine participation to the school's governing council or assume that it will materialize indirectly, outside formal decision-making processes, through the market or through the social pressure applied among or by the community members on each other and on both the local school council and on the local teachers. Furthermore, critics assert that, to the extent that neoliberalism relies on policies based on choice, competition and the market, it attempts to 'delegitimate and disengage government and society from any collective responsibility for social welfare' (Klees 1999, p. 3).

Liberal Perspective on Participation

Liberal perspectives on development also have faith in the market but recognize that for the market to be efficient and equitable substantial government intervention is often necessary. Liberal forms of participation, as we define them here, often occur in political and economic contexts marked by democracy and regulated markets, though this is not always necessarily so. For our purposes, the most important characteristic of participation in development and education governance from the liberal perspective is that existing institutions – be they governmental or non-governmental, national or international – mediate a form of participation which is short-term and instrumental in nature. As will be shown, liberal participation with these characteristics frequently includes and is managed by representatives from each of the four types of institutions mentioned above. Some of the most well-known and highly visible processes are funded and structured by donor institutions and international NGOs.

Furthermore, unlike the neoliberal paradigm, for which participation occurs primarily through market-based reforms, liberal forms of participation involve individuals, communities and civil society organisations (CSOs)[2] in processes with relevance for the development strategies pursued at local, national and international levels. Liberal approaches are concerned with how participation serves to inform, improve, strengthen and legitimate the policies and plans produced through these institutionally dependent processes (Weiler 1983). The processes to which we refer include, for example, participatory poverty assessments (PPAs) (Robb 2001), poverty reduction strategy papers (PRSPs) (World Bank 2000), civil society campaigns (Mundy *et al.* 2001; Mundy 2008) and instances of national policy formation or organisational strategy elabouration (Reimers *et al.* 1997).

Clearly, liberal forms of participation can vary greatly in terms of the actors involved and the level to which they pertain (i.e. local, national, international). The common denominators, however, are (a) that they occur in spaces, through processes, and with resources provided by a range of governmental, non-governmental and development institutions; (b) that they invite community members, their representatives and/or CSOs acting on their behalf to engage in dialogue, information-sharing, and (much less commonly) agenda-setting and policymaking; and (c) that they tend to permit and sustain participation only as a front-end process that does not carry over to the management or implementation of those programmes and policies which were reformed or elabourated while relying on the involvement of non-specialists. Participation is thus an input for official and/or otherwise institutionally circumscribed processes.

With regard to application, these processes are invoked in order to gather data on and design responses to a range of development issues, among which education is one. For example, a donor institution might hire consultants to perform a PPA. This could entail visiting various locales to record the desires and feedback of community members on the operation of a particular innovation, such as a school meals programme (Robb 2001). Alternatively, CSOs which represent girls education, or which advocate for quality education in rural areas, might participate in national level discussion that feeds into the construction of a country's PRSP (World Bank 2000). Separately, institutions such as USAID will sometimes provide the resources to contribute to formulation of a national education policy. This could include funding, among other things, a series of high-profile round table discussions with elected officials, senior Ministry of Education (MINED) personnel and CSO representatives (Reimers *et al.* 1997). A related example at the global level is provided by the World Bank, which in 2010 conducted a series of consultations with academics and governmental representatives from around the world to gather input for the development of its next sector-wide education strategy document.

More often than not, however, these forms of participation serve to reify, rather than alter or redirect, those processes and structures into which they feed. Put another way, liberal participation tends to maintain, not challenge, the status quo. Not surprisingly, liberal forms of participation have been criticized for this, for the nature of institutions and their representatives to ensure longevity and survival, despite calls for and claims of meaningful participation which will benefit those most in need. Liberal participation becomes an act which is managed, co-opted, and tokenistic, with 'the alleged beneficiaries treated "largely [as] objects rather than subjects"' (Kapoor 2004, p. 127). Recognising this, progressives seek to transform larger structures such that they foster more meaningful forms of participation, as will be discussed in the next section.

Neoliberals would also criticize liberal processes, though for entirely different reasons. Specifically, they interpret liberal mechanisms of participation as inefficient, ineffective and inequitable. From the neoliberal perspective, participation in education governance through market-based mechanisms is most desirable because they induce efficiency and therefore produce better outcomes. At the same time, liberal forms of participation are also critiqued by neoliberals because they act as a form of market interventionism.

Progressive Perspective on Participation

The progressive paradigm begins with a critique of current structures of development and governance (Fung *et al.* 2001; Hahnel 2005). These include the market and representative democracy, not only because they reduce participation to consumerism and periodic voting, but also because they tend to reproduce the existing social order and various systems of oppression, such as capitalism, patriarchy, racism, sexism and heterosexism, among others (Hahnel 2005; Andersen *et al.* 2007). Furthermore, the mainstream development approach of market liberalisation, privatisation, and conservative fiscal policy suppresses wages, cuts social programmes, promotes an export economy, and exacerbates inequalities (Korzeniewicz *et al.* 2000), and therefore is seen as a form of violence against the poor (Rahnema 1992). To the extent that current systems are reproductive and disenfranchising, they are seen as disempowering, and therefore inherently non-participatory.

Progressives, then, understand participation differently, in a way that goes beyond being an actor in the market or an instrumental input in an institutional process. For them, participation must lead to and reflect more just and democratic relations among peoples (Hickey *et al.* 2005). Participation must involve empowerment, where empowerment

> is regarded as a *process* which enables individuals or groups to *change* balances of power in social, economic and political relations in a society. It refers to many activities, including but not confined to awareness of the societal forces which oppress people and to actions which change *power relationships* (UNDP 1994, p. 86 [emphasis added], as cited in Ahmed 1999, pp. 86–7).

The progressive perspective thus understands empowerment as a process of change in which various social, economic, and political power relationships are addressed and replaced with alternative ways of orgainising a society. These alternative forms should not only exhibit more equal and equitable relationships, but should also facilitate the involvement of average people in the making and implementing of those decisions and policies which affect their lives (Edwards 2010a).

Accordingly, for progressives, participation in development generally and education specifically is about working toward these changes and the realisation of alternative systems of economic and political organisation.

Consequently, we can distill three broad points that guide this project: (a) personal transformation through the development of an awareness of oppression and a critical consciousness; (b) purposeful individual and group action against oppressive political, economic and social systems; and (c) working toward actual transformation of those systems. Though progressive approaches to participation ultimately have in common the above agenda, the strategies that proponents pursue vary widely. Furthermore, just as with the neoliberal and liberal approaches to development, we see that the principles guiding progressives are applied at multiple levels, from the local to the global.

A few examples make this clear. At the local level, popular education – a form of critical pedagogy – encourages students to investigate the world around them in order to recognize and then mobilize around unjust policies and structures (Kane 2001). Social movements, which often incorporate popular education as one prong of their activism strategies, operate on a larger scale, rely on the coordination of multiple groups, and may target one or many issues (Anyon 2005). The Landless People's Movement of Brazil is an example of such and shows how participation by teachers, students and the community is integral both to the governance of education and to the success of the movement as it engages in 'the struggle for land reform' and develops 'radical new forms of grassroots democracy, environmental care, and co-operative production' (McCowan 2003, p. 1). Separately, municipalities in Brazil such as Porto Alegre, the fourth-largest city in that country, have shown that it is possible to create within the state itself concentric democratic forums at the school, community and municipality levels that serve as spaces in which to determine curricula, elect principals and establish overarching normative goals (Edwards 2010b). Fung et al. (2001) refer governance approaches of this nature as empowered participatory governance.

Similarly, Reimers et al. (1997) elabourate and provide examples of an approach to policymaking at the national level known as informed dialogue, which is both liberal and progressive in nature. In that policymaking is here based on an institutionally dependent process of research-informed, national-level dialogue among a broad base of participants from across government, civil society and the private sector, it is liberal. However, in that the process of informed dialogue is iterative and emphasizes inclusiveness, deliberative democratic decision-making, the importance of trust between participants, and the social construction of knowledge, it is progressive. Honest deliberation can often lead to conscientisation, and an emphasis on the social construction of knowledge means that decision-making departs from the perspectives of those who face the challenges being addressed. Informed dialogue thus demonstrates improvement over more tokenistic versions of participation in policymaking and is at once liberal as well as progressive.

In contrast, a more radical approach to pursuing the progressive agenda is to act completely outside the state, as the Zapatistas have done. This group, comprised of a number of indigenous peoples in southern Mexico, engaged in armed resistance against the Mexican government in the 1990s to achieve full autonomy. Specifically, they fought against the injurious neoliberal economic policies and destructive bilingual education policies of the Mexican state to pursue instead political sovereignty, sustainable economic development, and alternative education policies (Flores 2003; Earle *et al.* 2005).

Lastly, CSOs, which have been mentioned above as participants in a number of official liberal and progressive processes, have also been known to function independently of the state. CSOs have shown that they, too, can mobilize the resources necessary to network and foster participation at multiple levels in order to raise the profile of certain issues, or in order to hold governments and international institutions accountable for commitments they have made (Mundy *et al.* 2001). Moreover, to the extent that they embody the participation of marginalized groups and push for, among other things, fundamental modifications to dominant approaches to development and the governance and provision of education, they can be classified as progressive. One example of this type of action is the sustained efforts of globally-networked NGOs and union associations such as Oxfam, ActionAid and Education International, which since 1999 have led the Global Campaign for Education (Mundy *et al.* 2001).

While each of the three points we lay out above are not present in all progressive approaches, what all progressive approaches do have in common is an emphasis on empowerment and transformation of individuals and groups to contribute meaningfully to alternative forms of development and education governance. Because progressive approaches to development and education governance respond to the status quo and seek alternatives to it, the strategies they engage with and the replacement structures they create look different across contexts and focus on one or many levels of engagement, ranging from the local to the global, as our examples have shown.

Like the neoliberal and liberal paradigms, progressive approaches are not without their flaws. In particular, progressive conceptions of development and education governance presuppose participation in various forms, but individuals and groups may not be predisposed to participate. Ideally, participation is a dialogical and negotiated process, not to be imposed, but to be developed from below. It may not always proceed in this fashion, however. In response, progressives would argue that the continuing economic, political, technological and cultural globalization will increasingly affect the day-to-day lives of the world's population, and that, as such, the challenge is to democratize this force, and this implies fostering widespread participation (Mundy 2007). That is, given the reality of globalization, many suggest that it is better to engage with it and transform it – preferably through participatory and democratic means – rather than to ignore it.

Table 3.1 Three Perspectives on Participation in Development and Education Governance

Characteristics	Neoliberal	Liberal	Progressive
Governance based on ...	– Consumerism – Reducing state responsibility – Increasing individual and/or community responsibility	– Existing institutions (governmental, non-governmental, national, international) – Institutionally-dependent participatory processes	– Meaningful decision-making power for individuals and groups – Ability to pursue alternative forms of development and governance – Critique of dominant governmental structures and development policy
Primary Principles	– Efficiency – Accountability – Competition	– Instrumental value of participation	– Agency – Personal empowerment – Group action – Structural transformation of political, economic, social and cultural systems
Central Strategies include ...	– Market-based policies/strategies – Accountability-based decentralization – Privatization	– Donor and NGO sponsored consultations (e.g., Poverty Reduction Strategy Papers, Participatory Poverty Assessments), summits, roundtables, workshops, and conferences – Representative democracy	– Conscientization – Social movements – Civil society organization campaigns – Informed policy dialogue – Deliberative democratic decision-making – Empowered participatory governance

Individual Participation in governance is …	– As part of invisible hand (vote with money, through school choice) – Through school councils (in decentralization) – Via social pressure (in decentralization)	– Via civil society organization representation – Voting (in representative democracy)	– Via personal empowerment – As member of social movement collective, or activist group – As participant in decision making rooted in deliberative democracy – Via civil society organization representation
Nature of Citizen	– Rational, utility-maximizing consumer	– Socially responsible citizen – Member of society with responsibility to participate in available processes	– Political being – Social-justice oriented activist – Member of collective
Primary Catalysts Bringing About Participatory Strategies	– International financial institutions – Multi–and bilateral development organizations – Conservative think tanks	– International financial institutions – Governmental institutions – Multi- and bilateral development organizations – Civil society organizations	– Critical pedagogues – Social movements, activist groups – Civil society organizations
Primary Actors Realizing Participatory Strategies	– Individuals as consumers or clients – Communities as accountability mechanisms – Reduced but strong state – The market	– Governmental institutions – International financial institutions – Multi- and bilateral development organizations – Civil society organizations	– Critical pedagogues – Communities as collectives – Social movements, activist groups – Civil society organizations – Transformed government and/or economy
Portrayal of State and Market	– State assumed to be inefficient and ineffective, but perspective relies on strong state to implement policies	– Not anti-market; liberal participation layered upon/ co-exists with market-based approach	– Critical of both state and market

Sources: Author.

Summary discussion of three approaches

The preceding discussion, summarized by Table 3.1, argues that the neoliberal perspective is founded on the principles of efficiency, account-ability and competition. It emphasizes market- and accountability-based forms of school management. In theory, community-based governance from this perspective could involve significant participation. In practice, however, school councils usually lack resources and the decision-making ability of these entities is restricted. Liberal forms overlap with the neoliberal approach. They generally use ad hoc approaches to participation as an instrumental means to compensate for the lack of formal participation by individuals and community members in macro-level policymaking or project design. Such efforts are often structured and facilitated by existing multilateral institutions and nongovernmental organisations, and thus often serve institutional needs more than those of the people for whom they enhance participation. In contrast to these perspectives, the progressive approach begins with a critique of the market and the state and seeks alternatives to them which allow for robust participatory governance and sustainable and just development. Consequently, this approach pursues strategies that result in personal conscientisation, group action, and struc-tural transformation.

Separately, a point can be made with regard to institutions. That is, our focus above on the reliance of liberal participation on existing institutions is not meant to suggest that the neoliberal and progressive perspectives on participation do not also include or assume the presence of institu-tions. The difference, however, is the ends sought through reliance on institutions. For example, the neoliberal perspective does not object to institutions, so long as their existence is guided by or furthers market principles in the governance of development and education initiatives. On the other hand, the progressive perspective – which also assumes the existence of institutions – begins from the premise that those institu-tions created by both liberals and neoliberals must be transformed such that they allow for empowerment and create opportunities for more meaningful participation.

Thus these three perspectives, while they overlap somewhat, clearly originate from and strive for distinct versions of development and education governance. Nevertheless, as the following section demonstrates, each perspective can be present in a single country context as various actors engage from disparate perspectives and on different levels in the contested terrain that is development and education governance.

Illustrative Examples of Participation

This section presents and analyses three examples of participation in education governance in El Salvador, one from each paradigm elaborated above. The examples include (a) education governance decentralisation policy in El Salvador; (b) the process of national education policy formation in El Salvador between 2003–05; and (c) the project of popular education and self-governance during the civil war of the 1980s. Each example is discussed in terms of its historical context and features, followed by commentary on how the case relates to each version of participation presented above.

EDUCO (Neoliberal)

Historical context

The Education with Community Participation programme (known as EDUCO) decentralized select decision-making responsibilities and administrative functions to the community level in rural areas of El Salvador. (Decentralisation would later be scaled up to include other areas as well.) This program, piloted in 1991 by the MINED and implemented on a large scale in 1994 through a loan from the World Bank, grew out of the context surrounding education as the twelve-year civil war (1980–92) was ending between the Salvadoran government and the FMLN (the Farabundo Marti National Liberation Front, a coalition of rebel groups fighting for land reform, among other things) (ADES 2005). Specifically, three factors contributed to the adoption of EDUCO. The first was a lack of access to MINED-provided preschool and primary education in rural areas, a result of the conflict. The second factor was the dysfunctional relationship between many rural communities and the MINED. These communities did not trust the MINED and MINED teachers were often unwilling to accept posts in the countryside. As a result, many communities created and managed their own schools. The third factor was the influence and pressure of international donor organisations. Not only did such organisations contribute over $552 million to the Salvadoran education system between 1991 and 2005, but these organisations also exhibited 'almost unflagging attention and support' for the EDUCO programme from the outset (Quijada *et al.* 2009, p. 16). Thus, while being pushed by the World Bank, the EDUCO programme was also seen as a way to increase access and address teacher placement issues. Critics, however, argue that the EDUCO strategy was meant simultaneously to legitimize (and hence control) the community schools in rural areas, delegitimize education provision by the state (by shifting responsibility to the community), and subvert the teachers' union (by requiring that the teachers hired not belong to the MINED official career system).

Features

Officially, increasing the number of schools by transferring responsibility for the management of education to the community level was a strategy to address a widespread lack of access. While there is nothing inherently neoliberal about a desire to increase access, it is the logic and mechanisms reinforcing this policy that reflect the neoliberal perspective on participation, that is, a preoccupation with narrow views of efficiency and effectiveness through community-based accountability relationships is what places EDUCO in the neoliberal realm.

Under EDUCO, each community selects a group of parents to comprise the Community Education Association (ACE, in Spanish), the legal entity at the community level which oversees the school. Each ACE, which operates on a year-to-year contract with the MINED, is responsible for hiring, firing and managing teachers; maintaining and furnishing the schools; negotiating with governmental and/or international agencies to obtain funds for building and/or repairing their schools (since the government-allocated budgets are insufficient for such expenditures); and spending any discretionary funds. There are five community members on each ACE, each elected for a period of two years. They are not compensated financially; instead, ACE members are intended to participate because they are interested in improving the socio-economic status of the community through education (Meza *et al.* 2004).

The policy assumes that by shifting the administrative functions of education management to the community level, decentralisation is more efficient than traditional centrally-controlled public schools (Di Gropello 2006). As well, because teachers are selected and managed directly by members of the community, education will be more effective because the teachers will be more responsive to the needs and demands of the community, especially since the teachers are non-union (a requirement of the policy) and do not have job security (Meza *et al.* 2004).

Discussion

In some communities, ACE members, and sometimes others from the community, will work together to organize social projects, improve roads, increase water and electric supply, construct schools and offer health programmes (Cuéllar-Marchelli 2003). From a critical perspective, and especially in the absence of governmental funding for such activities, this behavior represents the assumption of state responsibilities by poor and disadvantaged individuals and communities in rural areas. Furthermore, because there is great variation across communities with regard to this type of behavior, we have reason to believe that the full extent of ACE activity is limited to hiring and firing teachers, or handing them a paycheck (Cuéllar-Marchelli, 2003), despite the fact that proponents discuss EDUCO as a 'mechanism to promote community participation' more generally (Meza *et al.* 2004, p. 3). Moreover, where ACEs could assume or effect more meaningful community engagement, insufficient resources exist to do so because there are few, if any, discretionary funds. Thus, instead of implementing community-based projects, ACEs are reduced to motivating teachers and perhaps looking for funds to supplement government allocations.

Ultimately, the question is not if EDUCO creates space for community participation, for it certainly does, but rather how. The above discussion of EDUCO indicates that the policy's mechanisms are consistent with the neoliberal perspective because they rely on instrumental community management via a school council and social/parental pressure and through market mechanisms in order to make education more efficient, effective, and accountable.

Plan 2021 (Liberal)[3]

Historical Context

Between 2003 and 2005, the construction of Plan 2021, a national level education strategy document intended to guide education policy from 2005 to 2021, was a participatory process involving a broad range of international, national and local stakeholders. Just as with EDUCO, the nature of this process grew out of a distinct historical context, within which two aspects are especially relevant. The first is a precedent for participatory processes of policy dialogue established in the mid 1990s. This precedent was set by the first of these processes, which spanned 1993–95 and involved the conduct of an education sector assessment by the Harvard Institute for International Development, under contract with USAID, followed by a processes of debate and consultation, input from a presidential commission, and, finally, the publication of a long-term education policy strategy (the Ten-Year Plan) by the MINED. The second salient aspect of context was a confluence of process-facilitating factors mid-year 2003, just as the Ten-Year Plan began to wind down. On the one hand, USAID's education office in El Salvador designs its own country strategies for education to mirror the national political cycle, and, in the summer of 2003, USAID began to prepare its strategy for the country because presidential elections were less than a year away. At the same time, presidential candidates and the MINED also began thinking about next steps for identifying education policy priorities. The main actors were thus on the same wavelength regarding the need to begin again the process of national dialogue on the obstacles facing education and possible responses to them.

Features

Around this time, at least four separate and significant events occurred wherein representatives from the MINED, international donor institutions, civil society, the private sector and local community members had the opportunity to discuss issues in and directions for education within El Salvador. The first occurred in December 2003, through a series of round-table discussions co-sponsored by USAID, the Academy for Educational Development, and the World Bank, and which included over 70 key individuals from across the education sector, including representatives of the MINED, NGOs, universities and other organisations, as well as a few public school teachers and directors. However, reports indicate that teachers' union members and those groups which opposed the incumbent political party were not involved in the round tables.

The second opportunity for discussion by a broad cross-section of Salvadoran stakeholders on issues of education came in late August 2004. Recently elected President Antonio Saca created a Presidential Commission of sixteen 'notable people' representing the MINED, the business sector, academia, local think tanks, each political party and the Catholic Church. The Presidential Commission completed its work between 30 August and 30 November 2004. Officially the group's task was, through discussion, to elabourate recommendations for the MINED 2005–09 national education strategy. Unofficially, their task was also 'to search for consensus (and legitimacy) among principal political and social forces' (Edwards, forthcoming).

Third, concurrent with the Presidential Commission, was a process of national consultations between October–December 2004 that involved over 8,000 individuals from every sector and level of society, including students, parents, teachers, school directors and others from rural and urban areas. These consultations were financed by USAID, the World Bank and other international institutions who hired consultants to conduct community-level consultations throughout the country. Consultants compiled and provided reports to the MINED; these reports circulated only among senior MINED staff. These consultations served principally as a way for community members to participate and offer feedback, as opposed to formally involving them in the policymaking process.

Fourth, a seminar held at Harvard and financed by USAID in December 2004 provided an opportunity for discussion by fifteen prominent individuals selected by the Minister of Education. Participants included a third of the Presidential Commission members, numerous MINED officials, one legislative assembly member and NGO representatives. The purpose of the seminar was both to contribute feedback and input for Plan 2021 as well as monitoring strategies to accompany its implementation. Though neither school level personnel nor union members participated, the Harvard seminar included a diverse range of influential individuals, among whom consensus (or, at least the appearance of it) would be important for the adoption of Plan 2021.

Discussion

This process is most clearly consistent with a liberal perspective because a range of stakeholders was invited into a formal, governmental and institutionally dependent process. This process was also noteworthy for the amount and type of participation that it engendered. Two aspects in particular stand out: first, a wide range of actors and perspectives was consulted for their input; and second, they were consulted for the purpose of providing feedback and input that would lead to the development of the next national education strategy document. Despite these positive attributes, however, the process still reflects aspects of the managerialist critique described by Kapoor (2004, p. 126) in that participation was 'molded to fit bureaucratic or organisational needs'. The Plan 2021 policy formation process simultaneously gave rise to significant forms of partici-pation by a range of actors while circumscribing participation by others, such as unions and traditionally oppositional groups.

A final observation is that the occurrence of four separate events to foster discussion that fed into the creation of a national strategy paper sets this process apart from other liberal approaches in terms of the level and nature of participation. To be sure, the participation and dialogue that characterize the formation of Plan 2021 go beyond that which is typically found in education policymaking in low-income countries and thus place this instance of participation in education governance at the deep end of liberal participation strategies. This is because it was an iterative process of national-level policy dialogue among a broad base of participants from across government, civil society, the private sector, schools and local community members (Reimers *et al.* 1997). With regard to the instrumen-talist emphasis of liberal approaches, participation of various stakeholders in the development of Plan 2021 also served as a means to generate not only legitimacy for the Plan but also buy-in from constituents across the education sector and government and the private sector more broadly.

Popular Education in Santa Marta (Progressive)

Historical Context

Communities in the north of El Salvador engaged in a popular education project during and after the civil war as part of a larger socialist movement to create a more just and democratic society. These social-economic and educational projects grew out of a number of historical factors that go back to and include: post-World War II industrialisation and export-led growth, sharp increases in income inequality, the emergence of the liberation theology movement, and severe governmental repression and violence during the 1970s (ADES 2005). In the late 1970s, in response to this repression, and inspired by the liberation theology movement, rural communities in the north of El Salvador began to organize and search for responses to their dire situation. Increased repression by the National Guard followed, and in 1979, as the conflict escalated, teachers in these areas abandoned their positions. In northern communities, after the assassination of Monsignor Romero – influential Catholic priest and champion of the poor – in March 1980, more community members began to support grassroots resistance efforts. Armed conflict began in late 1980, shortly after which the residents of Santa Marta, a community in the north, were forced by the military to flee and set up refugee camps in Honduras (ADES 2005).

Features

While FMLN rebels fought against government forces, exiled community members in Honduras worked toward an alternative development model and implemented popular education from refugee camps. Although refugees would continue to attempt to realize these objectives upon returning to their communities in El Salvador, the most robust embodiment of progressive principles occurred in the mid 1980s, as thousands of Salvadorans lived 35km inside the Honduran border, in the camp known as Mesa Grande (ADES 2005). We focus primarily on this period, with an emphasis on issues of empowerment and self-governance.

Between 1981–87, 7,500 refugees from many communities across El Salvador were determined to continue the task of orgainising and self-governing, despite difficult psychological and physical living conditions, isolation, limited access to arable land, and economic dependence on international organisations. The refugees saw their time in the camp as practice for creation of an egalitarian society after the war. As such, seven sub-camps were created, each with its own elected Committee which organized work and held informational and consultative assemblies. Members from these committees reported to the larger refugee Camp Committee, which served as the official body representing all refugees in dealings with international agencies. One coordinator was also assigned to each group of ten tents to ensure that families' needs were met. All members of the camp between 15–54 years of age who were not caring for children (approximately 2,800 people) contributed to work in agriculture, health, construction or education. Instead of individual remuneration, members were fed, clothed and cared for by the work of the community, with each member receiving equal distribution of food, clothing, etc. (ADES 2005, p. 87).

Education was one of the strongest areas of self-governance. Over 100 instructors taught more than 2,500 students up to the sixth grade. Thousands of adults also took literacy courses based in the Freirean philosophy of learning simultaneously to read the word and read the world, thus being able to analyze critically their reality (Freire *et al*. 1987). Teachers planned together daily to teach language, math, nutrition and social studies. Minimal provision by the United Nations of physical space, didactic material and teacher training helped in this effort, but the 'heart of educational organisation' itself was the Education Teams created by the refugees (ADES 2005, p. 95). To be specific, teachers elected representatives to be on four different Education Teams (each one corresponding to a different level of education, e.g. 1st/2nd grade, 3rd/4th, etc.), and then each Team elected a Coordinator to assist the teachers in lesson plan implementation.

Moreover, in the Education Teams, elected teachers made decisions together. Refugees attribute success in this area to the dedication of the teachers, a high level of organisation, and the help of a few international consultants. While returnees in a few communities continued to implement popular education and strive for self-governance in the years after life in the refugee camps, the actions of exiled Salvadorans during these six years between 1981–87 exemplify to a fuller extent the realisation of progressive principles (ADES 2005).

Discussion

This case contrasts starkly with each of the previous two examples by reflecting each of the progressive perspective's three principles of participation in development and education governance. As mentioned previously, these principles are (a) personal transformation through the development of an awareness of oppression and a critical consciousness; (b) purposeful individual and group action against oppressive political, economic and social systems; and (c) working toward actual transformation of those systems. Specifically, then, the progressive case discussed above reflects these three principles through (a) the invocation of popular education teaching methods, (b) the structuration of multiple democratic spaces for decision-making generally and in governance of education specifically, (c) the organisation of communal work and provision of equal compensation, and (d) a determination to use their time in the camp as preparation for the realisation of a more just and equitable society after the war. Put another way, the preoccupation of those involved with the creation of a just and more deeply democratic alternative to dominant governmental and economic structures, combined with the purposeful elabouration of meaningful processes of decision-making and the empowerment of all adult refugees through Freirean literacy practices, demonstrates a comprehensive example of what progressives conceive of as the realisation of – and participation in – appropriate development and education governance.

The systems that the refugees established could not withstand the transition back to Santa Marta, however. This was because, in 1987, when refugees returned to their communities, they had to struggle amid ongoing conflict until 1992, at which point war ceased and the Peace Accords were signed. Furthermore, between 1987 and 1992, rural Salvadoran communities would lose almost all their international assistance and be forced to enter a market economy without the capital or skills necessary to work their land. Select communities in the northern region did continue to self-govern their schools democratically outside the MINED, just as they had done in the camps, although with less success due to changes in communities' economy and the toll that a protracted and unsuccessful conflict exacted. In time, not only did these communities formally reenter the MINED system, but they also converted to EDUCO schools. The unfortunate irony is that EDUCO schools represent a manifestation in the area of education of exactly the type of ideology and policies that these communities had fought to resist (ADES 2005). Santa Marta made the conversion out of the need for governmental funding. In an attempt to maintain some autonomy, however, through EDUCO, they were able to hire their own teachers and continued to implement a curriculum with critical elements.

Discussion of Three Examples

These examples align well with the three perspectives presented earlier. EDUCO schools reflect neoliberalism's preoccupation with a narrow version of efficiency and effectiveness through community-based accountability relationships. Community members apply pressure socially or participate in the ACE, which hires, fires and manages teachers. The Plan 2021 example corresponds closely with the liberal perspective through its reliance on existing institutions to formulate and propel multiple instances of dialogue and feedback with a broad range of stakeholders as an instrumental part of the process of constructing a national-level education strategy document. The process showed some depth in its participatory nature, though the involvement of traditionally oppositional groups may have been minimal, as was engagement with individuals from schools and communities themselves. Lastly, popular education and self-governance by Salvadorans in the refugee camps during the civil war of the 1980s mirrors the personal transformation and political economic alternative for which the progressive perspective calls.

Interestingly, within a country as small as El Salvador, prominent examples exist which represent each of the three perspectives delineated in this chapter. More than coincidence, this fact highlights the contested nature of both development and education governance, and the role of participation therein.

It is important to note that within this contested space one glimpses the multilevel politics of participation. For example, in the case of EDUCO, we see that international actors encourage and support more participation by local actors when that participation supplants government and occurs in spaces geared to engender market dynamics. The case of EDUCO also suggests that one principal reason that agents of the state agreed to such policies was because, under the circumstances, at the end of the Salvadoran civil war, the government lacked capacity and sufficient resources and was in need of external assistance. In this situation, local actors, though they had been transferred more responsibility, did not have a choice in whether the policy was adopted, and thus had to adapt to narrow forms of participation.

In the case of Plan 2021, the national actors were, from previous experience, familiar with the means of engagement that international donor organisations create to support the development of national education policy. Thus it was expected and accepted that these international actors would once again facilitate policy formation procedures. The long-term perspective taken regarding the case in this paper reveals this 'support' also has the effect of embedding the preferences, perspectives and language of international financial institutions and donor organisations. Certainly, international actors did not unilaterally influence national policy, but it is to be expected that a number of their perspectives and policy preferences would filter through each stage of the policy-making process, especially when many of these events and sub-processes are structured, financed and informed by the resources and inputs of these international institutions. This is not to say that national level political actors and senior officials from various ministries did not control and/or significantly contribute to many aspects of the policy formation process, but rather to point out that those actions were circumscribed both by the larger processes managed by donor organisations and by international political economy. As for local actors, in the development of Plan 2021, a sample of communities played a minimal role, having been given one opportunity to participate in a general feedback session in the latter stages of policy development.

What the progressive example shows is that resistance and civil war opened space for alternatives that both state actors and neoliberal development policies militated against at the end of the war. The new business elite in the late 1980s favoured economic policies advocated by the US government, USAID and the World Bank and adopted policies and development strategies that worked against both the larger progressive participatory project and the ability of individual communities to pursue or sustain that project after the war. Thus while certain participatory spaces have continued to exist in El Salvador throughout the 1990s and 2000s, they tend to be those initiated, endorsed and/or configured by international donor institutions and prominent national actors. This is not to say that contestation no longer occurs, only that support for participatory processes and mechanisms comes predominantly from non-progressive perspectives and favours non-progressive policies . As such, fewer and fundamentally different forms of participation currently occur at each level than would be called for from the progressive perspective.

Conclusion

We do not claim that the three perspectives delineated here to characterize participation in development and education governance are all-encompassing. Nor do we wish to claim that it is always clear within which framework a particular example of participation operates. What we do argue is that calls for and examples of participation are always political and ideological, and the application of these three frameworks focuses attention on that. This is extremely important. Calls for and attempts at participation have become ubiquitous, but they are usually undifferentiated and are often all assumed to be of positive value. Yet discussions of and reforms for participation in development and education governance are predominantly neoliberal–instrumentalist in purpose, limited in nature, and imbued with market ideology. It is important to recognize that neoliberal forms of participation may simply reproduce inequality (as do neoliberal reforms more generally). And it is also important to recognize that there are deeper, stronger forms of participation, as discussed throughout this chapter.

Notes

1 The diversity of perspectives on decentralization is equal to that for participation. For simplicity, we refer in this chapter to decentralization at the community level, as described by Meade et al. (2008) and World Bank (2003). These authors discuss 'accountability-based decentralization.' According to this model, in addition to decentralizing to the community level, an accountability mechanism is implemented whereby either the community can hold the school council responsible for the quality of education, or in which the state can hold the school council or teachers responsible for education quality (World Bank 2003; Meade and Gershberg 2008).

2 We use the term civil society organization to include NGOs as well as 'citizen groups, expert communities, and trade unions' (Mundy et al. 2001, p. 87).

3 This section draws from Edwards (forthcoming).

References

ADES (Asociación de Desarrollo Económico Social, Santa Marta) (2005), Una *Sistematización de la Educación Popular en el Cantón Santa Marta, Cabañas, El Salvador*, 1978–2001. San Salvador, El Salvador: ADES.

Ahmed, S. (1999), 'Empowering local communities: Comilla approaches and experiences'. In J. Mullen e.), *Rural Poverty, Empowerment and Sustainable Livelihoods*. Vermont: Ashgate Publishing Company, pp. 80–102.

Andersen, M. and Collins, P. (2007), *Race, Class, and Gender: An Anthology*, 6th edn. Belmont, CA: Wadsworth.

Anyon, J. (2005), *Radical Possibilities: Public Policy, Urban Education, and a New Social Movement*. New York: Routledge.

Chakrabarti, R. and Peterson, P. E. (eds) (2009), *School Choice International: Exploring Public-Private Partnerships*. Cambridge, MA: MIT.

Chubb, J. E. and Moe, T. M. (1990), *Politics, Markets and America's Schools*. Washington, DC: Brookings.

Cornwall, A. (2006), 'Historical perspectives on participation in development'. *Commonwealth & Comparative Politics*, 44, 49–65.

Cuéllar-Marchelli, H. (2003), 'Decentralization and privatization of education in El Salvador: assessing the experience'. *International Journal of Educational Development*, 23, (2), 145–66.

Di Gropello, E. (2006), A comparative analysis of school-based management in Central America, Washington, DC: World Bank. Working Paper 72/2006.

Earle, D. and Simonelli, J. (2005), *Uprising of Hope: Sharing the Zapatista Journey to Alternative Development*. New York: Altamira.

Edwards Jr., D. B. (2010a), 'Trends in governance and decision-making: a democratic analysis with attention to application in education'. *Policy Futures in Education*, 8, (1), 111–25.

—(2010b), 'A comparison of local empowerment in education: Porto Alegre, Brazil and Chicago, USA'. *Research in Comparative and International Education*, 5, (2), 176–84.

—(forthcoming), 'International processes of education policy formation: An analytic framework and the case of Plan 2021 in El Salvador'. *Comparative Education Review*.

Flores, R. (2003), 'From disillusionment and abandonment to autonomy: Zapatista bilingual indigenous education in Chiapas, Mexico' [Online] Available at: www.inmotionmagazine. com/auto/zbie1. html (Accessed: 10 December 2009)

Freire, P. and Macedo, D. (1987), *Literacy: Reading the Word and the World*. Westport, CT: Bergin & Garvey.

Fung, A. and Wright, E. O. (2001), 'Deepening Democracy: Innovations in Empowered Participatory Governance'. *Politics & Society*, 29, (1), 5–41.

Guzmán, J. L. (2005), 'Educational reform in post-war El Salvador', in E. Vargas-Barón and H. B. Alarcón (eds), *From Bullets to Blackboards: Education for Peace in Latin America and Asia*. Washington, DC: Inter-American Development Bank, pp. 43–62.

Hahnel, R. (2005), *Economic Justice and Democracy: From Competition to Cooperation*. New York: Routledge.

Hickey, S. and Mohan, G. (2005), 'Relocating participation within a radical politics of development'. *Development and Change*, 36, (2), 237–62.

Kane, L. (2001), *Popular Education and Social Change in Latin America*. London: Latin American Bureau.

Kapoor, I. (2004), 'Concluding remarks: the power of participation'. *Current Issues in Comparative Education*, 6, (2), 125–29.

Klees, S. J. (1999), 'Privatization and neoliberalism: ideology and evidence in rhetorical reforms'. *Current Issues in Comparative Education*, 1, (2), 19–26.

—(2008), 'A quarter century of neoliberal thinking in education: misleading analyses and failed policies'. *Globalisation, Societies and Education*, 6, (4), 311–48.

Korzeniewicz, R. P. and Smith, W. C. (2000), 'Poverty, inequality and growth in Latin America: searching for the high road to globalization'. *Latin American Review*, 35, (3), 7–54.

Leal, P. A. (2007), 'Participation: the ascendancy of a buzzword in the neo-liberal era'. *Development and Practice*, 17, (4–5), 539–48.

McCowan, T. (2003), 'Participation and education in the Landless People's Movement of Brazil'. *Journal for Critical Education Policy Studies*, 1, (1) [e-journal]. Available at: www. jceps. com/?pageID=article&articleID=6.

Meade, B. and Gershberg, A. I. (2008), 'Making education reform work for the poor: accountability and decentralization in Latin America'. *Journal of Education Policy*, 23, (3), 299–322.

Meza, D., Guzmán, J. L. and De Varela, L. (2004), 'EDUCO: a community-managed education programme in rural areas of El Salvador', paper presented to Scaling Up Poverty Reduction: A Global Learning Process and Conference, Shanghai, 25–27 May.

Mundy, K. (2007), 'Global governance, educational change'. *Comparative Education*, 43, (3), 339–57.

—(2008), 'Civil society and its role in the achievement and governance of Education for All', paper commissioned for the EFA Global Monitoring Report 2009 'Overcoming Inequality: why governance matters'. Available at: unesdoc. unesco. org/images/0017/001780/178020e. pdf (Accessed: 1 December 2011).

Mundy, K. and Murphy, L. (2001), 'Transnational advocacy, global civil society: emerging evidence from the field of education'. *Comparative Education Review*, 45, (1), 85–126.

Quijada, J., Harwood, A. and Gillies, J. (2009), *El Salvador Education Reform Case Study*. Washington, DC: Academy for Educational Development.

Rahnema, M. (1992), 'Participation', in W. Sachs e), *The Development Dictionary: A Guide to Knowledge as Power*. New Jersey: Zed Books, pp. 116–31.

Reimers, F. and McGinn, N. (1997), *Informed Dialogue: Using Research to Shape Education Policy Around the World*. Westport, CN: Praeger.

Robb, C. M. (2001), *Can the Poor Influence Policy? Participatory Poverty Assessments in the Developing World*, 2nd edn. Washington, DC: World Bank.

Thobani, M. (1984), 'Charging user fees for social services: education in Malawi'. *Comparative Education Review*, 28, (3), 302–423.

Weiler, H. (1983), 'Legalization, expertise, and participation: strategies of compensatory legitimation in educational policy'. *Comparative Education Review*, 27, (2), 259–77.

World Bank (2000), Poverty reduction strategies: a sourcebook. Washington, D.C.: World Bank.

—(2003), *World Development Report 2004*. Washington, D.C.: World Bank.

CHAPTER FOUR

Silences, Stereotypes and Local Selection: Negotiating Policy and Practice to Implement the MDGs and EFA

Elaine Unterhalter

Introduction

Addressing gender inequality has been a key concern of global policy on education and poverty for more than a decade (Unterhalter 2007; Rizvi *et al.* 2010). For ten years at the apex of the global initiatives have stood the Millennium Development Goals (MDGs) with three out of eight goals addressing these areas: MDG1 deals with poverty, MDG2 with universal primary education, and MDG 3 with gender equality and the empowerment of women. A second major global framework, put in place in 2000, the Dakar Platform for Action on Education for All (EFA), has goals on education and gender and, while not explicitly concerned with poverty, implicitly must address this because of the very large numbers of poor children out of school or not flourishing within it. However, there has been relatively little research on the implementation of global aspirations concerned with the interlinking of gender, education and poverty, despite the enormous literature on the implementation of EFA and the MDGs, as documented annually in the UNESCO *Global Monitoring Reports* (e.g. UNESCO 2011) and reviewed extensively through large academic programmes (e.g. Colclough 2011; Lewin *et al.* 2011; Tikly *et al.* 2012).

This chapter explores how global policy frameworks like the MDGs and EFA have been understood in a range of local settings, how these understandings bear on practice and what reflections on this practice might tell us about approaches to framing global obligation. The analysis develops partly through some discussion of the conceptual literature on global policy frameworks. It also draws on data from the *Gender, education and global poverty reduction initiatives* (GEGPRI) research project conducted between 2007 and 2011[1] which looked at understanding of global gender, education and poverty policy in two countries – South Africa and Kenya – and a number of global organisations. In such a short space, it is impossible to do justice to the nuance of the large body of data collected for this project, and a fuller exploration of a number of themes is made in other publications from the project (e.g. Dieltiens *et al.* 2009; Karlsson 2010; Unterhalter *et al.* 2011a; Unterhalter *et al.* 2011b; Unterhalter *et al.* 2011).

Conceptualising global frameworks

The formulation of global policy frameworks like the MDGs and EFA has generated a rich literature considering the nature of the claims made for global compact and the forms of realisation that emerge. Over the last ten years the debate about global obligation has moved from assessing whether this is feasible and desirable (Wallace Brown *et al.* 2010), to discussing how to achieve a transformation of unjust structures (Paul *et al.* 2006; Brock 2008) and what level of sufficiency in education or poverty reduction is required (Melamed *et al.* 2011). Central to this debate is a concern with the ethical form of the political relationship between global, national and local bodies.

In trying to distinguish different approaches to global obligation associated with the policy languages of a number of UN gatherings which gave prominence to gender, education and poverty reduction, I identified in earlier work (Unterhalter 2007) differences between a minimalist conception of securing only universal primary schooling, gender parity and reduction in poverty for a portion of the population and a maximalist vision of global responsibility and engagement with rights, capabilities and gender equity . Similar points have been made in assessments of the MDGs. Gore (2010, p. 71) considers the MDGs to represent a shift from a 'procedural conception' of international society with a 'common respect for a set of rules, norms and standard practices' such as those associated with the Universal Declaration of Human Rights or the Beijing Declaration on Women and Gender, to a 'purposive conception', where the stress is on a 'co-operative venture to promote common ends.' For Gore, a procedural conception entails a maximalist view of development. Here aspects of equality and flourishing are goals for rich and poor countries. A purposive conception is associated with a minimalist view, which ensures the most deprived cross a threshold of adequate provision. This might mean earning a dollar a day or completing a primary cycle of schooling.

By implication both the procedural and the purposive approach face a problem relating to the nature of the social contract that underpins them. The more demanding the social justice content of the procedural approach, the more difficult it becomes to secure full human rights or gender equality through agreements at all levels, from multinational conventions, to national governments, down to local assemblies. The more minimal the purposive agreement, the easier it might be for governments to sign up. However, this begs the question of whether governments are able to implement purposive agreements and how these are understood at sub-national level. This point is often made in relation to the difficulties of realising the MDGs in many countries in Africa, which came to the project in 2000 from a very low base (Collier 2007; Vandemoortele 2009). A separate question is whether the purposive agreements associated with the MDGs represent a wide enough range of ideas of wellbeing, and whether a more expansive purposive arrangement is feasible (Waage *et al.* 2010)

The rationale for the MDG approach, initially formulated by an inner circle of development assistance specialists, and then later endorsed by the majority of governments and international organisations, was that in focusing on a particularly delimited purposive development strategy, which just met some limited but universally agreed targets, many of the contentious issues of value associated with development could be bracketed somewhere else. The consensus on achieving sufficiency, it was suggested or implied, would be an important form of global glue to support poverty reduction, gender equality, education and health expansion, but the detail of the policy direction in these larger areas was not to be specified by global compact (Melamed *et al.* 2011, pp. 3–5). In an earlier article on the MDGs (Unterhalter 2005) I argued they might open the way for a wider engagement with rights, capabilities and equality, that is that they could be seen as necessary, but not sufficient to enable such a process to unfold. Thus while the political liberalism associated with the purposive agreements might offer a way through the difficulties with the comprehensive ethical visions associated with the procedural view, it might be the case that the overlapping consensus, which holds together the purposive view, is concerned with very minimal social provision, so that the gradations of crossing a line regarding level of schooling or income do not sufficiently open up further ethical actions and claims on national and international bodies, but in fact close them down. The comparative case studies conducted for the GEGPRI project of negotiations with gender, education and poverty reduction initiatives in Kenya and South Africa were partly conducted in order to investigate whether this was the case.

Kenya and South Africa: Context and Methods

The GEGPRI project aimed to examine empirically initiatives engaging with global aspirations to advance gender equality in and through schooling in contexts of poverty. Between 2007 and 2011 ten case studies were conducted. These comprised six government bodies, namely the national Department of Education in South Africa and the Ministry of Education in Kenya, a provincial department of education in each country, and a school in each country in a matched neighbourhood on the edge of a large city serving a poor population. In addition four case studies were made of non-statutory bodies: a NGO working on questions of poverty and schooling in a rural setting in each country, and an NGO working at the national level, engaged in discussions with global networks. The case studies were supported by a number of interviews with staff working on aspects of gender and education in selected global organisations. Research methods comprised documentary analysis (including a review of websites and publications over ten years), interviews and focus group discussions (133 hours), observations, field notes, and report-back meetings in each research site on preliminary findings. The research was conducted over three years to enable some documentation of change. In all the research settings, engagements with the global frameworks were examined, and the particular meanings attributed to gender, poverty and education explored. In analysing the data for this chapter a concern has been to consider the kinds of claims people concerned with the implementation of global frameworks make about global obligation.

Comparative case study has allowed investigation of similar kinds of relationship – negotiations with global policy agendas on gender, education and poverty reduction – in somewhat different sites, selected as locations of different levels of engagement with the global policy agenda (vertical comparisons) and different state and non-state formations (horizontal comparisons). Kenya and South Africa were selected as the research settings because both countries had put in place policies to address poverty reduction, the expansion of education provision, and gender equality, and were active players in relation to the global policy frameworks in these areas. However, their location in relation to global policy making is different, with South Africa a member of the UN Security Council and the G20, while Kenya has been the recipient of a substantial aid package and is subject to constant international scrutiny regarding corruption and threats of violence.

South Africa and Kenya are both highly unequal societies, with high gini coefficients and large populations of very poor people living close to people who are comfortably off and many who are very wealthy. Both have active women's movements, although their emphases have been different. In South Africa, gender equity has enjoyed policy attention since 1994, although the extent to which it is seen as a priority has fluctuated. Early post-apartheid policy discussion of gender equity in education expressed an early promise of non-discrimination and equality of opportunity. This orientation has moved through a phase with a stress on gender-neutrality to the current period where gender is often seen as a moral issue closely associated with sexuality. In Kenya, the movement for more gender equity in policy came from the bottom up and women's rights groups mobilising on a wide range of issues from political leadership to environmental degradation, and from the top down through global institutions engaging in different ways with ruling elites. A gender and education policy was developed in 2007, and gender equity figures prominently in the policy language associated with aid relationships. These similarities and differences between the two countries suggested potential to yield rich insight into how the cases did and did not vary.

Negotiating global frameworks

In line with many studies on global policy transfer (Steiner-Khamsi 2004; Cowen 2006; Bartlett *et al.* 2009), when all the case study sites were considered, it was evident that there was only a partial connection between practice in global, national and local sites and the procedural approach to global policy frameworks. That is, the stress was rather muted on the fuller ethical dimension of global policy, which brought together ideas about rights and substantive equality in response to poverty, discrimination against children and their exclusion from school. What was much more common than reflections on opening up procedural discussion through engagement with purposive implementation, was a more limited instrumental concern to 'cross the line' of sufficiency with regard to a particular element of poverty or school enrolment. Often this was accompanied with over-simplified ideas that gender was mainly about numbers of girls and boys, not social relations or power. The more reflective engagement with a larger procedural agenda was most articulated by staff working in global organisations, and some of those in national organisations, particularly some individuals in the South African national and provincial Department of Education who were networked into global discussion. The further national level implementation moved away from a global hub, generally close to a capital city, the less the language and frameworks of the global policy discourse in its most substantive procedural form was used, and the more limited the discussion of gender, education and poverty became. These restricted meanings took particular forms. Sometimes, they reflected difficulties in thinking about gender, education and poverty *together*, so that only one element of the linked problems emerged, and sometimes they reflected a concern to establish professional social distance from what were seen as the deficits of an excluded group, such as poor families or girls who did not attend school.

Purposive, rather than procedural?

In nearly all the case study sites the global frameworks, to the extent that participants were aware of them (in the rural NGO and school sites sometimes knowledge was limited), were most often or most actively understood in terms of measuring or accounting for performance. However, in some sites and for some individuals the purposive framework opened up, added weight to or helped frame more procedural concerns. Thus, while the argument is often made that global frameworks are re-contextualized in national settings, sometimes following global directives and sometimes diverging from them (Cowen 2006; Rizvi et al. 2010), placing the data from the different case studies side-by-side we see particular kinds of engagement, sometimes dutiful, sometimes dismissive and sometimes expansive and critical.

The national departments

In the two national departments the MDG and EFA frameworks were important for officials, as a 'guiding tool' or as a mechanism for exchanging information up and down the hierarchies of government (Kenya National Ministry Official 1, 17/10/2008; South African National Department Official 23, 10/11/2008). In Kenya, partly because of the importance for the whole Ministry of a substantial aid package, which drew heavily on the MDG and EFA frameworks, the MDGs, it was claimed, ensured a level of accountability to the global community by government and NGOs:

> Let me say, those goals and MDGs, they are very good because ... these goals keep the government and NGOs, all of us, on our toes. If we had no goals, we would go back and be in our own comfort and pretend everything is OK (Kenya National Ministry Official 5, 21/05/2008).

Officials acknowledged that working within the frameworks generally meant that there was little space for discussion and reflection on gender, other than through a concern with school enrolment and levels of learning, and virtually no consideration of gender and poverty together:

> ... the Ministry is doing much more than that – the gender policy – because there are many things that the Ministry is doing to coordinate the MDGs. ... When we are moving towards parity – and we want to have parity in enrolment – the Ministry from the top is addressing the MDGs (Kenya National Ministry Official 01, 17/10/2008).

Now the issue of poverty – we have not tackled the issue of poverty because it is not in our mandate to tackle the issues of poverty. For us as educationists is to offer education that is quality education, enhance retention, completion and transition rates to the next level (Kenya National Ministry Official 16, 10/11/2009)

By contrast, in South Africa, there was a sense that the national education priorities connected with the MDGs and EFA, but were not being driven by them. Indeed, there was a view articulated by a number of officials that deepening engagement with gender and poverty was needed, not because this was required by the global policy frameworks, but because of wider ethical concerns prompted by local complexity. One South African official acknowledged that:

... people often look at that kind of data [collected for MDG and EFA reports] and say 'we've achieved gender parity – in a sense that those don't apply to us.' But in a way that has been the problem, because they are very generalized and they have help[ed], but now they don't help enough. Because actually what needs to be done is actually quite complex, it is multi-faceted. We have to deal with really difficult issues that are not about saying we have just achieved this particular international benchmark ... We often have to report, but it's kind of routine. And I don't think we do it particularly well, it's an opportunity to showcase how brilliant we are and how much we have achieved, but actually not acknowledge the depth of some of the more complex problems (South Africa, National Department of Education, Official 13, 20/10/2008).

For another South African official, the MDG approach of using indicators could be useful in addressing issues, for example gender based violence, but the fact that there was no indicator on this in the MDG or EFA framework meant this was not being done:

... we don't have an indicator on how many girls are raped in schools. We're not tracking that. So what is not measured does not get done. What is measured gets done. It's about the indicators. What we have found is that indicators drive what becomes important. At an international UNESCO level, the MDGs, EFA, influence must be at the level of indicators. And that's where the money goes to ... (South Africa National department Focus Group Discussion, 19/08/2008)

It can be seen that while the purposive approach was used in both national departments, for some officials in South Africa this went together with reflections on how global frameworks might support more procedural engagements. The reasons this wider perspective was not voiced in

Kenya, and was only articulated by some officials in South Africa, may be associated with the professional backgrounds of staff in the two departments (Unterhalter *et al.* 2011a) or the ways in which members of the research team were seen by participants (Makinda *et al.* 2011). What is important to note for the argument in this chapter is that in the national departments there was a range of responses regarding how the global frameworks were seen, but that the language of the purposive approach was particularly compelling.

The provinces

In the two provinces, there was a strong sense that the global policy frameworks were set somewhere at a political distance, and that officials were tasked to deliver on behalf of national departments. In South Africa, a provincial official gave an account of a top-down process between tiers of government negotiating action on global goals:

> ... they [the MDGs and EFA] are very important in the sense that we are not a province in isolation to the national mandates or international mandates because it becomes the programme for implementation for all government departments. At the beginning of the year or when the financial period starts, these frameworks ... are always tabled to all government departments. Even in our own when we have branch meetings, they are tabled ... (South African Province Official 2, 06/02/2009).

This managed response, following a line of command in respect of a global directive sits slightly uncomfortably with the descriptions provincial officers gave of their work on education, gender and poverty initiatives, and a sense of enormously inadequate human, financial and policy resources to take forward what they believed in (Karlsson 2010). One official eloquently confessed she could never fulfil the expectations associated with the MDGs in the face of widespread poverty:

> We have been to those places, we took old clothes, our clothes, to give those. How do you feel when you drive your car passing? You see those people selling mangoes. How do you feel? You are busy telling people that 'no, we are addressing the millennium goals.' In what way? How do you do it? (South African Province Official 3, 23/02/2009).

In Kenya provincial officers felt the MDGs had been made a long way away from their day-to-day experiences. Some had heard about the MDGs, but did not know what they were. An officer said:

I tell you the first time I heard about the MDGs and you will not believe, it was last year when I went for a Ministry of Planning had a dissemination kind of workshop organised at the province here. I went to represent my boss and that's the first time I heard about MDGs and really it's like they belong to other people (Kenya Province Official 2, 16/09/2008).

A number of provincial officials articulated their responsibility to implement the MDGs, but felt achieving them was unlikely. Some argued that the top-down communication of the policies (largely given as directives) was responsible for difficulties in implementation. Communities, it was claimed, find it hard to own the otherwise good policies because they are viewed as alien. One officer said, 'we were just told "here are the papers come out with the proposals, vet them, send them to us"' (District Official 2, 28/11/2008). Apart from MDG 2, many participants at the district level did not foresee the realisation of the other MDGs by 2015. They stressed the challenges of achieving universal primary education because of poverty, drought, understaffing and overcrowding of schools, the long distances children had to travel from home to school, and what was repeatedly called 'culture', that is the lack of engagement with schooling by some communities. In contrast to the confidence of their South African counterparts about working to achieve the MDGs at the national level, Kenyan provincial officers appeared pessimistic. While South African provincial officials saw the MDGs as a top-down exercise that largely did not matter one way or the other to their work, for the Kenyan officials there seemed to be a sense that the very ambition of the MDGs in the face of the difficulties they encountered was a mockery. One official said:

Another thing to this MDG. We are operating like crisis as far as the human resource is concerned. For us we have a number of schools actually [and not enough teachers]. Even sometimes we doubt the quality of the curriculum that we are offering (Kenya District Official 7, 24/11/2008).

One provincial official expressed incredulity about the monitoring associated with EFA. When a member of the research team asked for the provincial figures on teachers by gender, the request was greeted with scorn:

Where do you think you can get such information? Does it really exist? Are you researching all the 22 districts in this province? ... I have not seen it. And I do not think there is an officer who is allocated that duty of collecting the information here. And I am not interested to know since I do not know what the end users of that information would be (Kenya Field Notes, 17/09/2008).

These data exist at the national level and are reported to UNESCO as part of its work on monitoring EFA. It is not clear how they are collected with accuracy at the provincial or district level without the involvement of local officers. But the response indicates both exasperation at the lack of staff to carry out many different administrative tasks, and also very limited interest in knowing about gender, teacher deployment and a global framework of accountability.

Thus for provincial officials in both countries the global frameworks were primarily understood in their purposive form, while the wider procedural issues about rights or equality were viewed either sympathetically or with exasperation as impossible to address adequately.

The schools

This sense of professional distance from engagement with the MDG project was even more pronounced at school level. In both schools teachers were aware of the poverty children experienced, but in the South African school, where a feeding scheme was in place, there was a stronger sense of the school's involvement with aspects of poverty, while teachers in Kenya tended to see the problem of hunger as a responsibility of the children's families; this was corroborated in a later round of data collected in 2010 (Brown, 2011). The Deputy Head noted the effects of hunger on learning, but did not feel able to venture a view on what should be done. She emphasized:

> There is a slum near the school [...] The children go without food the whole day. The children come from very poor homes and this is affecting their performance. If a child is hungry especially in the afternoon, the child may not understand anything (Kenya Deputy Head Teacher, date not known, 2008).

In both schools, gender was seen largely as a matter of equal numbers of girls and boys enrolled or taking responsibility as class monitors or members of sports teams. The South African Principal (2008/03/25) described gender equality as being 'like a quota' and maintaining a 'balance' and a teacher as being 'in the equal' (Teacher 1, 2010/07/26). In Kenya there was a similar sense that gender equality was parity:

> We encourage teachers to be gender sensitive, for example, at parade we encourage the girls to work hard and tell them that they can perform well. The whole staff in our school usually tries to make the boys and girls feel that they are equal and even when they are choosing prefects' body they know how to mix boy and girl. ... If the game captain is a boy, then we have a girl assisting, so we balance (Head teacher, 29/05/2009)

In both countries teachers noted the effects of gender and poverty on families, but were not able to explain how they might intersect and the kinds of support they and the school might provide to help to effect change. In South Africa, absenteeism among girls was associated with poverty and the sexual division of labour in the household:

> ... we find that there is a grade 7 learner who is a boy and there is a grade 5 learner who is a girl. They are coming from one family. If there is a problem at home which needs somebody to stay at home, you know who will stay: the girl; because she will look after this. [...] From grade 5 upwards girls have to do mother's work at home (South Africa Deputy Principal, 2010/09/15)

Similar connections were noted in Kenya:

> For the past five years is the fact that parents have given priority to their boy child. The boys are taken away to boarding and private schools that are numerous around this school (Kenya Teacher 13, 2008).

It can be seen that the effects of gender inequalities and poverty were very evident to the teachers, but they lacked a language of policy and practice to connect them. The MDGs and EFA, to the extent they knew of them, were considered very far away. The MDGs are seen as remote and spoken about in the public media, with little bearing on the things that people experience or have capacity to effect:

> I do heard about it [MDGs and EFA] but I've never given my time to get an explanation about it because it's never touched [me]. I've never get the real explanation about it (South Africa Principal, 2008/03/25)
> ... there is the Millennium Development Goals but where? And what the Millennium Development Goals say to whom too? You know that ... they must come down. Don't just say when we have TV and say that there is something, that there's change what, but we don't have that change! (South Africa Teacher 1, 2010/07/26)

In Kenya, there was a similar sense of policy handed down from somewhere far away.

> I have only heard some of the Millennium Development Goals like universal primary education. I think it was declared in Dakar (Teacher 14, 12/06/2010)

EFA and the MDGs had blurred together for one teacher, but she was one of only a handful who knew about the global policy framework. What these excerpts indicate is that teachers' sense of their work is about enrolling and retaining children in school. Wider connections between education, ending poverty and achieving gender equality are harder to make and do not appear as part of everyday discussion of practice at school. The global policy frameworks appear as far away, partly because the acronyms and processes are unfamiliar, but partly also because the ethical connection between ideas and institutional levels is not available to teachers. Provincial officials stressed purposive rather than procedural meanings of global goals because their work entailed them being responsible for results, but other perspectives (negative and positive) were available to them. The teachers in these schools, in contrast, did not voice a wider language of procedural aspiration. This may be partly because of the dynamic of how they saw the research team composed of elite outsiders from universities. It may also partly be because that language was not an everyday or familiar discourse. What was more readily available to them was a language of critique of poor families for keeping children, particularly girls, out of school.

The rural NGOs

The teachers' limited engagement with a procedural approach to development as a global project was echoed by staff employed in the rural NGO. In each country the NGO was working in a context of harsh poverty, limited access to transport, and worsening livelihoods because of lack of water and disputes over land. Each had established a particular niche around education support. In Kenya the NGO provided training for teachers and school management committees, some school infrastructure and learning materials. This education stream went together with work on health, livelihoods and a strong advocacy focus around ethnic rights. In South Africa, the NGO ran an after school club to encourage reading for children, a number of holiday programmes to accelerate learning, and a literacy group for mothers. Both thus complemented the work of the government in engaging with global policy on EFA and the MDGs.

In Kenya, the concerns of a global development community were communicated to the NGO primarily through aid relationships. An officer working on the livelihood programme explained the focus on women was because of 'donor requirements':

> The majority of the target groups are women, according also from the donor. So we have mixed groups, we have men and women, but the majority must be women (Kenya Local NGO staff member 3, 26/05/2010).

Unlike the relationship in South Africa, where the donor did not appear to be 'pushing' gender or poverty reduction, here there was a clear direction being given on both. NGO fieldworkers in Kenya spoke of their work being networked with global, national and local NGOs and bilateral or multilateral organisations and one donor from a G7 country. This sense of a connection through funding to a wider policy community was not that clearly articulated in South Africa, although one of the facilitators had represented the NGO at a number of international meetings. Evidently there is not just one global policy framework, and many international relations involving NGOs do not draw on the concerns of the MDGs or EFA.

For participants in the case studies in the NGOs in both countries, the global policy framework was either something they had heard of very generally or not at all. In South Africa most of the six village-based facilitators who participated in a focus group discussion (05/06/2009) had only heard of the global goals by name and did not know what they meant. Village-based NGO officials reluctantly recognized that gender equality was a legal right in the national Constitution (I, 05/06/2009), and that there were policies governing these rights in schools. But gender was not part of the NGO remit, even though much of their work was with women. A village facilitator said: 'the NGO never talks about the global goals' (Local NGO staff member 2, 03/06/2009).

In Kenya, there was a similar sense that the organisation's priorities were not being framed by or linked to the global policy framework. One NGO worker said 'there are so many policies around here [...] we don't disseminate those policies' (Local NGO staff member 5, 19/05/2010). On the MDGs the view was one of indifference and distance. One NGO worker noted sceptically, 'another issue is whether the people own the global declarations. The issue is not even whether they own the MDG's but rather understand, comprehend and know them.' In another exchange with an interviewer the issue of how the MDGs could be discussed at the grassroots, was raised. The view was that the MDGs were too particular, and that the nature of the work which the organisation did was general and integrated with its own programme of education, not the steer from the MDGs:

Interviewer: How do you make them comprehend these MDG's?
NGO worker: You see when you talk to people it is general. Among the people we have educated, semi-educated, illiterate, semi-illiterate and illiterate people [...]

While the NGO saw itself advocating to the Kenyan government to do more on the provision of schools, water and land policy, it did not see this as associated either for good or ill with an external process. They talked about a loose network with external actors or something 'whereby we share out what is really happening what is not working', so we can 'tailor-make or change activities' (Local NGO staff member 01, date not known). The organisation was thus being driven by its perception of need on the ground. Many NGO workers did not mention the global gender, education or poverty reduction framework at all. They constantly stressed 'policy for the pastoral communities' (Local NGO staff member 01, date not known), indicating a strong sense of local priorities that separated them from global and many national frameworks.

Thus, in contrast to the teachers at the school for whom some elements of EFA, particularly regarding enrolment and attainment, are very much part of daily practice, NGO workers who work on education, but are not formally employed in schools, see their remit as linked to local priorities with which national or global frameworks have only a contingent relationship. They might make gestures toward these frameworks in order to secure aid, but the discursive frame is not immediately familiar.

The global NGOs

There is a very different language spoken in NGOs which are located in large cities and are networked on a regular basis with global organisations. Both organisations where data regarding national NGOs was collected comprised the national offices of international NGOs working on education and gender in many countries, with considerable stature in global forums. Both were very active in promoting the MDGs and EFA nationally through workshops, circulating information, advocacy with national government, other NGOs and CSOs, and were directly involved in poverty reduction initiatives, such as supporting school vegetable gardens, distributing sanitary towels, and in education programmes for girls, supplementing the work of schools.

For both organisations the MDGs and EFA were central to their mission and were strongly associated with rights and gender equality. The connections that it was difficult for teachers and rural NGO workers to make came easily:

> Our starting point is that gender inequality is a key factor in poverty. Inequalities of race and imbalances of power between various socio-economic groups, whether racial, caste, or of course gender, are quite key. We make a very direct relationship between those two. If you want to address poverty, you must address inequalities and imbalances of power and gender inequalities are part of that. You must look both at public inequalities but also at inequalities in the household, how power is distributed (South Africa National NGO staff member 12, 09/12/2010).

The MDGs were seen to complement this:

> I think our work is already targeting aspects of the MDGs and the MDGs came along and happened. There were goals that were set, and I think the MDGs whether they were implemented or not is not

necessarily going to change the way [the NGO] is focused ... I tend to see the MDGs as a bit more of, it is a way to create more awareness, it's a potential way to get more government commitment and things like that (South Africa National NGO staff member 2, 23/07/2009).

The NGO in Kenya, although aware that the MDGs were difficult to realize still took them as a focal point in work at national and community level:

We usually sensitise the community members on importance of MDGs or education on that matter (Kenya National NGO staff member 3, 19/03/2009).

There are those particular two Millennium Development Goals, 2 and 3 addressing the issues of girls and women. You know a lot has been done towards it. But I must say there are a lot of challenges. Like in Kenya free primary education. When you look at societies one of the worst challenges facing the societies when it comes to opportunities towards the MDGs is pastoralist societies. But you will see a lot of challenges when you go to [rural area]. There are a few like distance to school, insecurity and cultural perception. But you will still see that the willingness of us being there. So I would say when we talk about the MDGs, there is hope (Kenya National NGO staff member 8, 19/03/2009).

Thus for both organisations the MDGs were an important component of how they oriented their work, but they did not form a straitjacket requiring particular results, as some government officials appeared to feel. This was most evident in the ways in which they explored a range of meanings of gender considerably beyond those expressed in the MDGs and EFA.

In the NGO studied in South Africa, 'gender' was considered a technical term, suggesting projects needed to include men, which was considered obfuscating as the priority for the organisation was women's rights:

Not that we're excluding – not saying do not to do anything with men – but men tend to get the lion's share of programmes anyway. So that's why we shifted the terminology (South African National NGO staff member 12, 09/12/2010).

It allows us to link women's economic empowerment, their reproductive roles with questions of resource equality and distribution, and the patterns that take place in one but are parallel to the contributions that are being made in another area. [But on gender and schooling] ... I think we haven't picked up that campaign – (South African National NGO 12, 09/12/2010).

In Kenya attending to local meaning was stressed:

One of the key actors towards education is the people themselves. Let us start from there. Sit with them, listen to them and build on the best practices. From there now you will be able to [act] based on what is happening globally and in the continent. They will now give their own perspective and ideas and would be able to design a programme (Kenya National NGO staff member 8, 19/03/2009).

It can be seen that, unlike government officials at national and provincial level, NGO workers are much more comfortable with the MDGs and EFA as one of a number of strategies they can attach to rights, empowerment or local meanings. The purposive stress is not pre-eminent for them, possibly because they do not have the responsibility for results-based development.

There was considerable congruence between the views of staff in the global NGOs in Kenya and South Africa and those in multilateral organisations and global civil society networks in Europe and North America. Often these groups shared education backgrounds and had many opportunities for networking in person or through electronic discussions. In the global organisations all participants except one – who said their work was locally defined – recognized that global frameworks were important in their work:

> ... what I think they have been useful for actually is uniting civil society, especially within education around a sense of global obligation. And the EFA declaration still has tremendous power in the global campaign for education movement and I think it's one reason why [it] doesn't suffer from some of the big ideological fractures that go on in other global coalitions because that baseline if you like, there is no serious dissent about that as the baseline (Staff member, International civil society network 5, 23/12/2008).

> I believe that global targets are extremely important because they allow for, if you will, international peer pressure ... I think that it is important that the international community has set certain standards and certain minimally acceptable behaviours with regard to their populations in general and also with regard to their children (Participant 1, Multilateral Institution 8, 27/06/2008).

Despite differences in terms of which frameworks participants identified with most closely as individuals and as institutions, all recognized the MDGs as playing a key role in shaping international policy and action on gender and education. While for some the MDGs could leverage action, a more critical view was that the MDG framework with its stress on gender parity, curtailed work on women's empowerment:

> I see that most of them are minimum standards because we are talking about basic education, it's a minimum standard. Gender parity, a minimum standard ... OK, those are starting points for discussion and I think that is good (Staff member, International NGO 1, 07/12/2007).

For me, for the type of work that I do, they are useful because … [it] forms a framework that can push us. It can help us engage with government, because governments have agendas they wish to meet … It can help us engage with partners on a more local level. We have a mandate. (Staff member, Bilateral Institution 3a, 03/03/2008).

It can be seen that in global organisations, as in the global NGOs, there is a confidence to work the MDG and EFA agenda regarding gender, education and poverty in ways they find strategic and satisfactory. They feel a sense of ownership of the agendas, and see the possibility to use them in ways that advance their ideas about gender equality, education and addressing poverty.

Conclusion

The data suggest that the global policy frameworks associated with the MDGs and EFA have catalysed some connections both of social policy, associated vocabularies, and of particular kinds of organisations. But this stops well short of building a broad global advocacy movement concerned with human rights and gender equality that reaches down to district education officers, primary school teachers or rural NGO staff. In these organisations the MDGs and EFA feel like other people's projects, and on that basis it is difficult to engage in substantive discussion about poverty, rights and gender equality. Exploration of these ideas and a ready conceptual vocabulary comes much more comfortably to some staff in government and those working in global NGOs and multilateral organisations.

A global process of networking is apparent but it connects only certain staff in national departments of education, national NGOs and global organisations in its critical procedural reflection on development. It is noticeable that these processes are much more evident in the national and provincial departments in South Africa than in Kenya, reflecting heightened capacity and confidence to define and reflect on education interests and agendas. By contrast, purposive claims of governments and the pressures these place on staff are the ways in which provincial officials and teachers express their connection to global frameworks. In the local rural NGO in both countries, neither purposive nor procedural vocabularies are deployed, and the stress is on local needs.

There is a clear contrast between those employed in global and national organisations who take the global frameworks as part of the landscape of their work, and who feel they can work both on and with the policy, and those who feel the frameworks and the vocabulary of rights and substantive equality, which they articulate, are not their project. Partly these are differences of location, particularly with regard to how much the first group has access to the internet, the meetings both actual and virtual, which have created a global community concerned with the MDGs and EFA. The second group, if they use the internet, do not do so for work. Their professional horizons with regard to poverty and gender tend to be framed more by the national press, radio and participation in Church. Apart from meetings where one or two may be invited occasionally to give a particular perspective, they have no purchase on the global discussion of frameworks. Partly these are also differences of education, in that all those in the first groups are graduates, and many are post-graduates, while most of those in the second group have post-school diploma level qualifications. In addition these are differences of location, so that in South Africa, which is less answerable to global agendas in their purposive form, there is more confidence to consider a procedural language by some government officials.

What does this tell us about claims to global obligation voiced by those working on gender, education and poverty? The political philosophical literature (Wallace Brown *et al.* 2010) highlights debates concerning conflicts of interest, procedural reason and the nature of mutuality and right. The data suggest that confidence in procedural reason and mutuality is most apparent for those whose professional biography and location supports the expression and examination of a vision of global obligation. Two senses of articulation express this relation. They are able to articulate, in the sense of express, such a project because their work articulates, in the sense of connects, the global, the national and the local. By contrast, those whose professional identities are squeezed by demands they fulfil certain purposive visions of a global education project, do not easily debate issues of right or mutuality, and more frequently portray the world in terms of conflicts of interest and disarticulation from a global gender, education or poverty reduction project. Practice clearly frames how meanings of global obligation are negotiated. It thus appears difficult to assume engaged work on addressing the connection between education, gender equality and poverty without critical, procedural reflection on practice in the light of global, national and local policy.

To what extent is this a problem of a failure to take the procedural reflection from the global to the local? And to what extent is it the lack of a strong procedural framing in the MDGs or EFA? In my view, these difficulties are linked. In going around the problem of securing widespread agreement for a procedural approach concerned with rights and equality, to stress 'a better way' of a minimal purposive achievements, the process of building the space for procedural reflection has stopped in its tracks. In the place of critical discussion of rights and equalities and consideration of the reasonable grounds on which they might rest has come a stress on meeting targets. This might get minimal achievement of social development, but it does not enhance processes of dialogue, reflection, strengthening of professional insight or enhancing critique. Indeed, implementing the purposive approach appears to work easily with silences, stereotypes and particular forms of local selection. To bring the procedural reflection down from ideal theory to real life implementation, what is needed is the hubbub of comment, examination of the reasonableness of claims, negotiation around plurality and critical reflection on the significance of local context in the intersection of gender, poverty and education.

Notes

1   GEGPRI was funded by the UK Economic and Social Research Council (ESRC) Award no. RES 167–25–260 under a partnership with the UK Department for International Development (DFID). The project ran from September 2007 to March 2011. The Institute of Education, University of London held the award and co-investigators were engaged in work for the project at the University of the Witwatersrand, University of KwaZulu-Natal, and the Catholic University of Eastern Africa. My thanks to all the members of the project team for the collabouration on the project, without which this chapter could not have been written.

References

Bartlett, L. and Vavrus, F. (eds) (2009), *Critical Approaches to Comparative Education: Vertical Case Studies from Africa, Europe, the Middle East, and the Americas*. Palgrave: Macmillan.

Brock, G. (2008), 'Taxation and Global Justice: Closing the Gap between Theory and Practice'. *Journal of Social Philosophy*, 39, (2), 161–84.

Brown, S. (2011), 'Do Kenyans consider nutrition a component of quality education? A case study in a peri-urban school'. MA dissertation, University of London, London.

Colclough, C. (2011), *Challenges for the optimal allocation of educational aid? Should MDG priorities be more prominent?* London: DFID. Working Paper 40/2011.

Collier, P. (2007), *The Bottom Billion*. Oxford: Oxford University Press.

Cowen, R., (2006), 'Acting comparatively upon the educational world: Puzzles and possibilities'. *Oxford Review of Education*, 32, (5), 561–73.

Dieltiens, V., Unterhalter, E., Letsatsi, S. and North, A. (2009), 'Gender blind, gender-lite: a critique of gender equity approaches in the South African Department of Education'. *Perspectives in Education*, 27, (4), 365–74.

Gore, C. (2010), 'The MDG Paradigm, Productive Capacities and the Future of Poverty Reduction'. *IDS Bulletin*, 41, 70–9.

Karlsson, J. (2010), 'Gender mainstreaming in a South African provincial education department: a transformative shift or technical fix for oppressive gender relations?' Compare, 40, (4), 497–514.

Lewin, K. and Little, A. (2011), 'Access to education revisited: Equity, drop out and transitions to secondary school in South Asia and Sub-Saharan Africa'. *International Journal of Educational Development*, 31, (4), 333–7.

Makinda, H. and Yates, C. (2011), 'Social exclusion and violence: researchers' experiences of vertical and horizontal disconnections in conducting naturalistic inquiry in Kenya', paper presented to UKFIET Conference, Oxford, 13–15 September.

Melamed, C. and Sumner, A. (2011), 'A post 2015 global development agreement: Why? What? Who?', paper presented to the ODI/UNDP Cairo workshop on a post-2015 Global Development Agreement, Cairo, 26–27 October.

Paul, E. F., Miller, F. D. and Paul, J. (eds) (2006), *Justice and Global Politics*. Cambridge: Cambridge University Press.

Rizvi, F. and Lingaard, B. (2010), *Globalizing Education Policy*. Abingdon: Routledge

Steiner-Khamsi, G. ed. (2004), *Global Politics of Educational Borrowing and Lending*. New York: Teachers' College Press.

Tikly, L. and Barrett, A. (2012 forthcoming), *Education Quality and Social Justice in the Global South*. Abingdon: Routledge

UNESCO (2011), *Global Monitoring Report 2011: The Hidden Crisis: Armed Conflict and Education*. Paris: UNESCO/Oxford University Press.

Unterhalter, E. (2005), 'Global inequality, capabilities, social justice and the Millennium Development Goal for gender equality in education'. *International Journal of Educational Development*, 25, 111–22.

—(2007), *Gender, Schooling and Global Social Justice*. London: Taylor Francis Routledge.

Unterhalter, E., Karlsson, J., Onsongo, J., Dieltiens, V., North, A., Makinda, H., and Yates, C. (2011), *Gender, Education and Global Poverty Reduction Initiatives. Report on Comparative Case Studies in Kenya, South Africa and Selected Global Organisations*. London: Institute of Education, University of London.

Unterhalter, E. and North, A. (2010), 'Assessing Gender mainstreaming in the education sector: depoliticised technique or a step towards women's rights and gender equality?'. *Compare*, 40, (4), 389–404.

—(2011a), 'Responding to the gender and education Millennium Development Goals in South Africa and Kenya: reflections on education rights, gender equality, capabilities and global justice'. *Compare*, 41, (4), 494–511.

—(2011b), ' "Girls" schooling, gender equity, and the global education and development agenda: Conceptual disconnections, political struggles, and the difficulties of practice'. *Feminist Formations*, 23, 3, 1–22.

Vandemoortele, J. (2009), 'The MDG Conundrum: Meeting the Targets Without Missing the Point'. *Development Policy Review*, 27, 355–71.

Waage, J., Banerji, R., Campbell, O., Chirwa, E., Collender, G., Dieltiens, V., Dorward, A., Godfrey-Faussett, P., Hanvoravongchai, P., Kingdon, G., Little, A., Mills, A., Mulholland, K., Mwinga, A.,North, A., Patcharanarumol, W., Poulton, C., Tangcharoensathien, W. and Unterhalter, E. (2010), 'The Millennium Development Goals: a cross sectoral analysis and principles for goal setting post 2015'. *The Lancet*, 376, (9745), 991–1023.

Wallace Brown, G. and Held, D. (2010), *The cosmopolitanism reader*. Cambridge: Polity.

CHAPTER FIVE

Education Decentralization in South Africa and Zimbabwe: The Gap Between Intention and Practice

Daryl Stenvoll-Wells and Yusuf Sayed

Introduction

School governance is crucial to ensuring that children, young people and adults access good quality education. Effective governance matters particularly for the marginalized and disadvantaged (UNESCO, 2009). Globally the governance reform agenda encompasses a range of strategies to improve the delivery of education services. This includes the decentralisation of education authority from the central level to sub-national bodies, extending participation at the school level through devolving responsibility to school governance committees, introducing more market-oriented measures such as choice and competition, and the partial or full privatisation of education.

Decentralisation as a reform strategy has become central to development thinking since the World Education Forum at Dakar in 2000. It is one of the few policies that strike a chord on both the right and the left of the political spectrum. From a market-focused human capital perspective, it offers expressions of client and consumer power and choice. From a rights-based perspective, it offers a participatory model of citizen action and local control. It is also argued to be a policy that improves education quality, increases transparency, and engenders public commitment to and support for education. Institutions within the international community profess somewhat opposing and overlapping justifications for backing Decentralisation initiatives. This is evident in the policies of international

NGOs such as ActionAid, finance institutions like the World Bank and international donors such as DFID. The complexity and competing rationales for education decentralisation is nowhere more apparent than in the EFA Framework of Action agreed at Dakar in 2000 which indicates:

> the need for better governance of education systems in terms of efficiency, accountability, transparency and flexibility so that they can respond more effectively to the diverse and continuously changing needs of learners. Reform of educational management is urgently needed, to move from highly centralised, standardised and command-driven forms of management to more decentralized and participatory decision-making, implementation and monitoring at lower levels of accountability (Framework of Action, para. 55).

This statement captures much of the promise and peril of policies of education decentralisation, that it will result in the redistribution of power, it will enhance participation and democracy, engender a more responsive education system, and improve education quality.

Most developing countries have embraced some form of decentralisation including in Sub Saharan Africa. In particular, efforts have been made to devolve educational decision-making through school governing bodies and school, management committees. These bodies serve as a useful unit of analysis on several levels. Exploring the declared and actual composition of such groups, the roles they have been assigned by higher levels of government, how responsibility is distributed among stakeholders, and their effectiveness at improving school governance may provide clues as to the cultural and social determinants necessary for successful democratic participation in education.

The region of southern Africa contains some of SSA's most challenging conditions as well as some of its most promising prospects. Observing several of the region's responses to decentralisation raises important questions about these policies and provides lessons for future implementation. This chapter analyses research regarding school governing bodies' roles in two neighbouring countries in Southern Africa, South Africa and Zimbabwe. It seeks to contextualize differing meanings and constructs within the notion of education decentralisation, noting (dis)similarities in how the policy of education decentralisation is constructed between and within governments, participants and development agencies. Zimbabwe and South Africa are regional neighbours who share some historical similarities, but have taken very different approaches to basic education reforms. Naidoo (2005) lists South Africa among several countries that are 'proceeding fast' toward education decentralisation, while Zimbabwe is listed among states that are proceeding 'more slowly' (p. 99). Although white supremacist policies left behind a divided legacy in both countries, stark differences over the past two decades of political rule have resulted in widely varying approaches and responses to the decentralisation process.

Acknowledging their unique contextual factors and the dynamic nature of implementation, this chapter compares the development of participatory governance strategies in these two neighbouring states. Using the composition and function of school governing bodies as units of analysis, it seeks to understand how and why the policies took shape as they did in the light of existing local and international socio-political conditions.

The chapter begins by providing a brief typology of decentralisation followed by a discussion of the contextual background of South Africa and Zimbabwe. This is followed by a comparative case study of both countries' efforts at participatory school governance, with a focus on the composition and function of school governing bodies. The final section synthesizes key elements of the policy approaches in the two countries and the lessons learnt.

Contextual Background

South Africa: Historical Perspective on the Evolution of Participatory Governance

1948's official apartheid ('separateness') legislation and the subsequent 1953 Bantu Education Act allowed the South African government to monitor closely any programmes which did not serve its existing socio-political agenda. The enforced inequality mandated by apartheid laws demanded the complicity of the education establishment in perpetuating a divided society. Schooling was 'designed to consolidate white power and privilege – and entrench black oppression and exploitation' (Weber 2002, p. 618). A key statement of resistance to these laws was the 1955 Freedom Charter, adopted by 3,000 delegates as an early public statement of opposition. However, it was the 1976 Soweto student uprising that awakened the world to the gravity of the situation in South Africa and planted the seed for global resistance to minority rule in the coming years. It also reflected the central position education would play in the opposition.

By the mid-1980s, resistance to apartheid education had been organized under the auspices of the National Education Crisis (later Coordinating) Committee (NECC). The NECC commissioned a National Education Policy Investigation (NEPI) to study available alternatives. The NEPI offered an analysis of existing policy documents, attempting to reconcile them within its framework of democratic, non-racist and non-sexist principles. Unfortunately, many critics found NEPI glossed over key issues of implementation. In the year before apartheid's demise, African primary school students residing in the ten homelands received the lowest public spending per capita – less than forty per cent that of White primary students – followed by non-homeland Africans (43 per cent) (Castro-Leal 1999, p. 19). While the greatest disparities were determined by race, public education spending was also poorly distributed across economic levels, such that 'the richest household quintile received almost twice its share of the population' (that is, 23.4 per cent of public resources for 12.5 per cent of the population) (ibid. p. 16).

Despite all the gross inequalities of apartheid's legacy, South Africa's anti-apartheid opposition engendered '[p]rinciples and values for democratic policy processes such as participation, consultation, redress, equity, representativity and accountability ... within the mass democratic movement' (Cross *et al.* 2002, p. 175). During the transition from minority to majority rule, protracted negotiations between the Nationalist Government and the ANC struck a participatory tone. It was believed that consensus would lend an air of legitimacy to the new government as a product of the South African peoples' will (Carrim 2001, p. 101). The 1996 Constitution of the Republic of South Africa reconfigured the country into 'a parliamentary democracy with powers and duties allocated to nine provinces' (ibid.). Legislation of the provinces' autonomy, in concert with an elected Parliament, could be considered one of the earliest manifestations of decentralisation.

The new government released a spate of documents outlining intended reforms to South African education policy[1], culminating in the *South African Schools Act* (quoted in Carrim 2001, p. 117) of 1996. This was the government's most specific plan to date for equitable funding of public schools. The South African Schools Act and the associated National Norms and Standards for School Funding dictated a weighted allotment of public education expenditure, with schools divided into five quintiles. Schools in the poorest quintile would receive 35 per cent of public education funding, while the wealthiest schools would receive 5 per cent (Bush *et al.* 2003, p. 131).

In the light of its plans for redistributive spending, the government was wary of the possible loss of support from middle-class stakeholders, which might lead to their withdrawal from the system[2]. Self-management and participatory school governance were ways of reassuring the public that all participants would have their say in individual schools' decision-making processes. The institution of school-based management (SBM) would become a yardstick of government's effectiveness at devolving power to local levels, and was seen as a way to 'promote greater accountability to the centre as well as to the community' (Abu-Duhou 1999, p. 22). While devolution of school management has been taken up to varying degrees by many LIDCs, South Africa's SBM project proceeded far more rapidly than that of its regional counterparts in the decade following apartheid's demise. By 2007, it had 'moved further than any other sub-Saharan African country in introducing, on a national level, school-based governance and financing' (Daun 2007, p. 134).

Zimbabwe

Education in pre-independence Zimbabwe consisted of two school systems: white and black. The colonial government warned missionaries not to 'overeducate' Africans, and were critical of attempts to teach them anything beyond the practical skills necessary to produce labourers in agriculture or industry. White schools received funding up to twenty times that of black schools. Like its neighbour to the south, Zimbabwe's pre-independence government evolved a highly complex school system characterized by geographic and racial division.

In the early years of independence, Zimbabwe undertook one of the continent's most remarkable expansions of schooling, in alignment with the government's adoption of the socialist principle 'growth with equity'. The sheer numbers demonstrating the system's expansion are astounding: the number of primary schools doubled between 1979–91. The government was especially concerned with building education infrastructure in neglected areas, training large numbers of teachers to work in new schools, and the provision of teacher resources.

The number of trained teachers more than tripled in the decade following independence, while primary school enrolment increased by 177 per cent. Public financing of education went from a pre-independence rate of 4.4 per cent to 22.6 per cent in 1980, facilitated by community contributions. Despite such support, the emphasis on access over quality led to falling pass rates. By the second decade of independence, the government could no longer bear the strain of previous policy. Pursuant to the International Monetary Fund (IMF)'s policies prescribed by its Economic Structural Adjustment Programme, cost-recovery strategies were put into place in the education sector, including the introduction of school fees.

Inspired by recommendations from the 1990 Jomtien EFA conference, the government rolled out several new education policies in the years that followed, including 1992's *Statutory Instrument 87* and the subsequent *Better Schools Programme Zimbabwe* (BSPZ) of 1993. Statutory Instrument 87 was the first official legislation designed to decentralize Zimbabwean schools, devolving school management to the local level.

While a 1993 report found 81 per cent of Zimbabwe's education decision-making was located with central government, Statutory Instrument 87 and BSPZ signalled a shift towards decentralisation, including a devolved management structure made up of local, district and provincial committees. Although the national-level Ministry of Sports, Education and Culture (MOESC) continued to hold responsibility for the infrastructure, financing and resourcing of all government schools, significant resourcing was devolved to localized clusters, usually consisting of five schools which share 'human, material and financial resources' (Chikoko 2008a, p. 2). One of the cluster's main objectives is to support School Development Committees (SDCs, serving non-government schools) and School Development Associations (SDAs, serving government schools) in becoming 'full partners' in school management. Most prevalent are the SDCs of non-government schools: 'government-aided institutions the majority of which are in the rural areas where most (about 80 per cent) of Zimbabweans live' (Chikoko 2009, p. 202). Since the early nineties' reforms, SDCs had been given significant powers in the day-to-day running of schools, and their roles have sometimes been pivotal to the continued operation of the basic education system (NEEDU 2009). Although designed to account for all stakeholders' interests, the government has been adamant that the success of school management hinges on the role of parents: the government has even gone so far as to state that 'though schools are owned by various responsible authorities, they actually belong to parents' (UNESCO 2008, p. 20).

Zimbabwe's mid-1990s economic downturn saw increasing unemployment and rising inflation, leading to 'rampant structural poverty' (GoZ 2009, p. 2) and heightened unrest. By 2002, land redistribution policies and the consequent decline in agricultural production had combined with a decline in manufacturing to cause hyperinflation. The number of people living below the food poverty (extreme poverty) line had risen to 63 per cent by 2003, and by 2008 'up to 80 per cent of the population survived on less than US$2 a day' (BWPI, 2009a).

Zimbabwe is now considered a fragile state – one in which 'state power is unable and/or unwilling to deliver core functions to the majority of its people: security, protection of property rights, basic public services and essential infrastructure' (OECD, cited by Makochekwana 2009, p. 4). The drastic situation has caused many of the country's most capable professionals to flee, often to neighbouring South Africa (DFID 2010), leading to serious capacity erosion in all sectors (UNDP 2006, p. 2). Basic school infrastructure, including water and sanitation, is crumbling (Williams 2010, p. 1), and schools lack 'everything from toilet paper to textbooks' (IPS 2007). The number of pupils who passed the primary (Grade 7) leaving exams dropped from 62 per cent in 2005 to 39 per cent in 2009 (MOESAC 2009). Government school fees, ranging from US$5–$10 per term, are prohibitively expensive for many families, and pupil drop-out is high (Williams 2010, p. 1).

Decentralisation and New Governance Models

Chambers (2004, p. 4) has listed a number of alterations to the development discourse as observed over twenty years, and has demonstrated how language helps set the parameters of development through its capacity to shape thinking about cultural contexts, responsibility and the limitations of intervention. A key factor highlighted by Chambers (2004) is the upward direction of accountability within the new governance model. One of the ultimate goals of accountability is the legitimation of government, which should have a self-reinforcing effect on political participation. Both Zimbabwe and South Africa had critical reasons to crave political legitimacy during the emergence of education reforms.

South Africa's African National Congress in its first years of power initiated a new school governance framework, the South African Schools Act. The government was concerned with continued participation in the education sector, and a need for legitimacy. During the final years of the apartheid regime, 'token or advisory forms of representation' were added to the political and educational structure, provoking derision toward black participants who were seen as 'giving legitimacy to organs of government which had no real power' (Weber 2002, pp. 629–30). Thus the new government was aware that public participation hinged on concrete evidence of transfer of power to lower levels.

The use of legislative means of transfer as seen in South African and Zimbabwe has been termed *juridification*. This is defined as a process wherein 'legislation is used as a constraining mechanism to control the actions of internal state actors' (Sayed 2002, p. 39). Juridification institutionalizes the link between accountability and a focus on outcomes. Powers granted by school governance legislation come with the responsibility to carry out the law according to government's norms and standards (Grant Lewis and Motala 2004).

While assumptions of shared decisional power contained within the 'governance' model appear in Zimbabwean education policy (Chikoko 2009), they do so with considerably less frequency than their South African counterparts. Selected documents contained a relatively infrequent use of the word in comparison with the South African literature. Part of this may be attributed to the differing labels for school governing committees, with South Africa's designation of School Governing Bodies as opposed to Zimbabwe's School Development Committees. However, given the significance of the source documents, it is hard to imagine that this difference in terminology is merely coincidental.

In analysing the evolution of school management reforms, it is striking to note the contrasting choice of labels for South Africa and Zimbabwe's respective school management groups. South Africa's appellation gives slightly greater significance to the governors' positions in terms of decisional power. The South African Schools Act's preferred wording pays heed to the 'governance' model, which at the time of its release was appearing with increasing prevalence in the discussions about decentralisation.

In Zimbabwe, ZANU-PF's deepening abuses of power were counteracted by public attempts to conceal the 'repressive political governance culture' (BWPI 2009a, p. 38) within the official rhetoric of human rights (UNESCO 2008). Thus, shared school 'management' is sanctioned, echoing the consumerist terminology of some new governance models;

however, 'governance', with its overtones of individual agency, is diminished in favour of a more functionary, bureaucratic designation. The new governance model's depiction of shared decisional power appears in Zimbabwean education policy, but with considerably less recurrence.

Another set of terms that appears often in development discourse is 'participatory development.' Participatory development strategies discouraged 'hierarchies of authority' (Brett 2003, citing Chambers 1983) and instead promote ideals of empowerment and individual agency associated with democracy and the open market. Discussions of participatory development are often conspicuous in their omission of elites; nevertheless, the phenomenon of elite capture has been an inescapable reality of decentralisation. To clarify whose participation should be sought, the qualifier of 'equity' was added to form newer frameworks of 'equitable participation', involving 'stakeholders' in 'redistribution' and 'redress'.

Absent from much of the discourse about education decentralisation is a genuine engagement with pedagogy (Alexander 2008). Arguments regarding decentralisation's beneficial effects on accountability, equity and participation optimistically describe a universalized solution for education, in which pursuit of a definitive education quality has contradictory effects on the course of decentralisation, as illustrated in the examples of South Africa and Zimbabwe.

School Governance Policy & Practice

This section analyses the make-up of School Governing Bodies in the case of South Africa, and School Management Committees in the case of Zimbabwe, analysing how decision-making power is exercised in context. The table 5.1 below provides a summary of the main nature of the devolved school governing structures in both countries.

Composition of School Governing Bodies and School Management Committees

Participants in School Management

There is considerable overlap in the composition of governing bodies in both countries, although they differ in a few significant ways. Both include the school head or principal, parents and school faculty. The number of parents on South African SGBs must constitute the majority – 50 per cent of the group plus one. Zimbabwean SDCs must also include the school head or principal, parents and school faculty. However, it prescribes the number of parents to be included (five). Zimbabwe also adds the school's deputy head to the membership, inserting increased representation for senior

Table 5.1 Elements of South African and Zimbabwean School Reform legislation established by SASA and S.A. 87.

	South Africa (SASA, 1996)	Zimbabwe (SI 87, 1992)
Name of School Management Group:	School Governing Bodies	School Development Committees
Composition + Proportions	– School Head or Principal – Parents (50% +1) – School Faculty (number determined by Member of the Executive Council)	– School Head or Principal – Deputy Head – Local Councillor (1) – Parents (5)
Method of Selection	Manner of election or appointment to be made public locally through publication in the Provincial Gazette. Elections held every three years through procedures determined by Member of the Executive Council.	Faculty appointments made by the Secretory. SDCs may apply to Secretary to include 'more or fewer' members. Parents elected by School Parents Assembly consisting of no less than 20% of School's parents.
Functions	– Setting School Fees – Fundraising – Managing School Finances – Maintaining School Facilities – Setting Disciplinary Policy – Determining Language of instruction – Volunteerism and Community Outreach	– Setting School Fees – Fundraising – Managing School Finances – Maintaining School Facilities (non-governmental schools) – Hiring Personnel 'with the approval of the Minister' (since revoked). – Volunteerism and Community Outreach
Compliance	SGBs may not refuse admission based on inability to pay or because parent does not subscribe to school's mission statement. Refused applications may be appealed and decisions may be reversed by Member of the Executive Council. Members must recuse themselves in cases of conflict of interest.	No recourse to recourse unpaid fees at non-government schools. Proposals to increase fees must be approved at meeting of school Parents Assembly. If Spa denies fee increase, responsible authority may appeal. Secretary may abolish committee if notified of noncompliance.

Sources: Based on GoZ (1992) and RSA (1996).

management; it also allots one space for a local councillor, introducing as well the influence of local political leadership.

The preamble to the South African Schools Act (1996) listed the government's rationales for setting out the new programme, which sought 'to uphold the rights of all, learners, parents, and educators' and 'promote their acceptance of responsibility for the organisation, governance and funding of schools in partnership with the state.' The South African Schools Act's goal of equitable representativity was based on a 'stakeholder' construct: as one school principal put it, stakeholders on an SGB 'need one another to advance the best interest of the school' (Grant Lewis and Naidoo 2004, p. 104). This stakeholder construct denies conflicting interests in favour of a homogenized group identity. Instead of representation along racial, social or gender lines, 'stakeholder' refers to a homogenous array of 'parents/ guardians', 'teachers/educators', 'administrators/ senior school leadership' and 'learners', a development which was justified as a reaction against the country's history of racial division. One SGB member states, 'South African schools tend to shy away from emphasising cultural differences and tend to focus on assimilation and similarities' (Moloi 2007, pp. 468–9). Reports from Zimbabwe reflect much more open division between stakeholder groups and low to non-existent uptake of a homogenized 'stakeholder' identity.

These two extremes illustrate the inherent contradictions in participatory development strategies, which discourage 'hierarchies of authority' (Brett 2003, p. 2 citing Chambers 1983) in favour of ideals of empowerment and individual agency.

Selection of Members, Inclusion and Representativity

Another difference in the two countries' legislation is the manner of school management group selection. The number of teachers on South African bodies is not fixed, instead being determined by a 'Member of the Executive Council'[3], and with the 'manner of election or appointment' made public locally. SGBs are elected every three years through 'election procedures ... determined by the provincial Member of the Executive Council' (Joubert 2006, p. 4). It is left to the community to run the elections 'in a manner that is transparent, free and fair' (ibid.). The SGB may also co-opt additional members of the community 'to assist in discharging any other function' (section 23, #6), but co-opted members do not have the right to vote on the SGB. The South African Schools Act does not prescribe the exact number of parents, teachers, or co-opted members, again reserving this power for a Member of the Executive Council, who must also determine the manner of election of SGB members 'by notice in the Provincial Gazette' (section 24, #2).

In Zimbabwe, teacher participants are not elected, but are appointed by the district's Secretary of Education. At the Secretary's discretion, the SDC may permit 'more or fewer' elected members than the number specified. Zimbabwean SDCs must apply to the Secretary to permit 'more or fewer elected members' than the legislation designates. SDCs are elected by a larger group known as a School Parents Assembly, which is made up at least twenty per cent of the parents and guardians of pupils. These Assemblies are expected to determine 'the composition, functions, duties, procedure and powers of the SDC' via a constitution (Education Act 25:04, section 36–2 & 3) created annually. If the assembly fails to create such a document in a manner the Ministry deems 'satisfactory', then these decisions are left to the Minister (ibid.).

While inclusivity is seen as one of the precepts of participatory school management reforms, some elements of these policies are unclear on how to ensure equitable participation of eligible members. Neither country's source documents – South African Schools Act or SI 87 – gives specifics on how to solicit marginalized members of the community. As previously discussed, the 'stakeholder' construct elides racial, gender and cultural differences in favour of more generalized role-based quotas. Section 27(e) of the South African Schools Act states that a Member of the Executive Council must establish 'guidelines for the achievement of the highest practicable level of representativity of members of the governing body'[4]. No further details are given.

Data is available on the distribution of various groups on South African SGBs: one study found female members were more likely to occupy 'positions of deputies and additional members whereas their male counterparts continued to dominate the position of power' on the SGB (Malada 2005, p. 4). Despite an increase in black student numbers, 'white parents continue to dominate' SGBs (ibid., p. 5). Language distribution favoured English speakers, followed by Afrikaans speakers, with only a small percentage of African indigenous speakers represented (ibid., p. 6). African members were found to occupy secondary positions to their white counterparts.

The source documents give unclear and sometimes contradictory instructions regarding member recusal. Section 26 of the South African Schools Act establishes the policy's position on SGB member recusal:

> A member of a governing body must withdraw from a meeting of the governing body for the duration of the discussion and decision-making on any issue in which the member has a personal interest.

The issue of establishing which policies constitute those of 'personal interest' to members is not clarified. The consequences of this section's lack of clarity on criteria for 'representativity' is seen in researchers' findings on the enactment of SGB policy.

What is often missing from school reform policies is acknowledgement of the conflicts that are 'endemic to organisational life' (Altrichter *et al.*

2000, p. 100). Recognising stakeholders' sometimes conflicting aims does not have to mean relinquishing the hope of consensus. It does necessitate an understanding of interactions and social roles as a basis for policy formation (ibid., p. 1010). Connections between increased participation and improved equity are called into doubt when participants' identities and rights become neutralized by the generic, market-framed formulations of 'stakeholder', 'customer' and 'consumer'.

Although a 1999 World Bank document outlined inequities in the South African school system by providing statistical data on participation at racial and socioeconomic levels (Castro-Leal 1999), a decade later key South African education monitoring documents present statistics on primary learners as distributed by province and gender, but not by race (RSA 2008). Such 'neutralization' seems to increase in the government's strategic plan outlines from year to year. The 2006 strategic plan makes no mention of an SGBs' importance in its goals of quality or efficiency, but SGBs are mentioned under the rubric of 'Race and Values': it sets the aim for 'SGBs in 10,000 public schools [to] have policies in place on how to govern schools in relation to non-racism and equity' by 2007 (RSA 2006, p. 56). The equivalent document in 2010 directs SGBs to develop 'a training manual that infuses Human Rights and values into SGB training' (RSA 2010, p. 158). No mention is made of racial inequity or redress.

Governing Body Functions: Financing

Setting School Fees

The documents sampled indicate the setting of school fees is by far the most contested decisional power of school governing bodies. A 2005 strategic plan recommends that SDCs 'review school fees regularly to reflect the economic reality' (UNICEF/MOESAC 2005, p. 13), but this does not seem to have taken effect by the time of a 2009 report on decentralisation in Zimbabwe. This cited 'a need for pro-poor budgeting ... The present system excludes the very poor and destitute' (BWPI2009a, p. 148). A government assessment of the same year decried the government policy's lack of transparency regarding school fees and levies, which it found 'should be united into one fee, governed by transparent regulations, and controlled at school level, with clear decision-making processes and responsibilities for both the school and the parental leadership structures' (NEAB 2009, pp. 61–2).

Although South Africa's NNSSF may have been adopted to prevent learners from poor backgrounds from exclusion due to their parents' inability to pay, it is clear that something about the existing system is not working. A 2007 strategic plan lists the need to 'monitor and support the implementation of the amended Norms and Standards for funding including fee levels, exemptions, and no-fee schools' (RSA 2007, p. 54); the strategic plan from 2010 persists in recommending further '[a]mendments to norms … (including fee levels, exemptions, no-fee schools, transfers etc.)' (ibid.). A recent statement by an SGB representative complains that the 'one-size-fits-all approach' of the quintile system is 'no longer appropriate', and espouses an alternate 'per-learner funding model' (FEDSAS 2010, p. 11).

Given the binary nature of Zimbabwe's system of government and non-government schools, it is hardly surprising that the fees situation is seen as 'confusing'. Although the 2005 Education Act dictates unnamed school 'authorities' must apply to institute increases, one teacher complained that 'government leaves this to the school and its SDC. It's not even aware of the fees and levies charged and does not follow up or audit.' (Chikoko 2008a, p. 7) This is compounded by an apparent lack of consequences for those who do not pay: 'parents who could pay decided not to do so when they learnt that children would not be sent away from school' (NEAB 2009, p. 2). A 2009 joint study found that most government school fees went unpaid. It went on to recommend that more emphasis should be placed 'on the levies which are decided upon by the parents themselves', suggesting further decentralisation of school fee policy is in order (NEAB 2009, p. 55). However, detractors in both countries have voiced suspicion that decentralisation of school fee policy is simply an elabourate means of passing responsibility for an inadequately managed system onto the stakeholders: 'the school bears responsibility for exclusion, rather than the state' (Sayed 2002, p. 41).

Fundraising

In addition to setting fees and levies, governing bodies are often tasked with raising additional funds for the school, which can be done in a variety of ways. South African SGBs have the right to charge fees for external use of school grounds, or raise funds through sales at the school tuck shop, but the low or non-existent income of parents severely constrains fundraising capacity for schools in poor communities. Even so, a study of township schools found some using innovative strategies for fund-raising, including making and selling school uniforms, screening videos in the township, raffles and cultural days, and collection of recyclable materials (Prew 2009, p. 837).

In Zimbabwe, 'state and donor grants provide an incentive for parents and communities to contribute in order to obtain more grants' (NEAB 2009, p. 55). The lack of valuable currency has led stakeholders to seek 'locally based answers … such as the provision of foodstuffs by parents in rural areas' to incentivize hungry teachers to stay at their posts (BWPI 2009b, p. 129). While this would appear a heartening solution to an intractable problem, sources show friction has arisen between parents and teachers 'due to the fact that parents, even very poor parents, were forced by circumstances to take over responsibility for teachers' remuneration' when the state neglected to pay (NEAB 2009). Parents were reportedly 'very unhappy' with the obligation to provide teachers' incentives, and 'complained that this was dividing parents and teachers' (ibid., p. 82).

Management of School Finances

Governing bodies have taken up extensive financial responsibilities allotted by the school governance legislation, including management of school infrastructure and funds. However, division between governing body stakeholders is high, with stakeholders frequently calling into question each other's capacity to make informed and equitable decisions.

Teachers in Zimbabwe lamented that financial decisions were 'monopolised by parents because they say they are the source of the school funds' (Chikoko 2009, p. 204). Efforts at developing the management capacity of SDCs have been hampered by the country's complex system of reporting and supervision, where non-government schools report to the local Rural District Council (RDC) rather than the ministry employing school faculty and leadership (Chikoko 2008b, p. 245; MOESAC 2009). This has led to exclusionary practices: 'the education ministry sometimes organized financial management skills workshops which [school heads] could attend. SDCs were not included in such workshops because ... they were not part of the structures of the latter ministry' (ibid., pp. 256–7).

While South African parents and teachers both consider it the SGB's duty to 'see to the smooth running of the school's administration', teachers felt the SGB should not be involved in 'managerial' matters (Grant Lewis and Naidoo 2004, p. 105). In fact, 'school personnel appear not to want parental involvement beyond token ... fund-raising and other support activities' (ibid., p. 106). However, this is largely due to a belief that SGB members lack the skills needed to execute other administrative duties.

Training school leaders in developing the capacity of their schools' governing bodies has paid off in some cases. A South African university distance education course aimed at furthering parental involvement in education mentioned the possibility of combining community outreach and SGB development. It cited positive results in a case where the manager of a local business was solicited by a principal to train the SGB in budgeting (Lemmer 2007).

Governing Body Functions: Issues of teaching and learning

Curriculum

In many respects, the area of curriculum appears to have been one of the more under-utilized functions of governing bodies. This has been attributed to limitations in capacity as well as the dominance of other school leadership in this role. In 2008, a Zimbabwean parent governor notes 'some parents cannot read and write so to ask them to come and look at their children's work is asking for too much sometimes' (Chikoko 2008b, p. 254). Even so, 'teachers and school heads felt that parents should play a more significant role in decisions about curriculum' (ibid., p. 260), and one of the BSPZ's aims was 'to extend the role of SDCs from that of providing physical infrastructure to full partners in the school system' (Chikoko 2009). There was no evidence of this coming to fruition within the sample.

In South Africa, both teachers and parents claimed 'teachers dictate the terms in the SGB. We have political power. The parents always endorse our [teachers] position' (Grant Lewis *et al.* 2004, p. 106). This single-stake-holder dominance may have consequences for the curriculum and overall learning. A 2005 survey found 'just over fifty per cent at most' of Grade 6 students were given homework 'most days' of the week, and only 'about half' received encouragement from parents in completing homework. It went on to recommend that 'principals, in collabouration with SGBs, should develop school policies that set minimum acceptable amounts of homework' (SACMEQ 2005, policy suggestion 3.12). This suggests the possibility of a curricular role for SGBs in reinforcing learning and ensuring teacher professionalism. Whether teachers in the habit of wielding decisional power would be willing to allow such changes is open to question.

Language Policy

After the setting of school fees, governing bodies' relationship to language policy is the second most contentious area of implementation. This is a multi-layered relationship, since the language used in legislation directly affects school governors' ability to interpret it correctly and enact it. In Zimbabwe, 'while SDCs conducted their business in the home language, the laws governing schools are written in English, so [parents] needed assistance from the school heads and teachers to interpret these laws and regulations ... parent governors are at the mercy of other stakeholders' (Chikoko 2008a, p. 15).

In South Africa, the South African Schools Act extended the number of recognized official languages from two to eleven, and the country's constitution now considers all of these languages 'equal' under the law (Brock-Utne *et al.* 2004, p. 71). However, 'when one reads the official government policy carefully, one sees that this policy does **not** state that a change of language instruction needs to take place' (ibid., p. 72). Sayed (2002) cites an extreme situation that arose from of the confusion over this element of the legislation: a formerly white Afrikaans school began admitting black learners, who were taught in English. When the SGB purchased a set of resources for Afrikaans-speaking students, the black community protested and the situation rapidly descended into provocation and police intervention (Sayed 2002, p. 43). This is but one example of the 'need for precise clarity about different levels of responsibility' (ibid), and the high emotions that school language policies may incite.

Governing Body Function: Staffing and community involvement

Employment of Faculty & Staff

The involvement of governing bodies in decisions related to school personnel has been another cause of friction, especially with respect to the hiring and firing of faculty and staff. Amendments to the South African Schools Act stress the importance of equity and representativity, but give no further criteria or recourse for stakeholders who feel their concerns are not being addressed. The document's unclear wording resulted in conflict soon after the original legislation, when several SGBs interpreted their power to make hiring recommendations differently from the Ministry (Sayed 2002, pp. 43–4). This resulted in amendments to the act, limiting SGBs' choice of teachers to selections from the provincial department of education (RSA 2006, section 7–1). The episode alerted policymakers to possible clashes between the rights of schools and the duty of the state to ensure uniform standards and equity (ibid., p. 44). Only wealthier 'Model C' SGBs have continued their involvement in hiring teachers, whose salaries they pay directly through fund-raising in their affluent communities. This enables them 'to maintain their teacher-learner ratio stable without having to wait for government to issue posts' (Malada 2005, p. 9).

In Zimbabwe, the involvement of SDCs in hiring and firing was a short-lived experiment. The groups' employment powers were quickly the subject of accusations and counter-accusations; district and provincial powers accused school governors of nepotism and corruption. SDCs insisted that the ministry and local education officials did not want to relinquish power for political reasons. Faculty have also expressed resentment over the notion of hiring decisions being made by uneducated parents, as voiced by one teacher, who complained, 'how can I go for training for three years only to come and be interviewed for a job by a semi-literate parent?' (Chikoko 2008b, p. 258) Interviews with Zimbabwean parents indicated they felt they lacked 'competence' to make decisions regarding teacher appraisal, and preferred the more straightforward tasks concerning management and infrastructure (Chikoko 2008b, p. 259). One parent even described it as 'disempowering' to be asked to short-list and interview candidates without being adequately trained (Chikoko 2009, p. 205).

Volunteerism and Community Outreach

A number of South African SGB members reported they placed great importance on their role in providing a link between the school and the community, not only through academic reinforcement but in establishing 'social, health, recreational, nutritional and transport programmes' (Malada 2005, p. 10). Several studies reported positive results when school leadership was given training in forms of community engagement (Lemmer 2007, Prew 2009). A course for teachers and school leaders sensitized them to parents' needs, leading them to provide more accessible meeting locations and times, better notifications on school activities for illiterate parents or those who spoke minority languages, and even childcare (Lemmer 2007). Some schools reported pay-offs in terms of school volunteerism, with parents providing free security for school grounds, cleaning toilets, and helping to reduce truancy and lateness. Teacher attitudes were also transformed by such training. While some teachers may carry resentful attitudes toward poorly educated, rural parents[5], a teacher participant came to see parents as 'a source of inspiration' (Lemmer 2007, p. 227). As one mother proudly remarked, 'I don't have money to offer the school but I have two hands and a brain to help teachers to stay in class and do other things' (ibid.).

Zimbabwean SDCs have been commended for keeping schools operational through the past decade of hardship (BWPI 2009b, p. 133). Despite their marginalisation with respect to other (non-financial) governing functions, parents seem to have taken ownership of their responsibilities to provide the school with a community liaison, as one parent testified: 'We only come to assist in linking the school with the community' (Chikoko 2008b, p. 253). A 2005 report encouraged SDCs to take up more responsibility for educating parents about the need to keep children in school, particularly girls who fall out of the system due to religious and cultural practices that prevent girls' participation (UNICEF/MOESAC 2005, p. 13).

In order for positive engagement to occur, community members needed to be given real responsibility rather than simple 'inclusion' in school activities (Prew 2009, p. 839). However, when contributions of time and skill are not matched by increased involvement in school decision-making, such practices can become 'extractive'. A Malawian study on similar themes noted that when community members are expected to offer services and funding to schools without having any real decisional power in how these are being used, 'they did not result in increased community ownership or accountability of schools to the community' (Rose 2003, p. 57).

Rifts between stakeholders can prevent the kind of trust necessary for governing bodies to make the most of their decisional powers and individual members' capacities, making their functionality less than the sum of their parts. This returns us to the problem of stakeholders' 'empowerment' and the decentralisation's divergent roots in neoliberal strategies and human rights approaches:

> There are conflicting views as to what empowerment means ... To neoliberals it means regarding people as consumers and customers ... To others, empowerment means the opposite: people are regarded as citizens (Therkildsen 2001, p. 29)

By way of conclusion

This paper has examined processes of education decentralisation in two countries in Southern Africa, both with a history of colonial rule. It argues that the policy of decentralisation, specifically the devolution of authority and control to school governing structures, was as much a reaction to colonial rule as it was a reaction to policy borrowing. A strong emphasis on democratic school governance in both countries was seen as a reaction to a system of political rule in which decisions affecting the majority were made by a minority white ruling government. Sayed (2002) argues that, specifically in the South African case, the policy of education decentralisation was chosen as it accords with the policy intentions of both the political right (the old ruling Apartheid government) and the progressive movement and the left (the new democratic government that came into power following the democratic election of 1994) while simultaneously projecting a vision of modernity.

Across both countries, what is striking is the discrepancy between the official justifications for participatory school governance and the actual effects on democracy at the local level in the form of school governance structures. The presumed equality of participation by all stakeholders at the local level is an illusion, as the evidence shows that in the past decade one or several stakeholder groups dominated decision-making within the school governing body. It is the powerful middle and professional classes who possess the necessary cultural capital that dominates such structures. Rose (2003) notes that it has proven especially difficult for school administrators to share power as '... opening the school to broader community involvement would take control away from the principal.' The global discourse of benign stakeholder equality in devolved governance structures comes unstuck on the reality of power. As Weiler (1993) notes, decentralisation can quite easily be a transfer of power from central to local elites, in contrast to the idea that it empowers local communities.

It is evident across both contexts that while the more democratic and participatory intent of decentralisation is laudable, the reality is that the state and teachers as professionals continue to exercise power over the curriculum and that often local structures are not able to have a major say about teaching and learning. Thus, participatory forms of school governance do not impact on the key aspect of improving quality, namely, teaching and learning (Sayed *et al.* 2011). The reality of participation masks the failure to devolve power and develop local structures so that they can take on an effective role with regard to curriculum issues.

Across both countries, it is evident that what was actually devolved to the school was the need to raise funds to supplement state resources in education – a strategy of financial downloading (Sayed 2002). This led, particularly in the case of South Africa, to a two-tier system of education whereby schools with a wealthier parent base were able to afford more resources (including teachers) compared to schools serving the marginalized and poor. This is why, in the case of South Africa, the government introduced in 2006 a 'no fee school policy' to ensure that the poor do not carry the burden of paying for their education; a policy that, while noble, does not fundamentally redress the inequalities in the system which were introduced as part of the South African School Act (Sayed *et al.* 2009).

In conclusion, this paper argues that decentralisation can enable local actors to facilitate the efficient delivery of context-relevant resources, infrastructure and (where possible) personnel. However, it does not always result in more equitable outcomes; decentralisation as an education policy needs to be introduced with caution in societies which are highly unequal. The putative global benefits of decentralisation cannot and should not be taken at face value without examining their impact on equity at the local level in diverse contexts.

Notes

1   These included the ANC's *Policy Framework on Education and Training* (1994, cited in Jansen 2002), the 1995 *White Paper on Education and Training* (cited by Grant Lewis and Motala 2004), and the 1996 *National Education Policy Act* (NEPA).

2   According to Pampallis (2003), withdrawal of middle-class stakeholders 'would deprive public schooling of its most influential advocates as [they] no longer depended on the public schools for the education of their own children and grandchildren.' (p. 151)

3   'Member of the Executive Council' means Member of the Executive Council of a province who is responsible for education in that province. (South African Schools Act 1996, Definitions, i–xi)

4   Defined in Chapter 1, xi: '"Member of the Executive Council" means the Member of the Executive Council of a Province who is responsible for education in that province.'

5   One teacher summarized her attitude towards the disadvantaged parent community at a farm school: "...Most of them can't read and write. They only speak their mother tongue and Afrikaans. They are interested in dancing,

fighting, gossiping, going to work, drinking liquor and not caring for children.' (Lemmer 2007, p. 223).

References

Abu-Duhou, X. (1999), 'School-Based Management'. Fundamentals of Education Planning 62, Paris: IIEP-UNESCO.

Alexander, R. (2008), *Education for All, the Quality Imperative and the Problem of Pedagogy*, Cambridge: CREATE-IOE University of London.

Altrichter, H. and Salzgeber, S. (2000), 'Some Elements of a Micro-Political Theory of School Development', in H. Altrichter and J. Elliott (eds), *Images of Educational Change*. Buckingham: Open University, pp. 99–110.

Brett, E. A. (2003), 'Participation and Accountability in Development and Management'. *The Journal of Development Studies*, 40, (2), 1–29.

Brock-Utne, B., and Halmarsdottir, H. (2004), 'Language Policies and Practices in Tanzania and South Africa: Problems and Challenges'. *International Journal of Educational Development*, 24, 67–83.

Bush, T. and Heystek, J. (2003), 'School Governance in the New South Africa'. *Compare*, 33, (2), 127–37.

BWPI (2009a), *Brooks World Poverty Institute Zimbabwe Report*. BWPI: Manchester.

—(2009b), *Moving Forward in Zimbabwe: Reducing Poverty and Promoting Growth. Appendix 1: Prioritisation of Recommendations for the Education Sector*. BWPI: Manchester.

Carrim, N. (2001), 'Democratic Participation, Decentralisation and Educational Reform', in D. Jansen and Y. Sayed (eds), *Implementing Education Policies: the South African Experience*. Lansdowne: UCT Press, pp. 98–111.

Castro-Leal, F. (1999), *Poverty and Inequality in the Distribution of Public Education Spending in South Africa*. Washington, DC: World Bank. Working Paper 19711/1999.

Chambers, R. (2004), *Ideas for Development: Reflecting Forwards*, Brighton: IDS. IDS Working Paper 238.

Chikoko, V. (2008a), 'Negotiating Roles and Responsibilities in the Context of Decentralised School Governance: A Case Study of One Cluster of Schools in Zimbabwe' [Online] Available at: www. topkinisis. com/conference/CCEAM/wib/index/outline/PDF/CHIKOKO per cent20Vitallis. pdf> (Accessed: 1 December 2011)

—(2008b), 'The Role of Parent Governors in School Governance in Zimbabwe: Perceptions of School Heads, Teachers and Parent Governors'. *International Review of Education*, 54, (2), 243–63.

—(2009), 'Educational Decentralisation in Zimbabwe and Malawi: A Study of Decisional Location and Process'. *International Journal of Educational Development*, 29, 201–11.

Cross, M., Mungadi, R. and Rouhani, S. (2002), 'From Policy to Practice: Curriculum Reform in South African Education'. *Comparative Education*, 38, (2), 171–187.

Daun, H. (2007), *School Decentralization in the Context of Globalizing Governance*. Netherlands: Springer.

DFID (2010), *Learning for All: DFID' Education Strategy 2010–2015*. London: Department for International Development.

FEDSAS (2010), 'FEDSAS Submission to the Parliamentary Portfolio Committee on Basic Education' [Online]. Available at: www. pmg. org. za/files/docs/100728fedsas_0. pdf> (Accessed: 1 December 2011).

GoZ (1992), *Statutory Instrument 87: Education (School Development Committees) (Non-Government Schools) Regulations*. Harare: Government of Zimbabwe.

—(2005), *Education Act 25:04. Law Development Commission*. Harare: Government of Zimbabwe.

—(2009), *Zimbabwe Millennium Development Goals 2000–2007 Mid-Term Progress Report*. Harare: Government of Zimbabwe.

Grant Lewis, S. and Motala, S. (2004), 'Educational De/centralization and the Quest for Equity, Democracy and Quality', in L. Chisholm ed., *Changing Class: Education and Social Change in Post-Apartheid South Africa*. Cape Town: Zed, pp. 115–42.

Grant Lewis, S. and Naidoo, J. (2004), 'Whose Theory of Participation? School Governance Policy and Practice in South Africa'. *Current Issues in Comparative Education*, 6, (2), 100–12.

Kwenda, S. (2007), 'It is all zero here. We have nothing'. IPS (Inter Press Service), Harare, 12 April.

—(2007), *It's All Zero Here. We Have Nothing*, [Online] Available at: www. kubatana. net/html/archive/edutra/070412ips. asp?sector=edutra&year=2007& range_start=181> (Accessed: 12 April 2007).

Joubert, R. (2006), 'School Governance in South Africa: Linking Policy and Praxis', paper presented to Conference of Commonwealth Council for Educational Administration and Management (CCEAM), Cyprus, 12–17 October.

Lemmer, E. (2007), 'Parent Involvement in Teacher Education in South Africa'. *International Journal about Parents in Education*, 1, (0), 218–29.

Makochekwana, A. (2009), 'State Fragility: Zimbabwe's horrific journey in the new millennium', paper presented to European Report on Development Conference, Accra, 21–23 May.

Malada, N. B (2005), 'Perspectives of School Governing Bodies on Best Practices in Desegregated Schools: Preliminary Findings', paper presented to Human Sciences Research Council Diversity and Integration Workshop, Johannesburg, 1–3 February.

MOESAC (2009), 'Presentation outline for Meeting with Education Partners'. PowerPoint slides, Harare, 23 February.

Moloi, K. (2007), 'An Overview of Education Management in South Africa', *South African Journal of Education*, 27, (3), 463–76.

Naidoo, J. (2005), 'Education Decentralization in Africa: Great Expectations and Unfulfilled Promises', in D. Baker and A. Wiseman (eds), *Global Trends in Education Policy*. Amsterdam: Elsevier, pp. 99–124.

NEAB (2009), *The Rapid Assessment of Primary and Secondary Schools Conducted by the National Education Advisory Board*. Harare: NEAB/EU.

NEEDU (2009), *Ministerial Committee on a National Education Evaluation and Development Unit. Final Report*. Pretoria: Department of Education.

Prew, M. (2009), 'Community Involvement in School Development: Modifying School Improvement Concepts to the Needs of South African Township Schools', *Educational Management Administration Leadership*, 37, 824–46.

Rose, P. (2003), 'Community Participation in School Policy and Practice: Balancing Local Knowledge, National Policies and International Agency Priorities', *Compare*, 33, (1), 47–64.

RSA (1996), *The South African Schools Act*. Cape Town: Government Printers.

—(2006), *Education Laws Amendment Act 24/2005. Government Gazette*, 487. Cape Town: Government Printers.

—(2007), *Strategic Plan 2007–2011*. Cape Town: Department of Basic Education.

—(2008), *Education Statistics in South Africa 2008*. Pretoria: Department of Education.

—(2010), *Strategic Plan 2010/11–2012/13*. Cape Town: Department of Basic Education.

SACMEQ (2005), *The SACMEQ II Project in South Africa: A Study of the Conditions of Schooling and the Quality of Education*. Harare: Southern African Consortium for Monitoring Educational Quality/ Ministry of Education, SA.

Sayed, Y. (2002), 'Democratising Education in a Decentralised System: South African Policy and Practice'. *Compare*, 32, (1), 35–46.

Sayed, Y. and Ahmed, R. (2009), 'Promoting access and enhancing education opportunities? The case of no-fees schools in South Africa'. *Compare*, 39, (2), 203–81.

—(2011), 'Education quality in post-apartheid South African policy: balancing equity, diversity, rights and participation'. *Comparative Education*, 47, (1), 103–18.

Therkildsen, O. (2001), *Efficiency, Accountability and Implementation: Public Sector Reform in East and Southern Africa*, Geneva: UNRISD. Democracy, Governance and Human Rights Programme Paper Number 3.

UNDP (2006), *Draft Country Programme Document for Zimbabwe (2007–2009)*. New York: UN.

UNESCO (2008), *National Report on the Status of Education by Zimbabwe. 48th Session of UNESCO International Conference on Education*. Geneva: UNESCO.

—(2009), *Overcoming Inequality: Why Governance Matters*. Oxford – Paris: Oxford University Press and UNESCO.

UNICEF/MOESAC (2005), *Zimbabwe National Strategic Plan for the Education of Girls, Orphans, and Other Vulnerable Children*. Harare: UNICEF.

Weber, E. (2002), 'An Ambiguous, Contests Terrain: Governance Models for a New South African Education System', *International Journal of Educational Development*, 22, 617–35.

Weiler, H. N. (1993), 'Control versus Legitimization: the politics of ambivalence', in J. Hannaway and M. Carnoy (eds), *Decentralization and School Improvement: Can we fulfil the promise?* San Francisco, CA: Jossey-Bass Publishers, pp. 55–83.

Williams, P. (2010), 'Educational Development, Assistance Flows and Co-ordination in Zimbabwe', paper presented to LINK/CCFE Conference. London, 22 July.

CHAPTER SIX

Implementing Global Policies in African Countries: Conceiving Lifelong Learning as Basic Education

Anja P. Jakobi

Introduction

Lifelong learning has become a central idea in many policy documents and reforms worldwide. States aim to educate citizens throughout the lifespan, and public as well as private providers target many different groups besides the traditional student. However, lifelong learning is often assumed to be limited to industrialized countries in their transformation into a knowledge society and the change to new modes of production. Yet many developing countries have also turned to lifelong-learning reforms, even under adverse conditions (Jakobi 2009b). In this chapter, I will illustrate how two African countries, namely South Africa and Nigeria, align with a global discourse on lifelong learning and the extent to which they refer to corresponding policies. Given the lack of resources for education in these countries, they represent 'hard cases' for the implementation of lifelong learning.

I shall begin with a short introduction to global education policy, based on the idea of a world society. In a further step, I will present the global discourse on lifelong learning, mainly created by international and regional organisations. In a third step, I will outline some quantitative indicators on the educational situation in African countries. In a fourth and fifth step, I will analyse the policies developed and implemented in South Africa and Nigeria. Both are Sub-Saharan countries, but in the light of their history, political and education systems, the countries vary widely according to the aspects of lifelong learning they can achieve. In a final step, I shall sum up the findings and delineate areas for further research. The chapter shows that countries can rapidly align with global policy discourses, but that such alignment does not mean similar policy implementation.[1]

Global Education Policy and the World Society

This chapter conceives world politics as being based on a shared world culture, as developed in the framework of sociological institutionalism (e.g. Meyer *et al.* 1997a; 1997b). Originally, sociological institutionalism was developed within the field of organisational sociology. Researchers found that organisations, for example, firms, are sometimes not structured according to a functional logic, but follow those principles that appear to be the most legitimate (Meyer *et al.* 1977). In the so-called organisational field, organisations are thus exposed to ideas of the wider environment that concern their identity, either by explicit or implicit rules. Under such conditions, they show the tendency to become more similar; so-called 'isomorphism' occurs (DiMaggio *et al.* 1983).

Later, sociological institutionalists transferred this approach to the world of states, based on the assumption that questions of legitimacy would also play a crucial role in this particular community of organisations. States are therefore considered to appear more legitimate if they feature the same characteristics as other states, for instance, a national constitution, an education system, a democratic order or the entitlement of individual rights (Meyer *et al.* 1997a). Examples include the worldwide establishment of welfare arrangements, globally spread environmental policies, and scientific bureaucracies (Finnemore 1996a; Meyer *et al.* 1997b). The struggle for individual rights and development as well as the quest for progress are almost universal characteristics across countries (Meyer *et al.* 1997a, p. 153). Modern societies seek to secure progress and justice (Finnemore 1996b) and the idea and coverage of rights is constantly expanded upon (Meyer 2000, p. 239). Contrary to what may be assumed, such diffusion is not caused by, for example, common economic development that states would face and that, in turn, would lead to the establishment of certain school curricula or environmental standards (Meyer *et al.* 1992; Meyer 2005). Instead, these phenomena can better be explained by the idea of a commonly shared world culture – a world society in which states participate while they are engaged in international exchange.

Members of the organisational field of world society are actors such as governmental or non-governmental organisations, states or epistemic communities: non-governmental organisations, lobby states and international organisations implement policies at local level and campaign for political aims. By doing so, they are concerned with 'enacting, codifying, modifying, and propagating world-cultural structures and principles' (Boli *et al.* 1999, p. 19). Powerful or otherwise successful states can act as role models for other states, thereby setting standards of what statehood encompasses in terms of substance and behaviour. Epistemic communities, as scientists, influence world politics as a major source for problem definition (Haas *et al.* 1977; Adler *et al.* 1992; Haas 1992). International governmental organisations have the capacity to link these different actors, and to provide forums wherein world society can meet and discuss global public policy, implement regimes, etc. Moreover, international organisations also have several means at hand for disseminating identified political aims across countries.

International organisations are thus not only a forum for exchange in world society, but they also seek to develop, support and disseminate policies internationally to countries and other organisations. The different means available to them not only allow for a variety of activities linked to a specific policy, but they also enable the organisation to intervene at different stages of the domestic policy process. As agenda-setters, international organisations mainly foster debate; however, through coordinating and monitoring, they also intervene in the implementation process, weighing up and identifying better ways to pursue the political goals. The following section will elaborate on different international organisations that disseminate lifelong-learning policies.

International Organisations and Lifelong Learning

Lifelong learning has not only become a key principle in education policy reforms, but it has also developed its meaning over time. While in the 1970s it was mainly linked to adult education, training and continuing education, nowadays it encompasses the whole spectrum of educational phases (from pre-schooling to higher education and adult education) as well as different forms of learning (from formal to informal and non-formal) (Jakobi 2009b). International organisations have long conducted activities linked to lifelong learning and disseminating this political goal with different means. An important precondition for these activities has been the burgeoning idea of a knowledge society, in which education is of paramount importance. Originally developed from the late 1960s onwards (Drucker 1969; Bell 1973), the idea of a knowledge society gained further momentum in the 1990s and today constitutes a central narrative in global education reforms (Jakobi 2007).

The consensus on lifelong learning has been 'one of the most remarkable features of the education policy discourse, nationally and internationally, of the past decade' (Papadopoulos 2002, p. 39). Many countries today refer to this idea or endeavour to implement corresponding reforms. An analysis of education policy reports submitted to the International Conference of Education – a major conference hosted by the UNESCO International Bureau of Education in Geneva – shows this development in figures: from the mid-1990s until 2004, countries have increasingly referred to lifelong learning in the context of education policy. However, while the share of countries that refer to this idea has steadily increased from 62.8 per cent in 1996 to 72 per cent in 2004, recent figures from 2008 point to a slight decrease in the number of countries to 65.5 per cent (the second row in Table 6.1. outlines the number of reports analysed in each respective year). Since this only represents a snapshot and the number of countries is still high, we cannot speak of a diminishing importance of this idea in education policy, but attention should be paid to its future development.

Table 6.1 Lifelong Learning in Education Policy Reports

Year	1996	2001	2004	2008
Percentage of Countries referring to Lifelong Learning in Education Policy	62.8	70.6	72	65.5
Number of Countries Analysed	43	51	82	84

Source: Jakobi 2009a.

In any case, approximately two-thirds of very different countries refer to this concept, despite significant discrepancies in their national background. At the same time, countries have also begun to implement related reforms (Jakobi 2009b). For example, national qualification frameworks have become one means of ensuring learning processes over the entire lifespan. First established in New Zealand, these frameworks have spread worldwide since the early 1990s. Moreover, early childhood education is flourishing across countries, delivering the first step in lifelong education processes.

UNESCO had already been involved in early debates on lifelong learning, for example, through the so-called Faure Report, in which lifelong learning was advocated as a master concept for shaping education systems (UNESCO 1972, p. 182, emphasis in original). This and other activities, however, were not achieved by increasing national activities and over the course of the 1980s organisations turned their back on the matter. Nevertheless, in the 1990s, this situation changed, beginning with the Jomtien Summit in 1990, where participants adopted the World Declaration on Education for All: Meeting Basic Learning Needs. The declaration included an emphasis both on pre-primary education and on the inclusion of adults as potential recipients of basic education (World Conference on Education for All 1990, Art 1[4], (3[1], 5).

In 1991, the UNESCO General Conference decided to set up a commission for reflecting on the future of education systems. The International Commission on Education for the Twenty-First Century published its report in 1996, underlining the importance of lifelong learning for future education systems (UNESCO 1996, Part 1). It was explicitly seen as the foundation of future education policy: 'The concept of learning throughout life is the key that gives access to the twenty-first century. It goes beyond the traditional distinction between initial and continuing education' (UNESCO 1996, p. 111). Learning over the lifespan included access to a variety of learning opportunities, the development of early learning in childhood and preschool (UNESCO 1996, p. 134; World Education Forum 2000, pp. 28–30; 64–6). Moreover, as a standard-setting activity, the 2001 Revised Recommendation concerning Technical and Vocational Education conceptualized vocational education and training as being one aspect of lifelong learning (UNESCO 2001, p.1). Consequently, barriers between different levels and kinds of education should widely be abolished, and flexible structures are required that guarantee individual entry and re-entry to education as well as continuous learning. The UNESCO also has regional offices in Africa where specialized missions, e.g. teacher training, take place. The recent mid-term strategy also identified Africa as the first geographical priority, and quality and lifelong learning as a main strategic goal (UNESCO 2008). We can therefore expect a growing UNESCO emphasis on lifelong learning in African countries. The renaming of the UNESCO Institute for Education to the Institute for Lifelong Learning and its emphasis on literacy and basic education further underlines this strategic move.

Summarising these and other activities that UNESCO has carried out over the years, it becomes clear that the organisation has made strenuous efforts to promote lifelong learning. The organisation's classic standard-setting instruments, declarations of world conferences or publications, all stressed the importance of the issue. The organisation highlights the importance of the idea for both developed and developing countries: 'Basic education is still an absolute priority. But adult education, which might seem irrelevant for countries that still have a long way to go to meet basic education needs, has nevertheless acquired decisive importance to be an essential condition for development' (UNESCO2005, pp. 24–25).

Besides UNESCO, the OECD also began working on lifelong learning at the end of the 1960s (Papadopoulos 1994, pp. 112–13; 119). It published an important conceptual report in 1973, which, did not, however engender many national changes (OECD 1973: see Schuller *et al.* 2002). The visible re-emergence of lifelong learning took place in the 1990s. The 1994 OECD Jobs Study had already drawn attention to the need for further qualifying the labour force and the results of the Adult Literacy Survey had further illustrated a somewhat serious lack of competencies among adults, which underlined the importance of further qualification (OECD 1995, p. 15; OECD 1996, pp. 237–8). The 1996 meeting of OECD Education Ministers concerned Lifelong Learning for All (OECD 1996, p. 21). This conference was an initial event for the success of lifelong learning within the OECD, its members and beyond. Summarising the overall development within the OECD, it can be stated that the organisation has carried out a wide range of initiatives, attempting to bring lifelong learning closer to countries. The organisation has become a key player in fostering the idea and it coordinated different countries' activities to calibrate their policies (see Jakobi *et al.* 2007).

Another important international actor is the European Union, which initiated activities in the early 1990s. A major public event was the European Year of Lifelong Learning in 1996, in which more than 500 projects were financed with an overall contribution of approximately eight million ECUs (EU Commission 1999, pp. 12–15). At the end of the European Year, the Council adopted conclusions on a strategy for lifelong learning. These conclusions were comprehensive and included diverse areas of education, from pre-school to the accreditation of teachers (European Council 1996). Since 1997, lifelong learning has been part of the European Employment Strategy, and the Lisbon Agenda further reinforced the central role of education and qualifications (EU Commission 2000, p. 5; European Council 2002, p. 1; European Council 2000). The Memorandum on Lifelong Learning, published in 2000, brings together thoughts on indicators, benchmarks, and best practices for each objective (EU Commission 2000, pp. 24–36; EU Commission 2001, p. 5). Recent years have continued the emphasis on lifelong learning, for example, the creation of a common qualification framework was decided, whose implementation began in 2007 (EU Commission 2005, p. 4). An additional peak was the 2006 decision of the European Parliament and the Council on establishing a lifelong-learning action programme. The agenda included programmes linked to educational phases from pre-primary and secondary to higher education, vocational education and adult education (EU Commission 2006, pp. 2–10).

Another important player, in particular with a view to developing countries, is the World Bank. The Bank was not involved in the movement of the early 1970s concerning lifelong learning and, compared to its earlier activities, the organisation's recent turn toward the issue was somewhat surprising. During the 1980s, the Bank's emphasis on primary education led to the closing of many adult and non-formal education programmes. During the preparations for the 1990 Jomtien Summit, the Bank was on the verge of withdrawing its contribution if the summit's focus on basic education included adult education. Moreover, adult education funding was further reduced during the 1990s (Klees 2002, p. 461). Thus explicit activities on the issue have only recently been initiated. In January 1999, for the first time, World Bank President Wolfensohn mentioned lifelong learning in the context of the comprehensive development framework (World Bank 1999, p. iii). Later that year, the Education Sector Strategy paper stated that 'countries that provide opportunities for people to learn at all ages – as their work or lives change, and as new knowledge replaces old – will have an edge over those who do not' (World Bank 1999, p. 8). Moreover, the need to recognize lifelong learning is expressed by its inclusion in one of the checklist questions that the World Bank integrates into its project developments (World Bank 1999, pp. 40–1). The Bank has prominently featured lifelong learning and it has become a concept disseminated in various contexts. The organisation stated that a 'lifelong-learning framework encompasses learning throughout the life-cycle, from birth to grave and in different learning environments, formal, non-formal and informal' (World Bank 2005). In its most prominent publication on the subject, the Bank identified four main issues that the countries need to address: it analysed the societal needs that arise from the knowledge economy to the education system, it formulated perspectives on how lifelong learning should be promoted, on what a governance framework should look like, and on how it should be financed (World Bank 2003). Moreover, the Bank also developed an approach to measuring a country's progress towards lifelong learning (World Bank 2003, pp. 104–7). The Bank once fostered lifelong learning through distance education, for example, by way of the African Virtual University or other means related to different educational stages (World Bank Institute 2001, p. 2).

Unlike the World Bank, the ILO had already been involved in the debate on lifelong learning during the 1970s, mainly through its discussion on paid educational leave. The organisation set up related standards with the 1974 Paid Educational Leave Convention, the 1975 Human Resources Development Convention, and their corresponding recommendations in 1974, 1975 and 2004. All are directly linked to issues of lifelong learning, both politically and historically. The recommendation on human resource development has recently been revised, also as a result of a new consensus that had emerged in developmental assistance during the 1990s, which perceived human resources development as a critical factor for successful economic development (Salt *et al.* 1996, p. 707). The new recommendation contains an explicit reference to private training providers and the governmental role in this context is seen as defining a framework for certification, identifying the role of government and social partners in training, quality assurance and quality standards.

Alongside its normative instruments, the ILO further provides technical assistance for countries in lifelong learning matters. Projects implemented include, for example, handicraft promotion in Jordan that aims at developing a handicraft sub-sector. It includes technical training, self-employment skills, design and marketing as well as 'core and lifelong-learning skills' (ILO 2005a); another project concerns supporting the Albanian employment service in its efforts to redeploy 'redundant public employees.' It comprises individual training and capacity-building at national level to enable the country to provide the service autonomously in future (ILO 2005b). In its endeavors to implement lifelong-learning policies, the ILO is linked to other UN agencies, for example, through a joint project with UNESCO in Botswana. There, additional vocational training and education was intended to build a broad skills base as well as the specialisation needed for higher-level skills and technician training. As a result, Botswana launched a technical education programme that was 'designed to a high international standard, includes strict quality assurance measures, prepares for first employment, opens doors for further and higher education, and provides a base for lifelong learning' (UNESCO 2003, Botswana). This is only one example that illustrates how measures currently promoted in industrialized countries – such as quality assurance, education in modules, qualification frameworks and lifelong learning in general – are transferred to the developing world through the activities of international organisations.

Global and Cross-Regional Developments in Lifelong Learning

Whether or not countries decide to pursue lifelong-learning ideas or to implement policies is certainly not determined by the state of their economy or current education system. Though specific developing countries face many difficulties in education, they have nonetheless introduced many similar policies, with the aim also of competing in a global knowledge society (compare Jakobi 2007). It is this overlap of educational aims that makes education a particularly important example of global trends within a one-world society (compare Meyer *et al.* 1992; Meyer *et al.* 1997a). Regions, however, differ greatly in the extent to which they can actually achieve lifelong learning in practice. For example, European and North American countries have many resources and a highly skilled workforce that benefits from learning by updating skills. In contrast, countries like China, even if willing to invest a great deal, can only provide educational opportunities in partnership with private or foreign educational institutions (Jakobi 2009b). As the following sections show, the situation is considerably different in African countries.

The Development of African Education

The use of the term 'African countries' does not imply one common education system exists on this continent: African countries show significant diversity in political, cultural and social terms. In my study, I focus on Sub-Saharan African countries; however, attempts to generalize across countries should be undertaken with caution. However, compared to other world regions, we can state that many African countries are still influenced by their colonial history, and with regard to their current linguistic and

Table 6.2 Financing of Education in 1999 and 2005

	Total Public Expenditure on Edu. as % of GNP		Education as % of Government Expenditure		Total Aid to Education (constant 2005 US$ million)	
	1999	2005	1999	2005	1999/ 2000 average	2005
World	4.5	4.9	...	14	...	...
Countries in Transition	3.7	3.6	...	16	...	...
Developed Countries	5.0	5.5	11	13	...	...
Developing Countries	4.4	4.7	...	...	...	...
Arab States	...	...	...	...	1057	1283
Central & Eastern Europe	4.3	4.9	...	...	396	295
Central Asia	3.7	3.2	...	...	104	118
East Asia & the Pacific	4.8	...	...	...	1252	1265
Latin America & the Caribbean	4.7	5.0	16	13	576	660
North America & West. Europe	5.0	5.7	12	13	3	1
South & West Asia	2.9	3.6	...	15	812	1101
Sub-Saharan Africa	3.7	5.0	...	...	2279	2810

Sources: EFA/UNESCO (2008, pp.355, 388); modified.

cultural orientation. In addition, most countries in the region are among the poorest in the world. Social indicators, ranging from life expectancy to school attendance and income, still point to many problems in a large number of African countries. In particular, financing of education continues to be a problem, on the individual, local and national levels. Table 6.2 shows a comparison of different types of countries and regions according to their education financing patterns in 1999 and 2005. As the figures reveal, the relative share of expenditure on education has increased in developed as well as in developing countries. However, the relative share is higher in developed countries, signifying a growing difference in spending. Moreover, the figures on total aid to education show that Sub-Saharan countries in particular are highly dependent on donors with regard to educational investment.

Historically speaking, many education systems have been influenced by colonial rule and were established according to the structure of the education system in the 'home country.' With the rise of international organisations as important education policymakers and the evolution of education as an important means for development, education systems have become increasingly modelled according to global ideas of how an accurate and adequate education system should be established (e.g. Finnemore 1996a). Nonetheless, educational problems are still severe, as a first look at literacy rates reveals. Table 6.3 illustrates the most populated Sub-Saharan countries and the percentage of illiterate adults. Causes of adult illiteracy are manifold and range from irregular or non-attendance at school in youth, to ineffective schooling, dropouts in early years, unaffordable school fees, the need for child labour by the family to the non-existence of schools. A recent UNESCO publication estimated that approximately 20 per cent of the whole Sub-Saharan population are illiterate adults, not to mention illiterate children and youth (Aitchinson *et al.* 2009, p. 2). This already reflects progress in literacy: literacy rates are generally developing positively, and have also received some attention in the framework of Education for All.

Despite the existing problems in politics, economy and society, the idea of lifelong learning and corresponding reforms can also be found in Sub-Saharan countries, although with a very different understanding of what is meant by lifelong learning compared to highly industrialized countries in Europe. While industrialized countries often mention the knowledge society, and strive for a competitive workforce with up-to-date skills in their concepts of lifelong learning, African concepts are far more focused on basic education. Only some countries have a broader notion of the knowledge society in mind when drawing up lifelong-learning policies (Aitchinson *et al.* 2009, p. 7). What is more, educational governance is often restricted, which implies that formulating laws and enforcing them might prove difficult. For example, only a few countries have legislative frameworks in place when it comes to adult education, and only South Africa and the Seychelles have legislation explicitly dealing with lifelong learning (Aitchinson *et al.* 2009, p. 9). Regardless of these difficulties, countries have tackled the inception of complex educational governance instruments, and most comprehensively national qualification frameworks. South Africa established such a framework in 1994 and the Seychelles in 2005. Kenya, Namibia, Botswana and Lesotho plan to introduce such a framework in the near future; the latter has even already linked its existent qualification with the South African framework. Zambia has established a central regulatory authority (Aitchinson *et al.* 2009, pp. 36–9).

Table 6.3 Illiteracy in Sub-Saharan Africa

Country	Percentage of Illiterate Adults
Angola	32.6
Burkina Faso	71.3
Cameroon	32.1
Côte d'Ivoire	51.3
Democratic Republic of Congo	32.8
Ethiopia	64.1
Ghana	35.0
Kenya	26.4
Madagascar	29.3
Malawi	28.2
Mali	76.7
Mozambique	55.6
Niger	69.6
Nigeria	28.0
Senegal	57.4
South Africa	12.0
Uganda	26.4
United Republic of Tanzania	27.7
Zambia	32.0
Zimbabwe	8.88

Source: Based on Aitchinson et al. 2009, p. 2.

Below I present two countries and their approaches to implementing lifelong learning, namely, South Africa and Nigeria (compare Jakobi 2009b). Although both countries experience severe problems with regard to the scope and quality of their education system, they differ greatly in terms of their history, their political system and current status of development

(Mazrui 2006). The analysis is illustrative in the sense that it focuses on how the countries endeavor to align with the global idea of lifelong learning and how the education system is referring to global, world culture aspects. This is not to say that these elements always deliver the intended results or that only the macro level would shape these systems. Instead, the policies are a result of local and world culture ideas. Given this chapter's emphasis on the latter, I limit the analysis mainly to these aspects.

South Africa

After the fall of the apartheid regime, South Africa introduced many reforms to establish an education system that breaks with the former system of discrimination and the low literacy and schooling rate. The Constitution declares a right to basic education, including adult education, and to further education which the state has to implement over time. The Ministry of Education was established in 1994, and important bodies, such as the Department of Education, the South African Qualifications Authority, councils and institutes followed immediately or in the following years (UNESCO 2003, South Africa). All sectors of education policy have been reformed in phases, and an extensive restructuring was carried out in early childhood, adult and higher education. For this purpose, South Africa has cooperated with international organisations and engaged in bilateral cooperation to establish a comprehensive education system (e.g. South African Department of Education 2007, p. 18). Lifelong learning was rapidly identified as a central concept in reforming education policy, and international policy ideas were adopted (see Aitchison 2004, pp. 518–19).

Today, the system is classified into three levels: general basic education, further education and training, and higher education (South African Government Information 2008). Lifelong learning is a prominent concept in education policy reforms, ranging from preparation in early education to adult basic education and continuing education. The Department of Education's vision is 'a South Africa in which all people will have access to lifelong learning, education and training opportunities, which will, in turn, contribute toward improving the quality of life and building a peaceful, prosperous and democratic South Africa' (South African Department of Education 2007, p. 9). In 2001, South Africa outlined its human resources strategy, and two of its four objectives are directly linked to the education system; a third concerns the labour market demand for education (South African Ministry of Education and Ministry of Labour 2001a, pp. 11–17).

In early childhood education, South Africa has introduced the so-called reception year. Since 1997, the last year of pre-primary education prepares children for school and makes an additional year of education possible (South African Ministry of Education and Ministry of Labour 2001a, p. 21; UNESCO 2003, South Africa). The year is not yet compulsory, but it is nonetheless intended to cover all children by 2010 (South African Ministry of Education 2001, p. 5). Increasing access to early childhood education is one of the current educational priorities, and early childhood education is viewed as preparation for schooling and the basis for future lifelong learning (South African Department of Education 2007, p. 4; South African Ministry of Education 2001, pp. 8–10).

Like other countries, South Africa is attempting to integrate its quali-fication structure into one framework and, in doing so, is also trying to dissolve the strict separation of academic and vocational paths (UNESCO 2003, South Africa; South African Department of Education 2001, p. 9). The country has begun with the implementation of a qualification framework in 1995, building upon discussions on more equal training in an education system under apartheid (South African Ministry of Education and Ministry of Labour 2001b, p. i). Although the intended targets of qualification levels could barely be achieved (Aitchison 2004, p. 533) and the implementation proved to be difficult, the framework has been perceived to be an important tool to unify the fragmented education system and to enable ongoing learning processes. Its implementation has, in turn, been supported by international organisations and several bilateral contacts (South African Ministry of Education and Ministry of Labour, 2001b, p. 3; 10; 21–34). Non-governmental actors also supported the framework's establishment, deeming it to be an opportunity for disad-vantaged groups to proceed along the different educational levels (Fehnel 2006, p. 229).

As well as the formal adult education covered in the framework, South Africa is also investing in adult basic education, a widely perceived need given that a large number of adults never attended school or left within the first few years. Adult basic education is perceived both as a right as well as a necessity in the changing economy. Moreover, it is not only seen as a compensatory experience for basic schooling, but efforts are being made to make this basic level the starting point for further education and training. Hence it 'progressively initiates adult learners onto a path of lifelong learning and development' (South African Department of Education 2001, pp. 1–2, 5). Several organisational steps have been taken to implement this policy. For example, a literacy agency had been founded, while an act on adult basic education regulated the establishment and quality of training centres, and multiple projects have been created to support the basic education of adults (South African Government Information 2008; see also South African Department of Education 2001, pp. 15–19).

Addressing higher education is also part of the efforts to put the principles of lifelong learning into practice. A first phase of restructuring the higher education sphere entailed the integration of the college sector and the merger of many institutions in order to create a more coherent system (UNESCO 2003, South Africa). Additionally, private higher education has become more widespread, and boundaries between academic versus vocational and contact versus distance education have blurred since the 1990s (Cloete *et al.* 2006, pp. 246–7; Fehnel 2006). The reform processes sought to allow for broader and more representative access from all spheres of society, and were also linked to the establishment of the qualification framework and its different means of defining qualifications. The system was supposed to 'open its doors, in the spirit of lifelong learning, to workers and professionals in pursuit of multiskilling and reskilling, and adult learners whose access to higher education had been thwarted in the past' (South African Ministry of Education 1997, p. 17; see also Cloete *et al.* 2006). The system is intended to serve the country's human resources development by updating knowledge, and it provides high-level skills training for the younger generation (South African Government Information 2008).

Overall, lifelong-learning debates are prominent in the South African education system and many efforts have been undertaken to implement its principles in different sectors of the education system, even if implementation has proven to be difficult and has only been achieved to a small degree (see Aitchison 2004). The country is well aware of the ongoing global debates on lifelong learning, for example, in the case of the qualifications framework, and has continuously worked with international collabourators to develop its education system.

Nigeria

Nigeria is one of the poorest countries in the world, with a GNI of only 390 US $ per capita in 2004 and a history of independence strongly influenced by coups d'état and non-democratic regimes. Despite rich crude oil resources, policymakers usually did not place education high on the agenda, and the World Bank criticized sports events that cost more than the annual national budgets of education and health combined (BBC 2003; see also Lewis 2007, p. 249). The country is internally divided along religious borders, but also with regard to its plethora of languages and dialects which amount to approximately 300 (Aitchison *et al.* 2009, p. 1).

Despite these conditions, Nigeria aligns with the global discourse, and in its reports to the International Bureau of Education, the country acknowledges the importance of lifelong learning: 'there is the urgent need to ensure relevance of educational content and a reorientation of education philosophy, teaching and learning strategies, and the infusion of knowledge and skills beyond schooling for lifelong learning, for a knowledge and information society' (Nigerian Federal Ministry of Education 2004, p. 25). The country's first education system was established by the British colonists; later, the model was reformed to conform to the US structure (Aborisade *et al.* 2002, pp. 78–9) and still today the Nigerian education policy considers itself to be oriented toward international trends and to be linked to educational developments all over the world (Nigerian Federal Ministry of Education 2001, p. 6).

The attention afforded to pre-primary education grew in previous years but the bulk of pre-primary education is financed by parents. In recent years, the government evaluated ways of increasing the participation rate, since pre-primary education is seen as an advantageous 'early start' (Nigerian Federal Ministry of Education 2004, p. 10). In 2007, the goal was set to increase participation rates in specific early education programmes to 70 per cent by 2015 (Nigerian Federal Ministry of Education 2008, p. 10). The professionalisation of early childhood education in the country began in the early 1990s through co-operation with UNICEF on an Early Childhood Care Development and Education Project. Early childhood care has been taught in university courses and there have been plans to expand such teaching to colleges throughout the country (UNESCO 2003, Nigeria). Moreover, curricula for infants and children aged up to five years have been drawn up (Nigerian Federal Ministry of Education 2008, p. 35). Nonetheless, participation in pre-primary education is still low: in 1999, approximately 18 per cent of the children aged three to five were enrolled in pre-primary education, with significant differences between urban and rural areas, which amounted to 37 per cent and 12 per cent respectively (Nigerian Federal Ministry of Education 2004, p. 10). For 2001, the UNESCO Institute for Statistics estimated a gross enrolment rate of 8.2 per cent for the entire country (EFA/UNESCO 2005, p. 276). Nigeria has only been exposed to a small degree to international organisations: in the 1990s, the World Bank had even been the only organisation that dealt with the primary school sector in the country (Moja 2000, p. 14). The World Bank also held workshops on education policy in the country in more recent years (World Bank 2008).

However, even the limited exposure to international discourses has led to some changes: since 1999, Nigeria has defined 'basic education' to include adult education. It introduced the basic education scheme that focuses on the provision of primary and junior secondary education for youth, as well as on functional literacy programmes for adults (Nigerian Federal Ministry of Education 2004, p. 4). This is an extension of primary education to later life and exceeds the regulation of the former Universal Primary Education Programme that only concerned schoolchildren. Moreover, the Nigerian scheme explicitly mentions flexible exits and entrance points to education, the inclusion of non-formal education and, eventually, the transition from the non-formal to the formal level (Nigerian Federal Ministry of Education 2004, p. 5). Non-formal programmes were established to educate illiterate people or out-of-school youth. No current data are available, but there was a considerable increase during the 1990s: in 1991, approximately half a million adults were enrolled, while in 1996 more than one million learners took such courses (UNESCO 2003, Nigeria). Such courses nonetheless differed significantly, ranging from basic literacy to continuing education, vocational education or prison education. In the context of Education for All, UNESCO has made agreements with Nigeria on several programmes, including adult literacy or technical and vocational training (UNESCO 2011). In brief, Nigeria has taken the first steps towards ensuring increased learning activities, but the scope of the political aims and the implementation process are not comparable to other countries, both in Africa and beyond (see Jakobi 2009b).

Comparison and Conclusion

The examples of African countries reveal that very different countries are implementing lifelong-learning concepts. On the one hand, this takes place in a universal manner when countries align themselves with the global discourse on lifelong learning. On the other hand, they frequently adapt the significance of lifelong learning to their national needs, which means that they often lay the emphasis on adult literacy and basic education, which are less pronounced in European countries. Yet countries such as South Africa have nonetheless introduced large-scale reforms such as qualification frameworks. Overall, the educational level has increased in African countries over time. Besides Southern Asia, where countries like Bangladesh only have a small literate population, Africa has remained a region with many illiterate people, but the percentage has dropped remarkably over the last ten years, resulting in an average increase in literacy of nearly ten per cent. In Nigeria, the literacy rate has risen by approximately 20 per cent in the same timeframe. Such figures show the effects of education; however, the extent to which lifelong learning is responsible for this progress remains to be seen. Comparative data on these developments are hard to find, but growing gross enrolment rates in pre-primary education (see table 6.4) at least give rise to the assumption that Africans are spending more time in education than they used to do some years ago.

To summarize the development of lifelong learning in African countries, we can assert that they are part of a global policy discourse and target of a worldwide norm of lifelong learning that has been established internationally (see Jakobi 2009b). From the perspective of world society theory, lifelong learning thus represents a further example of a common world culture in which specific aspects – lifelong educational processes in this case – are disseminated across countries. However, the examples show that the implementation of lifelong-learning principles differs widely and is closely linked to the political, social and economic preconditions of a country. World culture is thus interpreted regionally and nationally, and this interpretation is not only a cultural one, but is also heavily shaped by material conditions.

Table 6.4 Gross Enrolment Rates and School Life Expectancy 1999 and 2005

	Pre-Primary Education		Tertiary Education		School Life Expectancy Primary to Tertiary Edu.	
	1999	2005	1999	2005	1999	2005
World	33	40	18	24	10	11
Countries in Transition	46	60	41	56	12	13
Developed Countries	73	78	55	66	15	16
Developing Countries	28	34	11	17	9	10
Arab States	15	17	19	21	10	11
Central & Eastern Europe	49	59	39	57	12	13
Central Asia	22	28	19	27	11	12
East Asia & the Pacific	40	43	14	24	10	12
Latin America & the Caribbean	56	62	21	29	13	13
North America & West. Europe	76	79	61	70	16	16
South & West Asia	22	37	8	11	8	10
Sub-Saharan Africa	10	14	4	5	7	8

Sources: EFA/UNESCO (2008, pp. 274–5; 322; 283), modified (all weighted averages, rates in per cent, expectancy in years).

It is thus important to analyse world culture both with regard to similarities and differences, and to examine which factors are likely to cause the former or the latter. The cases described herein illustrate that the worldwide discourse on lifelong learning has also borne an impact on these African countries, in a sense that lifelong learning nowadays appears to be an important principle even in countries with limited resources for its implementation. This fact is then mirrored in how lifelong learning is connected to the national education system: in the cases analysed here, it has led to organisational changes such as the qualification framework, but it may also mean little more than the improvement of basic education.

Further research is required to analyse the creation, dissemination and implementation of global policy discourses more closely. With a view to national case studies, the translation of global norms should be subject to more in-depth examination, both by way of a cross-national comparison, but also an analysis of which global education policy ideas are translated easily, which are not, and why. In particular, colonial history still exerts an impact on African education systems, including access, financing and content. Nevertheless, implementation studies on global norms still lack effective and reliable data. Measuring the success and failure of global policies is particularly difficult. Therefore many research steps are yet to be taken before a comprehensive picture of the implementation of global policies can be provided.

Note

1 The chapter partly draws on Jakobi (2009a, 2009b).

References

Aborisade, O. and Mundt, R. J. (2002), *Politics in Nigeria*, New York: Longman.

Adler, E. and Haas, P. M. (1992), 'Conclusion: Epistemic Communities, World Order and the Creation of A Reflective Research Program'. *International Organization*, 46, 367–90.

Aitchison, J. (2004), 'Lifelong Learning in South Africa: dreams and delusions'. *International Journal of Lifelong Education*, 23, 517–44.

Aitchison, J. and Alidou, H. (2009), 'GRALE: Global Report on Adult Education and Literacy. Regional Synthesis Report on Subsaharan Africa' [Online] Available at: graleconfintea6.net/ (Accessed:20December 2009).

BBC (2003), 'Nigerian star defends Games cost' [Online] Available at: news.bbc.co.uk/2/hi/africa/3195424.stm (Accessed: 1 December 2011).

Bell, D. (1973) *The Coming of Post-Industrial Society*, 1999 edn. New York: Basic Books.

Boli, J. and Thomas, G. M. (1999), 'INGOs and the Organization of World Culture', in J. Boli and G. Thomas (eds), *Constructing World Culture. International Nongovernmental Organizations since 1875*. Stanford: Stanford University Press, pp. 13–49.

Cloete, N. and Fehnel, R. (2006), 'The Emergent Landscape', in N. Cloete, P. Maassen, R. Fehnel, T. Moja, T. Gibbon and H. Perold (eds), *Transformation in Higher Education. Global Pressures and Local Realities*. Dordrecht: Springer, pp. 245–60.

DiMaggio, P. and Powell, W. W. (1983) 'The Iron Cage Revisited: Institutional Isomorphism and Collective Rationality in Organizational Fields.' *American Sociological Review*, 48 (April), 147–60.

Drucker, P. F. (1969) 'The Knowledge Society'. *New Society*, (24 April 1969), 629–31.

EFA/UNESCO (2005), *EFA Global Monitoring Report 2005: The Quality Imperative*, Paris: UNESCO.

EU Commission (1999), *Implementation, results and overall assessment of the European Year of Lifelong Learning (1996). Report from the Commission to the Council, the European Parliament, the Economic and Social Committee and the Committee of the Regions submitted in accordance with Article 8 of European Parliament and Council Decision No 2493/95/EC.* COM (99) 447 final, 15.09.1999.

—(2000), *A Memorandum on Lifelong Learning*. Brussels: EC. Commission Staff Working Paper SEC (2000) 1832.

—(2001), *Making A European Area of Lifelong Learning A Reality*. Brussels: EC.COM(2001) 678 final, 21/11/2001.

—(2005), *Towards a European Qualification Framework for Lifelong Learning*. Brussels: EC. Commission Staff Working Document SEC (2005) 957, 08/07/2005.

European Council (1996), *Council Conclusions of 20 December on a Strategy for Lifelong Learning (97/C 7/02)*. Brussels: EC.

—(2000),'Presidency Conclusions of the Council of the European Union' [Online] Available at: www.europarl.europa.eu/summits/lis1_en.htm (Accessed: 1 December 2001).

—(2002), *Council Resolution of 27 June 2002 on Lifelong Learning (2002/ C 163/ 01)*. Brussels: EC.

Fehnel, R. (2006), 'Private Higher Education', in. N. Cloete, P. Maassen, R. Fehnel, T. Moja, T. Gibbon and H. Perold (eds), *Transformation in Higher Education. Global Pressures and Local Realities*. Dordrecht: Springer, pp. 227–43.

Finnemore, M (1996a), *National Interests in International Society*, Ithaca, London:Cornell University Press.

—(1996b), 'Norms, Culture and World Politics: Insights from Sociology's Institutionalism'. *International Organiziation*, 50, 325–47.

Haas, E. B., Williams, M. P. and Babai, D. (1977), *Scientists and World Order. The Use of Technical Knowledge in International Organizations*, Berkeley, California: University of California Press.

Haas, P. M. (1992), 'Introduction: Epistemic Communities and International Policy Coordination'. *International Organization*, 46, 1–35.

ILO (2005a), *Technical Cooperation Project: Handicraft Promotion in Jordan (Project Code JOR/96/017ITA)* [Online] Available at: www.ilo.org/public/english/employment/skills/technical/project/tcp_21.htm (Accessed: 20 September 2005).

—(2005b), *Technical Cooperation Project: Programme for the Redeployment of Redundant Public Employees (Project Code ALB/00/01/ITA)* [Online] Available at: www.ilo.org/public/english/employment/skills/technical/project/tcp_20.htm (Accessed: 20 September 2005).

Jakobi, A. P. (2007), 'The Knowledge Society and Global Dynamics in Education Politics'. *European Educational Research Journal*, 6, (1), 39–51.

—(2009a), 'Global Education Policy in the Making: International Organizations and Lifelong Learning'. *Globalisation, Education and Societies*, 7, 473–87.

—(2009b), *International Organizations and Lifelong Learning: From Global Agendas to Policy Diffusion*. Houndsmill: Palgrave.

Jakobi, A. and Martens, K. (2007), 'Diffusion durch Internationale Organisationen: Die Bildungspolitik der OECD'. *Politische Vierteljahresschrift, Sonderband 'Transfer, Diffusion und Konvergenz von Politiken'*, 247–70.

Klees, S. J. (2002), 'World Bank Education Policy: new Rhetoric, old Ideology'. *International Journal of Educational Development*, 22, 451–74.

Lewis, P. M. (2007), *Growing Apart. Oil, Politics and Economic Change in Indonesia and Nigeria*. Michigan: The University of Michigan Press.

Mazrui, A. A. (2006), *A Tale of Two Africas: Nigeria and South Africa as contrasting Visions*. London: Adonis & Abbey Publishers Ltd.

Meyer, J. W. (2000), 'Globalization. Sources and Effects on National States and Societies'. *International Sociology*, 15, 233–48.

Meyer, J. W., Boli, J., Thomas, G. M. and Ramirez, F. O. (1997a), 'World Society and the Nation-State'. American Journal of Sociology, 103, 144–81.

Meyer, J. W., Frank, D. J., Hironaka, A., Schofer, E. and Tuma, N. B. (1997b), 'The Structuring of a World Environmental Regime, 1870–1990'. *International Organization*, 51, 623–51.

Meyer, J. W., Kamens, D. and Benavot, A. (1992), *School Knowledge for the Masses*. Washington: Falmer.

Moja, T. (2000), *Nigeria Education Sector Analysis: An Analytical Synthesis of the Performance and Main Issues*. Washington: World Bank.

Nigerian Federal Ministry of Education (2001), 'Country Report to UNESCO Forty-Sixth session of the International Conference on Education', Geneva, 5–8 September. Available at: www.ibe.unesco.org/International/ ICE/46english/46natrape.htm (Accessed: 8 August 2005).

—(2004), 'Our Youth, Our Hope. Report to the forty-seventh International Conference on Education', Geneva, 8–11 September. Available at: www.ibe. unesco.org/International/ICE47/English/Natreps/Nrep_main.htm (Accessed: 8 August 2005).

—(2008), 'The Development of Education in Nigeria. Report Submitted to the International Conference on Education', Geneva, 25–28 November. Available at: www.ibe.unesco.org/en/ice/48th-session-2008/national-reports.html (Accessed: 15 December 2008).

OECD (1995), *The OECD Jobs Study. Implementing the Strategy*. Paris: OECD.

—(1996), *Lifelong Learning for All*. Paris: OECD.

Papadopoulos, G. (1994), *Education 1960–1990. The OECD Perspective*, Paris: OECD.

—(2002), 'Lifelong Learning and the Changing Policy Environment', in D. Istance, H. Schuetze, G. Hans and T. Schuller (eds), *International Perspectives on Lifelong Learning. From Recurrent Education to the Knowledge Society*. Buckingham: Open University Press, pp. 39–46.

Salt, A. and Bowland, D. (1996), 'International Labour Organization', in A. C. Tuijnman ed., *International Encyclopedia of Adult Education and Training*, 2nd edn. Oxford, New York and Tokyo: Pergamon, pp. 704–9.

Schuller, T., Schuetze, H. G. and Istance, D. (2002), 'From Recurrent Education to the Knowledge Society: An Introduction', in D. Istance, H. Schuetze, G. Hans and T. Schuller (eds), *International Perspectives on Lifelong Learning. From Recurrent Education to the Knowledge Society*. Buckingham: Open University Press, pp. 1–21.

South African Department of Education (2001), 'Policy Document on Adult Basic Education and Training' [Online] Available at: www.education.gov.za/ Documents/policies/PolicyDocumentABET.pdf (Accessed: 5 March 2008).

—(2007), *Strategic Plan 2007–2011*. Pretoria:Department of Education.

South African Government Information (2008), *Education* [Online] Available at: www.info.gov.za/aboutsa/education.htm (Accessed: 5 March 2008).

South African Ministry of Education (1997), 'Education White Paper 3. A Programme for Higher Education Transformation'. *Government Gazette*, 18207, 15 August. [Online] Available at: www.info.gov.za/whitepapers/1997/ educ3.pdf (Accessed: 12 December 2008).

—(2001), 'Education White Paper on Early Childhood Education', presented to Meeting the Challenge of Early Childhood Development in South Africa, Pretoria, 5 May.

South African Ministry of Education and Ministry of Labour (2001a), *Human Resource Development Strategy for South Africa: A Nation at Work for a Better Life for All*. Pretoria: Ministry of Labour.

—(2001b), *Report of the Study Team of the Implementation of the National Qualifications Framework*. Pretoria: Department of Education.

UNESCO (1972), *Learning to Be. The World of Education Today and Tomorrow*. Paris: UNESCO.

—(1996), *Learning: The Treasure Within*. Paris: UNESCO.

—(2001), 'Revised Recommendation Concerning Technical and Vocational Education' [Online] Available at: portal.unesco.org/en/ev.php-URL_ ID=13145&URL_DO=DO_TOPIC&URL_SECTION=201.html (Accessed: 1 December 2011).

—(2003), *World Data on Education*, 5th edn. CD-ROM, Geneva: UNESCO/IBE.

—(2005), *Towards Knowledge Societies*. Paris: UNESCO.

—(2008), *Midterm Strategy 2008–2013*. Paris: UNESCO.

—(2011), Nigeria and UNESCO launch $6 million national literacy programme, [Online]. Available at: www.unesco.org/new/en/media-services/single-view/ news/nigeria_and_unesco_launch_6_million_national_literacy_programme/ (Accessed: 5 August 2011).

World Bank (1999), *Education Sector Strategy*. Washington, DC: World Bank.

—(2003), *Lifelong Learning in the Global Knowledge Economy. Challenges for Developing Countries*. Washington, DC: World Bank.

World Bank (2008), 'Strategic Choices for Education Reform in Nigeria', Workshop, Abuja, 20–26 January. Available at: go.worldbank.org/ PE24054RT0 (Accessed: 10 August 2011).

World Bank – Children & Youth (2005),Available at: <www1.worldbank.org/ education/lifelong_learning/> (Accessed: 18 November 2005).

World Conference on Education for All (1990), 'World Declaration on Education for All: Framework for Action Meeting Basic Learning Needs', Jomtien, 5–9 March.Available at: www.unesco.org/education/pdf/JOMTIE_E.PDF (Accessed: 1 December 2011).

World Education Forum (2000), 'The Dakar Framework for Action. Education for All: Meeting our Collective Commitments', Dakar, 26–28 April.Available at:

unesdoc.unesco.org/images/0012/001211/121147e.pdf (Accessed: 1 December 2011).

World Bank Institute (2001), 'The Global Forum on Fighting Corruption and Safeguarding Integrity'. *WBI News*, Spring 2001, 2–3 [Online] Available at: siteresources.worldbank.org/WBI/Resources/wbinewsFall01.pdf (Accessed: 1 December 2011).

CHAPTER SEVEN

Conditional Cash Transfers in Education for Development: Emergence, Policy Dilemmas and Diversity of Impacts

Xavier Bonal, Aina Tarabini and Xavier Rambla

The Context for the Emergence of CCTs

In recent decades, international organisations have commented broadly on the connection between poverty reduction and the potential of the poorest people for resilience. In the late 1980s, UNICEF responded to the alarming perverse effects of Structural Adjustment Programmes (SAPs), asking for 'adjustment with a human face' underpinned by social emergency funds (Cornia 2001). One of the most visible reactions to the failure of SAPs was the identification of poverty alleviation as the most salient objective of international organisations in shaping the global development agenda. The 2004 World Development Report, *Making Services Work for Poor People*, is a clear example of the inclusion of poverty alleviation vis-à-vis economic growth among the main priorities for development. The report is also an example of the idea of 'activating' the poor to help them change their circumstances. Thus the role of policy in this framework entails empowering the poor and giving them the necessary tools to take advantage of existing economic and social opportunities. The centrality of poverty reduction was also visible when *Poverty Reduction Strategy Papers* (PRSP) became the most significant instrument through which international organisations would support governments in the fight against poverty. In fact, PRSP became a necessary tool for highly indebted poor countries to continue borrowing funds from international finance organisations and a new form of conditionality.

Thus in the first decade of the twenty-first century the World Bank (WB) advised donors and governments to manage social risk by assessing the vulnerability to potential poverty-inducing shocks and providing the necessary economic and social resources for victims to withstand these shocks (Holzmann *et al.* 2003, p. 10). The idea is generally associated with a hypothetical 'generative mechanism' (Pawson 2006) grounded on social capital theories: the point is that the poor may lessen their multi-dimensional deprivation by mobilising their own social networks and making their voice heard in social policy consultation bodies (Narayan 1999; Atria 2003).

Naturally, this understanding of poverty reduction affords a central role to education among *the best* policies. If poor people have to be empowered to develop social and human capital, there is nothing like education. In fact, education is one of the central strategies in PRSP and has also remained one of the central sectors in the WB's lending portfolio. Since the MDGs were established, the Bank's support for education has constantly increased, reaching $5 billion in 2010 (World Bank 2011, p. vi).

That is the context in which Conditional Cash Transfer Programmes (CCTs) in education emerged. Interestingly enough, these programmes were not part of any system of lending conditionalities nor were they were part of international organisations' global agenda for education development. CCTs are an example of an inverse policy path, from the bottom up. State or federal governments in Brazil and Mexico initiated CCTs in education on a large scale in the mid-1990s. In Brazil, the Federal District began the first *Bolsa Escola* in 1995. After two years, the *Bolsa Escola Federal* was initiated. *Progresa* – then renamed *Oportunidades* – started in Mexico in 1997. Since then, different programmes have been extended, especially in Latin American countries but there are also recent examples in Asia and some African countries. Curiously enough, these programmes are part of the South-South cooperation policies. Indeed, the First World has also learned from the Mexican or Brazilian experience, as is illustrated by the CCT programme developed in New York City. The WB did not promote the two most important CCT programmes in the world and it was actually highly reactive to these new policies in closely observing and evaluating processes of implementation and their impacts (Peck *et al.* 2010).

One of the reasons for this passivity can be explained by the focus of the Bank's lending on investment and infrastructure on the one hand, and on school supply policies on the other. The WB has never financed the current costs of education and concentrated its project lending activity on capital costs. However, nor did the WB include CCTs among their policy recommendations. The Bank has contemplated demand-side policies such as school vouchers or educational loans, but has not traditionally included CCTs as a good policy practice to enhance school access or school performance.

Interestingly, this is not the case anymore, since the Bank is currently supporting programmes such as *Bolsa Familia* in Brazil. There might be different reasons for this change but a plausible explanation is related to the adequacy of CCTs within the framework of the anti-poverty agenda for development. CCTs are designed as a policy tool to break the inter-generational reproduction of poverty through education and as a method of empowering the poor to overcome their circumstances. In this sense, CCTs do fit in with the ideas of the WB and other international organisations with regard to fighting poverty by bypassing the inefficient state of developing countries and by delivering resources directly to those most in need (Tarabini 2008). This is especially significant since CCTs have not shown a clear impact on school performance. What we know today is that there is mixed evidence concerning the effects of CCTs in several educational dimensions. There is evidence of substantial improvements in school access or in access to school meals (a very important effect in contexts of extreme poverty). Some authors even positively value the effects of CCTs in reducing child labour (Rawlings 2005). On the other hand, other authors have expressed doubts over how useful these programmes are in improving learning and performance (Schwartzman 2005). Significantly, by examining different countries, Reimers *et al.* (2006) ascertained that the logical framework of CCT programmes was often focused on attainment, assistance and enrolment, but its instantiation seldom concerned dropouts, learning, the quality of instruction, repetition and promotion and school improvement. In short, this sample of experiences shows that the alleged impact of these programmes on other sectors beyond social protection ultimately remains unclear, at least in the area of such a prominent area as education policy has become.

In spite of this uncertainty, one significant policy question that remains unanswered is whether CCTs are or are not a worthy tool to break the reproduction of poverty. The answer to this question is not at all simple. It depends on how a CCT programme is designed, who the beneficiaries are and how we assess the impact of these programmes. Although the latter question is particularly important – and would reveal the many limitations of impact evaluation methodologies – we will concentrate in this paper on the first two. We argue that the uncertain effects of CCT programmes are closely linked to two sets of factors. On the one hand, policymakers face significant dilemmas when designing CCTs. Options taken in the programme design may prove crucial to understanding the orientation of the programme and its effectiveness in terms of school access, school performance and other effects. On the other hand, the social conditions of educational demand explain why different families and different pupils react differently to the same type of input. The transfer can have an entirely different impact depending on who the beneficiary is, even when all of them are poor.

In this paper, we explore the main dilemmas faced by policymakers when designing a CCT programme. Our arguments can be considered as generic, although reflections and examples are mainly taken from an analysis of the Bolsa Escola programmes (PBE) developed in Brazil (both in its federal and local forms) from the mid-1990s until they were absorbed by the federal programme Bolsa Familia (PBF) in the year 2003. The dilemmas, short-comings and possibilities of a CCT programme can be found in the realm of institutional design, in the technical processes of beneficiary selection and coverage and in the implementation systems developed. Our analysis will encompass all these dimensions, and is thus fed by the empirical evidence available in the different evaluations of the programme, sometimes performed by specialists from international organisations (UNESCO, the WB and the ILO), at other times by scholars, and even occasionally by personnel from the programme itself. As data for our analysis, we have also added the studies our research group conducted during the years 2003–06, and in particular we shall take into account the evidence from a study regarding the impact of PBE on the conditions of educability of the beneficiaries in the town of Belo Horizonte.[1]

The chapter is structured as follows. In the next section, a description of the PBE is provided, with special attention afforded to variations between the federal and the municipal versions of the programme. The third section explores technical dilemmas involved in the programme design and intro-duces reflections on the changes generated following the implementation of the PBF. The fourth section provides examples of how different the impact of the transfer can be depending on the social and living conditions of beneficiaries. Finally, a concluding section underlines the main deficiencies in mainstream evaluation when assessing CCT programmes and provides guidelines for a 'realistic' evaluation of CCTs (Pawson 2006).

Characteristics of the *Bolsa Escola* Programme

The PBE was a demand-side education programme based on income transfers to poor families, on the condition of their children attending school. This programme was part of the Minimum Income Guarantee Programmes initiated in Brazil in the first half of the 1990s and, from the very beginning, it was developed in a decentralized fashion on a municipal scale.

The programme was first implemented in 1995 in the Federal District with the aim of achieving three goals: 1) increasing the families' standard of living in the short-term; 2) lowering child labour rates; and 3) optimising children's staying in school with the ultimate goal of reducing future

poverty. The highly favourable evaluation of the earliest proposals implemented and the spread of the debates on this type of programme drove
many other municipal governments – many of them governed by the PT
(Workers' Party) – to develop education-associated minimum income
programmes, which became widespread in the country during the second
half of the 1990s.

The manner in which the programme was implemented on a municipal
scale showed differences in both design and management; however, generally
speaking both their goals and the criteria used to select the population
converged. In terms of the goals, there was a general overlap with those
set by the pioneering programme in Brasilia. In terms of the selection
systems, the programmes shared a series of criteria including family income,
children's ages and period of time residing in the town, with potentially
eligible families being those with a per capita family income lower than
a certain pre-defined level (generally, the poverty line) with at least one
school-aged child and a minimum time of residence in the town ranging
from one to five years. The families fulfilling the requisites that were
accepted for participation in the programme received a monthly income
transfer, usually an amount varying between one-half and one minimum
salary, provided their child regularly attended school.

Starting in 1997, and in the light of the success of the municipal experiences, a type of federal programme began to be implemented. In 2001,
the federal PBE spread to a nationwide scale, leaving its management and
implementation in the hands of the town education councillors, with the
financing and monetary transfers to the beneficiaries remaining under the
aegis of the National Secretariat. Table 7.1 summarizes the main characteristics of the municipal PBE in Belo Horizonte, and its comparison with the
federal programme is explained below.

Until the end of 2001, the PBE in Belo Horizonte operated in the town
autonomously, managing to assist a total of 9,311 families. In 2002, the
federal PBE began to be implemented in the city. The main difference
between the programmes concerned the sum of the transfer. The Belo
Horizonte PBE transferred a fixed monthly sum (R$168, equivalent to €71)
per family, while the Federal PBE assigned a variable benefit according to
the number of children in each family (up to a maximum of R$45 for three
children or more, equivalent to €19).

In 2003, and due to the federal government change in Brazil, the
PBE underwent a significant change: it was incorporated into a new
programme targeting the poor, *Bolsa Familia* (PBF). This modification
brought changes both in the functioning and in the features of the
programme. The PBF is part of the *Fome Zero Programme,* a public
policy aimed at combating hunger and social exclusion in the country.
This programme has combined all the income transfer programmes
existing in the country and implies, in general terms, the disappearance
of the PBE as an independent programme. On average, the PBF transfers

Table 7.1 Design of the municipal PBE in Belo Horizonte

Start of programme	1997
Selection criteria	Per capita family income < average minimum salary Children aged 7–14 (6–15 starting in 2001) Minimum time residing in town: 5 years *Priority given to families with minors living in situations of social risk.
Value of the transfer	R$168 per month per family (equivalent to €71 in 2011)
Conditions	Children's minimum attendance of 85%
Timeframe	Indefinite
Management and implementation	Municipal Education Secretariat
Budget	1.67% of the municipal education budget
Methodology of Family Assistance	• Socio-educational actions • Education and professional training for young people and adults • Special attention to families with minors in situations of social risk

Source: compiled by the authors of this paper.

R$77 per family per month (equivalent to €25) and thus substantially increases the transfer sum provided by the federal PBE. At the same time, the programme introduces a three-pronged action that includes education, health and food. This approach allows the programme to extend beyond educational conditionality and includes additional benefits for pregnant women and small children or food subsides. Moreover, the merging of the previous independent programmes has reduced administrative costs and bureaucratic complexity for both the beneficiary families and the administration of the programme. Prior to the unification of the programmes under the PBF, each of them had its own implementing agency, information system and source of financing. This meant that it was possible for one family to receive benefits from all the programmes simultaneously while another family, displaying an identical socioeconomic profile, could be excluded from all of them (Soares 2010, p. 2).

Despite the generalisation of the PBF, this programme co-existed for a few years with some of the former independent programmes, such as the local PBE. In recent years, however, a number of municipal forms of the programme disappeared (including the Belo Horizonte PBE), as did the benefits provided by them. Nowadays, the PBF has been consolidated as the main national strategy for the fight against poverty in Brazil. Moreover, as

Draibe (2006) indicates, 'it has monopolised pro-poor policies in the whole country'. In 2006, it benefited 11 million families in the whole country, 18.6 per cent of the total population (Villatoro 2007). Its estimated cost is 0.5 per cent of GNP and approximately 2.5 per cent of total government expenditure (Lindert 2006).

Finally, it is important to appreciate the role of the WB in the programme. The WB's loan for the programme in its first phase (2004–09) was US$572 million; in its second phase (2010–15), a total amount of US$200 million. There is no doubt that the WB's involvement in the PBF does not only indicate the priority given to targeting in the WB portfolio, but also its growing influence in shaping the directions that targeting programmes have to follow.

Dilemmas in the PBE: An Analysis from the Standpoint of Supply

In this section we shall analyse the shortcomings and possibilities of the PBE from the standpoint of its institutional design, identifying certain dilemmas on whose resolution the equity and efficacy of the programme may depend. We shall first refer to the dilemmas linked to the process of targeting and the coverage of benefits; secondly, to the options related to the amount of the benefit; and finally to the possible consequences generated from investing greater or lesser effort in monitoring and family assistance measures.

Dilemmas of Targeting and Coverage: Who Benefits?

From the experience of targeting programmes, three criteria operate to define the beneficiary population: territorial, vulnerability and institutional criteria. The projects undertaken in the region have tended to use one of these criteria (or the combination of more than one) to select the target population. The efficacy of the programmes and volume and characteristics of the population excluded from them largely depend on this selection process.

In the case of the PBE, the targeting method was based on a combination of territorial and vulnerability criteria, while institutional criteria were totally excluded. The first phase of targeting in both the federal programme and its municipal variants was based on the territorial criterion, hinging on which areas with high levels of social exclusion were identified as places where intervention should be targeted. The second phase of targeting entailed identifying the potential beneficiaries based on gathering information on families' economic status and calculating a vulnerability index.

The available evaluations of the different forms of the PBE all coincide in highlighting that the targeting was appropriate and that the selection process tended to be targeted to the neediest people in each territorial area (Sabóia *et al.* 1998; Lavinas *et al.* 2001). On the other hand, it is important to take into account a number of risks linked to the geographical targeting associated with some CCTs. The main risk of this targeting criterion is creating an 'ecological fallacy' by regarding the entire territorial unit as if it displayed social homogeneity (Brodershon 1999). To rectify this fallacy, one can operationally resort to defining very small territorial units that tend to minimize the lack of homogeneity. This, however, does not take into account the fact that small pockets of poverty might remain outside the programme if they are located in territories with average values on the social indicators.

Finally, the criteria of targeting must inevitably be related to the programme's coverage capacity. Indeed, the different forms of the PBE tended to generate situations of 'over-targeting', that is, selecting beneficiaries from amongst the population that met the requirements, but that for budgetary reasons remained excluded from the programme. This need to select among the potential beneficiaries is usually resolved by endeavouring to give priority to the most vulnerable families. This process, which is ethically indisputable, may, however, have consequences on the efficacy of the transfer in terms of its potential impact on creating income autonomy. Some evaluations have pointed out that the PBE enabled many families to escape from destitution, though not poverty (Lavinas 2000). Only a small percentage of families, in certain municipal programmes, managed to change their living conditions sufficiently to rise above the poverty line. Paradoxically, sound targeting might reduce the efficacy of the programme in terms of the possibilities of effectively reducing poverty and generating better conditions of educability in the children.

The dilemmas mentioned might also have an effect on the social cohesion between the populations that do and do not benefit from the programme in the poor communities where it is implemented. The situations of over-targeting could generate a logical disgruntlement between those families that remain excluded from the programme though they meet the eligibility requirements. Likewise, the discretional nature of whether one was a beneficiary of the federal or the municipal varieties of the PBE generated a logical disgruntlement in the families benefiting from the federal programme who do not understand why they received less than other families in an identical situation of poverty. Here we can identify one of the most obvious contradictions in the discourses on education and poverty. While these discourses place great importance on community social cohesion as a mechanism to combat poverty (World Bank 2001, 2004; Putnam 2004), due to their very design, the targeting programmes with their coverage limitations generate disparities that make this social cohesion difficult to achieve.

Dilemmas concerning the Benefit: How Much to Transfer?

Decisions on the transfer sums are important since the programme's efficacy in achieving its goals largely depends on them. A first factor to take into account centres on what many authors call the trade-off between breadth and intensity (World Bank 2004). Indeed, targeting programmes debate the breadth of the coverage and the intensity of the benefit, and both the PBE and the PBF are no exceptions. The federal PBE variant, for example, offered broad coverage but limited benefit, while the municipal variant in Belo Horizonte offered a higher benefit, which consequently hindered the programme's chances of breadth (though obviously that depends on the amount of resources invested.) Broader coverage can ensure greater equitableness in access to the benefit but lower efficacy in achieving the goals, and conversely, a higher amount transferred may enable certain families to escape from their situation of poverty and generate mechanisms for creating income autonomy, but it could also generate inequality amongst sectors of the population that meet the eligibility criteria yet do not manage to be aided by the programme.

Within a context of clear financial limitations (on both a federal and municipal scale), the choice of either type of strategy clearly involves a political decision. One of the considerations to be borne in mind when fixing the sum of the benefit thus entails defining the goal to be achieved by the transfer. For example, a transfer may be chosen that manages to situate the families above the poverty line, or one may be chosen according to the opportunity cost associated with attending school (Sedlaeck *et al.* 2001). Some evaluations of the programme make it possible to determine the relationship between the amount transferred and the educational career of the beneficiaries, thus determining not only the amount of the transfer based on families' overcoming their material poverty but also based on knowledge of the relationship between the transfer and achievement of the goals, such as school attainment and the eradication of child labour. The consideration of which goals are given greatest priority is thus fundamental for considering the extent to which a targeting programme like the PBE is exclusively envisioned to alleviate the problems of lack of schooling and poverty (or even as an instrument of social control), or as a social policy that strives to use education as a key mechanism in the struggle against chronic poverty. Choosing one decision over the other will provide objective criteria for fixing the amount of the transfer and assessing the coverage needs based on criteria that are not exclusively conditioned by the available budget, a predominant criterion in almost all the targeting programmes.

Finally, the disjunctions are also related to the fixed or variable nature of the transfer. Most versions of the PBE have opted for a fixed transfer, although the federal form of the programme introduced a variable transfer depending on the number of 'eligible' children within the family unit. The decision for either type of option is generally related to the added costs that might be involved in introducing variability in the systems of selecting and monitoring the beneficiary population. The choice of the simple transfer model, recommended by some authors (Sedlaeck *et al.* 2001) may enable administrative costs to be saved; yet it might also lead to problems of equity and efficacy. The problems of equity are the result of offering identical amounts to family units with very different circumstances in terms of the ways they experience poverty. The problems of efficacy derive from witnessing the impact of very different transfers among the beneficiary families. Below we examine this issue in greater depth when we refer to the programme's shortcomings and possibilities from the standpoint of demand.

Dilemmas concerning Monitoring and Assistance: Is Transference Alone Enough?

A final set of dilemmas present in the design of the PBE centres on the least quantifiable but no less important terrain of ensuring its efficacy. These are measures that the programme can incorporate for the purpose of assisting and monitoring the beneficiary families. This is one of the realms in which the more help-oriented or redistributive orientation of the programmes can be seen. Logically, the chances for a greater breadth and/or intensity of the programme depend on the funds earmarked for the assistance measures, yet effective use of the transfer can also break the reproduction of the poverty cycle.

The decisions in this area are indicative of the possible political orientations the programmes might have with regard to defining poverty and the mechanisms needed to combat it. In other words, the more comprehensive the monitoring and family assistance measures, the greater the inter-sectoral actions related to the programme. Likewise, the more actions there are parallel to the transfers aimed at increasing the quality of the educational process, the more evidence there will be that the programme's design does not limit the concept of poverty solely to material factors but also extends it to other aspects. Underpinning the design, then, is some kind of interpretation of the relationship between education and poverty, or, what amounts to the same, the choice of a vision of the relationship as either exclusively unidirectional (in which education is conceived as a causal factor in the situation of poverty) or recursive (in which education and poverty mutually influence one another). The more funds are earmarked to actions such as adult literacy, visits to healthcare centres, occupational training policies, meetings with the beneficiary families and follow-up of the students' school career, the closer the programme will approach a recursive vision of the relationship between education and poverty, in which factors that could determine the possibilities for taking advantage of the educational experience are as important as school attendance and the quality of the education.

The variants of the PBE differed considerably in their planning of the monitoring measures and complementary actions for the beneficiaries. The federal type was limited to targeting and ensuring the income transference and left the design of the monitoring and assistance services to the municipalities, while the Belo Horizonte PBE applied a broad, diverse assistance methodology which included action in labour, social, educational and personal areas. In this regard, the PBF clearly draws its inspiration from the municipal forms of the PBE and combines the monetary transference with several complementary actions for beneficiary families. These actions, oriented toward maximising the effects of CCTs in reducing poverty, could be both specifically designed to cater for PBF families or other existing programmes, and include four main categories: access to knowledge (young and adult literacy programmes, vocational training, etc.), access to employment and income (professional qualification, access to micro-credit, etc.), improvement of housing and infrastructure (basic services programmes) and citizenship rights (programmes related to the exercise of civil and political rights) (www.mds.gov.br/bolsafamilia). Actually, the national debate surrounding the new federal educational plans to be implemented between 2011 and 2021 has essentially assumed this multi-dimensional, bi-directional view of poverty reduction (CONAE 2010).

The reflections in this section point to the possible political options that underpin the characteristics of the programmes' supply. However, the efficacy of the programme in terms of meeting its goals does not only depend on the political orientation implicit in their design. Our studies highlight how the impact of the transfer has different effects according to the social conditions of the beneficiaries and their representations of poverty and education. The efficacy of a targeting programme must thus be seen as not only based on the characteristics of the supply side but also the demand side, and especially from the standpoint of the possibility the transfer and other complementary actions may alter the conditions of educability of poor students.

Limits and Opportunities of the PBE: An Analysis from the Demand

The conditions of educability have been defined by López and Tedesco (2002) as the set of resources (both material and otherwise) that make possible the development of both educational practices and their potential success. From this perspective, it is claimed that if everyone is potentially educable, it is crucial to take into account the role played by both the socio-family and the school context in developing or hindering this potentiality. The idea of educability, thus, is not linked to an individual's capacity to learn, but rather to the characteristics of the educational and socio-family system, mainly centring on the relationships between the two.

In this section, we focus on the impact of the PBE programme on the conditions of poor students' educability, exploring their limits and opportunities in this area.

Impact of the PBE on Education and Educability

The PBE, in both its federal and municipal variants, aims to ensure school access and school attendance for poor children through the provision of financial support to their families. On account of its very nature, then, it can be assumed that one of its immediate impacts will be an increase in school attendance of beneficiary students, since if they do not meet the minimum requirements in this area, the family's monetary transfer is stopped. The rise in school attendance and the fall in dropouts during the period of primary education are therefore direct educational impacts of this type of programme, resulting from their very design.

Indeed, our studies allow us to confirm the positive effects of the PBE in terms of school attendance, an aspect acknowledged in both family accounts and in student and teacher interviews (Bonal et al. 2010). For the case examined, it can also be claimed that the improvement in school attendance is due not only to the programme's conditionality but is also linked, in turn, to the economic and socio-cultural changes registered in the families as a result of their participation in the programme.

The monetary transfer associated with the PBE, of varying amounts, constitutes an improvement in the beneficiary families' living conditions inasmuch as it entails a fixed, sure and steady income that can be used to cater for the different material and educational needs. The interviews held with the beneficiary families reflect how this monetary benefit is a means for them to cover their most immediate needs, such as food, clothing or health. Having good nutrition, the clothing needed or school supplies are clearly necessary pre-requisites for the development of educational practices and are crucial factors in making regular school attendance possible.

The PBE implies an improvement in the educability of the beneficiary students. This is not only because the programme requires them to attend school (direct educational effect) but precisely because it makes it possible for them to do so in that it guarantees the necessary conditions (indirect educational effect). It cannot be forgotten that although education is a necessary condition for equity, good educational development cannot be ensured without previously ensuring a minimum level of equity (López et al. 2002). Regular school attendance and children's potential educational success are closely associated with a series of family characteristics that affect the positions and dispositions adopted towards education: the availability of material resources, the possibility of assisting children's educational development, a proper physical context to accommodate school routines, and the family's cultural and educational climate and values are just some of the key factors in this process.

All the mothers interviewed stressed the influence of the improved living conditions on their children's school opportunities, highlighting different consequences of this economic improvement on their children's chances of being educated:

> To me the PBE was a great help, now I can at least send my children to school well fed (...) before, my youngest daughter was malnourished, and only when I joined the programme did she begin to develop, and why is that? Because I could feed her better and don't you think this contributes to her education? It's like a car without gas, a car without gas doesn't move, does it? Well, a malnourished child can't go to school, it's the same, exactly the same (Jacqueline, beneficiary of the Belo Horizonte Municipal PBE).

The improvement in the family's living conditions clearly influences the children's educational opportunities inasmuch as it makes it possible for them to meet the minimum requirements to carry out school practices and increases their chances of taking advantage of their education. Indeed, schools assume that students come with a series of predispositions, attitudes and behaviour learned before starting school; they expect that families ensure that their children are given the resources, values and habits needed for their education; and they trust that the students will arrive in their classrooms with the school supplies needed, the predisposition to study, the possibility of doing homework at home and a positive attitude toward school. The PBE enables families at the very least to provide the basic material requirements to make their children's education possible, thus ensuring the minimum needed for their educational development.

Limits of the Programme to Ensure Conditions of Educability

The positive effects we have just examined, however, are not equally present throughout social, educational and family settings. In this section, we will illustrate the shortcomings of the programme in two fundamental aspects: the difficulty of generating positive impacts in the realm of educability in all the beneficiary families, and the difficulty of ensuring improvement in educability conditions from the school standpoint.

The Diversity of Impacts according to Family Characteristics

Despite the fact that all the beneficiary families share a common situation of poverty, their living conditions differ broadly according to factors such as income levels prior to the implementation of the programme, the composition and stability of the family structure, the situation of the different family members, both adults and minors, in the labour market, the neighbourhood in which they live and the level of education of the adult family members. These factors identify different situations of social exclusion and, in short, they determine the type and intensity of impacts of the monetary transfer on different family and social settings. Although the monetary transfer is in itself positive from the standpoint of material living conditions, its effects on other non-material dimensions of poverty are completely different according to the different types of family situations (Bonal *et al.* 2010).

In terms of the usefulness and destination of the benefit, there is a clear difference between families who, in addition to the PBE, also receive income from activity in the labour market and those who live exclusively on the monetary transfer. Although in both cases most of the benefit is used for things such as food, housing or healthcare, in the former there is the possibility of earmarking part of the grant to purchase educational materials. That is, only the families that have better relative living conditions manage to allocate part of the benefit to purchasing school supplies and even low-cost tuition or extracurricular activities, while those living in a situation of greater instability have very few chances of using the benefit to pay for such materials or activities. The use of the monetary benefit, then, and its repercussions on the children's conditions of educability, are strongly influenced by the baseline socioeconomic situation and, for many families, the sum transferred proves insufficient simultaneously to meet subsistence and educational needs:

> I would like to find a course for him because he has some problems in maths but it is difficult because you have to pay for it and I do not have enough money to do so. I got the PBE, yes, but this is the only income we have at home ... and it is not enough at all. It is a help, a big help, it ensures the basic, you know, the basic food, and this stuff, but I have to pay for gas, water, housing, everything and I am on my own ... (Mother benefiting from the Belo Horizonte Municipal PBE).

In terms of school attendance, the diverse range of situations is similar. While for some families the PBE is the first chance to ensure their children's regular school attendance, for others it is an incentive that improves a pre-existing situation, and yet for others, due to their situation of deprivation, it is an insufficient stimulus in itself to generate significant, permanent changes in this area. It follows that, though higher school attendance is a key factor in changing children's educational and life trajectories in families with relatively superior living conditions, for others it is unlikely to lead to significant and permanent changes in their relationship with, expectations of and strategies towards schools, if other types of action are not simultaneously undertaken. The level of poverty in which some families live is so extreme that improvements in their children's school attendance, despite its inherent importance, has a limited capacity to change substantially both the current situation and their future social and educational prospects. Moreover, in some cases, the awareness of the social stigma related to poverty is so strong that it clearly limits the educational expectations and opportunities of young students:

> If you go to find a job and tell them you're from the slum, they are not going to hire you ... I've seen this with other people, people here in the slum with studies but they could not find a job in the city ... So, you can have education, but what for? They do not want us (Joao, 14-year-old student).

The diversity of impacts of the PBE is reflected in all the dimensions that define the conditions of educability from the family standpoint – educational assistance, help with homework, among others – enabling us to claim that the families' living conditions prior to joining the programme are key to understanding the different intensity of its educational impacts, not to mention the potential permanence and stability of these impacts.

Despite the fact that the Belo Horizonte PBE is one of the most ambitious of its kind, its impact on education and educability is extremely varied if other complementary measures or policies are not implemented that enable the families in the greatest situation of vulnerability to raise their standard of living. Likewise, we must highlight the existence of situations of 'ineducability' (Bonal *et al.* 2010) which continue to be perpetuated despite the programme's actions, and which cannot be overcome without the intervention of other types of policies. Drug dealing, lack of public investment in the *favelas*, lack of stable employment, insalubrious dwellings and child labour are just some of the factors characterising the everyday lives of these families, which continue to hinder them not only from the point of view of the possibilities of educational integration but more especially social integration.

Diversity of Impacts according to the School Characteristics

School attendance itself does not presuppose greater educational attainment, nor does it automatically generate a change in the attitudes and positions of adults and minors towards education. On the contrary, the role played by educational institutions, their way of dealing with learning difficulties and their way of forging relations with students' families are key to improving or hindering the educational trajectories of the students participating in the PBE.

On the one hand, it is crucial to take the structure of opportunities of different schools into account to cater effectively for the students from impoverished family backgrounds. The schools' social composition and their geographical location are two crucial factors in this regard. Some schools are located in the middle of highly dangerous slums and are entirely made up of poor or extremely poor students. Consequently, these types of schools present a 'concentration of difficulties' that, without the support of complementary public resources, could make it difficult to guarantee the learning of the students. As this teacher clearly explains:

> In this school all the students are poor. I'd say that 100 per cent of the students are poor. This is one of the poorest neighbourhoods in the whole country, this is a very poor community, there is a high level of unemployment, a high level of illiteracy ... and so this is a school in which a lot of difficulties are concentrated. The level of difficulty of our students is very high in every sense: in cognitive terms, in relational terms, in personal terms ... so, in my opinion, this school would need much more resources, human resources, economic resources ... the level of difficulty is so high ... so high, that sometimes nothing is enough (Teacher in a public school with a high concentration of poor students).

On the other hand, it is crucial to consider the processes of stigmatisation toward poor students that exist in many schools. School is still considered as the 'natural place' for the middle classes and the poor are constantly accused of not having the interest, the capacity or the motivation to support their schooling process; they are accused of their own poverty. Moreover, programmes like the PBE are explicitly rejected by some teachers due to the stereotypes they have with regard to poor students and their families. According to this view, the PBE focuses on school attendance but not on educational achievement, and the students who benefit from the programme are accused of not having a better attitude and better results. In fact, many teachers expect a kind of mechanical adhesion of poor students to the school institution simply on account of being grant beneficiaries. They consider that affording poor students the opportunity to stay in school is enough for them to take advantage of this situation, thus disregarding the number of socioeconomic difficulties they have to face in their daily lives, the role of the school itself in reducing the distance between poor students and the school institution and its demands, and the fact that for poor students to rely on school it is first necessary for the school to rely on them:

> The PBE families only live to complain, their only motivation with the school is that we justify the regular attendance of their children because,

if not, they lose the grant. But that's all, they do not participate in anything else, they do not take part in the school life, they do not help or assist their children's education process. Perhaps the PBE can ensure that the child goes to school, but nothing else, and just coming is useless (…) their only concern is getting the money each month, there is no commitment either on the part of the child or their families, they come without having done the homework, they don't listen in class, they're not motivated, they disturb the entire classroom … (Teacher in a public school).

Of course, programmes such as PBE are not directly responsible for situations like these, but if it is expected that educational investment is key to poor people having the opportunity to escape poverty, the very role of the school in this process cannot be ignored. If poor students continue to attend 'poor schools' and 'schools for the poor', it will not be their educational investment that will open opportunities up to them.

Conclusions

For the last decade, CCTs have become a 'fast social policy' in the developing world. Whether these programmes can be considered a progressive or regressive social policy is a highly controversial issue. Are CCTs a good policy for the poor? Are they redistributive or are they part of the new faces of neoliberalism in social policies? Do they have positive effects for poverty alleviation?

Answering these questions is no simple task. As this paper has shown, programme design is a central aspect in assessing the impact of CCTs. In fact by examining the programme design we can infer what Pawson or Dale have called the 'programme ontology' (Robertson *et al.* 2007): that is, the values underlining specific public policies are implicit in the very design of the programme. In the case of the PBE and the PBF, we have looked at aspects such as the programme extension, the value of the transfer, the targeting system, the follow-up monitoring procedures and the support methodology. We have observed significant differences among programme variants, and we have illustrated tensions and dilemmas that policymakers face when designing a CCT programme. Within this diversity, it would be erroneous to qualify or disqualify CCT programmes as inherently 'good' or 'bad' policies for the poor. To investigate the effects of these programmes further, we have observed how they are "appropriated" by those that benefit from the transfer. Again, there is a notable diversity of impacts, which hinge on the wide diversity of educational demand. Although all the beneficiaries are poor, they differ in the way they experience poverty. Their family structure and characteristics are different, as are the educational contexts of poor children, the different forms of using non-school time and the school cultures they experience. These factors are decisive in understanding what we call 'conditions of educability.' The existence of the transfer means nothing if we cannot observe the role it can play within specific living conditions.

Reflecting on the conditions of educability is a necessary task to explore further the nature of CCTs and their usefulness as a policy to reduce the intergenerational reproduction of poverty. Focusing only on the educational results of beneficiaries is a very reductionist policy evaluation methodology to dismiss these programmes as efficient social policies. There are effects that can only be assessed in the long term, especially those that cannot be directly considered strictly 'educational' effects. In fact, conditions of educability point out 'what else' is necessary for a child to learn at school besides the transfer. While a few more interventions are necessary in some cases, there are cases which require an intensive follow-up methodology and a multidimensional supportive strategy to help children learn at school.

Observing conditions of educability is also useful in drawing the conclusion that CCTs may constitute a very poor social or educational policy when not included within a larger strategy to reduce poverty through education. Those approaches that see CCTs as an inexpensive and useful social policy ignore the fact that poverty reduction is undoubtedly an expensive objective. Most determinants of poverty call for intensive intervention strategies, among which CCTs can be an important part, but not the only one.

Note

1 This study carried out under the Spanish project *Progresos y Limitaciones de la Educación para Todos* (EDU2008-60816), assessed the impacts of the living conditions of poor children on their conditions of educability. Interviews were carried out with teachers and beneficiary families (mothers and children) of the PBE. See the complete study in Bonal and Tarabini (2010).

References

Atria, R. (2003), 'Capital social: concepto, dimensiones y estrategias para su desarrollo', in R. Atria ed., *Capital social y reducción de la pobreza en América Latina y el Caribe: en busca de un nuevo paradigma*. Santiago de Chile: CEPAL, pp. 581–90.

Bonal, X. and Tarabini, A. (2010), *Ser pobre en la escuela. Habitus de pobreza y condiciones de educabilidad*. Buenos Aires: Miño y Dávila.

Brodershon, V. (1999), 'Focalización de programas de superación de la pobreza', in UNICEF ed., *Derecho a tener derecho: infancia, derecho y política social en América Latina*. Montevideo: UNICEF – Instituto Internacional del Niño (IIN) – Instituto Ayrton Senna, pp. 1–25.

CONAE – Conferência Nacional de Educação (2010), *Construindo o Sistema Nacional Articulado de Educação: O Plano Nacional de Educação, suas Diretrizes e Estratégias de Ação*. Brasilia: Ministério da Educação.

Cornia, G. A. (2001), 'Social Funds in Stabilization and Adjustment Programmes: A Critique'. *Development and Change*, 32, 1–32.

Draibe, S. (2006), 'Brasil: Bolsa Escola y Bolsa Familia', in E. Cohen and R. Franco (eds), *Transferencias con responsabilidad. Una mirada latinoamericana*, Mexico D.F.: FLACSO, pp. 137–78.

Holzmann R., Sherburne-Benz, L. and Tesliuc, E. (2003), *Social Risk Management: The World Bank's Approach to Social Protection in a Globalizing World*. Washington, DC: World Bank.

Lavinas, L. (2000), 'The Appeal of Minimum Income Programmes in Latin America', paper presented to the Meeting on Socio Economic Security, Bellagio, 6–10 March.

Lavinas, L., Barbosa, M. L. and Tourinho, O. (2001), *Assessing Local Minimum Income Programmes in Brazil*. Geneva: ILO, Brazil Regional Office, World Bank and IPEA.

Lindert, K. (2006), 'Brazil: Bolsa Escola Program. Scaling-up Cash Transfers for the Poor', in OECD-WB (ed), *Emerging good practice in managing for development results: Sourcebook*, Washington D.C.: OECD-WB, pp. 67–74.

López, N. and Tedesco, J. C. (2002), *Las condiciones de educabilidad de los niños y adolescentes en América Latina*. Buenos Aires: IIPE-UNESCO.

Narayan, D. (1999), 'Bonds and Bridges. Social Capital and Poverty'. *Policy Research Working Paper*, 2167, 1–50.

Pawson, R. (2006), *Evidence-Based Policy: A Realist Perspective*. London: Sage Publications Ltd.

Peck, J. and Theodore, N. (2010), 'Recombinant workfare, across the Americas: Transnationalizing 'fast' social policy'. *Goforum*, 41, (2), 195–208.

Putnam, R. (2004), 'Education, Diversity, Social Cohesion and Social Capital', paper presented to the OECD Meeting: Raising the Quality of Learning for all, Dublin, 18–19 March.

Rawlings, L. B. (2005), 'A new approach to social assistance: Latin America's experience with conditional cash transfer programmes'. *International Social Security Review*, 58, (2–3), 133–61.

Reimers, F., Silva, C. S. and Trevino, E. (2006), 'Where is the "education" in Conditional Cash Transfers in Education?'. *UIS Working Papers*, 4, 1–80.

Robertson, S., Novelli, M., Dale, R., Tikly, L., Dachi, H. and Alphonce, N. (2007), *Globalisation, Education and Development: ideas, actors and dynamics*. London: DFID.

Sabóia, J. and Rocha, S. (1998), 'Programas de garantia de renda minima-linhas gerais de uma metodologia de avaliaçao a partir da experiencia pioneira do Paranoá, no Distrito Federal', *IPEA texto para discussao*, 582, 1–37.

Schwartzman, S. (2005), 'Education-oriented social programmes in Brazil: the impact of Bolsa Escola', paper presented to the Global Conference on Education Research in Developing Countries (Research for Results on Education), Prague, 31 March–02 April.

Sedlaeck, G., Gustafsson-Wright, E., Ilahi, N. and Lannon, M. (2001), *Brazil: as assessment of the Bolsa Escola Programmes*. Washington DC: World Bank.

Soares, S. (2010), 'Targeting and coverage of the Bolsa Família Programme: What is the meaning of eleven million families', *One Pager*, 117.

Tarabini, A. (2008), 'Educational targeting in the fight against poverty: limits, omissions and opportunities'. *Globalisation, Societies and Education*, 6, (4), 415–29.

Villatoro, P. (2007), 'Las transferencias condicionadas en América Latina: luces y sombras', paper presented to the Seminario Internacional Evolución y desafíos de los programas de transferencias condicionadas, Brasilia, 20–21 November.

World Bank (2001), *World Development Report 2000/2001. Attacking Poverty.* Washington DC: Oxford University Press.

—(2004), *Inequality in Latin America and the Caribbean: Breaking with History?* Washington DC: World Bank.

—(2011), *Learning for All: Investing in People's Knowledge and Skills to Promote Development. World Bank Groups Education Strategy 2020.* Washington DC: World Bank.

CHAPTER EIGHT

School-Based Management in Post-Conflict Central America: Undermining Civil Society and Making the Poorest Parents Pay

Margriet Poppema

Introduction

School-based management (SBM) has been on the educational reform agenda of International Organisations (IOs) since the 1990s and is regarded as the most radical form of educational decentralisation. Although the models might differ, the main rationale given for the implementation of SBM is that by enhancing the participation of local stakeholders, decentralisation will lead to more efficient services and boost educational achievement. Most analysis of SBM programmes (SBMPs) evaluate the functioning of the programmes and their main outcomes. In this chapter, the focus shall be placed on the specific political and economic context that gave rise to the two first SBMPs in the Global South, namely, the Autonomous Schools Programme (ASP) in Nicaragua and the EDUCO Community-Managed Schools Programme in El Salvador. They were implemented at a time when major (post) conflict transformation processes in Central America (CA) were driven through the direct intervention by the Unites States (US) and their Agency for International Development (USAID).

Since then, these SBMPs have been implemented in countries where IOs have great leverage, as in (post-) conflict countries (Afghanistan, the Democratic Republic of the Congo, Nepal, Philippines, Sri Lanka, etc.) or in countries that are undergoing significant political, social and economic change. Next to USAID, the World Bank is the major promoter of SBM and has continuously expanded its support for this kind of decentralized reform. A review of World Bank's lending portfolio over the years 2000–2006 shows that SBM projects amount to US$1.7 billion, representing approximately 18 per cent of total education financing (Barrera-Osorio *et al.* 2009).

The EDUCO programme in particular has been cited as the *best practice*, arguing that the project was built on the experience of at least 500 community-run schools operating in conflict-affected areas in the 1980s.'When the country emerged from war, the new Ministry of Education launched Education with Community Participation (EDUCO), a programme that gave these schools official recognition and financial support.' (UNESCO 2011, p. 224). This appreciation has been highlighted in all the World Bank documents on the topic (see Jimenez *et al.* 1999; Meza *et al.* 2004; Sawada *et al.* 2005; Gropello 2006).

According to the World Bank website, SBMPs take on many different forms:

> both in terms of who has the power to make decisions as well as the degree of decision-making devolved to the school level. While some programmes transfer authority to principals or teachers only, others encourage or mandate parental and community participation, often in school committees (sometimes known as school councils). In general, SBM programmes transfer authority over one or more of the following activities: budget allocation, hiring and firing of teachers and other school staff, curriculum development, textbook and other educational material procurement, infrastructure improvement, setting the school calendar to better meet the specific needs of the local community, and monitoring and evaluation of teacher performance and student learning outcomes.

World Bank reports mention that 'SBM emphasizes the individual school [...] as the decision-making authority' (Barrera-Osorio *et al.* 2009, p. ix) and continues that 'by giving voice and decision-making power to local stakeholders who know more [...] decentralization can improve educational outcomes and increase client satisfaction' (2009, p. 1). SBM has been implemented in high-income countries as well[1]. However, after more than fifteen years of implementation, there is still no conclusive evidence that SBM yields significantly higher student achievement, either in the US (Cook 2007) nor in the Global South. This is even recognized by the Director of Education at the World Bank, Elizabeth King, who states that the evidence base that SBM can improve the quality of teaching and learning is limited (2009, p. ix). Nonetheless, SBMPs continue to be promoted by the World Bank.

If SBMPs do not foster higher student achievement, why are they propagated and financed by USAID and the World Bank? In recent years, five major background reports were published which uses the examples of

EDUCO and ASP for dissemination purposes (World Bank 2007; 2008a; 2008b; Barrera-Osorio *et al.* 2009; USAID 2010). In this chapter, I will examine the implementation of these first SBMPs in countries that were hot spots of US government intervention. The SBMPs were developed as a solution to counter the educational legacy of the left wing Sandinista government in Nicaragua, and to undermine the influence of educational civil society organisations in El Salvador. The US, through USAID and in conjunction with International Financing Institutions (IFIs), played an early role in mediating overall change in the region. Here, I will first outline the historical and contextual background of CA, and then will look at the two countries, beginning with the changes in the decade preceding the implementation of SBMPs. This will be followed by a short history of the education system and an appraisal of the contextual aspects of the SBMPs, identifying the actors that were key for the conceptualisation, implementation and prolongation of the programmes, as well as which stakeholders were excluded. This will be done in chronological order for each country, although the processes in the different countries are closely interlinked. In the conclusion, the major changes, the main stakeholders and the consequences of the two SBMPs are analysed.

Contextual Background of Central America

The first SBMPs were implemented in two very small countries, both with a current population of around six million[2]. These CA countries share the history of Spanish colonialism until 1821 and, since the end of the nineteenth century; the US has played a dominant role in the region in order to secure their commercial and political interests. The successive authoritarian leaders and the policies of accumulation led to a highly unequal land ownership and deeply rooted relations of injustice, with high rates of poverty among the majority of the population. Even the booming agro-export model of economic growth from 1950 to the 1970s only enriched foreign investors and a handful of national families[3], while landlessness, a skewed income distribution, and lack of education for the greater part of the rural population continued, leading to growing discontent among popular sectors and other politically and economically excluded groups (Pearce 1998; Robinson 2003).

During the Cold War period, the US did not tolerate any moderately progressive or nationalistic government in the region, framing any progressive movement as communist, and acting upon it[4]. Many popular movements and civil society protests challenged the socio-economic injustices, the lack of political freedom and human rights. The fierce repression of any opposition movement strengthened the armed liberation movements until in 1979 the Sandinista National Liberation Front (FSNL) in Nicaragua unexpectedly overthrew the Somoza dynasty and installed a left wing revolutionary Sandinista government[5]. In El Salvador a similar kind of opposition was active, posing a revolutionary challenge to the authoritarian and US-supported right wing government.

In the aftermath of the US military defeat in Vietnam in 1975, these small CA countries became the hot spots for US intervention, combating the so-called 'Soviet beachheads' in order to keep the region open to free-market principles. El Salvador, in particular, became the laboratory of the most extensive US *low-intensity-warfare* up to that moment; while in Nicaragua the US organized a massive destabilisation programme and financed the Contra military forces. Many researchers on CA point out that analysing the US counter-insurgency is crucial for understanding the current international post-war strategies of liberal peace building (Foley 1996; Robinson2003; Quan 2005; Kurtenbach 2010). Here it will be shown that this is also valid for the post-conflict educational strategies.

Nicaragua: From the Sandinista Educational Reform to the Autonomous School Programme (ASP)

The Political and Socio-Economic Context of the 1980s

When the Sandinista National Liberation Front (FSLN) came to power in 1979, they tried to install an alternative development model to free-market capitalism. Their political view was based on nationalism, popular democracy and anti-imperialism, and included a commitment to a mixed economy, political pluralism and a non-aligned foreign policy (Carnoy *et al.* 1990; Arnove 1995; Robinson 2003). Their main policies focussed on a long-demanded land reform and the expansion of social programmes in the areas of education, health and housing, together with some more direct forms of income distribution (Forsberg 2007).

Just shortly after the installation of the Sandinista government, the US started a complex interventionist strategy, organising a massive destabilisation campaign to undermine the national cohesion and to isolate the government from international markets and credits (Robinson 2003, p. 72). In 1981, all aid from the US to the government was suspended, while aid and assistance was given to opposing groups and parties. At the same time, international diplomatic pressure was intensified, resulting in the World Bank and IMF withholding all loans, and culminating in a full trade embargo in 1985, and under the banner of 'democracy promotion', the US organized and financed the Contra military force (Posner 2004)[6].

When the Sandinista project collapsed and the right wing National Opposition Union (UNO) won the elections in 1990, all the sanctions were lifted and the US, jointly with the IFIs, returned with their grants, loans and prescriptions. They had great leverage as the foreign debt had grown from US$1.6 billion in 1979 to around US$10 billion by 1990. The restructuring of the debt with the IFIs was followed up by structural adjustment policies, fiscal austerity and the opening up of the economy to the global market. In addition the UNO government gave ample space to USAID who laid down the US policy for Nicaragua in a Strategy Statement that took a year of study and 'which involved a counterreform in every institutional and policy arena'[7] (Robinson 2003, p. 75). All neoliberal measures were stoutly implemented, including public sector reconstruction, social spending cuts, privatisation and deregulation of the economy.

Education during the Sandinista Period (1979–1990)

Under the Somoza regime (1933–1979), poverty was widespread and spending on education was limited. In the late 1970s, only 65 per cent children were enrolled in primary education and just 22 per cent of them would complete six years (Carnoy et al. 1990). Most rural schools would only offer one or two years of schooling, and more than 50 per cent of the population was illiterate. Due to this historical neglect, education became a prime focus of the Sandinista government; their policies were based on the right to education for all, defined as 'popular'[8], and seen as an important element in the creation of a 'new person'[9] and in the construction of a more equal and just society (Arnove 1995).

The Ministry of Education (MINED) worked closely together with the teacher union ANDEN as well as with many popular civil society organisations. The education budget more than doubled from 2.9 per cent to 6 per cent of GNP, and the main objectives were the expansion of the public education system, the promotion of qualitative change, and the transformation of the system (Carnoy et al. 1990). They were inspired by socialist thinking and both educational and political objectives were a central part of the process of social change and liberation (Forsberg 2007).

Education was thus given a key role in political socialisation, focussing on critical and participatory citizenship, especially in adult education. The establishment of a basic education system for adults (PBEA) and the National Literacy Crusade were some of the major accomplishments (Arnove 1995). More than 13,000 PBEAs were established and illiteracy was reduced from 50 per cent to 23 per cent. International recognition came from the United Nations as access to the different levels of the education system between 1979–1984 more than doubled and the teaching force tripled. After 1985, the growth slowed down due to the US-sponsored Contra war that conceived schools and hospitals as key military targets[10].

The role of the World Bank during the Sandinista period was notorious for its absence; even though they had strongly supported the Somoza dictatorship with two educational loans in 1968 and in 1976, a third loan to the Sandinista government was unilaterally suspended in 1981 in accordance with US policies. This occurred in spite of the World Bank's recognition that the Sandinista government had 'education among the top development priorities of the country' (World Bank 1981, p. 1).

The Autonomous Schools Programme (ASP) from 1990 to 2007

When the UNO government took over in 1990 and the support of the US and the IFIs returned, USAID took the lead in the field of education to wipe out any political and ideological legacies of the Sandinistas. With the support of USAID and the IFIs, the conservative Minister of Education, Humberto Belli, transformed the education system in three ways: first, by dismantling the strong role of the state through decentralisation and privatisation of the public school system; secondly, by abolishing the adult education system and focusing mainly on pre- and primary education; and thirdly, by introducing a conservative agenda reinforcing religious and patriarchal values through the introduction of civics, morality and politeness.

The ideological approach was sweeping; all textbooks developed during the Sandinista period were shredded or burned, and USAID allocated $12.5 million to replace them with 7.6 million new textbooks copied from other LA countries (Arnove 1995). The new textbooks emphasized strong conservative and Catholic values, and women were invariably depicted as housewives and men as productive workers. This stood in stark contrast to the strong participation of women during the Sandinista period, and the fact that 80 per cent of the teaching force was female.

The reorganisation of the role of the state in education was facilitated by the USAID-financed redundancy pay for the massive lay-offs in the public sector. The Ministry of Education (MINED) staff was cut by more than 50 per cent, the regional offices were dismantled, the teaching force reduced, and teacher salaries decreased (Arnove 1994). This had direct consequences for student enrolment, which declined by nearly 25 per cent (150,000 children) in 1990 (Picón *et al.* 1994). The educational policy changed toward decentralisation and privatisation of the public school system, of which the ASP became the main strategy (Arnove 1995).

The ASP programme started in 1991 with 20 secondary schools and was steadily extended to include 63 per cent of all students in urban and rural areas by 2005. The idea of *school autonomy* was based on the introduction of market mechanisms, cost efficiency and the creation of some accountability through parent participation in school councils. The introduction of school fees was a sensitive issue; hence the introduction of the ASP was carefully prepared by the MINED. With the support of USAID, a cadre of loyal local representatives was trained to become the intermediary educational staff in the municipalities. They were educated in the philosophy, goals and components of the reform and the strategies for promoting it, 'making sure that its ideology was presented in the most attractive possible light' and that they could counter the opposition to the ASP programme (Gershberg 1999, p. 16).

These municipal delegates played an important role in the establishment of the autonomous schools. With the promise of better salaries on the basis of school fees, the principal and teachers were persuaded to become an autonomous school[11]. Other mechanisms used were higher pay for the pro-autonomy teachers and for their schools, or sometimes dismissal of teachers if they voted against autonomy. This located the political battle at the school level as the teachers that would vote against the ASP were members of the teacher union ANDEN (Fuller et al. 1998; Gershberg 1999). Although teacher approval was formally needed, together with sufficient enrolment, it would be the principal alone who would sign the school co-management agreement at the central MINED office. Within the ASP-system, the individual school received monthly transfers that were earmarked for teacher salaries. This funding was to be supplemented with fees, donations and other incomes to complement teacher salaries and to acquire educational resources. In the beginning, the fees were mandatory; however, after much controversy they were abolished for primary education in 1999. Notwithstanding, parents were still expected to pay quotas and the average parent expenditures represented approximately half the total cost of sending a child to school (Arcia 2000, cited in Gershberg 2005, p. 300). This system privileged parents and schools with greater capacities and resources, as poorer parents were less able to contribute significantly.

The management of the autonomous school itself was delegated to the principal jointly with the school council (principal, teachers and parents) in which the elected parents had a voting majority, though, in practice, it was the principal who had the real power (Forsberg 2007, p. 103). The school council was charged with the management of the budget and personnel, and (officially) some curricular decisions and evaluation and planning functions. However, they were under the strict control of the MINED. According to Forsberg, 'the central office has the right to dismiss the school principal and to suspend members of the school council if they do not adhere to the norms and procedures laid down in the General Regulation for Education' (MINED 1999, p. 31 cited in Forsberg 2007, p. 101). All these policies were strongly contested by organized civil society actors such as the teacher union ANDEN and by women's organisations due to the high cost of education for the poor, the highly conservative curriculum and the marginalisation of civil society organisations. This left the ASP for more than a decade without any legislation, which was only enacted in 2002 via the Education Participation Law (Forsberg 2007).

Within the international context, the ASP has been considered to be the most radical educational reform in Latin America, and USAID and the World Bank have played a central role in advising the reform and making loans available (Gershberg 1999; Robinson 2003; Forsberg 2007). Moreover, it is framed as part of the pacification and democratisation attempt (Gropello 2004), where democracy is defined in terms of individual freedom from state indoctrination and intervention, in areas best left to the family and intermediate associations (Arnove 1995, p. 37). The ASP programme remained controversial during the entire period of implementation and was abolished on the first day the new Minister of Education of the reformed Sandinista party FSLN took office in 2007.

To sum up, I have argued that education in Nicaragua has been part of an intense economic and political struggle. The enormous effort of the Sandinista government during the 1980s to expand and improve all levels of education was strongly based on collective action together with mass organisations, such as the teacher union and civil society actors. Nevertheless, as soon as the UNO government came to power in 1990, this enormous expansion of education and the participatory manner of decision-making was eliminated. Education became key in a well thought-out counter strategy developed by USAID, which was further implemented by the World Bank, aiming to dismantle fully the Sandinista education system in every aspect. The main elements were the restructuring of the role of the state, the introduction of market mechanisms through ASP, the abolition of the adult education system, the introduction of conservative values and the marginalisation of all civil society organisations. The new SBM system of *autonomous* schools demanded *voluntary* funding and labour from (poor) parents through a hierarchically controlled system of so-called *participation*. Through ASP, a top-down and highly regulated form of participation by parents and teachers was installed in each individual school, without any possibility of representation to influence national education politics and policies.

El Salvador in the 1980s and the Community-Managed Schools Programme EDUCO

The Political and Economic Context of the 1980s

During the 1970s, the circumstances in El Salvador were quite similar to the Nicaraguan situation with the presence of a massive popular movement that struggled to change the highly unequal socio-economic system. Yet the victory of the Sandinistas in 1979 and the perceived threat of an insurrectionary triumph of its Salvadorian counterpart, the Farabundo Marti National Liberation Front (FMLN), substantially changed the conditions in El Salvador. As in Nicaragua, the US instigated a massive intervention;

however, in this case, not attacking but rather supporting the government, leading to a full civil war that was waged between the armed forces, death squads and right-wing supporters on one side and a guerrilla army of the FMLN and its mass-based supporters on the other side (Robinson 2003, p. 87). During the next 12 years, El Salvador became the laboratory for the most important and expensive *low-intensity-warfare* developed by the US after the Vietnam defeat (Schwarz 1991; Sepp 2005; Nelson 2008). An investment of US$6 billion was made in economic, military and covert aid, while approximately US$1 billion from the IFIs was mobilized to transform Salvadorian society (Robinson 2003, p. 89). This approach has later served as a template for Iraq (Maass 2005)[12].

These massive investments created the opportunity for USAID to play an important role in the restructuring of society. A detailed study by Foley (1996) gives a revealing insight into the key role of USAID in the transformation of civil society. USAID developed a dual strategy: on the one hand, building political power and influencing a segment of the Salvadorian business class to establish private foundations, while on the other hand supporting the government's fierce attacks on all popular organisations associated with the leftist opposition[13]. At the national level, USAID supported the foundation of the Salvadorian Foundation for Social and Economic Development (FUSADES)[14] led by the wealthiest members of society and, in the field of education, the Business Foundation for Educational Development (FEPADE) was created in 1986 (1996, p. 73). Moreover, with funds from the USAID programme Strengthening Associations (FORTAS), many mini-foundations headed by local landlords were established throughout the country to carry out social services in rural areas (1996, p. 77). This overall strategy permitted these new private foundations to develop a vast network within the civil society sector. At the same time, all unions and popular organisations suffered fierce repression, and many leaders were persecuted, murdered or joined the FMLN. The violence increased exponentially leading to the killing of more than 75,000 people, 95 per cent of whom were killed by the US-supported military or related forces (Amnesty International 2001). The education sector and especially the public teacher union ANDES were not excluded from repression[15].

Not surprisingly, owing to the marginalisation and the physical silencing of almost all oppositional civil society organisations, FUSADES could rapidly become the most influential neoliberal socio-economic think-tank in El Salvador. In the field of education, FUSADES, alongside FEPADE, played an early role in the establishment of the EDUCO educational programme (World Bank 1994).

Educational Situation during the Period of Violence

During the twelve-year armed conflict, the already poor socio-economic and educational situation of the 1970s deteriorated and became even worse as finances for public expenditures were diverted to the defence budget. Education as a percentage of BNP dropped from 3.7 per cent in 1980 to 1.9 per cent in 1992 (Cuéllar-Marchelli 2003, p. 149). During the 1980s, more than 800 schools were closed down, particularly in the rural areas, affecting around 1,500 teachers, while leaving more than 100,000 students without education (Alvear-Galindo 2002, p. 87). Dropout rates in 1986 reached approximately 90 per cent of the student population in certain areas and the illiteracy rate was in the vicinity of 40 per cent in 1985 (Moncada-Davidson 1995).

Education was especially neglected in the regions in conflict, thus different communities and popular organisations assumed the responsibility and became active actors in organising their own education. This alternative movement for education was based on the principle of 'education of, by and for the people' and developed in Christian-base communities[16], in refugee camps, and in FMLN controlled areas. The popular schools fostered a political and emancipatory vision of education based on the work and methodology of Paulo Freire, combining education with participation in the struggle for social justice and dignity (Hammond 1999). According to Reimers (1997), they provided education to some 17,000 students in rural areas during the conflict.

The Peace Accords and the Establishment of EDUCO

Following the electoral defeat of Nicaragua's Sandinista government in 1990 and the US presidential change, the US lost its main rationale to interfere in El Salvador and the stage was set to embrace the peace negotiations between the government and the FMLN. In the meantime, the ultra right-wing Nationalist Republican Alliance (ARENA) won the elections in 1989 and would stay on for the following 20 years[17]. The new president Alfredo Cristiani invited the USAID-funded FUSADES to join his administration and to implement a set of proposals to tackle socio-economic issues, including the educational sector. The previous general manager of FEPADE was appointed Minister of Education and would remain in office for almost a decade (1989–98) while the World Bank stepped up financial and technical support for education. As in Nicaragua, education became one of the key areas of socio-economic and political reform, through decentralisation, privatisation and a strong focus on building new forms of socio-economic co-existence at the local level. However, public investment in education remained low: 1.9 per cent of GNP in 1991, to 2.4 per cent in 2002 and 3.1 per cent in 2007 (UNESCO 2009).

The new education policy and the EDUCO programme were developed with 'exceptionally close relations and trust between USAID, the implementing partners, and MINED officials' (USAID 2010, p. 81). The overall vision was, like the Nicaraguan ASP, inspired by cost-effectiveness and human capital theory. EDUCO started in the 78 poorest municipalities with the lowest health/nutrition and education indicators, and expanded primarily to the former conflict regions (World Bank 1994, p. 1; Cuéllar-Marchelli 2003, p. 146). USAID was directly involved in the conceptualisation of the EDUCO strategy. Their subsequent funding was channelled through the 1990–1999 Strengthening Achievement in Basic Education (SABE) project, funded with US$33 million (2010, p. 70) and focussing on the problematic parts of the education system: the quality of the curriculum and textbooks; pre- and in-service teacher training to support curriculum implementation; and achievement tests to assess the new core curriculum. According to Darlyn Mesa, Minister of Education, 'the main support and the life of the Ministry revolved around the SABE project' (USAID 2010, p. 70). Thereafter the EDUCO programme became actively supported by the World Bank and the IADB, and although the Bank reduced its direct financing of EDUCO in 1996, it continued supporting the long term sectorwide educational reform process with technical and financial assistance. The total World Bank loans for education in El Salvador from 1991–2005 were US$271 million (Meza et al. 2004, p. 16; World Bank 2004) and jointly with the loans of the IADB, the total amount was well over the US$ 552 million for the Salvadoran education sector (USAID 2010).

Within the EDUCO schools, the management and administration were transferred to community education associations (ACEs)[18] each consisting of five parents. The ACEs receive per pupil financing directly from MINED, and they supplement the state funds with their labour, material resources and through school fees. The ACEs are responsible for the hiring, firing and monitoring of teachers on an annual basis and for buying the necessary resources (Cuéllar-Marchelli 2003; Meza et al. 2004, p. 3). The parents in the ACEs are not paid for their work, and the contract between MINED and the EDUCO schools has to be renewed each year[19]. Furthermore, MINED controls the curriculum, provides the textbooks and organizes the national assessments as well as teacher training; however, in practice the execution of these educational services is often contracted out to private institutions (Cuéllar-Marchelli 2003, p. 152). The EDUCO schools are established in the existing local infrastructure, either in schools or private institutions. EDUCO teachers, contracted by the ACEs, are not part of the Ministry's teaching staff like public school teachers and have no job security; they lack freedom of association and have no pension rights. This has led to a high turnover rate in EDUCO schools, because teachers leave for official positions whenever they have the chance.

Over the past decades, EDUCO has become the main schooling option for approximately 80 per cent of the municipalities in extreme poverty

(UNESCO 2009, p. 153), enrolling around 50 per cent of all children in rural areas (World Bank 2003). With EDUCO, the total enrolment has increased from 76 per cent to 83 per cent (Gropello 2006), and internationally EDUCO has gained recognition for its promises to be the *best policy option*. It was honoured with the World Bank's Presidential Award for Excellence (1997) and considered a successful programme by the IADB (Cuéllar-Marchelli 2003, p. 156). The World Bank states that 'the EDUCO model [...] has been successful in improving efficiency and effectiveness as a result of strong leadership and government commitment, consensus-building across communities, teacher unions and opposition leaders, and a culture of institutional and pedagogical innovation.' (2005, pp. 118–19). Nevertheless, in spite of the fact that teachers spend more time in schools, this has not resulted in promoting higher achievement scores (Sawada *et al.* 2005; Barrera-Osorio *et al.* 2009).

Criticism of EDUCO

The claim that EDUCO is based on the experiences of popular education in rural areas during the 1980s has been questioned by many. Reimers (1997) mentions that EDUCO was perceived as a policy to neutralize the network of popular teachers, who identified with the opposition. Moncada-Davidson (1995, p. 65) states that in communities EDUCO was seen as an imposition by the government attempting to weaken the political power they had gained during the 1980s and as 'a strategy to propagate the government's political and economic ideology to the population' (Moncada-Davidson 1995, p. 68). Moreover, EDUCO was established disproportionately in the conflict-ridden areas of the eastern part of the country, in spite of the fact that there were higher percentages of out-of-school children in the western part of the country. Thus it can be argued that the experiences of popular education have merely been used as a discursive justification.

Cuéllar-Marchelli considers EDUCO to be a 'very particular privatisation strategy, through which "not-for-profit parents" associations are contracted to administer schools financed by the state' (2003, p. 146). These parents are the only ones not paid within the education system, while the amount of time parents of one school would spend on administration and training was 576 hours per year. The sum of parent labour constitutes 805 full-time jobs, representing 28 per cent of the work done by all the MINED staff (Cuéllar-Marchelli 2003, p. 159). Thus if parents' time investment had been included in the unit costs in 1993, the cost of official public schools and EDUCO schools would be the same (World Bank 1994, p. 48).

These labour donations *are* paid by the poorest parents as EDUCO schools operate in the most disadvantaged areas. Only 39 per cent of EDUCO children's households have electricity and 18 per cent have piped water; 70 per cent of their households do not have built floors and only

3 per cent have sanitary services available. This contrasts with official public schools' households of which 71 per cent have electricity; 37 per cent have piped water and 51 per cent of their houses have built floors (Cuéllar-Marchelli 2003, p. 158). In 2006, nearly 90 per cent of the EDUCO parents were working in the agricultural sector, two-thirds of whom work as day labourers under very precarious conditions in terms of income and access to social services. These parents have very low levels of education as more than 50 per cent have had less than three years of schooling (Briones 2007, p. 14). However, as EDUCO is the only option, it makes the poorest parents work *voluntarily* to guarantee some education for their children.

The best organized opposition against EDUCO has come from the teachers union ANDES that opposed the programme from the beginning as a move to privatize education and to eliminate job security and tenureship. The many teacher strikes have demanded free education for all, an increase in educational investment, an increase in salaries and the unification of the labour conditions for all teachers (Polo 2007, pp. 99–100)[20].

To sum up, as in Nicaragua, EDUCO can be deemed to be part of a much broader USAID and World Bank driven socio-economic and political reform. USAID financed the neoliberal think tanks, such as FUSADES and FEPADE, which together with MINED and USAID itself have been strategic in the development of EDUCO. The EDUCO reform has a clear political and ideological framework; it is *finance-driven* as it locates the highest cost for education with the poorest families. It introduces top-down structures of technical *participation* of the poorest parents. Furthermore, it establishes *market mechanisms* in education with the introduction of per pupil financing and the outsourcing of intermediate services to the private sector. EDUCO is also part of a political strategy to undermine popular forms of education and to marginalize the teachers and communities involved. It is not surprising that as soon as the new FMLN government came to power in 2009 and the former teacher and ANDEN union leader, Salvador Sánchez Cerén, was appointed Minister of Education, steps were taken to abolish EDUCO.

Comparing the ASP in Nicaragua and EDUCO in El Salvador

Both SBM reforms were introduced after a decade-long *low-intensity-war* that was supported by the US to keep the CA region open for their free-market interests and to oppose any initiative that would endeavour to redress the highly unequal socio-economic order. In Nicaragua, the educational gains at all levels of the education system during the 1980s were countered by neoliberal shock therapy to wipe out the Sandinista legacy and to introduce a conservative ideology. The highly successful adult education system was abolished and the main strategy to restructure the education system was the introduction of the ASP in secondary and primary education. In El Salvador, the EDUCO programme was introduced in parallel to the existing official public system to promote educational services in rural and war-affected areas. Both educational reforms aimed at undermining and sidelining any form of civil society collective action, by replacing it with a system of vertically delegated management responsibilities to parent councils. In Nicaragua, the ASP reform was mainly concentrated within the MINED, from the central offices to the municipalities and then directly in the school councils. In El Salvador, the EDUCO office would directly fund the school councils, while the intermediate education services were outsourced to the private sector. The functions of the school councils in both SBMPs coincide, giving not-for-profit parents the responsibility to administer the budget, raise extra funds and to hire, fire and control teachers.

Following nearly two decades of implementation of these internationally celebrated SBMPs, enrolments show expansion in the first years of primary school while the equity and quality of the education system is especially worrying. According to the latest statistics, enrolments up to the fifth grade have increased to 95 per cent. However, only 69 per cent of all students in El Salvador and just 50 per cent in Nicaragua will survive to the last grade of primary education (UNESCO 2009). In the field of quality, the second regional study of LLECE (2008) shows that both countries are among the least performing in terms of learning outcomes in Latin America[21]. They show poor achievement in language and mathematics in grades 3 and 6, with only two out of ten students reaching the high level in El Salvador and Nicaragua, while in Cuba and Uruguay this accounts for 75 per cent of students.

The figures are also characterized by deep inequalities; rural urban differences in performance are more than double in El Salvador, to the disadvantage of the rural students of whom 50 per cent are enrolled in EDUCO. An urban student has a six time better chance of achieving at the highest level. In Nicaragua, there are huge disparities in wealth, revealing a difference of seven years of education between the richest and the poorest households from 9.2 to 2.2 years (UNESCO 2009, p. 74), reflecting the great inequalities in financial capacities of families to contribute to the education of their children.

Thus nearly two decades of school-based reform has delivered neither quality nor equity in education. The low achievement reflects the low investments in SBMPs and the high costs for the poorest population. Probably the political and socio-economic motives behind the programmes are likely to account for these meagre results, as the labour market for the agricultural and the manufacturing sector in the region mainly calls for a cheap and low-skilled labour force and not a well educated population.

Conclusion

This chapter can be taken as a post-analysis of the origins, objectives, outcomes and the main stakeholders involved in the SBMPs in Central America, as the ASP and EDUCO programmes were abolished shortly after the FSLN and the FMLN governments came to power in 2007 and 2009.

The first and most radical forms of SBM in the Global South emerged under the very specific contextual conditions of CA. El Salvador was the main testing ground for the political and economic restructuring of society, and USAID was the key sponsor behind these major changes. During the 1980s, USAID started to build a new framework of allies in the region through the creation and support of new right-wing private sector organisations at national and local level: from the creation of the social economic think tank FUSADES, to directly involving private enterprise within the education sector through FEPADE. These *soft* policies of stimulating private sector organisations worked in unison with the US-backed Salvadorian armed forces that fought the *hard* battle by terrorising all civil society organisations that were thought to be associated with the FMLN opposition. In Nicaragua, during the same period, the US financed a Contra War to destabilize the Sandinista government, which led to the right-wing UNO government in 1990. Accompanying this change, USAID developed a counter strategy to break down all the vestiges of the successful public Sandinista education system. In addition, the enormous debt burden created much leverage for the reinforcement of economic and political conditionality according to the Washington Consensus.

Within this context, USAID stimulated the development of the most radical SBMPs, and the World Bank took up its financing, at times jointly with the IADB. USAID continued their further involvement through the funding of the SABE project in El Salvador and BASE in Nicaragua, addressing the most problematic sectors of the education system. Moreover, USAID, jointly with the World Bank, the IADB and some private US Foundations, supported the creation of a regional neoliberal think-tank called Partnership for Educational Revitalization in the Americas (PREAL) in 1995. This has become, as is stated, 'the strongest private voice on education in Latin America to build a new constituency for education reform.' (PREAL 2011). Regionally, PREAL works in close collabouration with national organisations like FUSADES and FEPADE and, in Nicaragua, with EDUQUEMOS and FUNIDES, as well as with similar organisations in Guatemala, Honduras, Panama and Costa Rica. At the same time, it has intimate relations with Washington-based global stakeholders. This powerful network of think-tanks and aid agencies is consolidating a long-term neoliberal influence through its presence within the educational sector with policy advice, the financing of research and the organisation of seminars[22].

This multi-scalar financial and discursive power explains why the EDUCO model has been promoted in the Global South as a *best practice*, arguing that the project was built on the experience of at least 500 community-run schools. At the local level, these celebrated SBMPs turn out to be much less *empowering for communities* than has been claimed. In fact, EDUCO opposes everything popular community schools had fought for. The popular experiences were participatory and communitarian, it was education 'of, by and for the people', with voluntary teachers fostering a political and emancipatory vision of education through collective participation in the struggle for social and economic justice. EDUCO is the mirror opposite of these popular experiences as it was used to neutralize or weaken the power of these communities, their teachers, as well as the teacher unions.

These SBMPs should be analysed as part of top-down decentralisation and privatisation strategies that have focussed on the depoliticisation of socio-economic relations and on the building of new forms of socio-economic co-existence at the local level. *Participation* only includes parents of children that attend the school, and thus the broader *community* is not included. The participation of these parents is controlled through a strongly regulated form of decision-making in each school, and non-compliance with rules and regulations can lead to the withdrawal of educational funding. The direct financing of individual school councils makes it hard to organize collectively and to formulate alternative proposals for changing the policies. It is the poverty of parents that keeps them hooked to EDUCO and ASP as it is the only option of guaranteeing at least some form of education for their children. In practice, these SBMPs contradict the title of the 2004 World Bank Development Report 'Making Services Work for Poor People', as in this case *the poorest parents have paid the highest price to make the educational services work for their children.*

Notes

1 Mainly in Anglo-Saxon countries like the US, UK, Australia and New Zealand.

2 In 1996, the SBM PRONADE programme was implemented in Guatemala. For a contextual analysis, see Poppema, M. 2009. It was followed in 1999 by PROHECO in Honduras.

3 Fourteen families in El Salvador and, in Nicaragua, the Somoza family was the main owner of most of the arable land.

4 Like the 1954 CIA-backed military coup in Guatemala against the democratic nationalist president Jacobo Arbenz in order to stop a moderate land reform.

5 The party was named after Augusto César Sandino who led the Nicaraguan resistance against the US occupation in the 1930s.

6 The US secret involvement in Nicaragua, 'the Iran-Contra Affair', became a

major political scandal in 1986, when it was discovered that President Reagan had permitted the CIA to use the profits from the sale of illegal arms to Iran to finance the Contra military forces in Nicaragua. In 1986, the International Court of Justice (ICJ) ruled in favour of Nicaragua and against the US, which was judged to have violated international law by supporting Contra guerrillas. The US did not recognize the jurisdiction of the ICJ and, after 1991, the new UNO government withdrew the complaint (Posner, E.A.2004).

7 At the beginning of the 1990s, the USAID mission became the largest in the world, staffed with over 300 diplomats. Since then, USAID has provided Nicaragua with over US$2 billion in assistance.

8 The term 'popular' education was widespread in Latin America. Generally speaking, it means that education is the right of all (especially the peasant and working classes) and that 'educación popular' should be constructed with active and conscious political participation and the mobilisation of mass organisations (Carnoy et al. 1990).

9 An altruistic, cooperative, critically conscious and participatory citizen, motivated by collective goals.

10 In 1984 alone, 98 teachers were killed and 171 were kidnapped (Prevost 1987).

11 The salary benefit could range somewhere from 0 to 50 per cent for secondary schools and from 0 to 30 per cent for primary schools.

12 'After the invasion the US soldiers and officers are increasingly moving to a Salvador-style advisory role' (Maass 2005).

13 The 'Reagan administration didn't leave any space for left-wing organisations out of fear of an "inevitable" communist takeover' (Nelson 2008).

14 From 1984 to 1992, USAID contributed US$150 million to FUSADES alone.

15 ANDES 21 claims that during the war 376 teachers were killed, 106 disappeared and 500 were jailed (Alvear Galindo 2002).

16 Many Catholic priests were inspired by 'liberation theology' and supported popular education. They also suffered from the repression; most well-known was the killing of Archbishop Oscar Romero in 1980.

17 According to Robinson (2003), the US(AID) intervention, jointly with FUSADES, was able to create a consensus of the private sector and civil society for the new economic and political model. This made it possible for ARENA to continue until the current global economic crisis.

18 From the Spanish 'Asociación Comunal para la Educación.'

19 This in contrast to the 50-year contract that FEPADE obtained in 1990 to manage a post-secondary technical institution (ITCA).

20 As teacher salaries had fallen by 50 per cent during the period 1984–92 while the per capita income rose by 5.4 per cent.

21 Jointly with Guatemala, Haiti and the Dominican Republic.

22 Many of the consultants of these think-tanks had high ministerial positions during the implementation period of the SBMPs, reflecting a sort of revolving door between the Ministries and these private sector organisations.

References

Alvear Galindo, V. (2002), 'La Educación Popular en Morazán, El Salvador, durante la Guerra Civil de 1981 a 1992: ¿Parte de una Estrategia de Supervivencia?', PhD thesis, Freie Universität, Berlin.

Amnesty International (2001), *El Salvador: Peace can only be Achieved with Justice*. London: Amnesty International, AMR 29/001/2001.

Arnove, R. F. (1994), *Education as Contested Terrain: Nicaragua, 1979–1993*. Boulder: Westview Press.

—(1995), 'Education as contested terrain in Nicaragua', *Comparative Education Review*, 39, (1), 28–53.

Barrera-Osorio, F., Fasih, T., Patrinos, H. A. and Santibáñez, L. (2009), *Decentralized Decision-Making in Schools. The Theory and Evidence on School-Based Management*. Washington DC: Directions in Development – Human Development, World Bank

Briones, C. (2007), *EDUCO y Capital Social Comunitario: una agenda nueva para el desarrollo local*. San Salvador: FLACSO.

Carnoy, M. and Torres, C. A. (1990), 'Education and social transformation in Nicaragua 1979–1989', in M. Carnoy and J. Samoff (eds), *Education and Social Transition in the Third World*. New Jersey: Princeton University Press, pp. 315–55.

Cook, T. D. (2007), 'School-based management: a concept of modest entitivity with modest results'. *Journal of Personnel Evaluation in Education*, 20, 129–45.

Cuéllar-Marchelli, H. (2003), 'Decentralization and privatization of education in El Salvador: assessing the experience', *International Journal of Educational development*, 23, (2), 145–66.

Foley, M. W. (1996), 'Laying the groundwork: the struggle for civil society in El Salvador'. *Journal of interamerican studies and world affairs*, 38, (1), 67–104.

Forsberg, N. R. D. (2007), 'School autonomy in Nicaragua: two case studies', in H. Daun ed., *School decentralization in the context of globalizing governance*. Dordrecht: Singer, pp. 95–114.

Fuller, B. and Rivarola, M. (1998), *Nicaragua's experiment to decentralize schools: views of parents, teachers, and directors*, Washington, DC: World Bank. World Bank Working Paper no. 5, Impact Evaluation of Education Reforms.

Gershberg, A. I. (1999), 'Decentralization, citizen participation, and the role of the state – the autonomous schools programme in Nicaragua'. *Latin American Perspectives*, 26, (4), 8–38.

Gershberg A. I. and Meade B. (2005), 'Parental contributions, school-level finances and decentralization: an analysis of Nicaraguan autonomous school budgets'. *Comparative Education*, 41, (3), 291–308.

Gropello E. di (2004), *Education decentralization and accountability relationships in Latin America*, Washington, DC: World Bank. World Bank Policy Research Working Paper 3453/2004.

—(2006), *A comparative analysis of school-based management in Central America*, Washington, DC: World Bank. Working Paper 72/2006.

Hammond, J. L. (1999), 'Popular education as community organizing in El Salvador'. *Latin American Perspectives*, 26, (4), 69–94.

Jimenez, E. and Sawada, Y. (1999), 'Do community-managed schools work? An evaluation of El Salvador's EDUCO program'. *World Bank Economic Review*, 13, (3), 415–41.

—(2003), *Does community management help keep kids in schools? Evidence using panel data from El Salvador's EDUCO program*, Washington, DC: World Bank. World Bank Discussion Paper CIRJEF–236.

Kurtenbach, S. (2010), 'Why is liberal peace-building so difficult? Some lessons from Central America'. *European Review of Latin American and Caribbean Studies*, 88, 95–110.

La Belle, T. J. (1986), *Nonformal Education in Latin America and the Caribbean: Stability, Reform or Revolution?* New York: Praeger.

LLECE (2008), *Los Aprendizajes de los Estudiantes de América Latina y el Caribe. Primer Reporte de los Resultados del Segundo Estudio Regional Comparativo y Explicativo*. Santiago de Chile: UNESCO-OREALC

Maass, P. (2005), 'The way of the commandos'. *New York Times* [Online], 1 May. Available at: www.nytimes.com/2005/05/01/magazine/01ARMY.html (Accessed: 16 May 2011).

McEwan, P. J. and Trowbridge, M. (2007), 'The achievement of indigenous students in Guatemalan primary schools'. *International Journal of Educational Development*, 27, (1), 61–76.

Meza, D., Guzmán, J. L. and De Varela, L. (2004), 'EDUCO: a community-managed education programme in rural El Salvador (1991–2003)'. *En Breve*, 51, 30731, 1–4.

Moncada-Davidson, L. (1995), 'Education and its limitations in the maintenance of peace in El Salvador'. *Comparative Education Review*, 39, (1), 54–75.

Nelson, M. G. (2008), 'The Durability of Cultural Influences: How American Foreign Policy Reinforced Historical Biases in El Salvador.' Monograph – Army command and general staff Coll. Fort Leavenworth Ks School of Advanced Military Studies. oai.dtic.mil/oai/oai?verb=getRecord&metadataPrefix=html&id entifier=ADA485562 (Accessed 18 May 2011).

Paris, R. (2002), 'Peacebuilding in Central America: reproducing the sources of conflict?' *InternationalPeacekeeping*, 9, (4), 39–68.

Pearce, J. (1998), 'From civil war to 'civil society': has the end of the Cold War brought peace to Central America?' *International Affairs*, 74, (3), 587–615.

—(1999), 'Peace-building in the periphery: lessons from Central America.' *Third World Quarterly*, 20, (1), 51–68.

Picón, C., Montenegro, J. J. and Poppema, M. (1994), *Informe de la misión de evaluación del proyecto UNESCO/Países Bajos/519/Nic/10*, Managua: Dutch Ministry of Foreign Affairs, UNESCO and the Ministry of Education in Nicaragua.

Polo, P. (2007), 'Una mirada a Centroamérica: la educación en El Salvador, Honduras y Guatemala', in P. Polo and A. Verger (eds), *Globalización y Desigualdades Educativas*. Palma: Escola de Formació en Mitjans Didàctics, pp. 86–129.

Poppema, M. (2009), 'Guatemala, the Peace Accords and education: a post-conflict struggle for equal opportunities, cultural recognition and participation in education', *Globalisation, Societies & Education*, 7, (4), 383–408.

Posner, E. A. (2004), *The Decline of the International Court of Justice*, Chicago: University of Chicago Law & Economics. Olin Working Paper 233/2004.

PREAL – Programa de Promoción de la Reforma Educativa de America Latina y el Caribe (2011), Available at: www.preal.org/ (Accessed: 10 April 2011).

Quan, A. (2005), 'Through the looking glass: U.S. aid to El Salvador and the politics of national identity', *American Ethnologist* 32, (2), 276–93.

Reimers, F. (1997), 'The role of the community in expanding educational opportunities: the EDUCO schools in El Salvador', in J. Lynch, C. Modgil and S. Modgil (eds), *Education and Development: Tradition and Innovation*. London: Cassell, pp. 146–62

Robinson, W. I. (2003), *Transnational Conflicts: Central America, Social Change, and Globalization*. London: Verso.

Sawada, Y. (1999), *Community participation, teacher effort, and educational outcome: the case of El Salvador's EDUCO program*, Washington, DC: World Bank. Development Research Group Working Paper 307/1999.

Sawada, Y. and Ragatz, A. B. (2005), 'Decentralization of education, teacher behavior, and outcomes the case of El Salvador's EDUCO program', in E. Vegas ed., *Incentives to Improve Teaching Lessons from Latin America*, Washington, DC: World Bank, pp. 255–306

Schwarz, B. C. (1991), *American counter insurgency doctrine and El Salvador: the frustrations of reform and the illusions of nation building*, Santa Mónica, CA: RAND

Sepp, K. I. (2005), 'Best practices in counter insurgency'. *Military Review*, May–June, 8–12.

UNESCO (2009), *EFA Global Monitoring Report 'Overcoming Inequality: Why Governance Matters'*. Paris: UNESCO.

—(2011), *EFA Global Monitoring Report 'The Hidden Crisis: Armed Conflict and Education'*. Paris: UNESCO.

USAID (2010), *The Power of Persistence. Education System Reform and Aid Effectiveness Case Studies in Long-Term Education Reform*. Washington DC: USAID.

World Bank (1981), *Nicaragua Basic Education Project. Staff Appraisal Report*, Washington DC: World Bank Latin America and Caribbean Regional Office.

—(1994), *El Salvador Community Education Strategy: Decentralized School Management*. Washington DC. World Bank. Report 13502–ES.

—(2003), 'El Salvador: participation in macroeconomic policy making and reform', *Social Development Notes*, March, 79.

—(2004), 'EDUCO: A community-managed education programme in rural El Salvador (1991–2003)', *En Breve*, June, 51, 1–4.

—(2005), *Education Sector Strategy Update* 'Achieving Education For All, Broadening our Perspective, Maximizing our Effectiveness', Presented to the Board of Directors on November 17.

—(2007), Impact Evaluation for School-Based Management Reform. Doing Impact Evaluation, nr. 10. Washington.

—(2008a), *What is School-Based Management? Education – Human Development Network*. Washington DC: IBRD.

—(2008b), *What Do We Know About School-Based Management?* Washington: IBRD . Education-Human Development Network.

—(2011), *School-Based Management*. [Online] Available at: go.worldbank. org/9EX3ZU6O90 (Accessed 9 March 2011).

CHAPTER NINE

Ethnic/Racial Diversity and Education Policy: The Role of the Black Movement and Multi-Scalar Processes within the Public Agenda in Brazil

Renato Emerson dos Santos and
Inti Soeterik

Introduction

During the first decade of the twenty-first century, policies to combat racism and racial inequalities have emerged in Brazil in a range of fields, and this has been especially visible in education. Throughout almost the entire twentieth century, Brazil officially claimed to be a 'racial democracy', and these policies appeared to be (or were based on) a negation of this idea. This chapter will examine the relationship between this emergence and global processes of constructing and disseminating anti-racist agendas, including in the realm of education.

In Brazil, the decisive protagonist role within the emergence process of a national public policy agenda against racial inequality is currently subject to intense debate. A longstanding explanation in Brazil (as part of the ideology of racial democracy itself) claims that these policies, known as 'affirmative action', are the fruit of artificially copying or importing an agenda developed in the United States. This explanation appears in the famous article entitled 'As Artimanhas da Razão Imperialista' ('On the Cunning of Imperialist Reason'), written by Pierre Bourdieu and Loïc

Wacquant (2002). These authors point to North American 'new imperialism' (through cooperative foundations and agencies) as a vector of the exportation of agendas, translating a comprehension of US race relations that is incompatible with the historic pattern of development in Brazil, where 'race' does not make sense. These arguments have strongly influenced Brazilian social thought as they offer a line of reasoning for how such international agendas, actors and processes are imposed on intranational agendas, actors and processes.

This chapter proposes two critiques of this perspective. Firstly, the 'imperialist import' explanation leads to a reflection on the processes of forming scales. In this argument, scales are understood as fields, arenas and spheres of power wherein political behaviour defines plans, practices and uses of and within a territory, while indicating a certain relation of primacy between them: the global (American imperialism) imposing itself on the national using its 'cunning.' In other words, scales are seen as distinct, separate 'levels', with independent logic and a hierarchical relationship between them. This chapter proposes then a critique on this understanding of scale. Secondly, we argue that the aforementioned perspective overrates the role of international organisations (so-called 'global actors') and overlooks the existence of the historic struggles of social movements, in this case that of the Black Movement in Brazil, as if it were not a causal force in the emergence of racial policies. Therefore another aim of this chapter is to discuss the role of this specific social movement in these developments.

With these objectives in mind, first the approach to the concept of 'scale' adopted in the chapter will be explained, pointing to the importance of understanding multi- and inter-scalar processes while investigating the emergence of race-based public policies[1] in Brazil. Then in the second section, the focus will turn to a discussion on the emergence of the national public policy agenda against ethnic/racial inequality in Brazil, offering a brief historic overview. The key role of the Brazilian Black Movement (BBM) on different scales will be highlighted, introducing the concept of 'area of movement.' In the third part, the relation between the emergence of ethnic/race issues in public policies in Brazil and on the global agenda will be examined critically. In so doing, the process of the World Conference Against Racism, Racial Discrimination, Xenophobia and Related Intolerance (WCAR) held in Durban, South Africa, in 2001 under the auspices of the United Nations will be discussed as an example of how the BBM used a 'politics of scales.' This process is considered especially interesting as it was characterized by the widespread participation of both official and civil society delegations from Brazil and all around the world in both the conference, parallel events and the preparatory process. To strengthen the argument that events and actions on a global scale have not played a significant direct role on the shaping of anti-racist education policies in Brazil, we subsequently discuss two World Bank documents and analyse the rationales and frameworks on ethnicity/race issues of this international organization. In the fourth and final section, in order to attempt to identify which global and local factors have contributed to the emergence and reinforcement of this agenda in Brazil, the applicability, in this case of concepts such as the 'boomerang effect', 'short-circuit', 'jumping scales' and 'embedding-disembedding' of scales of politics, is discussed.

Multi-Scale Processes and the Definition of Political Agendas

Scale is a concept that lies at the heart of understanding the contemporary world. The almost omnipresent use of the idea of globalization to explain phenomena and processes in a wide variety of areas brings scale to the centre of many narratives. The idea of globalization is in itself a scale-based narrative, pointing to scalar redefinition of processes. When the idea of 'thinking globally and acting locally' is proposed, this implies redefining scalar relationships in organising strategies and actions. Accordingly, one increasingly speaks of relations between the global, regional, national and local in order to understand recent processes and transformations. However, this raises a number of questions. The way in which one understands the concept of scale has itself a major influence on constructing explanations for phenomena. There is a current tendency to view things in a manner dissociated from preconceived and reified scales interrelating hierarchically (see Lacoste 1988).

The traditional vision of scalar ordering in the world, based on relations of contiguity, hierarchy and articulation, considers that a set of locations forms a region, a set of regions forms a country, a set of countries forms a continent and a set of continents forms the world. The emerging image is always somehow similar: spatial groups or entities relating and uniting to form new groups or entities on another scale. Each scale would correspond to a 'level of aggregation', which could be identified whenever the problem or phenomenon observed undergoes significant changes through redefining the size of the spatial area. This representation leads to the perception of these levels of aggregation, which are scales thought of as articulated 'spatial levels' but are in essence differentiated and dissociated. This is because the metaphor of the level (as a vertical overlapping of different horizontal planes) constructs an image of hierarchy and the subordination of spatial scales: each level is formed by the summation and embedding of territorial divisions on the scale immediately below in terms of area covered. This world appears, therefore, as the result of the 'embedding' of scales (Vainer 2001).

It has become clear that this hierarchical model of the world that dissociates scales and thereby makes processes and actors autonomous (making local processes and actors separate from others that are called national or global, for example) is insufficient. The very idea of scale needs to be revised. Scale is a social construction based on power relations; it is a container of power. In this sense, scale, as a heuristic instrument, enables levels of analysis of the real to be distinguished; yet, in the real, such levels are not levels, but rather simultaneities – of social actors, objects and actions that construct geographic space (Santos R. E. 2006).

What justifies scalar narratives is, in fact, the assertion that phenomena, as interrelated simultaneities, have impacts and effects on distinct environments and spatial units. Local, regional, national and global are in the same place, so that elements (actors, processes, phenomena and objects) are multi-scalar, with one scale influenced by other phenomena within other scales. This is the magic (and the importance) of the scalar organisation of political relations: it enables actors, relations, processes and phenomena that co-exist in space to be ordered so as to establish systems of domination and power. This is true both when one considers scale as a heuristic instrument (that explains the world while valuing the global over the local, the universal over the specific, and consequently that which one wishes to affirm as global/universal and that which one wishes to criticize as local/specific: see Santos B. S. 2004) and as the organisation of the experiences of individuals, groups and social actors, which are hierarchically ordered, and included in or excluded from power games.

The scalarity of political games is therefore related to the hierarchy of social actors, of arenas in which they participate and of contexts of interaction that serve or do not serve as arenas. It is also clearly related to legitimations and exclusions imposed on social actors in each 'scale.' It is thereby understood as an ordered power game, with defined spatial coverage, recognized actors (and others not recognized), its own rules and standards of conduct and specific objects of dispute. To be a global actor, one must be recognized globally by other actors, cause global impact, and be capable of engaging in dialogue and imposing one's projects in environments where others are not able to. Despite this, what has become increasingly clear is that social actors 'confined' to local or national scales have learned to manipulate and use this form of scalar organisation of power games. That is how expressions such as 'jumping scales' (Swyngedouw 1997), 'disembedding' and 're-embedding' (Giddens 1991), unpredicted linkages or 'short circuits' (Silveira 1996) and 'boomerang effect'[2] have arisen.

This multiplicity of terms shows the diversity of ways in which subordinate social actors use the 'scales of politics' to produce a 'politics of scales.' When speaking of 'cross-border activism' or multinationals, therefore, one must consider that this means more than 'going beyond' the national, but rather articulating a variety of scales (national, global, regional and local) and mobilising other actors, resources (financial, legal, etc.) and processes allocated in a power-scaled order.

In the case of the emergence of race issues in Brazil, we propose that it is most appropriate to think in terms of a 'politics of scales' of the Black Movement, given that, at different times and in different spaces, it is this movement that has been at the forefront in constructing, maintaining and imposing the agenda. There has been no international pressure, nor intra-national pressure, but rather the mobilisation of resources and processes by the social movement on different scales, and the use of processes on different scales as a justification for the Black Movement to strengthen the racial agenda. The value of thinking in terms of 'politics of scales' is that this concept enables a combination of the complexity of political games organized in multi-scale form and an emphasis on the leading role played by the social movement in creating and maintaining the agenda in the public debate and the spheres of social coordination.

It can be observed that a large share of the public policies that were initiated in the twenty-first century had been demanded and fought for by the Black Movement for a long time, and that some had already been implemented as public policies by municipal and state governments in previous decades. Therefore it is interesting, in our view, to investigate the role of the internal leadership of the Black Movement (on the local, regional and national scale) vis-à-vis global dynamics of policy dissemination, including with regard to policies on diversity and multiculturalism.

The Emergence of Race on the Education Agenda in Brazil

The incorporation of race issues as a foundation for education policies has been intensely debated over the last ten years in Brazil. Some policies, such as that of reserving quotas for black people at universities, have provoked some of the most controversial debates seen recently in the country. Within the framework of the development of anti-racism policies in several sectors[3], and developments such as the establishment of a Secretary for Racial Equality (SEPPIR) in 2003, and the creation of more than one hundred municipal and state bodies of a similar kind, the field that has experienced the most profound changes is that of education.

The two main areas in which race-based policies are being created in the Brazilian education system are (i) access to higher education and (ii) the combating of racism in the school environment. Starting in 2003, quotas have now been implemented at approximately forty universities throughout the country. In addition, the Ministry of Education is providing scholarships for black students to attend private universities, and both national government and some state and municipal governments are funding university admission preparatory courses for black and socio-economically disadvantaged youngsters. Furthermore, the Ministry of Education is funding university institutes and groups researching issues related to racial inequality. In terms of combating racism in education institutions, in 2003, Law 10.639 was approved that modified the Law of Guidelines and Foundations for National Education (MEC 1996). This law defined the teaching of issues related to ethnicity/race, African and Afro-Brazilian history and culture, and the inclusion of contents on the contributions of the BBM's struggles over the course of history as obligatory.

The construction of this agenda has involved historic struggles of the BBM on different scales, as well as international processes and actors more recently. These multi-scale processes are examined in this chapter. However, first the context wherein race issues started to emerge in Brazil will be briefly discussed. In our view, such information is key to understanding the internal processes in Brazil which contributed to these developments.

New Forms of Social Coordination in Brazil of the 1980s and 1990s

In this section we will argue that it is the emergence process of new forms of social coordination (Lechner 1997) that led to the incorporation of new agendas by the Brazilian state. In addition, we point to the key role played by the BBM as responsible for the strengthening of the anti-racist agenda. The emergence of new forms of social coordination can be understood when considering important factors which influenced Brazilian society, such as the re-democratisation process in the 1980s and the spread of neoliberal ideas and policies in the 1990s.

First of all, the emergence of race as a foundation on which to construct public policies in Brazil has to be understood as part of transformations in the relation between the state and civil society in recent decades. Starting in the late 1970s, Brazilian society experienced a process of re-democratisation, which culminated in the transition from the military regime to democracy in 1985. This process of democratisation generated the need to form social coalitions as an alternative to hegemonic forces and made it possible for social struggles to emerge. New social movements were organized, new mechanisms were created to represent sectors of civil society within the structure of the executive power (Burity 2006, p. 70) and, while some of civil society's social demands began to find an environment conducive to the creation of public policies, new agendas promoted by social movements were incorporated by spheres of the state.

The 1980s also witnessed some crucial moments for the Black Movement's actions in the field of education. While during this period discussion on the theme of race relations was still taboo in many sectors of society, the centenary of the abolition of slavery in 1988 turned race into a national issue. In that same year, a new federal constitution was being drawn up. This created an environment in which it was possible for the Black Movement to set out grievances against and demands to the state. In the process of constructing the new constitution, the education agenda of the Black Movement was strengthened by initiatives such as the Black National Constitutional Convention, held in Brasilia in August 1986. As a result, the new constitution included, for the first time, the criminalisation of racial discrimination. Furthermore, a small portion of the movement's demands in relation to education was also incorporated in the 1988 Constitution.[4]

The activities of different organisations and actors in the Black Movement in the re-democratisation process also led some state and municipal governments to create councils, commissions, coordination boards and advisory posts in order to tackle issues of racism and racial inequality. Jaccoud *et al.* (2002) and Jaccoud (2008) point to the fact that in the 1980s these councils and advisory bodies created a base for dialogue and pressure for the Black Movement, culminating in the creation, at the federal level, of the *Fundação Cultural Palmares* in 1988, entrusted with the task of formulating and implementing public policies to promote the participation of the black population in development processes.

Specifically in the field of education, beginning at the end of the 1980s, politicians of diverse ideological tendencies in different states and municipalities across Brazil began to recognize the need to reformulate state and municipal instruments regulating the education system (Santos S. A. 2005, p. 25). Consequently, even before the federal government formulated national and regional policies in this area, various municipalities introduced measures to ban the use of textbooks that spread prejudice and racial discrimination, and initiatives were implemented to include the history of black people in Brazil and the history of the African continent in primary and secondary school curricula at state and municipal schools (Santos S. A. 2005, p. 26).

Thus far, the discussion highlights the importance of considering the multi-scale process of producing public education policies in Brazil for understanding the construction of anti-racism public policies in the 2000s. Initiated in the 1980s, this process was strengthened by other factors, such as the process surrounding the Durban Conference, which shall be discussed later on.

Besides a strengthening of democracy, the 1990s in Latin America were marked in the economic sphere by a deepening of the technical and scientific revolution, globalization and the spread of neoliberal ideas and policies. In this dispute, it is important to recognize the presence and influential role of international and regional agencies (such as the International Monetary Fund, the World Bank, the Inter-American Development Bank and the UN Economic Commission on Latin America and the Caribbean.) Accordingly, during this period, education changes, such as the creation in Brazil of the new Law of Guidelines and Foundations for National Education (MEC 1996), found logical coherence with the project of adjusting Brazilian society to the demands of the neoliberal agenda of multilateral agencies like the International Monetary Fund, the World Bank and the Inter-American

Development Bank. Reforms in the field of education, such as decentralisation, were characterized by objectives defined by an agenda that placed an emphasis on assessment, merit, private property and the rules of the market (Frigotto 2003; see also Frigotto *et al.* 2003; Sarubi 2005) and were therefore resisted by a significant number of social actors campaigning in the education field (such as labour unions, the school community, etc.).

Paradoxically, however, the neoliberal prescription in this period also involved creating channels for dialogue with private actors, including civil society, which enabled tensions to be established around the opening up of movement agendas (see also Burity 2006). It was in this context that it became possible for the state to recognize not only the social movements' agendas, but also the movements' (and their activists') capacity and store of experience and knowledge, which could be used to help formulate, implement and evaluate new policies. Consequently, despite domination by hegemonic forces, the state's sphere of social coordination was strengthened.

The multiple recognition of social movements by the state (recognition of both agendas and expertise) allowed the movements to perform functions inside (or alongside) the state as well as to provide parliamentary assistance. One example is the Inter-ministerial Working Group to Value the Black Population, created as a response to demands expressed during the Zumbi dos Palmares March Against Racism, For Citizenship and Life, the largest ever mobilisation of the BBM held in 1995 in Brasilia. This working group, formed by representatives from eight ministries, the Secretary for Social Communication of the Presidency of the Republic, and eight representatives from the BBM received the task of preparing policy proposals to combat racism and racial inequality. S. A. Santos (2005, p. 25) claims that some of the historic demands made by the Black Social Movement were granted by the Brazilian government in subsequent years. In relation to education, he mentions, for example, the policy of reviewing textbooks, with the elimination of those containing material representing or encouraging racial discrimination.

Although the participation of movements inside the state apparatus was intermittent and subject to the political, institutional and financial fragility in which many policies are created and implemented, the passage through the state apparatus of some militant leaders of social struggles helped build the knowledge and capacity of these movements, with activists gradually learning to deal with state bureaucracy and navigate the institutional and political intricacies in the formulation of public policies (see Alves dos Santos 2006). In the case of the BBM, Jaccoud (2008) points out that the creation of state and municipal councils to tackle racial inequalities and other issues faced by the black population starting in the 1980s acted as an agent to build and develop relations between this movement and the state. According to this author, the creation of the councils represented the first generation of affirmative action policies in Brazil, and had a major influence on ensuing events, culminating in the profusion of actions experienced in the 2000s (such as the enactment of the aforementioned Law 10.639 in 2003).

As becomes clear from the discussion above, it is in this period of the 1990s, a period marked by profound clashes between projects and distrust from a significant number of social actors campaigning in the education field, that concern for the race issue emerged. The fact that some factors and developments in this neoliberalising context facilitated the inclusion of race issues on the political (education) agenda in Brazil also strengthened negative reactions to it, as some education militants pointed to this development as another item in the neoliberal prescription. One of the challenges in the effort to understand this process is then, in our view, to demonstrate that these are not developments created 'from the top down' or 'from the outside to the inside' but, in the first instance, are the fruit of the Black Movement's historic struggles in the field of education.

The Brazilian Black Movement and the Construction of an Anti-Racist Education Agenda

As stated in the introduction to this section, education has always been an active battlefield for the Black Movement. Demands in relation to education already featured on the agenda of Black Movement initiatives such as the statute of the *Frente Negra Brasileira* (the Brazilian Black Front), created in 1931. This struggle intensified after the Black Social Movement underwent transformations – for example, with the creation of *Movimento Negro Unificado* (the Unified Black Movement) in 1978 – as the military dictatorship weakened and Brazil entered the re-democratisation process. To understand the role of the BBM in the emergence of race-based public policies, as well as the new forms of social coordination that emerged in Brazil in the 1980s and 1990s, it is also necessary to consider processes internal to the movement. Two of these processes are highlighted in this section: the transformation of the forms of collective social action; and the redefinition of priority and hegemonic foci in the fight against racism.

The Black Movement is characterized by a multiplicity of forms of action, as it is composed of many participants linked to entities of different natures (for example, political, social or cultural), acting in different forms of institutionalisation, operating in different ways (individual or collective, more or less formal, more or less autonomous, more or less continuous, etc.). Recognising the fact that, at various times there have indeed been attempts to build a national entity to bring together all initiatives, the BBM, beyond an 'entity', needs to be seen as a specific kind of social struggle in which different forms of action (individual and collective) are mixed. These multiple forms act and engage in dialogue in various spaces: there are local, regional, national and supranational entities and forums; there are actors that participate in actions on different scales; and there are actors (individual and collective, institutionalized and informal) that communicate with local, regional and national entities, among others. In a country such as Brazil, with a political and administrative structure comprising three levels (federal, state and municipal)[5] and with a history marked by a federalism that oscillates between federal centralisation, autonomy for state governments and municipal localism, an understanding of the spatiality of actors is of great importance. Their spatiality will determine what dialogues are possible, and this in turn leads to varying correlations and possibilities of power. In the case of the Black Movement in Brazil, there are individuals, groups and entities acting and interacting in power relations on the full range of scales, from local to supranational. Such interactions at the supranational scale include, for example, meetings of black parliamentarians of the Americas and the Caribbean held in 2003 and 2004, as well as the 'Durban Process' activities that we will discuss in the next section.

From this perspective, the BBM resembles an 'area of movement', a set of forms of action constituting a field for dialogue, which moves in a direction that is the result of interrelated stances taken by (and public demands made by) its actors (Melucci 1994). According to Burity (2001), this concept endeavours to:

> [...] provide empirical concreteness to the study of these multiple actors that are usually described as social movements. The areas would correspond to fields for **structuring** collective identities and spaces for **recomposing** identity (which would be continuously exposed to fragmentation in a complex society.) In this case, however, individuals and groups would find the area of movement to be a space in which to recompose the identity divided by multiple belonging and by the different periods and roles experienced in society (p. 18, emphasis by the author).

This interpretation enables us to undertake a unified analysis of all individuals and groups that take a stance and act against racism, and that present themselves in society as black, within a pluralist social movement called the Black Movement. Consequently, divisions and differences (in terms of organisation, activities and even plans) within the field should be understood as a sign of diversity within the unity.[6] Nevertheless, diversity does not imply an absence of hegemonies. In terms of the organisational format of action, it is worth highlighting the trend termed the 'NGO-isation' of the Black Movement (see Silva 2004). It is noted that this trend of NGO-isation is part of a process of steering collective action and diverse forms of activism, which uses relations with the state as a way of achieving its demands, plans and desires. This creates a political culture that values participation and establishes a sphere of social coordination via social networks directly related to social coordination via the state. In the present case, it enables the encounter of the neoliberal state with activist sectors and social movements that have grown in Latin America since the

1960s: in both the former and the latter, 'single' or 'local' experiences are valued and understood as concrete actions to combat society's problems.

Although the tendency of accommodating the Black Movement's activist sectors inside this form of structuring action may be open to criticism of many kinds (see Silva, op. cit.), it brought fundamental changes for the emergence of affirmative action in Brazil in the 2000s. First, NGO-isation strengthens the focus of anti-racism action in relation to the state, and increasingly holds the construction of public projects and policies as an objective. Secondly, NGO-type action 'professionalises' militant sectors so that, although they are now required to pursue resources to sustain their activism, at the same time they gain practical knowledge regarding the formulation, implementation and evaluation of policies, as well as the functioning of the state. The latter aspect is fundamental, since it extends militants' capabilities, enabling participants in the Black Movement to be prepared to operate together with and inside the state, insofar as the latter recognizes their agenda and initiates measures to introduce anti-racism policies. Consequently, recognition of the agenda is accompanied by recognition of expertise, allowing activists to be channelled into the different spaces for formulating and implementing policies within the diverse spheres of the state.

The processes inherent to the Black Movement described above – the transformation of the forms of collective social action and the redefinition of priority and hegemonic foci in the fight against racism – contributed to a new focus of the movement on the construction of public policies.

The Emergence of Ethnic/Race Issues in Brazil and the Global Agenda

In Brazil, there is a consensus that the emergence of public policies incorporating race issues originated to a large extent after the third World Conference Against Racism, Racial Discrimination, Xenophobia and Related Intolerance (WCAR) held in Durban in 2001. The often-cited explanation is that the Durban Conference was a moment in which nation states came together with civil society entities to discuss racism and, as such, were obliged to take a stance with regard to race relations. It is then argued that this moment saw a build-up in tension in the Brazilian state from which policies emerged.

We agree with the idea that the Durban Conference has proven fundamental in the recent process of inclusion of race issues in formulating education policies in Brazil. Promoted by the United Nations, it was an important arena of discussion on racial injustices and policies on a global scale. Nevertheless, we would like to highlight here that the main outcomes of the conference on the creation of public policies in Brazil were not due to the declaration signed by the Brazilian government, but much more to the actions (on local/municipal, regional/state and national scales) carried out by the BBM during the process that surrounded the Durban Conference (see also Santos *et al.* 2010). In this reading of the Durban conference, there was a complex multi- and inter-scalar process of strengthening and pressure, in which the Black Movement used the existence of a global occurrence to implement its local, regional and national agenda.

It therefore becomes necessary to view the Durban Conference not only as an *event*, a moment in time, in which a convention was signed and the Brazilian state complied with the international treaty to which it was a signatory. This perspective enables us to consider that it was the heightened tension in the global agenda that allowed the nation state to initiate policies against racism. Considering the Durban Conference and its subsequent consequences, we argue that the conference needs to be under-stood, for Brazil, as a *process*, something that was initiated beforehand, through regional conferences, a national conference and a preparatory South American conference. These conferences became opportunities to articulate and strengthen the Black Movement on various scales. Within this process of strengthening the movement and increasing pressure on the state on various scales (local/municipal, regional/state, as well as national), anti-racism agendas and policies were constructed and strengthened.

In Brazil, the preparatory phase of the Durban Conference was accom-panied by the organisation of civil society movements and cooperation between them and different state actors (such as the Ministry of Foreign Affairs and the Ministry of Justice) and civil society actors (such as social movements, particularly the Black Movement, and universities). Thereby leadership roles were given to new organisations such as the aforementioned Inter-Ministerial Working Group to Value the Black Population. The plural composition of the National Preparation Committee, including political parties, government representatives and representatives of non-govern-mental organisations, contributed to more in-depth discussions regarding priorities within the Brazilian state in relation to the conference. The preparatory process for the Durban Conference was seen by representatives of different social movements as a unique opportunity to incorporate issues related to the fight against racism and discrimination and the promotion of racial equality as priority items on the national political agenda. Also on a regional level, the creation of the Strategic Afro-Latin American and Caribbean Alliance Pro-Third World Conference Against Racism played an important role in the preparatory phase of the Durban Conference. It was this alliance that, together with other organisations, led to the Citizens' Conference Against Racism, Xenophobia, Intolerance and Discrimination, held in Santiago, Chile in December 2000.

However, when the manner in which national and regional agendas were included in the international Durban agenda is investigated, the complexity of international consensus on the theme of racism becomes apparent.

Albuquerque (2008) explains that the work of the UN Secretary who prepared the international meetings seemed to be guided by the criterion to avoid dealing with issues with major potential to stir controversy. In addition, referring to the 'explosive load' of the Durban conference, Carneiro (2002, p. 211) writes:

> In many ways [ ] we can speak of the 'Battle of Durban'. The ethnic/racial problem surfaced in every dimension in the international arena, leading to the almost impossibility of reaching the minimum of consensus among nations to face it. What seemed to be anti-racist activist rhetoric was manifested in Durban: the ethnic, racial, cultural and religious issues, and all the problems in which they unfold – racism, racial discrimination, xenophobia, exclusion and social marginalisation of a large contingent of humans considered 'different' – have the potential to polarise the contemporary world.[7]

Carneiro (2002) explains that, underlying these controversial issues, was another element, not directly expressed, that characterized the (non) participation[8] of the Western countries in the Conference. She states:

> Beyond the objective of preventing the approval of any proposal that would open loopholes for reparations, they [delegations from Western countries] also fought to impede the condemnation of the colonial past, especially because this would signify questioning and criticising the grounds that justified colonisation and the economic expansion of the West (p. 212)

It is a fact that in relation to certain specific issues, such as Afro-descendents of the Americas and particularly Afro-Brazilians, the final Durban Declaration and Plan of Action can be considered a victory (see Albuquerque 2008). However, when one wonders in which specific manner the Durban Conference influenced policymaking on national and regional scales, it can be argued that the conference and its Declaration and Plan of Action in itself have exerted little direct influence on the shaping of public education policies in Brazil. As is confirmed by the concluding statement of the Civil Society Conference of the Americas held in June 2008 with the purpose of assessing compliance with the Durban Declaration and Programme of Action:

> Seven years after the approval of the Durban Declaration and Programme of Action, despite the efforts of civil society and some states in the region, there is still not enough institutionally nor the necessary financial resources for implementing the initiatives established to combat racism and all forms of discrimination (Sociedad Civil de las Américas 2008, p. 1)

Similar conclusions can be drawn in relation to the role of multilateral agencies such as the World Bank in agenda-setting on race in education. When examining the role the World Bank played with regard to these developments, it can indeed be perceived that, while it played a significant role in spreading a neoliberal agenda around the world in the 1990s, this agency began in the same decade to express a growing interest in and emphasis on implementing focused or compensatory policies for certain excluded groups in society (Burity 2006; Rocha 2006; Almeida 2008). Whereas multilateral agencies in this sense helped promote discussion on issues such as racism and ethnic/racial inequality in some contexts, the frameworks and rationale this focus was based on was distinct from those of the social movements that campaigned for the issues in the first place. By way of example, we briefly discuss two World Bank documents below.

Inclusion of the issue of racial inequality can be recognized in World Bank documents such as *The Costs of Discrimination in Latin America* (1994) and *Brasil: Justo, Competitivo e Sustentável* (2002). In the latter document, the World Bank acknowledges the existence of racism in Brazilian society and formulates recommendations in relation to this type of exclusion. Consequently, the statement cited below even seems to point to a dialogue with (ideas expressed by) the BBM, as the World Bank here openly criticizes the idea of Brazil being a racial democracy:

> Racial heterogeneity, combined with diffuse limits existing between racial groups, has induced many people to label Brazil a 'racial democracy'. However, there is no doubt that in the country race plays a significant role in determining opportunities in employment, education, housing and other areas, something that is increasingly recognised in public discourse. [...] [T]here is evidence that social mobility is lower among black people, in control of education and other characteristics. This latter observation suggests that an unnoticed characteristic may be less compensated for by Brazilian markets: racial discrimination is the most probable explanation (p. 89)

While recognising the fact that, since the mid-1990s, a concern with ethnicity/race issues has been increasingly incorporated into the agenda of multilateral agencies such as the World Bank, the dominant economic-oriented focus on 'investment' still remains. Issues such as those related to (inequality in) education are not discussed with reference to rights in the first instance, but with reference to investment: education for all should generate human and social capital. As such, in the discourse of these entities, ethnicity/race issues are also often incorporated into overall discussions on development and poverty (reduction) (see also Rocha 2006; Almeida 2008), and considered 'a loss of human capital' rather than a crime (for example, see also Patrinos 1994, p. 20). The 'costs of discrimination to society' (Patrinos 1994) is then often the fundamental concern of multilateral agencies in relation to ethnic racial inequalities. This argument, in the view of these agencies, is especially valid for Brazil, where non-white people account for at least half the population and, as such, discrimination would clearly harm the country's economic growth. Not surprisingly, then, in the case of Brazil, the World Bank identifies the issue as being 'clearly a priority research area' (1994, p. 20). As such, when recognising the fact that agencies like the World Bank may have played a role in placing race on the agenda, the rationale and frameworks used are very different to those brought forward by actors such as the BBM. The fact that this has direct policy implications becomes clear on analysing the same documents referred to above and comparing these with education policies developed in Brazil at the time. In these documents, even when it is stated that mere 'investment' in (universal) education policies would not be sufficient to eradicate racial exclusion in Brazil (Patrinos 1994, pp. 5 and 18) – an argument implying that affirmative policies could be necessary – policies and policy recommendations are formulated against quota policies (for example, see World Bank 2002, p. 90).

Several studies show (e.g. Moehlecke 2002; Rocha 2006; Almeida 2008) how in the same period, influential parties in the Brazilian government, such as the Minister for Education, positioned themselves against affirmative action policies, using similar arguments to those used by agencies such as the World Bank. Despite the international trend to discuss ethnic/racial inequalities and consider them as problematic, in line with discourses of agencies such as the World Bank, the dominant argument at the time in the Brazilian government and mass media was that the problem of racial inequalities in education should be combated through policies designed to improve public sector education in general and not through policies such as quotas. This is confirmed by Almeida (2008) in her study on the development of the Brazilian Government Diversity in the University Programme at the beginning of this century, a programme financed by the Inter-American Development Bank. Her study illustrates how this programme, while it played an important role in the development of the discussion on racial and ethnic diversity in Brazil, represented a 'compromise' of government between claims for affirmative action policies – expressed by the BBM and in the Durban process and its outcomes such as the Plan of Action – on the one hand, and the strong resistance still present in society, government and international entities against these types of policies on the other. This led to the fact that, besides financing already existent – mostly Black Movement linked – NGO initiatives like the aforementioned university admission preparatory courses, the programme did not at the time lead to the design and implementation of new anti-racist education policies that would transform the education institutions, processes and contents in a more structural manner.

This first analysis of the global agenda on the theme of racial inequality and education shows that global mobilisation did indeed grow around the

Durban Conference in 2001 and that the recognition of racial inequality and racism has been increasingly present in documents produced by multilateral agencies since the beginning of the 1990s. The inclusion of ethnicity/race issues on the national agenda should, then, without a doubt, be understood in the context of mounting international tension around the issue, wherein these organisations, like nation states, were obliged to position themselves in one way or another. However, we argue that the agendas coming from these 'global dynamics' rarely consider (solutions in relation to) the root causes of this type of exclusion. Contrary to the frameworks used by the BBM, the frameworks that dominate in global contexts do not include critical reflection on processes that contribute(d) to race becoming a structuring principle in many contemporary societies, such as the history of colonisation and the economic expansion of the West in the first place. The central question in the dominant global discourse remains to be: To what extent do these 'social issues' interfere with or obstruct development? This approach clearly does not involve a rethinking of what is (or could be) development *starting from* reflection on these social issues.

While global processes and actors in some cases seem to fulfil a bureaucratic role (for example, by financing or coordinating programmes and events) in relation to initiatives that aim to foster the inclusion of race issues on the agenda, they do not play a political protagonist role. It would be inaccurate to claim, then, that tensions on the global political agenda have determined the emergence of policies to combat racism and racial inequalities in education in Brazil. One might say that global processes helped to provide opportunities, as seen for example in the case of the Durban Conference, that were taken advantage of by social movement activism, in the BBM in this case. In endeavouring to understand the complex multi- and inter-scalar process surrounding agenda-setting and the inclusion of race issues in education in Brazil, we therefore observe that the decisive role does not seem to lie on the international, but much more on the local/municipal, regional/state and national scale, in a process stimulated primarily by actions of the BBM.

Conclusion

This chapter has attempted to show that the emergence of race as a foundation for public policies in Brazil, in particular in the field of education, is the fruit of a complex process involving conditions, opportunities and advocacy on different scales. By examining the ensuing debate, reflecting on the complexity of multi-scalar processes in setting agendas, and rethinking the concept of scale itself and relations between scales of politics, three distinct rationales can be identified when considering scales and the action of social movements.

First, the global (global actors and interests) conditions the local: from this perspective, racial/ethnicity agendas are the result of an imperialism related to the 'neoliberal wave' in which multilateral agencies are the heralds or protagonists. This rationale is the basis for a series of interpretations of the construction of education policies in the 1990s in Brazil (and in Latin America), in which multiculturalism, respect for diversity and greater value placed on issues and policies of identity and race are the fruit of a wave coming from elsewhere (both outside and within, global and national, with many different opposing parties appearing.)

Secondly, the movement implements its agenda by manipulating the construction of political agendas and processes on different scales; in other words, the movement operates a 'politics of scales'. This interpretation points to the centrality of the movement's advocacy in constructing education agendas.

Thirdly, the local benefits from a global context. This perspective states that the movement is a key actor in constructing the anti-racist education agenda, but the effective construction of policies only becomes possible within a global context that strengthens the movement in its struggle. In other words, policies are not constructed exclusively by the movement, and if it were not for the global context and actors, the movement would perhaps not be able to place race issues on the education policy agenda.

We advocate an understanding that incorporates aspects of the second and third premises described above. It would be insufficient to state that the global conditions the local, that race-based policies are the fruit of 'imperialism' or a result of an importation or copying of a global agenda. In this chapter, we argue that the Brazilian movement uses a 'politics of scale', taking advantage of opportunities opened up by global processes; it harnesses global instruments (multilateral agencies, conventions and international law, events, international political processes, etc.) to exert pressure on the state in order to construct policies. In this interpretation, the relationship between 'national/local' and 'global' processes is not a one-way street, nor something which is disassociated, as in 'levels', but an intertwining of tensions between agencies of political struggle, where the simultaneity of processes lends extra complexity to outcomes on different scales. It therefore becomes difficult to speak of a process of successive facts, in which a domestic process of construction influences a global process, or vice versa. Instead, multi- and international processes are ongoing, unfolding simultaneously on various scales.

Moreover, it has also been shown that the use of multi-scalarity in understanding processes linked to the Brazilian Black Movement does not only refer to national and global processes, but also to local and regional (intra-national) ones – all scales and arenas in which the movement participates. Therefore recognising the organisational complexity of the social movement revealed in this chapter is the only way of understanding this multi-scalarity.

Notes

1 To facilitate reading we will mostly employ the concept race (race-based policies, racial inequality, race issues, race relations) instead of concepts of both ethnicity and race. However, we do understand that often these concepts are interrelated. The ethnicity component then serves to indicate that the tense relations, due to differences in skin colour and other physical characteristics, also exist due to differences in culture expressed in different world visions, values and principles (see Brasil 2005 p. 13).

2 'Boomerang effect' or 'indirect pressure' are concepts Keck *et al.* (1998, in Smith 2005) use when referring to the situation in which groups within a repressive political context forge alliances with transnational actors that can exert pressure on that state through international institutions.

3 Anti-racist policies were developed in sectors such as health, human rights, the labour market, urban planning and heritage preservation.

4 The first paragraph of article 242 states: 'The teaching of Brazilian history shall take into consideration the contributions of different cultures and ethnicities to the formation of the Brazilian people.' (Senado Federal Governo do Brasil 1988, p. 151)

5 These often even become four, five or even six levels, for example, through local coordination entities and micro-, meso- and macro-regional planning organisations.

6 We therefore disagree with the views expressed by other authors that there are 'black movements' in Brazil.

7 Conflict surged especially around the situation in the Middle East, the legacy of colonialism and slavery and the claim for reparations by certain groups, and agreement on the definition of the list of victims of racism and different sources of discrimination (Carneiro 2002; Albuquerque 2008).

8 In protest at debates regarding the Israeli state and the situation in the Middle East, the European Union delegation threatened to leave the Conference, and Canada, the US and Israel did in fact leave before it concluded, without signing the declaration (Albuquerque 2008).

References

Albuquerque, S. J. (2008), *Combate ao Racismo*. Brasília: Fundação Alexandre de Gusmão.

Almeida, N. P. (2008), 'Diversidade na universidade: O BID e as políticas educacionais de Inclusão étnico-racial no Brasil', MA thesis, Universidade Federal do Rio de Janeiro, Río de Janeiro.

Alves dos Santos, I. A. (2006), *O Movimento Negro e o Estado (1983–1987)*. São Paulo: Prefeitura de São Paulo.

Bourdieu, P. and Wacquant, L. (2002), 'Sobre as Artimanhas da Razão Imperialista'. *Estudos Afro-Asiáticos*, 4, (1), 15–33.

BRASIL (2005), *Diretrizes Curriculares Nacionais para a Educação das Relações Étnico-Raciais e para o Ensino de Historia e Cultura Afro-Brasileira e Africana*. Brasília: Ministério da Educação.

Burity, J. A. (2001), *Identidade e múltiplo pertencimento nas práticas associativas locais*. Recife: Fundação Joaquim Nabuco.

—(2006), 'Reform of the State and the New Discourse on Social Policy in Brazil'. *Latin american perspectives*, 33, 67–88.

Carneiro, S. (2002), 'A Batalha de Durban'. *Revista Estudos Feministas*, 1, (10), 209–14.

Frigotto, G. (2003), *Educação e a Crise do Capitalismo Real*, 5th edn. São Paulo: Cortez.

Frigotto, G. and Ciavatta, M. (2003), 'Educação básica no Brasil na década de 1990: subordinação ativa e consentida a lógica do mercado'. *Educação e sociedade*, 24, (82), 39–130.

Giddens, A. (1991), *As Conseqüências da Modernidade*. São Paulo: EDUNESP.

Jaccoud, L. (2008), 'O combate ao racismo e à desigualdade: o desafio das políticas públicas de promoção da igualdade racial', in M. Theodoro ed., *As Políticas Públicas e a Desigualdade Racial no Brasil: 120 anos*. Brasília: IPEA, pp. 45–64.

Jaccoud, L. B. and Beghin, N. (2002), *Desigualdades Raciais no Brasil: um Balanço da Intervenção Governamental*. Brasília: IPEA.

Lacoste, Y. (1988), *A Geografia – isso serve, em primeiro lugar, para fazer a Guerra*. Campinas: Papirus.

Lechner, N. (1997), 'Tres formas de coordinación social'. *Revista de la Cepal*, 61, 7–17.

Melucci, A. (1994), 'Qué hay de nuevo en los nuevos movimientos sociales?', in E. Laraña and J. Gusfield (eds), *Los Nuevos Movimientos Sociales: de la Ideología a la Identidad*. Madrid: Centro de Investigaciones Sociológicas, pp. 119–50.

MEC – Ministério da Educação e do Desporto(1996) *Lei nº 9.394, de 20 de dezembro 1996* [Online] Available at: www.planalto.gov.br/ccivil_03/LEIS/l9394.htm (Accessed: 27 April 2010).

Moehlecke, S. (2002), 'Ação Afirmativa: Historia e debates no Brasil'. *Cadernos de Pesquisa*, 117, (11), 197–217.

Patrinos, H. A. (1994), *The Costs of Discrimination in Latin America*. Washington, DC: World Bank. Working Paper HCO.

Rocha, L. C. P. (2006), 'Políticas Afirmativas e Educação: A lei 10639/0 no contexto das políticas educacionais no Brasil contemporâneo', MA thesis, Universidade Federal de Paraná, Curitiba.

Santos, B. S. (2004), 'Para uma sociologia das ausências e uma sociologia das emergências'. In B. S. Santos ed., *Conhecimento Prudente para uma Vida Decente: um Discurso sobre as Ciências Revisitado*. São Paulo: Cortez, pp. 17–59.

Santos, R. E. (2006), 'Agendas & Agências: a espacialidade dos movimentos sociais a partir do Pré-Vestibular para Negros e Carentes', PhD thesis, Universidade Federal Fluminense, Niterói.

Santos, R. E. and Soeterik, I. M. (2010), 'Brazilian Civil Society in Global Politics? The Durban Process and its Effects on the Anti-Racist Education Agenda in Brazil', paper presented to Seminar Civil Society Advocacy and Education For All, Amsterdam, 4 February.

Santos, S. A. (2005), 'A Lei 10.639/2003 como fruto da luta anti-racista do Movimento Negro', in SECAD-MEC (ed.), *Educação Anti-racista: Caminhos Abertos pela Lei Federal n. 10.639/903*, Brasília: Ministério da Educação, pp. 21–37.

Sarubi, E. R. (2005), 'A gestão democrática da educação no Brasil: Alguns apontamentos'. *Revista eletrônica trabalho e educação em perspectiva* [e-journal] Available at: www.fae.ufmg.br/cadernotextos/backup/artigos/artigoVIII.pdf (Accessed: 21 April 2010).

Senado Federal Governo do Brasil (1988) *Constituição da República Federativa do Brasil* [Online] Available at: www.senado.gov.br/sf/legislacao/const/ (Accessed: 14 May 2010).

Silva, A. C. C. (2004), 'Agenciamentos coletivos, territórios existenciais e capturas uma etnografia de movimentos negros em Ilhéus'. PhD thesis, Universidade Federal do Rio de Janeiro/ Museu Nacional, Rio de Janeiro.

Silveira, M. L. (1996), 'Escala geográfica: da ação ao império?', paper presented to seminar O Discurso Geográfico na Aurora do Século XXI. São Carlos, 1–7 November.

Smith, J. (2005), 'The uneven Geography of Global Civil Society: National and Global Influences on Transnational Association'. *Social forces*, 84, (2), 621–52.

Sociedad Civil de las Américas (2008), *Declaración de la Sociedad Civil de las Américas de cara a la ConferenciaMundial de Revisión de Durban*. Brasilia: Sociedad Civil de las Américas.

Swyngedouw, E. (1997), 'Neither Global nor Local: 'Glocalization' and the politics of scale', in K. Cox ed., *Spaces of Globalization: Reasserting the Power of the Local*. New York/London: The Guilford Press, pp. 137–66.

Vainer, C. (2001), 'As escalas do poder e o poder das escalas: o que pode o Poder Local?', in ANPUR ed., *Ética, planejamento e construção democrática do espaço – Anais do IX Encontro Nacional da ANPUR*. Rio de Janeiro, Brasil. Niterói –RJ: ANPUR / IPPUR, pp. 140–51.

World Bank (2002), *Brasil: Justo, Competitivo e Sustentável: contribuições para debate: visão geral*. Washington, DC: World Bank.

CHAPTER TEN

A Converging Pedagogy in the Developing World? Insights from Uganda and Turkey

Hülya Kosa Altinyelken

Introduction

In recent decades, school pedagogy has assumed central importance in education reforms that are designed to enhance the quality of education. It has been increasingly linked to economic growth, international competitiveness (Alexander 2008) and political democratisation (Tabulawa 2003). Particularly after the 1990s, the global political discourse on pedagogy has been progressively shaped by approaches that are based on constructivism. Such approaches have become 'part of a discursive repertoire of international rights and quality education' (Chisholm *et al.* 2008, p. 4). Donor agencies have also proven influential in placing the notions of constructivism on the international reform agenda (Tabulawa 2003; Ginsburg *et al.* 2008). Indeed, an overview of policy documents by influential international organisations reveals that skills-based and learner-centred curricula have increasingly become the default position internationally.

Over the years, constructivism has largely influenced educational reforms in low-income countries as many have endorsed reform programmes that are couched in the rhetoric of constructivism. It has been characterized differently in diverse contexts as student-centred pedagogy (SCP), child-centred pedagogy (CCP), learner-centred pedagogy, active learning or collaborative learning. By the late twentieth century, reforms introducing CCP, student participation, democracy in the classroom, hands-on learning and cooperative learning groups have become globally ubiquitous (Anderson-Levitt 2003). Constructivism has been 'increasingly taken for granted as part of notions of educational quality' (Ginsburg *et al.* 2008, 106).

There are several examples of countries endorsing such pedagogical reforms in recent history. In Asia, examples include China (Carney 2008; Dello-Iacovo 2009), Russia (Schweisfurth 2002), Kyrgyzstan (Price-Rom *et al.* 2009) and Taiwan (Yang *et al.* 2008); in Sub-Saharan Africa, South Africa (Nykiel-Herbert 2004), Botswana (Tabulawa 2003), Namibia (O'Sullivan 2004; Chisholm *et al.* 2008), Ethiopia (Serbessa 2006), Malawi (Croft 2002) and Tanzania (Barrett 2007); in the Middle East, Egypt (Ginsburg *et al.* 2008) and Jordan (Roggemann *et al.* 2009); and in Latin America, Brazil (Luschei 2004), Guatemala, Nicaragua and El Salvador (de Baessa *et al.* 2002).

The spread of pedagogical approaches based on constructivism has rekindled the debate on globalization and curriculum, as scholars enquired whether convergence around discourses and national education policies has resulted in the convergence of educational practices around the world (Anderson-Levitt 2003, 2008; Carson 2009). In other words, has the convergence at the level of global policy talk on pedagogy led to convergence at the classroom level? And to what extent have the global and the official national discourses on pedagogy reshaped teaching and learning practices in classrooms? This chapter aims to reflect on such questions and seeks to provide an empirical examination of the practice of global education policy by focusing on the implementation of pedagogical reforms in two countries, namely, Uganda and Turkey.

These two countries are similar in terms of undergoing major curriculum review processes within similar timeframes and scope, and for being 'late adopters' of pedagogical approaches couched in the rhetoric of constructivism, defined as CCP in Uganda and SCP in Turkey (CCP shall be used to refer to both of them throughout the chapter.) However, they differ significantly in many other ways, including their geographical size, population, history, political economy, donor involvement and education system. Choosing cases that are very different from one other is considered appropriate, since the chapter is aimed at analysing how context (structural aspects) and agents (teachers) mediate 'global' policies, and what kind of indigenized implementation profiles emerge as such policies are implemented at school level. In other words, the nature and type of pedagogical reforms that Uganda and Turkey have recently experienced offer sufficient similarities to warrant comparison, with large differences to help highlight the influence of contextual factors and teacher agency[9].

Constructivism

Constructivism is not a pedagogical approach but a theory regarding how people learn. It associates knowledge directly with individual learners and considers it to be the product of students' activities. Through processes of assimilation and accommodation, knowledge is constructed by students as they relate the new information to their already existing cognitive structures (Bruer 1993). In other words, learning is conceived as 'an active process in which learners are active sense-makers who seek to build coherent and organized knowledge' (Mayer 2004, p. 14). Accordingly, knowledge is created by undergoing, researching and actively experiencing reality. Since learning is perceived as a self-regulated activity, emphasis is placed on providing students with ample opportunities for discovery and the interpretation of events. Learning to learn is perceived to be as important as mastering content. The role of teachers in this context is mainly geared toward stimulating and coaching students in their learning activities.

New paradigms of learning and teaching based on the principles of constructivism are characterized by minimal teacher lecturing or direct transmission of factual knowledge, individual and small-group activities, frequent student questions, and extensive dialogue among students (Leu *et al.* 2006). Since learning is viewed as a process during which students must be active, passive media such as books, lectures and presentations are often classified as non-constructivist teaching, whereas active media such as group discussions, hands-on learning and interactive games are classified as constructivist teaching (Mayer 2004).

The global diffusion of CCP

Why do different countries around the world seem to be engaging in a similar dialogue on how pedagogy should be reformed? Why are official discourses converging around the same pedagogical model? Different and often competing answers have been provided to these questions. According to modernisation theorists, countries borrow educational reforms from elsewhere because they are superior. The emerging global curriculum (and the pedagogical approach as an integral part of the curriculum) is a response to the demands of globalized economies and knowledge societies (Anderson-Levitt 2008). Pedagogical approaches based on constructivism have become popular since they represent the best way of organising teaching and learning in schools in the contemporary world. However, the outcomes of such pedagogies are contested, or the results are perceived as inconclusive in many developed countries where these pedagogies had a better chance of being implemented because of resource availability, smaller class sizes and improved teacher training (Alexander 2001; Gauthier *et al.* 2004; Mayer 2004; UNESCO 2005).

A second view is proposed by world culture theorists. According to them, countries have more or less freely adopted a global culture of schooling because a set of ideas and practices are perceived as the best and the most modern way, even though they may not actually be the best way to run schools. In other words, nations adopt ideas not because they are truly better, but because policymakers perceive them as modern, progressive and inevitable (Meyer *et al.* 2000). For instance, constructivism is perceived as effective in improving learning achievements and preparing children and young people for the labour market. In the current globalized, increasingly competitive knowledge economy, the business community demands employees who think creatively, adapt flexibly to new work demands, identify and solve problems, and cooperate with colleagues in effective ways to create complex products (Windschitl 2002).

The assumption that constructivist learning environments are superior in developing and reinforcing such skills and competencies therefore appears to have contributed to its greater appeal. Indeed, research has shown that approaches rooted in constructivism have been endorsed in many countries on the assumption that such approaches would better prepare workers for the global economy, in which 'the new rules of wealth creation are replacing the logic of Fordist mass production with new "knowledge-based" systems of flexible production' (Ball 1998, p. 120). Moreover, constructivism is associated with educating citizens who would effectively participate in democratic politics (Ginsburg 2009), and with creating more capable consumers through education.

The two theories presented above assume that countries import education policies more or less voluntarily, and they downplay the power asymmetries among them. Furthermore, the world culture theory, due to its structuralist ontology, fails to recognize the role of particular international actors who have been involved in disseminating such pedagogies in different parts of the world. These include bilateral organisations (e.g. DANIDA and USAID), international organisations (e.g. the World Bank and UNICEF), or other agencies (e.g. the Aga Khan Foundation and some international NGOs) that had different motives and agendas in promoting CCP.

The world system theory, in contrast, considers power central to the discussion. Here, convergence represents power, rather than progress. Hence, if pedagogical practices are converging around the world (at least in the official curricula), it is because a certain pedagogical approach is in the interests of powerful states or international organisations (Guthrie 1990; Tabulawa 2003; Carney 2008). These perspectives emphasize imposition or coercion as educational transfer mechanisms, and highlight the role of international aid agencies (such as USAID) as major players that have contributed to the spread of constructivism by advocating it as a prescription through educational projects and consultancies they funded (Tabulawa 2003). Although aid agencies frame their interest by focusing on the assumed effectiveness of constructivism in improving learning outcomes, this perspective points to a hidden agenda which is disguised as 'better' teaching. According to this view, the efficacy of constructivism lies in its political and ideological nature. Although the world system theory captures some of the complexities ignored by the world culture theory, it overemphasizes the role of international actors, disregards the agency of the recipient countries, and overstates imposition and coercion as policy transfer mechanisms.

Furthermore, Steiner-Khamsi underlines the importance of the 'politics' and 'economics' of educational borrowing and lending (Steiner-Khamsi 2010). The politics of educational transfer is relevant for both the lender and the borrower, and implies political reasons for exporting and disseminating specific education policies or reforms (e.g. by donor agencies, NGOs and consultants), as well as political motives at the local level for importing a set of education reforms. Steiner-Khamsi argues that borrowing can work as a means to de-contextualize and de-territorialize educational reforms that are contested in a given country (Steiner-Khamsi *et al.* 2000; Steiner-Khamsi 2004). She suggests that 'borrowing does not occur because reforms from elsewhere are better, but because the very act of borrowing has a salutary effect on domestic policy conflict' (Steiner-Khamsi 2006, p. 671). The economics of policy borrowing and lending, on the other hand, points to the economic reasons for borrowing a specific education reform. The economics of policy borrowing is particularly salient for low-income countries that are dependent on external aid. Indeed, the time has come for a specific reform when international funding for implementing that particular reform is secured (Steiner-Khamsi 2006). The economics of policy lending and borrowing also helps to explain why education reforms in low-income countries increasingly bear a resemblance to those in developed countries.

Educational transfer: Why and how are Western pedagogies imported?

The rationale

In both Turkey and Uganda, the new pedagogies were imported within the framework of improving the quality of education, and pedagogical renewal constituted an integral part of broader curriculum review and change processes. While adopting CCP, both countries have also instigated changes in curriculum content and student assessment.

In Uganda, following a one-year pilot phase, the Thematic Curriculum for primary schools was implemented nationwide in February 2007 (NCDC 2006a). Likewise, in Turkey, Curriculum 2004 was piloted for a year in a select number of schools and has been implemented nationwide since September 2005 (Educational Reform Initiative 2005). In Uganda, the content has been reorganized according to a number of thematic areas, and in Turkey, the content load has been reduced and a thematic approach has been considered in content organisation. Both curricula have adopted a competency-based approach as opposed to the traditional knowledge-based curriculum approach, and have emphasized the development of specific competencies and skills. In terms of student assessment, both countries attempted to move beyond testing, and adopted continuous assessment.

The official account as to why new pedagogies are adopted points to dissatisfaction with student learning achievements, the inefficiency of the education system, and the urge to restructure pedagogical practices in line with the imperatives of the knowledge-based economy. In Uganda, the primary concern is related to the very low achievement levels in literacy and numeracy (UNEB 2005) and the inefficiencies of the system as indicated by high drop-out and repetition rates (Read *et al.* 2005). CCP appears to have been embraced as an antidote to traditional teaching in the hope that learning achievements and competencies will consequently improve, particularly in literacy and numeracy. A literate and numerate population is seen as critical to economic growth, sustainable development and poverty reduction.

In Turkey, on the other hand, globalization, the knowledge-based economy, the EU membership process and harmonisation with the EU education system, the changing social and economic needs of Turkish society, concerns with low student motivation and disappointment with the results of Turkish students in international tests (particularly PISA) are highlighted as important motives. The new pedagogies that are based on constructivist principles are considered to be progressive and advanced, and viewed as the only alternative to the traditional teaching practices in both countries (see Altinyelken 2011). Furthermore, the discourses on the rationale for a new pedagogy reflect the primacy of economic considerations in both contexts. This does not come as a surprise, since such considerations have come to characterize many of the education policies initiated in different parts of the world.

Mechanisms

Both in Uganda and Turkey, the perceptions and the assumptions linking CCP with improved student learning and better preparation of workers for the contemporary labour markets appear to have strongly influenced education policymakers. Furthermore, Uganda exemplifies a country where the economics of education transfer have proven critical. The Ugandan education system is highly dependent on external assistance, as more than half the budget is paid for by donors (DGIS 2003). In turn, this creates 'a situation in which "voluntary policy transfer" is enmeshed with "coercive policy transfer"' (Dolowitz *et al.* 2000, p. 6). Donor aid is often accompanied by the lending of reform ideas, and even with the wholesale transfer of a comprehensive reform package formulated by the lender (Steiner-Khamsi 2006). Indeed, in Uganda, USAID and the Aga Khan Foundation have been actively involved in disseminating and institutionalising CCP in primary schools. For this purpose, they have developed and implemented projects in primary schools and teacher-training institutes in different parts of the country. According to some accounts, they have been very influential during the curriculum change process and in endorsing CCP as the official pedagogical approach in the new curriculum (see Altinyelken 2010).

The case of Turkey is interesting in terms of understanding both the politics and economics of educational transfer. The restructuring of the Turkish economy in line with neoliberalism was initiated in the 1980s, and the influence of such policies was also felt in the education system. However, an adaptation of the content of the primary school curriculum to the market was achieved by means of Curriculum 2004 (Akkaymak 2010). The curriculum change was initiated in the two years after the Justice and Development Party (JDP) came to power, so the adoption of CCP coincides with significant political change in Turkey. The political change is noteworthy in the sense that the JDP is the only party with Islamist roots that came to power as a single party in the history of the Republic. They had their own distinct vision of Turkish society and the education system. Even prior to their rise to power, they announced that they would bring about wide-ranging structural changes to the education system, which included changing the primary school curriculum. Since they were able to form a single-party government, they also had the political power to instigate fundamental changes (Akkaymak 2010).

In addition, accession to the EU has constituted another strong political motive in Turkey. In this sense, 'harmonisation' as a mechanism of policy transfer (Dale 1999) appears to have been influential in the adoption of CCP. Education, training and youth are considered to be the responsibilities of the Member States; however, the Community contributes to developing the quality of education in EU countries (Commission of the European Communities 2004). The Union's 2002 annual progress report considered the principles of the Turkish education system to be generally consistent with those of the EU. However, the report pointed towards reviewing the curricula and teaching methods as 'major issues to be addressed to increase the efficiency of the education system' (Commission of the European Communities 2002, p. 104).

Furthermore, the role of TÜSİAD (the largest corporate lobby in the country) merits attention. TÜSİAD has published a number of reports on education since the 1990s, urging governments to initiate major changes in the education system. Their reports have often formulated the role of education in economic terms, and suggested that the education system's primary responsibility is to produce an adequate workforce for the labour market. As early as in their 1990 Report, CCP was highlighted as the pedagogical model to be adopted, since it was considered to facilitate learning to learn and to develop important skills such as problem-solving, teamwork, research, and entrepreneurship (TÜSİAD 1990). Indeed, the role of TÜSİAD or the market in general has been considered strong in changing the curriculum and the pedagogical approach (Akkaymak 2010).

The economics of policy transfer is also highly relevant in the Turkish case, since the curriculum review was funded by the EU through the Support to Basic Education Programme. The programme was begun in 2002 and phased out in 2007, and had a budget of €100 million. The aim of the programme was to enhance the quality of formal and non-formal education and to increase access to education in Turkey (MONE 2008). The funding raised questions among teachers, as they enquired whether the funding was accompanied by the lending of educational ideas. Such a possibility was strongly refuted by policymakers, yet considered seriously by some of the teachers, headteachers and other stakeholders who shared their opinions on this topic. Indeed, both in Uganda and Turkey, policy-makers appeared rather defensive about any implications of outside imposition.

Main features of the new pedagogies

Despite their different characterisations, the new pedagogical approaches in Uganda and Turkey present several common features. The Ugandan curriculum interprets CCP as interaction among children, and between children and their teacher; emphasising classroom activities that enable children to handle materials and learn by doing; encouraging greater use of learning and teaching materials during lessons; advising that lessons be organized around the interests, concerns and abilities of children; and giving children the opportunity to influence the direction of the lessons. Active student participation in lessons, student talking time and group and pair work are emphasized. Learning by way of exploring, observing, experimenting and practicing are highlighted. In the Turkish curriculum, CCP is also defined along very similar lines as student participation, classroom activities, the use of learning aids, hands-on-learning and cooperative learning. Curriculum documents in both countries clearly suggest that the majority of lesson time should be spent on classroom activities. The four discernible differences between the two cases relate to the emphasis in Turkey on research activities, project-based learning (project and perfor-mance assignments), the use of ICT in classrooms and the integration of learning activities in and outside school, which anticipates and requires greater involvement of parents in education.

In both countries, the curriculum focuses on the development of specific competencies, and it is believed that CCP would prove highly conducive to this goal. The Ugandan curriculum focuses on the devel-opment of six life skills, which should occur in every theme and sub-theme. They include effective communication, critical thinking, decision-making, creative thinking, problem-solving and self-esteem (NCDC 2006b). The

Turkish curriculum, on the other hand, prioritizes the development of eight competencies: critical thinking, creativity, communication, problem-solving, research, using information technologies, entrepreneurship and language skills in Turkish (MONE 2005). The common features among the selected competencies are particularly notable, as four (out of six) competencies prioritized in the Ugandan curriculum are also prioritized in the new Turkish curriculum, i.e. critical thinking, problem-solving, creative thinking and effective communication skills. In addition, decision-making and self-esteem, two other competencies targeted by the Ugandan curriculum are also highlighted throughout revised educational programmes in Turkey. In both countries, CCP also aims at stimulating teamwork, cooperation and dialogue.

These findings support the idea that there is an international convergence in curriculum policy. The similarities in curriculum content (e.g. thematic organisation and the focus on the development of specific competencies), student evaluation (e.g. the introduction of alternative assessment methods that evaluate learning processes) and pedagogical approach (e.g. an emphasis on classroom activities, student participation, cooperation and hands-on-learning) support world culture theorists (Ramirez 2003). Does this evidence, then, point to a single global curriculum model or pedagogical approach? Indeed, it indicates the prevalence of pedagogical reforms couched in the rhetoric of constructivism, and convergence around how education policies are formulated in this area. However, since official curricula and mediated curricula tend to differ substantially, it cannot be taken as proof of convergence at the level of practice.

Teachers' views: Is CCP desirable?

CCP alters the role of teachers and appears to have wide-ranging implications for their profession. According to this pedagogical approach, teachers are expected to play facilitating roles within classrooms. Their primary role is no longer to convey knowledge but to mediate students' learning processes, and provide adequate guidance and support to these supposedly autonomous learners as they embark on constructing their knowledge. The students' role has become critical to educational processes since they are expected to assume much more responsibility in their learning and to be active in classroom processes. More importantly, it is now students who are required to direct learning (e.g. their interests, needs, learning styles, capacities, motivation and readiness), not teachers.

Since the old was critiqued and discredited in an effort to glorify and legitimize the new, having teachers at the centre was increasingly claimed to be authoritarian, uncaring, inefficient and morally wrong. Several teachers gave credit to this discourse both in Turkey and Uganda, arguing that education is about children, so they are the legitimate centres of schooling.

The majority of them also believed that increased student active engagement in learning processes would lead to higher learning achievements and better outcomes in competencies and skills; and greater student involvement would improve motivation, concentration and attendance. A pedagogical approach based on the transmission model has been attacked in both countries to the extent that some Turkish teachers appeared uncomfortable during interviews when they disclosed that they occasionally lectured in their classes. Yet, as Alexander (2008, p. 79) insists: 'Transmission teaching is ubiquitous [...] because there are undoubtedly circumstances in which the transmission of information and skill is a defensible objective, in any context.' Both in Uganda and Turkey, a polarized understanding of pedagogy was prevalent, not only among teachers but also among other key stakeholders. Such an approach appeared to have forced teachers to align with either the old teacher-centred (or subject-centred) approach, or with the new child/student-centred approach. Only a few dared to suggest that educationalists could instead move beyond such a dichotomous perspective.

In both countries, the proposed pedagogical approaches enjoyed a high level of receptiveness. In Uganda, CCP was viewed as the modern and progressive pedagogical approach. With the exception of one, none of the teachers appeared to be critical of the pedagogical approach and they seemed to shy away from questioning its underlying assumptions and main principles. It was simply perceived as a much superior pedagogical approach than traditional teaching. In other words, the Ugandan teachers did not question the desirability or the appropriateness of the new pedagogical approach, and appeared to welcome it as an example of Western best practice. However, they appeared to be overwhelmed by its implementation.

Likewise, CCP was perceived as the more advanced and progressive pedagogical approach by the majority of Turkish teachers. Some even explicitly noted that 'no one could be against it as no one can openly oppose development and improvement'. Furthermore, like Ugandan teachers, CCP was perceived by many as the only alternative to the traditional teaching methods that were criticized by policymakers, teachers and parents alike for being ineffective and boring. Some earlier studies have also identified overwhelmingly positive opinions and attitudes among Turkish teachers towards constructivism (Çınar et al. 2006; Işıkoğlu et al. 2007).

Such a positive attitude was mainly based on the belief that CCP was the dominant pedagogical approach in schools across Western Europe. The West was viewed as advanced, developed, rich and successful. Implicit assumptions were made about the link between Europe's level of development and school pedagogy. Although research studies have not established a clear link between economic development and teaching and learning approaches (Alexander 2008), teachers as well as policymakers believed that CCP could potentially stimulate economic development and boost the competitiveness of the Turkish economy. Adopting a Western 'best practice' was also deemed to be logical and practical. After all, in the past three centuries,

Turkey has often turned to the West to modernize and reform its military, legal, economic, political or educational system (Ulusoy 2009). In fact, teachers' accounts in both countries suggest that the West was viewed as the 'reference society' (Schriewer *et al.* 2004). Hence the pedagogical approach the Westerners might be using had credibility, legitimacy, and enjoyed a certain reputation.

Nevertheless, Turkish teachers' accounts are not so uniform, as strong criticism was also voiced by them. Indeed, some teachers expressed explicit resentment at and frustration with trying out foreign ideas. These teachers believed that educational ideas might work well in the countries of origin, but might fail when they were transplanted into new contexts. In this respect, teachers also pointed out that Turkish society is very different to Western European societies with regard to its vast socio-economic disparities between urban and rural citizens, the competitiveness of the education system, the hierarchical nature of relationships that involve an element of authority, the dynamics of parent-child relationships, the status attached to having a university degree, parental involvement in education, and so on.

Classroom practices: A case for convergence or divergence?

An examination of how the new pedagogical approaches imported from the West were re-contextualized and adapted locally in Uganda and Turkey reveals convergence at a superficial level around new rituals and practices, such as greater efforts to employ learning aids, or to involve children during lessons. However, the findings point more strongly to the persistence of divergences across nations. Divergence was not only manifest when the implementation profiles of the two countries were compared, but was also persistent when schools within a country or even classrooms within a school were compared. In other words, significant differences across schools and classrooms were noted as reform practices were embraced unevenly, interpreted differently and adaptations to classroom realities and student backgrounds have given rise to distinct implementation practices.

An overview of implementation profiles in Uganda and Turkey points to differing as well as some common features. In Uganda, the three most common indicators of change in classrooms included student talking time, the use of learning materials and group seating arrangements. However, these changes were often formalistic and interpreted differently from the manner intended by policymakers. For instance, student participation was regularly praised by teachers, and has become a buzzword among them. Although teachers reported increased student talking time, students were observed during classroom observations as giving answers in chorus to teachers' questions. The lessons were often dominated by teachers' questions, which were limited to basic information recall, requiring one- or two-word answers. Likewise, a formalistic adoption of group work was observed in classes visited in Uganda. Studies in other Sub-Saharan African countries have shown that changes in seating arrangements were the first – and in many cases the only – sign that teachers were implementing CCP (Nykiel-Herbert 2004). In the majority of Ugandan classrooms, children were seated in very large groups (up to 30 students in one group) and conducting meaningful learning activities proved difficult in such large groups. Furthermore, singing was a very common practice in Ugandan classrooms, as in several other Sub-Saharan African countries (Croft 2002). It was often used as a strategy to separate learning areas, to introduce children to new themes, and to improve their motivation and concentration.

In Turkey, as in Uganda, student talking time and the use of aids were common indicators of change. However, unlike Uganda, there was also much emphasis placed on classroom activities, the use of ICT, project, performance and research assignments. During lessons, teachers devoted the greater part of lesson time to activities listed in student workbooks. The activities were varied, and needed to be carried out individually, in pairs, or in groups. Teachers suggested that the noise level in classrooms has risen on account of such activities, and challenges associated with classroom management have increased. Turkish teachers demonstrated great enthusiasm for the benefits yielded by the use of ICT. The ICT tools concerned were used to screen documentaries, to practice using educational programmes for teaching language skills or mathematics, and for teacher and student presentations. Moreover, project and performance assignments were expected to stimulate learning through discovery and hands-on learning. Although some teachers appreciated their value in terms of stimulating creativity and learning, several others complained that students delegated such assignments to their parents so the objectives of the assignments were not achieved in practice. Parents' excessive involvement in project/performance assignments has become such a phenomenon that many referred to the new curriculum as 'parent-centred education.'

Although student talking time and the use of aids appear to be common implementation practices in both countries, the way they are interpreted and practiced differed significantly. As explained above, in Uganda, student talking time often meant posing questions to students that required one or two-word responses in chorus. In Turkey as well, teacher questions and short student answers were common, yet students were also given more opportunities to tell stories, or to talk about their experiences, such as their background, families, hobbies and so on. Likewise, the use of learning aids conveyed different meanings and practices in Uganda and Turkey. In Uganda, it often meant making use of printed materials (flash cards and wall charts), demonstrating specific objects while teaching words in English or literacy lessons, or counting with natural objects in Mathematics. In Turkey, on the other hand, it often meant the use of stationery for frequent classroom activities involving cutting and pasting, drawing and colouring, and the use of TV, computers or the internet.

Such implementation differences tell us a great deal about context (teachers and structural realities), as they are highly indicative of local circumstances. Indeed, Steiner-Khamsi *et al.* (2000) suggest that understanding how a transferred education model or policy has been re-contextualized and locally adapted conveys much about the local conditions and realities. For instance, resource availability predetermines what kind of learning materials will be used in classrooms, and how. Likewise, culture, student language proficiency and class size exert a considerable influence on the nature, frequency or duration of student talking time and participation. Moreover, teachers' own interpretations and choices lead to differences, as in the case of grouping and group work. For instance, while in Uganda all teachers organized group seating arrangements, only two teachers out of a larger sample in Turkey followed suit. For Ugandan teachers, group seating was a pragmatic way of dividing a large class characterized by significant differences in children's ability levels. In Turkey, even though group seating was not popular, teachers also organized ad hoc groups for specific classroom activities. In addition, group work also involved group activities and cooperation between children outside of lesson hours.

Implementation challenges: Are the new pedagogies feasible?

The classroom realities observed in Uganda and Turkey differed significantly in terms of resource availability and class sizes. For instance, although some classrooms had computers and internet access in Turkey, Uganda showed deficiencies in even the most basic needs, such as adequate chairs for students. Nevertheless, the Ugandan and Turkish teachers appeared almost equally puzzled and overwhelmed by the implementation of CCP. The majority of teachers in both countries considered the new approach complex, and viewed its implementation in their national contexts as highly problematic. They believed that the implementation process was constrained by a multitude of issues and problems, raising critical questions with regard to its feasibility. These included inadequate teacher training, large classes, the shortage of material, the examination system, language proficiency in English (in Uganda), teacher-related factors, and parental opposition. These challenges should be borne in mind since they have shaped the indigenized versions of CCP in Uganda and Turkey. They are briefly outlined below (see Altinyelken 2010, 2011 for a broader discussion on them).

Most Ugandan and Turkish teachers received ten days of training prior to the piloting, which enabled them to be only minimally acquainted with the main features of the new curricula. Teachers in both contexts appeared very critical of teacher training because of its short duration and low quality. The lack of a sound and thorough basis for CCP led to confusion, frustration and wide discrepancies in interpretation and teacher practices. Moreover, class size was mentioned as one of the biggest implementation challenges in both countries. In Uganda, the average class size in visited schools was 70, and some classrooms had up to 108 students. In Turkey, the average class size was 36 in visited schools, and the maximum was 49. Teachers described the difficulties of teaching in such overcrowded classes, and suggested that CCP has intensified those challenges, as the recommended teaching methods, such as student participation, learning by doing, and group work were time-consuming and difficult to organize. The expectations of policymakers regarding the implementation of CCP in large classes were perceived to be simply unrealistic.

Furthermore, CCP appeared to step up the demand for learning aids in both countries. Nevertheless, teachers were frustrated over the lack of adequate materials, even though they were in a more advantageous situation as pilot schools in comparison to other public schools. Material needs were framed differently since Ugandan teachers were more concerned over the lack of textbooks, visual aids and storybooks, while Turkish teachers made frequent references to computers, the internet, TV, digital learning materials and stationery needs. Ugandan teachers complained about the high cost of materials, the limited supply of printed materials, the inadequacy of the school budget allocation for the purchase of learning aids, the inability of students to provide some of the basic materials, and the time and effort expended by teachers on developing learning aids. Teachers in Turkey also commented on insufficient school budgets for providing learning aids and the implications of resorting to parents to provide for material needs. Indeed, despite the rhetoric on free public education at primary level, parents have been increasingly required to provide financial means for a range of items, including desks, seats, curtains, storybooks and ICT hardware. Such practices have not only raised the financial burden of education on family budgets but also created new forms of inequality within the education system. This has led to great discrepancies in school conditions and has led to visible differences and inequalities between schools, or even between classrooms in a single school.

Nationwide entrance exams to post-primary education pose an important challenge to the implementation of CCP in many contexts because of contradictions between the objectives of a constructivist curriculum (e.g. the development of skills and competencies) and what is assessed during exams (knowledge acquisition). Such contradictions and tensions persist in both Uganda and Turkey, pointing to a lack of educational policy alignment. In both countries, success is defined by exam performance. So even if school management, teachers and parents value the development of abilities, skills and competencies, if students cannot make the transition to good-quality post-primary educational institutions, then the intrinsic value of such competencies becomes questionable.

The language of instruction was raised as an important concern among Ugandan teachers. As in several other African countries, Uganda adopted the colonial language, English, as the official language and the language of instruction in schools. The Thematic Curriculum introduced the use of local languages as the language of instruction at lower grades; however, all schools continued to teach in English in Kampala due to the city's ethnic and linguistic diversity. The use of English was perceived as an obstacle to practicing CCP since several children, particularly those who had migrated from rural areas, had a poor level of English. Consequently, their participation and interaction with teachers and other students were limited. In observed classrooms, some students appeared to be fluent in English, while some others had had no prior exposure to English. Children who had been to nursery schools spoke better English, and those who migrated from the North or the East had the most difficulty in comprehending it.

In Uganda, teacher-related issues that hindered the implementation of CCP include low teacher motivation and morale, inadequate salaries, low teacher status and unfavourable living conditions. Ugandan teachers indicated that CCP made further demands on teachers by asking them to engage children in learning to a greater extent, and by being more innovative and creative in their teaching. However, teachers suggested that many of them lacked the motivation and energy to engage fully in educational change processes.

In Turkey, few teachers raised such issues as a challenge to curriculum implementation, yet they alluded to teacher resistance to proposals for change as a critical issue. Resistance to change was typically attributed to teachers who were relatively senior in age and who had many years of experience, i.e. more than 20 years. Some teachers argued that instead of organising classroom activities, senior teachers continued to rely on more traditional methods of direct teaching, because they viewed change as tiring and demanding. These teachers were also seen as problematic during interviews with policymakers, who openly suggested that once senior teachers had left the system, constructivism would be more widely endorsed. However, interview accounts have shown that extensive reliance on classroom activities and over-emphasis on competencies were criticized by teachers of all ages. Indeed, the majority of them did not approve of the substantial reductions in content load and tended to supplement it with direct teaching due to concerns with students' academic success, nationwide examinations, the increasing demand for private tutoring and deepening educational inequalities. These teachers therefore demonstrated *principled resistance* (Achinstein *et al.* 2006), since they perceived curriculum change proposals as detrimental to their students and to society in general.

Furthermore, in both countries, teachers encountered some parental opposition to the revised curriculum and concerns associated with CCP. In Uganda, partly because of inadequate public awareness-raising prior to the implementation, parents were reported to be confused, ambivalent or displeased with the new curriculum. Parental complaints involved a number of issues, such as the replacement of a subject-based system with learning areas, the overlap with early-childhood education, and the assessment system. For these parents, the new curriculum was a simplified version of the previous one; hence, it was viewed as less challenging. In addition, since the new system encouraged active learning, learning by doing, group activities and play, children were less involved with copying things from the blackboard. However, for several parents written exercises were primary indicators of teaching and learning.

In Turkey, teachers also reported some parental dissatisfaction with the new curriculum. Several parents appeared to be concerned with the quality of education: they were critical of the new curriculum for over-emphasising competencies, and paying inadequate attention to knowledge acquisition. Parents believed that children did not learn much in the new system, as an excessive amount of classroom time was spent on classroom activities. Some parents openly challenged the teachers, arguing that 'children are empty, they do not learn', and they endeavoured to exert pressure on teachers to supplement the curriculum with additional information and to spend more time on lecturing. This kind of pressure particularly came from parents who perceived education as an important social mobility mechanism, and who seemed to be concerned over the incongruity between mainstream schooling and secondary school entrance exams.

Conclusion

This chapter attempted to provide a critical and empirical analysis of how a global policy (pedagogical approaches based on constructivism) has been adapted locally in two different country contexts, i.e. Uganda and Turkey. The chapter provided an analysis on how context and local actors mediated education policies that are imported from the West.

The educational transfer process appears to entail distinct forces and mechanisms in the case-study countries, involving a combination of the global and the local. In Uganda, the active role of some international donors (USAID and the Aga Khan Foundation) and the dependence on external aid (which is often accompanied by the lending of reform ideas) seem to be critical to the adoption of CCP. The case of Turkey, on the other hand, demonstrates harmonisation as the policy transfer mechanism, because of the role of the EU, the most influential international organisation in Turkey (Dale 1999). Since the EU also provided funding for the curriculum change process, both harmonisation and imposition operated simultaneously. In Turkey, enchantment with the West, three hundred years of the policy-borrowing tradition from Western countries, and the status of EU countries as 'reference societies' (Schriewer *et al.* 2004) have also contributed to educational borrowing. The interplay of different factors in both cases gives credit to diverse theories that explain the relationship between globalization and educational transfer, yet in different degrees.

Educational policies are adapted and re-contextualized through multiple processes (Dale 1999); therefore, at the level of practice, there appears to be some convergence and many divergences in Uganda and Turkey. In both countries, CCP enjoyed a high level of receptiveness among teachers as the modern and progressive pedagogical approach. At the level of practice, implementation profiles reveal palpable differences because CCP is framed differently in curricular documents by accentuating different aspects of the pedagogy (e.g. research and ICT in Turkey and group work in Uganda), and, more importantly, because it is practiced differently by Ugandan and Turkish teachers. Therefore CCP assumed different forms in the case-study countries. This is not surprising, as an implementation process always involves the application and distortion of what is formally proposed by policymakers and curriculum designers (Lopes *et al.* 2009), and leads to discernible differences, even within the same country. Historical and comparative evidence suggests that continuities, especially at the level of pedagogy, prevail through successive education reforms (Schweisfurth 2002).'Convergence often occurs exclusively at the level of policy talk, in some instances also at the level of policy action, but rarely at the level of implementation' (Steiner-Khamsi *et al.* 2006, p. 9), because global policies are mediated and re-contextualized (sometimes beyond recognition), undermined or openly resisted by local actors.

It is also important to note that a one-size-fits-all approach to pedagogy fails to recognize that pedagogy is 'both the act of teaching and the discourse in which it is embedded' (Alexander 2001, p. 507). Since teaching and learning are contextualized activities, there can indeed be no justification for a universal and homogenising pedagogy (Tabulawa 2003). Furthermore, positioning the notions of teacher-centred and student-centred learning in opposition and making bipolar comparisons between them poses the risk of oversimplification (Edwards *et al.* 2008). As Alexander (2001) suggests, the pedagogical models should be as far removed as possible from the crude and normative polarising of 'teacher-centred' and 'child-centred' teaching and therefore, mainstream comparative research should abandon this dichotomy. According to Alexander (2001, p. 512), 'Perhaps the most damaging residue of this sort of thinking can still be found in the reports of some development education consultants, who happily commend Western 'child-centred' pedagogy to non-Western governments without regard for local cultural and educational circumstances.'

Note

1 The chapter is based on fieldwork in both countries; data collection took place in June–July 2007 in Uganda and February–May 2009 in Turkey. In both countries, public schools that were selected to pilot the new curriculum in the capital cities were chosen as research sites, and eight schools were visited per country, in Kampala and Ankara respectively. Two forms of data collection, interviews and classroom observation were used. At the school site, interviews were conducted with headteachers and deputy headteachers, and classroom teachers from Grades One and Two in Uganda, and One, Two and Five in Turkey. Interviews with school management amounted to a total of 24 (10 in Uganda and 14 in Turkey), and to 103 with teachers (34 in Uganda and 69 in Turkey). Interviews were also conducted with key informants within the field of education, including ministry officials, international organisations, academics, teacher unions and educational institutions. Furthermore, lessons were observed in Primary One and Two in Uganda (in total 28) and Primary One, Two and Five in Turkey (76 in total), by using a checklist which included items on the level of interaction between students and teachers, student talking time, classroom management and atmosphere.

References

Achinstein, B. and Ogawa, R. T. (2006), '(In)fidelity: what the resistance of new teachers reveals about professional principles and prescriptive educational policies', *Harvard Educational Review*, 76, (1), 30–63.

Akkaymak, G. (2010), 'Neoliberalism and education: Analysis of representation of neoliberal ideology in the primary school Social Studies curriculum in Turkey', MA thesis, Koç University, Istanbul.

Alexander, R. (2008), *Essays on pedagogy*. London: Routledge.

—(2001), 'Border crossing: towards a comparative pedagogy'. *Comparative Education*, 37, (4), 507–23.

Altinyelken, H. K. (2011), 'Student-centered pedagogy in Turkey: conceptualisations, interpretations and practices', *Journal of Education Policy*, 26, (2), 137–60.

—(2010), 'Pedagogical renewal in sub-Saharan Africa: the case of Uganda', *Comparative Education*, 46, (2), 151–71.

Anderson-Levitt, K. (2003), 'A world culture of schooling?', in K. M. Anderson-Levitt ed. *Local meanings, global schooling: anthropology and world culture theory*, New York: Palgrave Macmillan, pp. 1–26.

—(2008), 'Globalization and curriculum', in F. M. Connelly ed., *The Sage handbook of curriculum and instruction*. London: Sage, pp. 349–68.

Ball, S. J. (1998), 'Big policies/small world: an introduction to international perspectives in education policy', *Comparative Education*, 34, (2), 119–30.

Barrett, A. (2007), 'Beyond the polarization of pedagogy: models of classroom practice in Tanzanian primary schools', *Comparative Education*, 4, (2), 273–94.

Bruer, J. T. (1993), *Schools for thought: A science of learning in the classroom*. Cambridge: MIT Press.

Carney, S. (2008), 'Learner-centred pedagogy in Tibet: international education reform in a local context', *Comparative Education*, 44, (1), 39–55.

Carson, T. R. (2009), 'Internationalizing curriculum: globalization and the worldliness of curriculum studies', *Curriculum Inquiry*, 39, (1), 145–58.

Chisholm, L., and Leyendecker, R. (2008), 'Curriculum reform in the post-1990s sub-Saharan Africa', *International Journal of Educational Development*, 28, (2), 195–205.

Çınar, O., Tefur, E. and Mehmet, E. (2006), 'İlköğretim okulu öğretmen ve yöneticilerinin yapılandırmacı eğitim yaklaşımı ve programı hakkındaki görüşleri'. *Eğitim Fakültesi Dergisi* 7, (11), 47–64.

Commission of the European Communities (2002), *2002 Regular report on Turkey's progress towards accession*. Brussels: Commission of the European Communities.

—(2004), *2004 Regular report on Turkey's progress towards accession*. Brussels: Commission of the European Communities.

Croft, A. (2002), 'Singing under a tree: does oral culture help lower primary teachers be learner-centred?' *International Journal of Educational Development*, 22, (3–4), 321–37.

Dale, R. (1999), 'Specifying globalization effects on national policy: a focus on the mechanisms'. *Journal of Education Policy*, 14, (1), 1–17.

De Baessa, Y., Chesterfield, R., and Ramos, T. (2002), 'Active learning and democratic behaviour in Guatemalan rural primary schools', *Compare*, 32, (2), 205–18.

Dello-Iacovo, B. (2009), 'Curriculum reform and "Quality Education" in China: An overview', *International Journal of Educational Development*, 29, (3), 241–9.

DGIS (2003), *Local solutions to global challenges: towards effective partnership in basic education, country study report – Uganda*. Joint evaluation of external support to basic education in developing countries. The Hague: DGIS.

Dolowitz, D. P. and Marsh, D. (2000), 'Learning from abroad: the role of policy transfer in contemporary policy-making'. *Governance: An International Journal of Policy and Administration*, 13, (1), 5–24.

Educational Reform Initiative (2005), 'Yeni Öğretim Programlarını İnceleme ve Değerlendirme Raporu'. [Online] Available at www.erg.sabanciuniv.edu.tr/ (Accessed: 17 August 2010).

Edwards, R. and Usher, R. (2008), *Globalisation and pedagogy: space, place and identity*, 2nd edn. London and New York: Routledge.

Gauthier, C. and Dembele, M. (2004), 'Quality of teaching and quality of education: A review of research findings', paper commissioned for the EFA Global Monitoring Report 2005 'The Quality Imperative'. Available at: unesdoc.unesco.org/images/0014/001466/146641e.pdf (Accessed: 25 April 2010).

Ginsburg, M. (2009), 'Active-learning pedagogies as a reform initiative: synthesis of case studies' [Online] Available at www.equip123.net/docs/ e1-ActiveLearningSynthesis (Accessed: 7 April 2010).

Ginsburg, M. B. and Megahed, N. M. (2008), 'Global discourses and educational reform in Egypt: The case of active learning pedagogies'. *Mediterranean Journal of Educational Studies*, 13, (2), 91–115.

Guthrie, G. (1990), 'To the defence of traditional teaching in lesser-developed countries', in V. D. Rurst and P. Dalin eds., *Teachers and Teaching in the Developing World*. New York & London: Garland, pp. 219–32.

Işıkoğlu, N. and Bastürk, R. (2007), 'İlköğretim öğretmenlerinin yapılandırmacı yaklaşımla ilgili öğretim stratejileri hakkında görüşleri', paper presented to IV Eğitimde Yeni Yönelimler Sempozyumu, 17 November.

Leu, E. and Price-Rom, A. (2006), *Quality of education and teacher learning: A review of the literature*. Washington, DC: USAID.

Lopes, A. C. and De Macedo, E. F. (2009), 'A critical perspective on managing curriculum', *Curriculum Inquiry*, 39, (1), 57–74.

Luschei, T. F. (2004), 'Timing is everything: the intersection of borrowing and lending in Brazil's adoption of Escuela Nueva', in G. Steiner-Khamsi ed., *The global politics of educational borrowing and lending*. New York and London: Teachers College Press, pp. 154–67.

Mayer, R. (2004), 'Should there be a three-strikes rule against pure discovery learning? The case for guided methods of instruction'. *American Psychologist*, 59, (1), 14–19.

Meyer, J. W. and Ramirez, F. O. (2000), 'The world institutionalization of education', in J. Schriewer ed., *Discourse formation in comparative education*. Frankfurt: Peter Lang, pp. 111–32.

MONE (2008), 'Temel Eğitime Destek Programı' [Online] Available at projeler. meb.gov.tr/pkm1/index.php?view=article&catid=22:yaptik&id=63:temel-eitime-destek-programtedp&option=com_content&Itemid=64 (Accessed: 20 March 2010).

—(2005), *İlköğretim 1–5 sınıf programları tanıtım el kitabı*. Ankara: Ministry of National Education.

NCDC – National Curriculum Development Centre (2006a), *The National Primary School Curriculum for Uganda, Primary 1*. Kampala: NCDC.

—(2006b), *The National Primary School Curriculum for Uganda, Teacher's Guide Primary 1*. Kampala: NCDC.

Nykiel-Herbert, B. (2004), 'Mis-constructing knowledge: the case of learner-centred pedagogy in South Africa', *Prospects*, XXXIV, (3), 249–65.

O'Sullivan, M. (2004), 'The re-conceptualisation of learner-centred approaches: a Namibian case study', *International Journal of Educational Development*, 24, (6), 585–602.

Price-Rom, A. and Sainazarov, K. (2009), *Active-learning pedagogies as a reform initiative: the case of Kyrgyzstan*, Washington, DC: American Institutes for Research.

Ramirez, F. O. (2003), 'The global model and national legacies', in K. Alexander-Levitt ed., *Local meanings, global schooling: Anthropology and world culture theory*. New York: Palgrave Macmillan, pp. 239–54.

Read, T. and Enyutu, S. (2005), *Road map for the implementation of the curriculum reforms recommended by the primary curriculum review report and approved by the Ministry of Education and Sports*. Kampala: Ministry of Education and Sports.

Roggemann, K., and Shukri, M. (2009), *Active-learning pedagogies as a reform initiative: The case of Jordan*, Washington DC: American Institutes for Research.

Schriewer, J. and Martinez, C. (2004), 'Constructions of internationality in education', in G. Steiner- Khamsi ed., *The global politics of educational borrowing and lending*. New York: Teachers College Press, pp. 29–53.

Schweisfurth, M. (2002), *Teachers, democratisation and educational reform in Russia and South Africa*. Oxford: Symposium Books.

Serbessa, D. D. (2006), 'Tension between traditional and modern teaching-learning approaches in Ethiopian primary schools', *Journal of International Co-operation in Education*, 9, (1), 123–40.

Steiner-Khamsi, G. (2004), 'Conclusion: Blazing a trail for policy theory and practice', in G. Steiner-Khamsi ed., *The global politics of educational borrowing and lending*. New York and London: Teachers College Press, pp. 201–20.

—(2006), 'The economics of policy borrowing and lending: a study of late adopters', *Oxford Review of Education*, 32, (5), 665–78.

—(2010), 'The politics and economics of comparison', *Comparative Education Review*, 54, (3), 323–42.

Steiner-Khamsi, G. and Quist, H. O. (2000), 'The politics of educational borrowing: reopening the case of Achimota in British Ghana', *Comparative Education Review*, 44, (3), 272–99.

Steiner-Khamsi, G. and Stolpe, I. (2006), *Educational import: local encounters with global forces in Mongolia*. New York: Palgrave Macmillan.

Tabulawa, R. (2003), 'International aid agencies, learner-centred pedagogy and political democratisation: a critique', *Comparative Education*, 39, (1), 7–26.

TÜSİAD (1990), 'Türkiye'de eğitim: sorunlar ve değişime yapısal uyum önerileri' [Online] Available at www.tusiad.org/FileArchive/turkiyedeegitim.pdf (Accessed: 10 April 2010).

Ulusoy, K. (2009), 'The changing challenge of Europeanization to politics and governance in Turkey', *International Political Science Review*, 30, (4), 363–84.

UNEB – Uganda National Examinations Board (2005), *The achievements of primary school pupils in Uganda in English and Numeracy*. Kampala: UNEB.

UNESCO (2005), *Education for all global monitoring report 2005 – the quality imperative*. Paris: UNESCO.

Windschitl, M. (2002), 'Framing constructivism in practice as the negotiation of dilemmas: an analysis of the conceptual, pedagogical, cultural, and political challenges facing teachers', *Review of Educational Research*, 72, (2), 131–75.

Yang, F., Chang, A. and Hsu, Y. (2008), 'Teacher views about constructivist instruction and personal epistemology: a national study in Taiwan', *Educational Studies*, 34, (5), 527–42.

CHAPTER ELEVEN

Globalizing Educational Interventions in Zones of Conflict: The Role of Dutch Aid to Education and Conflict

Mario Novelli and

Mieke Lopes Cardozo

Introduction

This paper seeks to understand the rising tide of interest and action in the area of education and conflict by the international donor and development community since 2000, and to hone in on one key bilateral donor, the Netherlands. In line with the book's overall objective we are seeking to understand how a global education and conflict agenda emerged within the field of international education and development and the role of Dutch aid to education within this process. While much contemporary research has been done relating to the transfer of ideas and policies and the role of the World Bank, the IMF and other powerful agencies, from various perspectives (Cammack 2004, 2007), less is written about the role of smaller bilateral donors in these processes, either as catalysts for the spread of the global education agenda or as mediators. On this issue we draw insights from the potential differences between US and European interests, and consequently their approaches on the international stage, and theoretical debates on whether tensions can best be understood through triadic understandings of global politics (Asia, Europe, USA); bipolar (North versus South) or class factions and the rise of a transnational capitalist class (Robinson 1996; Amin 2004; Hardt *et al.* 2006; Negri 2008).

The chapter will proceed as follows: first, we will explore the broader development literature to chart the rise of the conflict and development agenda and the role of education therein. Secondly, we will explore the particular role of Dutch involvement in these processes and its critiques. This section draws on 15 interviews conducted in April and June 2010 with both Dutch ministry officials and civil society actors working on the theme of education and conflict, as well as a range of policy documents. We analyse the role of several related departments within the Dutch Ministry of Foreign Affairs (MFA) that are involved in the area, the most important or active one being the social department DSO/OO, who are responsible for the themes of education and research, health and civil society, followed by the Fragility and Peace Building Unit (EFV) and the humanitarian aid department (DMH/HH). In addition, we also include some initial insights into the role of and relationship with the Dutch Ministry of Defence. Finally we will reflect on the contradictory role of the Dutch in the global governance of education and conflict, linking the chapter back to broader debates contained in this book.

Understanding the Rise of Interest in Conflict and Development

In this section we aim to tell the story of the rise of interest in education and conflict in the global education agenda. This begins in the early 1990s in the period after the end of the Cold War. This led to the end of bipolarism in international relations, which in turn resulted in a drop in overall development aid, but also a shift of focus in development policy and education policy toward the least developed countries and population groups. The removal of Cold War tensions also produced a noticeable, albeit partial, shift away from the overwhelmingly partisan and highly political allocation of aid during the cold war (Lundborg 1998; Wang 1999; Christian Aid 2004).

These post-Cold War shifts led to an increased focus on Sub-Saharan Africa and joint donor efforts to improve the coordination of international development policy during the 1990s. These efforts culminated in the Millennium Development Goals and aspects of the Education For All objectives it contains. As part of a global education agenda, donors agreed in the Paris Declaration of 2005 to 'harmonise' their aid efforts in developing contexts, for instance through mechanisms such as the Sector Wide Approaches (Swaps) to education ensuring ownership and alignment with aid recipients' development strategies (Mundy 2002, 2006; King 2007; OECD 2005/2008). While not without both critics and critiques, there was a feeling that the architecture of aid was becoming more coherent and being targeted toward those areas of most need (Cosgrave 2005), even if the rhetoric often outpaced the financing (GCE 2009). On the other hand, this period also represented the rise of US hegemony and the broader consolidation of the neoliberal global project. This had the effect in the field of education and development of globalising a set of neoliberal-inspired education policy recipes including decentralisation, privatisation, new public management, etc. These policies were initiated in the heat of the Cold War under World Bank/IMF-sponsored structural adjustment policies but continue on to the present in different forms (Robertson *et al.* 2007).

Parallel to these post-Cold War developments of increased donor coordination and consensus and neoliberal hegemony was also a rise in Western interventionism, often under the leadership of the United States, in high profile conflicts from the Balkans to Rwanda, Somalia, Sudan, Iraq and Afghanistan. The post-Cold War peace dividend appeared to be ending before it had begun. Importantly, Western interventions in these conflicts were also discursively framed as 'humanitarian interventions' (Fearon 2008, p. 52), drawing on issues of human security, human rights, democracy and freedom for their justification (Roberts 2000; Forsythe 2000). The previous UN gospel of non-interventionism in the sovereign affairs of member states became tempered by the right of the international community to intervene in cases where the 'human security' of the population was at risk. Critics saw this new humanitarianism as a new mode of imperialism (Chomsky 1994; Chossudovsky 1997; Chomsky 1999; Chossudovsky 2002).

Increased intervention into conflict zones was also catalysed by the fallout from the 9/11 attacks. Suddenly the insecurity and conflict occurring outside the core global powers was recognized as producing insecurity at home (Duffield 2007). This led to an increased push to merge issues of international development with national security concerns – the merging of security and development – a logic that had of course been present throughout the Cold War. Almost immediately the US and other Western powers began to prioritize concerns over 'terrorism' and sought to integrate all other aspects of government policy under this overarching objective. During the Bush administration, development and humanitarian organisations were often simplistically treated as 'force multipliers' (Novelli 2010), and while the language has softened under the Obama administration, the central thrust of linking development aid to national security objectives has remained intact (Southern Aid Effectiveness Commission 2010). In June 2008, USAID released their new 'civil military cooperation policy' (2008), explaining their 3D-approach, incorporating Defence, Diplomacy and Development and stating that: 'Development is also recognized as a key element of any successful whole-of-government counterterrorism and counter-insurgency effort' (USAID 2008, p. 1). While the US was and remains the most vigorous agent in the process of merging security and development, the EU and other donors (including DFID, AUSAID, Japan and the Dutch, as this paper will show) have similar policies (EU 2003, p. 13).

While the renewed funding (see below) and commitment of Western governments to the importance of international development might be welcomed, this joined up whole-of-government 3D-approach brought with it dangers for the development and humanitarian community of being taken over by the generally more powerful security wing of national governments.Moreover, as noted recently by the Southern Aid Effectiveness Commission (2010), mixing development cooperation with other policies or 'commercial, security or geopolitical interests' undermines the possibilities of aligning overseas development assistance with internationally agreed aid effectiveness principles, like the Paris Agenda. Similarly, as the failure of both the Iraq and Afghanistan occupations is becoming increasingly evident, so it appears that there is a shift in military strategy from counter-terrorism to counter-insurgency. This shift has important implications for development practices and actors as counterinsurgency strategy seeks to control population groups and within this strategy is a component of winning hearts and minds through strategies such as social investments in health and education. This process blurs lines between aid worker and soldier, development issues and military strategy; this has a range of implications, not least the fact that it fuels accusations of western aid agency collabouration with occupying forces, which has increased the number of attacks on aid workers (Stoddard *et al.* 2006, 2009).

While the dynamics and nature of the development and conflict agenda remain hotly debated, what is less contested is the fact that conflict is now at the centre of the development policy and debate. Since the 1990's there has been a massive increase in the number of UN peacekeeping troops and humanitarian and development actors operating in conflict situations. By 1995, humanitarian agencies were responding to a total of 28 complex emergencies around the world, increasing from just five in 1985 (Bradbury 1995; Slim 1996). By the mid-1990s emergency spending had increased by over 600 per cent from its mid 1980s point to over US$3.5 billion and has continued to rise (Fearon 2008). Personnel had increased by over 700 per cent since 1999 to 110,000 personnel with a budget of US$7 billion in 2008. According to the 2008 Reality of Aid Report (2008, p. 8): 'aid allocations to the most severely conflict-affected countries ... increased from 9.3 per cent of total ODA in 2000 (for 12 countries) to 20.4 per cent (for 10 countries) in 2006.' Coupled with a general increase in ODA during the same period, aid to conflict-affected countries has nearly tripled in real terms between 2000–2006. In 2007, according to a recent OECD/DAC report (2008, p. 8) 38.4 per cent of total ODA (US$ 37.2 billion) went to conflict and fragile states.

What is also clear from the literature is that the distribution of aid among severely conflict-affected countries was, and remains, highly unequal and reflects the rise of the security agenda. In 2006 Iraq and Afghanistan accounted for over 60 per cent of all aid to severely conflict-affected countries (Reality of Aid 2008, p. 217). In 2007, (OECD/DAC 2008, p. 8) of the 38.4 per cent of total ODA (US$ 37.2 billion) that went to conflict and fragile states, over half was directed to just five countries: Iraq (23 per cent), Afghanistan (9.9 per cent), and Ethiopia, Pakistan and Sudan (sharing 17 per cent of the total).

Understanding the Rise of Education and Conflict

Since the late 1990s and in tandem with the expansion of development and humanitarian intervention in conflict zones, there has been a parallel increase in interest and recognition of the importance of education delivery in conflict and post-conflict zones. This we believe has been the result of three key drivers.

First, education, like food and shelter, has come to be seen as part of the core building blocks of human development and a necessary and vital part of humanitarian response in conflict situations in particular (Save the Children 2010). Since 2008, there has also been a Global Education Cluster, headed by UNICEF and the International Save the Children Alliance that coordinates the educational response in emergency situations, as part of the Inter-Agency Standing Committee (IASC) that assumes overall coordination, and develops policy involving UN and non-UN humanitarian partners operating in conflict zones. Central to the rise in prominence of education within conflict situations have been the actions of the Inter-Agency Network on Education in Emergencies (INEE), which emerged out of the World Education Forum in Dakar. INEE is a network created to improve inter-agency communication and collabouration within the context of education in emergencies, and has proved an effective lobbying, advocacy and policy-coordination and development institution. As with the more general increases in development aid to conflict effected zones (Fearon 2008, p. 72), increases in aid to education are at least partly due to the success of organisations like Save the Children, INEE and UNICEF in successfully lobbying for an expansion of their own mandates and activities in education, within a growing conflict and development funding regime.

Secondly, the success of these linked organisations and practitioners in placing education and conflict firmly on the international development agenda has been aided by a recognition from bilateral donors that a large proportion of the world's out-of-school children are located in conflict and post-conflict countries, and thus this issue needs to be addressed if the EFA goals are to be achieved (Stewart 2003; Save the Children 2007, 2008). This has also led to a growing awareness of the relationship between education and conflict, and its potentially catalytic and preventative roles (Bush *et al.* 2000; DFID 2003), though we would argue that the technical politics of delivering education in contexts of conflict rather than its political/cultural nature is highlighted in donor engagement to date. The Dutch, as we will show below, in the period 2007–10 have been very much part of this bilateral donor involvement to get education in conflict affected areas on the international agenda.

Thirdly, the merging of security and development outlined above has also penetrated the field of education and development. In education this emerges as a process of reinterpreting both the purposes and the practices of both education and development as having potential 'security benefits.' An illustration of this is the prevalence of references to the role of education in the US's counter-terrorism strategies elabourated in Patterns of Global Terrorism Annual Reports (since 2004 renamed Country Reports on Terrorism). As an example, the 2007 report, in Chapter 5, 'Terrorist Safe Havens', sub-section 7 focuses on Basic Education in Muslim Countries. In this section it notes that:

> The Department of State, USAID, and other US agencies continued to support an increased focus on education in predominantly Muslim countries and those with significant Muslim populations. The United States' approach stresses mobilising public and private resources as partners to improve access, quality and the relevance of education, with a specific emphasis on developing civic-mindedness in young people. In many Muslim-majority countries, such as Afghanistan and Yemen, the challenge was to increase country capacity to provide universal access to primary education and literacy (US State Department 2008, p. 243).

Similarly, as part of the US military's counterinsurgency strategy in places such as Iraq and Afghanistan, humanitarian and civic assistance 'can include such non-emergency services as constructing schools, performing dental procedures, and even vaccinating the livestock of farmers' (Brigety 2008). Crucially for us, it appears that educational provision (particularly for girls) became a key discursive justification for the military intervention in Afghanistan, and educational progress as a means of demonstrating the alleged success of the occupation.

These combined reasons have led to a growing commitment to the area of education and conflict, and have, not surprisingly, led to increased funds being allocated to education in conflict zones. While Save the Children see this as insufficient to meet the challenges ahead (noting that while 39 million of the 56 million out-of-school children live in conflict-affected countries, only 33 per cent of funding was allocated to them in 2006; Save the Children 2007, 2008, 2010), the funds allocated are increasing. DFID in its recent Education Strategy Paper (2010) notes that in the coming five years, 50 per cent of all aid to education will be directed to education in conflict and 'fragile states'[1]. What should also be noted is that, as with the general aid disbursements to conflict and fragile states, the distribution of educational aid between countries is highly uneven, with several high profile countries such as Iraq, Pakistan, Sudan and Afghanistan receiving large portions of the cake.

In conclusion what we can say at this point is that the rise of the education and conflict agenda has been facilitated by a range of external and internal factors: by post-Cold War and post-9/11 (geo)political realities and intentions; by EFA and MDG goals; by the advocacy of organisations like Save the Children, UNICEF and INEE, pushing for the humanitarian and human rights agenda of education; and finally also through the agency of military and security sectors that see building schools and strengthening education in certain conflict zones as part of their military strategy to win the hearts and minds of the civilian populations. Many of these issues and actors appear to clash with each other and produce unlikely bedfellows. In the next section we will begin to unravel where the Netherlands government fits into this complicated picture.

Dutch aid to education in emergencies and conflicts

Within the field of educational aid to conflict-affected states the Dutch are widely seen as playing an important leadership role, in terms not only of their funding commitment, but also their receptivity and support for educational interventions in conflicts, and for their innovation in developing new funding mechanisms to deliver aid to conflict-affected countries. Save the Children in their background paper (2009, p. 20) for UNESCOs Global Monitoring Report 2010 wrote how 'the Netherlands' substantial weight as one of the key education donors has given them considerable sway in influencing the shape of the international aid architecture.' They refer particularly to the Dutch influence as the largest donor to the Fast Track Initiative (FTI)[2] catalytic fund in opening up the system for countries under fragile or conflictive conditions, and the biggest Dutch investment in education and conflict, the UNICEF Education in Emergencies and Post-Crisis Transition (EEPCT) Programme, totalling US$ 201 million.

Historically, the Dutch see themselves as pioneers in the field of international relations. Until the 1950s, they held on strongly to their neutrality in international affairs, while during the Cold War this relatively small European country saw itself forced to become part of two important strategic alliances: NATO and what is now called the European Union. Dutch membership of NATO and its strong loyalty to the United States were seen as counterweights to either a Russian invasion or domination from the continental powers of Germany or France. This position gave the Dutch a relatively strong voice in the international arena during the Cold War.

The end of the Cold War meant a drastic shift in this balance of power, as NATO lost its original function. Subsequently, the attacks of 9/11 transformed both NATO and the Dutch-US relationship into an unequal and unilateral US dominated situation based on the idea of mutual insecurity, which continues to date. Instead of the former Dutch international position of neutrality and international stability (linked to its export-oriented trade system), the military has again become a major instrument of foreign policy, as was exemplified by the Dutch participation in the wars in Iraq and Afghanistan. In addition, ongoing processes of globalization and regionalisation resulted in the creation of a more regulated European market and community, where Dutch influence diminished rapidly (Tromp 2006). The Dutch thus find themselves in a subservient position in both a US and a European pact. Current foreign policies seem to be based on the idea that there is no other choice then to 'go with the flow or drop out of the game' (Tromp 2006, translated by authors). As we now move on to explore the Dutch role in education and conflict, we seek to highlight how the contemporary positive, yet also contradictory, role of the Dutch in the field of education can at least be partially understood from the changing position of the Netherlands in this historical geopolitical context.

The education and development department (DSO) of the MFA started to work actively on the theme of education and conflict around 2005, although earlier interest in the theme became apparent in the wake of the World Education Forum in Dakar in 2000. Based on the interviews and policy documents, we found four main reasons why the social department of the MFA started to invest in education in conflict situations over the last five years, which both tie into rationales already highlighted and bring in new local dimensions. First, for most Ministry officials of the social development department, reaching the MDGs was the main reason to prioritize education in conflicts and emergencies. As one of them said: 'our motivation was inspired by reaching the MDGs, considering the fact that most school children falling outside the [education] system live in conflict areas' (interview 06/04/2010). Second, the social development staff members also confirmed that by 2007 there was a financial opportunity to open up resources for this theme. The Dutch government had committed itself to allocating 15 per cent of total ODA to education (around €600 million per annum), and the Minister of Development Cooperation, Koenders (2007–February 2010) was prioritising aid to conflict-affected areas and fragile states in his policy note 'Our Common Concern' (MFA 2007a). Thirdly, this financial opportunity paved the way for the Dutch government to aim for strategic international leadership on the issue. The Dutch were frustrated with the rigidity of the FTI funding mechanism, particularly for conflict-affected states, seeking first to reform the FTI and then to bypass it via an innovative partnership with UNICEF. Another ministry official explained that:

we were able to show other donors that it was possible to do something.

That we shouldn't just wait for the FTI. We had the courage to explore new possibilities to fund education in conflict-affected areas through UNICEF (Interview 06/04/2010).

Fourth, there was an enabling international and national/institutional context for the rise of interest in education in conflict situations. As has been shown above, since Dakar in 2000 and the emergence of INEE, awareness of the need to invest in education in emergencies and conflict grew rapidly. At the level of the Dutch MFA, we observe how individual institutional factors also might have played a role in pushing the theme of conflict up the development agenda, because fragile states and development cooperation in conflict areas was a major priority of ex-minister Koenders. The enabling context was thus the product of a combination of international factors and personal interests and agenda-setting processes. This enabling context was also closely linked to the 'security agenda', which saw the development sector as an additional tool in strengthening and addressing security concerns. While the social development department saw its engagement as inspired by the MDGs, the conducive environment for engagement in conflict zones was no doubt facilitated by Minister Koenders' enthusiasm for an 'integrated 3D approach' to development, with much resemblance to USAIDs 3D-approach discussed above. This resulted in the creation of the Fragility and Peace Building Unit within the Dutch MFA, which explicitly sought to link Dutch military, diplomacy and development policies around the world. Parallel to this, the Dutch Ministry of Defence, caught up in the unpopular war in Afghanistan, was seeking social policies to assist in their counterinsurgency strategies in their zone of control in Afghanistan (Uruzgan), which included building schools (Ministry of Defense 2011a).[3] In the next section, we will look more closely at Dutch engagement in education in conflict-affected countries, trying to understand further the motivations, the practices and the underlying rationales.

Dutch policy and practice on education and conflict in action: From MDGs to Security?

The Dutch are guided in their policy formation and aid allocation by the policy ideas of various other international actors, particularly the World Bank and the OECD/DAC. With regard to the World Bank, apart from being a key development partner at country level, the Dutch also rely heavily on the Bank's reports and guidelines. In 2007, the OECD/DAC (2007) drafted an influential set of guidelines for policy and implementation called 'Principles for Good International Engagement in Fragile States and Situations.' The guiding policy principles as formulated by a staff member of the social department in a draft IIEP paper are closely related to these OECD/DAC principles:

> The guiding policy principles of [Government of the Netherlands] are: 1) an integrated approach; 2) local partners, local priorities; 3) context-specific approach and political sensitivity; 4) fast, flexible and long-term involvement; 5) multilateral where possible, bilateral where needed; 6) prevention and 7) taking responsible risks (Eijkholt 2011).

As well as immediate and short-term emergency relief, for a large part through the UNICEF-EEPCT programme, the government of the Netherlands emphasizes the importance of longer-term capacity-building strategies in fragile environments. They were actively involved in the development of Guidelines for Capacity Development in the Education Sector within the Education for All Fast Track Initiative Framework, which aims to implement the OECD/DAC and Paris principles. Capacity development has been at the core of the Dutch bilateral aid development programme in Afghanistan, particularly with regard to the creation of technical and vocational training centres in agricultural education. However, based on earlier policy experiences, the Dutch see it as one of their major challenges to balance these immediate and longer-term priorities of education in conflict situations, because of demands for results from Parliament and tax-payers (Eijkholt 2011).

Influenced by the World Bank's 'Assessing Aid' report (1998), the Dutch have limited the number of partner countries drastically over the last decade from over 100 to around 33 in 2007, with currently only 15 partner countries, due to a recent change of government and development policy.[4] The Dutch have recognized that a former focus on 'good governance' as a selection norm led to the neglect of countries that do not fulfil those criteria: countries that are 'fragile' or affected by conflicts (Save the Children 2009, p. 23). The policy notes on Dutch Development Cooperation 'Our Common Concern' (2007a) and the New Policy Letter to the House of Representatives (2011b) specify the partner countries in three different types: in profile 1, countries are selected on criteria linked to the 'accelerated achievement of MDGs'; in profile 2 countries belong to the 'security and development' group; and in profile 3 countries have a 'broad-based relationship' with the Netherlands. The current government has, however, announced it is to cut down on its development aid to education and health because they see less surplus value in these sectors, while they are prioritising security, agriculture and climate issues (MFA 2011a). Education is no longer a policy priority for development cooperation, but, in line with our former discussion of global prioritisation of education and conflict, Dutch development policy commitment to 'education in weak states will continue or even increase' (MFA 2011b).

The major financing innovation of the Dutch in the area of education and conflict has been the creation of the UNICEF-EEPCT programme. The first proposal for this US$ 201 million programme was written in 2006, and in that same year the Dutch were involved in working toward opening up the FTI system for fragile states. This programme came about mainly because of four reasons: at the time there was enough money available in the Dutch MFA to invest in this area; the FTI Catalytic Fund as it was designed then did not allow allocations for fragile states and the Dutch sought an alternative route; it was a response to the void between humanitarian and development stages of aid; and there were good connections and former experiences between the Dutch and UNICEF:

> The programme seeks to establish innovative strategies and delivery mechanisms so that educational interventions in fragile countries are a first step in a continuous reform process that will get countries back on a development path. Flexible funding is provided to accommodate the changing needs of a country (Eijkholt 2011).

In the initial design of the programme, 50 per cent was allocated to education in emergencies/crisis, 24 per cent to strengthening 'resilience' of education systems, 16 per cent to preparedness education systems, and 10 per cent to knowledge on reliable policy interventions and instruments. Most (75 per cent) of this funding was channelled to the national level, 15 per cent to the regional and 10 per cent to the international level (MFA, 2006). UNICEF is solely responsible for country selection, and UNICEF's strategies are aligned with CAPs and JAMs.[5] According to Save the Children's recent report *The Future is Now* (2010, p. 49), the UNICEF-EEPCT programme has contributed to a range of activities, including 'rebuilding and revitalising education systems in post-crises contexts, [...] investing in Education Management Information Systems, curriculum reform, systems to develop teacher capacity, and a teacher payroll system in Southern Sudan'. So far, education activities have been supported by the EEPCT programme in around 37 countries (MFA 2007a; UNICEF 2011).

Along with these multilateral programmes, the Dutch have also supported education in conflict situations through bilateral aid flows (particularly with regards to higher education) and through non-governmental/private aid channels. The social development department is actively involved in the INEE working group on Education and Fragility (Branelly *et al.* 2009) which brings together bilateral donors, multilateral organisations and INGOs working in the field of education and conflict. Although the government of the Netherlands does not directly support INEE on a multilateral basis, INEE is indirectly funded by the Dutch through the UNICEF-EEPCT programme: over the period September 2007–July 2010 this indirect funding to INEE was US$ 1,258,591). In the last few years, like many other bilateral donors, there has also been a shift from focussing mostly on basic education to supporting the whole education sector, including post-secondary forms of education and technical and vocational training. This broader approach to the education sector is also reflected in the various programmes for education in conflict areas that include, for instance, technical and vocational training projects and support to higher education institutes.

As for the other two relevant departments in the MFA, the Humanitarian Department and the Fragility and Peace Building Unit, this enabling context has also played a role in their efforts for education in emergencies or conflict areas. However, for the humanitarian department education is still not seen as a priority when providing basic human needs to people in emergency situations, even though Save the Children's 'Last in Line, Last in School' Report as well as IIEPs 'Donor's Engagement' publication both urge the Dutch Government to include education in its official humanitarian strategy (Save the Children 2007, p. 32; Branelly *et al.* 2009, p. 131). Here we see a difference with the general international recognition of the need to include education as a key humanitarian need that we considered above and the internal policies of the Dutch MFA. The Fragility and Peace Building Unit EFV has begun to acknowledge education's pivotal role in conflict prevention and reconciliation processes and is seeking to find ways to engage with and in the education sector.

Despite the active involvement in supporting education in conflict affected regions, there has been no official policy documentation developed within the social development department. Still, there are a number of internal policy documents, and the social development department has been involved in supporting the publication and dissemination of several UNESCO-IIEP publications, together with the 'IS Academie' research group on Education and Development of the University of Amsterdam[6]. The humanitarian department does not see education as a humanitarian priority, and thus has not included this in its policy documents. The Fragility and Peace Building Unit do have a policy document on fragile states and development in conflict areas which include some references to the need to support the education sector. Within this part of the MFA, education is seen as an instrument to create a peace dividend (MFA 2007b). Providing schooling to local populations in conflict areas is seen as part of the 'integral 3D-approach', through cooperation with the military as well as with civil society and the private sector. This cooperation is also reflected in the inclusion of these actors in so-called 'knowledge circles' that are promoted in the Netherlands by EFV and DSO/OO.

Although the 2007 policy note 'Our Common Concern' recognizes that a focus on fragile states is necessary because they lag behind in reaching the MDGs (Eijkholt 2011), EFVs policy on Fragile States and the (Ex-)Minister of Development Cooperation Koenders' discourse show similarities to the US counter-terrorism strategy reportfor an integral 3D state approach, and the importance of education as a peace dividend in cases such as Afghanistan. Based on the principles of this approach, Koenders claims

> we cannot solve the problem of fragile states through development cooperation alone. [...] In tackling the multiple causes of fragility, my colleagues and I seek to integrate three aspects: development, diplomacy and defence (the three Ds). This consistent multi-track strategy involves a solid, joint analysis of the problem; intensive international cooperation; investment of sufficient resources and people; long-term political commitment; support for parliaments and other countervailing powers; and unflagging attention to state performance. We also need to bear Western businesses and governments in mind, as they sometimes play a role in the abuse of power by elites in fragile states (MFA 2007c).

Linking back to the section on the global agenda on education and conflict, when Koenders talks about his 'colleagues' here, he seems to refer not only to his Dutch colleagues within the MFA but also to colleagues abroad (DFID, USAID) who similarly align with the 3D approach. In the province of Uruzgan in Afghanistan, the Dutch actively promote an integrated approach to security, governance, reconstruction and construction as part of the International Security Assistance Force (ISAF). Furthermore, 'the Netherlands is keen for all relevant parts of government, civil society and the private sector to be involved in formulating and implementing policy (Eijkholt 2011).

This integrated approach is also present outside the MFA, for instance through the Civil Military Cooperation (CIMIC) mission of the Ministry of Defence (2011a). In CIMIC, education is seen as a crucial instrument for development and to stimulate hope for the future. The network of Cultural Affairs and Education consists of reservists who are experts in the education or cultural sectors: 'The network ensures a contextualised understanding of the socio-cultural aspects of development projects' (2011a). This CIMIC network is involved in defence missions to Iraq, Afghanistan and the African continent.

The Dutch integrated 3D approach in Afghanistan

Returning to the Afghanistan case, we will now look at some concrete examples of the Dutch integrated approach that was implemented during the Dutch military presence in the Afghan province of Uruzgan until 2010. Over the past four years, the Dutch ministers of Development Coordination, of Foreign Affairs and of Defence worked together, because 'stability and reconstruction in Afghanistan is not only important for the country itself, but also contribute to more security in the Netherlands and the rest of the world' (MFA 2010a). In February 2011, the last Dutch soldiers left Uruzgan as part of the ISAF (International Security and Assistance Force). Dutch political and development advisors of the MFA work in the country as well, and Dutch money is invested in reconstruction projects at the local and national level. This combined security-development strategy is seen as 'a powerful tool in the struggle against radicalisation' (2010b).

At the national level, €25 million per year is invested through the Afghanistan Reconstruction Trust Fund (ARTF), managed by the World Bank, to cover salaries of ministry officials, offer microcredit loans, support the national solidarity programme (NSP), the Afghan National Development Strategy (ANDS) and the EQUIP education programme[7]. An amount of 50 million is invested until 2011 to support the judicial system and policy through the Law and Order Trust Fund Afghanistan, managed by the UNDP (Ministry of Defence 2011b).

The 3D approach with its civil-military cooperation in Uruzgan is perceived as a success story, since 'development aid reaches most of the local communities, which consequently choose to turn against the insurgents [the Taliban].'[8] It can thus be argued that education has been part of a Dutch counter-insurgency strategy in the Uruzgan province. The Provincial Reconstruction Teams (PRTs) of the Dutch military worked through a so-called 'inkblot method', where they first support the Afghan military in creating safe areas and consequently work on reconstruction of infrastructure, school buildings and basic healthcare facilities. According to the MFA, this is also called 'the Dutch Approach', which means:

> a combination of respect for the local population, an understanding of religion, local values and customs, and acting in as least aggressive a way as possible. Still, there are situations in which the army has to act forcefully in their struggle against the Taliban. It is essential for every success to be an Afghan success. Therefore we act together as much as possible with the Afghan military and police (2010b).

Schools were being (re)built as part of the ISAF or the civil-military CIMIC activities. A captain explains 'we have built five brand-new schools, and one protective wall for an existing school against floods. [...] These quick projects are psychologically important because they create goodwill with the local population. We call them force-acceptance activities' (2010b). Longer term reconstruction projects are also funded by the Dutch but implemented by the Afghan government or international multilateral or non-governmental organisations.

In conclusion to this section, we would like to recall the warning signs of integrating development into the area of security, particularly considering the current Dutch political decision to enter a new and highly debated 'police mission' in the province of Kunduz. The Southern Aid Effectiveness Commission in a recent report wrote:

> Mixing development cooperation with other policies, or even subor-dinating it, makes ODA hard to align with internationally agreed aid effectiveness principles. Although this practice is more profound in the USA than in the European countries visited by this Commission, the impor-tance of delinking development cooperation from commercial, security or geopolitical interests cannot be overemphasised (SAEC 2010, p. 24).

Arguing for the 'security benefits' of education might open up funding to (re)build schools in conflict zones. However, we see this as a potentially dangerous road. Is building schools to win the hearts and minds of the local population a good strategy when it is unclear what will happen within these schools afterwards? Will local and international development workers be safe when they would have to cooperate with the military in zones of violent conflict? And what if the merging of development and security provides more arguments to cut down on development spending because the military will take care of 'building back better' education systems in (post)-war situations? Both the sustainability and the ethics of military involvement in development delivery remains highly contentious.

Conclusions: The role of the Dutch in Aid to Education in Conflict affected Countries – globalizer or globalized?

In line with other publications that analyse Dutch aid to education and conflict (Save the Children 2009; Brannelly 2009; Save the Children 2010; Southern Aid Effectiveness Commission 2010), we agree that there are a number of positive sides to the Dutch way of supporting education in conflict-affected countries, such as their flexibility, short- and longer-term programmes, and their attempts to innovate and to provide international leadership in this area. Committed to the OECD/DAC principles and the Paris Declaration, the Dutch appear less interested than some donors in branding their aid, and more willing than most to pool funds, align aid with others and work collectively in the field of education (Lopes Cardozo *et al.* 2011).However, the current shift toward national (economic) interests (2011) at the expense of social investments of the new Dutch development cooperation strategy show warning signs of how former prioritisation of education based on the principles of solidarity and poverty reduction are rapidly being undermined.

We also note several potential dangers of the emerging 'integrated 3D-approach' and the increasing encroachment of more powerful sections of the Ministry of Foreign Affairs that threaten to undermine the developmental aspects of education in conflict-affected zones and subordinate them to military or diplomatic short-term objectives, including Dutch self-interest in terms of their economy and national security. This process appears both as an internal dynamic, but also as a reflection of the more global security agenda that threatens long-term and sustainable investments in education in conflict affected countries.

Beyond these struggles, there is also a broader issue of the intellectual dependency of the Dutch MFA on other international players, not least the World Bank and DFID. While the Dutch appear innovative in developing modes of delivery of aid, they are less innovative in producing alternative policies on projects and practices, of raising issues on the content of education in conflict-affected zones, opening up the issue of the drivers of both war and peace within the education systems themselves and how to address these issues. Instead, they reproduce a service delivery rationale for education in conflict zones without addressing the particularities of conflict and context. This might be a problem of a lack of independent knowledge production within the Netherlands in this policy field, but also perhaps a sense of dealing with the 'how' rather than the 'why' of policy intervention, which may be problematic, particularly when the agendas of the World Bank, DFID and USAID might be in tension with the broader foreign policy and development objectives of the Dutch on the international stage.

In conclusion, we can say that Dutch activity in the field of education and conflict is contradictory. While on the one hand they lead on the practicalities and funding issues, on the other they follow in terms of the content of global agenda-setting. They are both a key catalyst and contributor to the global agenda on education and conflict as well as a consumer of the core ideas that frame this agenda, produced by the World Bank, DFID and the OECD. Returning to the theoretical debates on ways to understand the tensions in the global politics of international development, this paper demonstrates the Dutch state's subordinate position within global power relations (vis-a-vis the USA and the UK), but also their ongoing influence in North-South development relations.

Notes

1 We consider 'fragile states' as a complicated and value laden concept; however we chose to use the term for this chapter in order to stay close to the discourse used in the global and Dutch policy environment.

2 For more information on the Education for All Fast-track Initiative (EFA FTI) see www.educationfasttrack.org/.

3 There is relatively low public support for Dutch involvement in Afghanistan (NOS nieuws, 21 April 2008). When the Dutch government decided to prolong its stay in the Uruzgan province from 2007 to August 2010, 60 per

cent of the Dutch public thought this extra investment would not be well spent, and 43 per cent were against the decision (TNS NIPO 2007).

4 Profile 1 partner countries include: Benin, Ethiopia, Mali, Mozambique, Uganda and Rwanda. Profile 2 partner countries are: Afghanistan, Burundi, Yemen, Palestinian Territories and Sudan. Profile 3 partner countries include: Bangladesh, Ghana, Indonesia and Kenya.

5 CAP = Consolidated Appeals Process; JAM = Joint Assessment Mission.

6 See www.iiep.unesco.org/information-services/publications/search-iiep-publications.html for *Certification counts: recognizing the learning attainments of displaced and refugee children*, edited by Jackie Kirk, and *Opportunties for change: Education innovation and reform during and after conflict*, edited by Susan Nicolai.

7 Education Quality Improvement Project, together with the Afghan Ministry of Education and also funded by the World Bank (Eijkholt 2011).

8 MFA, Presentation of the 3D approach by the Netherlands in Afghanistan (no longer available online).

References

Amin, S. (1997), *Capitalism in the Age of Globalization: the Management of Contemporary Society*. London: Zed Books.

—(2004), 'US imperialism, Europe, and the Middle East'. *Monthly Review – an Independent Socialist Magazine*, 56, (6), 13–33.

Bradbury, M. (1995), *Aid Under Fire: Redefining Relief and Development*, London: HMSO.

Branelly, L., Ndaruhutse, S. and Rigaud, C. (2009), *Donor's Engagement, Supporting Education in Fragile and Conflict Affected States*, París: IIEP-UNESCO and CFBT Education Trust.

Brigety, R. E. (2008), *Humanity as a Weapon of War: Sustainable Security and the Role of the U.S. Military*. Washington: Centre for American Progress.

Bush, J. and Saltarelli, D. (2000), *The Two Faces of Education in Ethnic Conflict*. New York: UNICEF

Cammack, P. (2004), 'What the World Bank means by poverty reduction, and why it matters'. *New Political Economy*, 9, (2), 189–211.

—(2007), 'Imperial nature: the World Bank and struggles for social justice in the age of globalization'. *Progress in Human Geography*, 31, (1), 124–6.

Chomsky, N. (1994), *World Orders, Old and New*. London: Pluto.

—(1999), *The New Military Humanism: Lessons from Kosovo*. London: Pluto.

Chossudovsky, M. (1997), *The Globalisation of Poverty: Impacts of IMF and World Bank Reforms*. London: Zed Books, Penang: Third World Network.

—(2002), *War and Globalisation: the Truth behind September 11*. Shanty Bay, Ont.: Global Outlook.

Christian Aid (2004), *The Politics of Poverty; Aid in the new Cold War*, London: Christian Aid.

Collier, P. (1999), 'On the economic consequences of civil war'. *Oxford Economic Papers-New Series*, 51, (1), 168–83.

Collier, P. and Hoeffler, A. (1998), 'On economic causes of civil war'. *Oxford Economic Papers-New Series*, 50, (4), 563–73.

—(2004), 'Greed and grievance in civil war'. *Oxford Economic Papers-New Series*, 56, (4), 563–95.

Cosgrave, J. (2005), *The Impact of the War on Terror on Aid Flows*, London: Action Aid.

Dale, R. (1989), *The State and Education Policy*. Buckingham: Open University Press.

—(1999), 'Specifying globalization effects on national policy: a focus on the mechanisms'. *Journal of Education Policy*, 14, (1), 1–17.

—(2000), 'Globalization and Education: Demonstrating a 'Common World Educational Culture' or Locating a 'Globally Structured Educational Agenda?' *Educational Theory*, 50, (4), 427–48.

Dezalay, Y. and Garth, B. G. (2002), *The internationalization of palace wars: lawyers, economists, and the contest to transform Latin American states*. Chicago, Ill.; London: University of Chicago Press.

DFID (2003), *Education, Conflict and Development*. London: DFID.

Duffield, M. R. (2007), *Development, security and unending war: governing the world of peoples*. Cambridge: Polity.

Eijkholt, C. (2011), 'A Donors Perspective on Capacity Development in the Education Sector in Afghanistan', in M. Sigsgaard ed., *On the road to resilience, capacity development with the Ministry of Education in Afghanistan*. Paris: UNESCO-IIEP, pp. 133–48.

EU (2003), *A Secure Europe In a Better World*. Brussels: European Union.

Fearon, D. (2008), 'The rise of emergency relief aid', in M. N. Barnett and T. G. Weiss (eds), *Humanitarianism in Question*. Ithaca: Cornell University Press, pp. 49–72.

Fine, B., Lapavitsas, C. and Pincus, J. (2001), *Development policy in the twenty-first century: beyond the post-Washington consensus*. New York, London: Routledge.

Forsythe, D. P. (2000), *Human Rights in International Relations*, Cambridge: Cambridge University Press.

GCE (2009), *Education on the Brink: Will the IMF's New Lease on Life Ease or Block Progress towards Education Goals?* Johannesburg: Global Campaing for Education.

Hardt, M. and Negri, A. (2006), *Multitude: War and Democracy in the Age of Empire*. London, NY: Penguin Books.

Harvey, D. (2005), *A Brief History of Neoliberalism*. Oxford: Oxford University Press.

King, K. (2007), 'Multilateral agencies in the construction of the global agenda on education'. *Comparative Education*, 43, (3), 377–91.

Larner, W. and Walters, W. (2004), *Global Governmentality: Governing International Spaces*. London: Routledge.

Lipschutz, R. D. and Rowe, J. K. (2005), *Globalization, Govermentality and Global Politics: Regulation for the Rest of Us?* New York: London, Routledge.

Lopes Cardozo, M. T. A. and Novelli, M. (2011), 'Dutch aid to education and conflict', paper commissioned for the EFA Global Monitoring Report 2011 'The hidden crisis: Armed conflict and Education'. Available at:unesdoc.unesco. org/images/0019/001907/190708e.pdf (Accessed: 1/12/2011).

Lundborg, P. (1998), 'Foreign Aid and International Support as a Gift Exchange'. *Economics and Politics*, 10, (2), 127–42.

Ministry of Defence (2011a),Available at: www.defensie.nl/onderwerpen/cimic/cultural_affairs__education (Accessed: 1/12/2011).

—(2011b),Available at: www.defensie.nl/missies/afghanistan/wederopbouw/ (Accessed: 1/12/2011).

MFA – Ministry of Foreign Affairs the Netherlands (2006), *Boordelingsmemorandum UNICEF proposal 2006, activity number 15070*, unpublished policy document. The Hague: DSO.

—(2007a), Our Common Concern, Policy Note [pdf]. The Hague: MFA. Available at: www.minbuza.nl/dsresource?objectid=buzabeheer:32207&type=pdf (Accessed: 01/08/2010)

—(2007b), Veiligheid en ontwikkeling in fragiele staten, Strategie voor Nederlandse inzet 2008–2011, policy note on Fragile States. The Hague: MFA.

—(2007c), Engagement in Fragile States: A Balancing Act, unpublished speech by Minister Koenders, 2 October 2007, internal documentation MFA.

—(2010a), Available at: www.minbuza.nl/nl/Onderwerpen/Afghanistan (Accessed: 1/12/2011).

—(2010b), *Information brochure Netherlands in Afghanistan*, [Online] Available at: www.minbuza.nl/dsresource?objectid=buzabeheer:80875&type=org (Accessed: 1/08/2010).

—(2011a), *Hervorming Ontwikkelingssamenwerking*, [Online] Available at: www.rijksoverheid.nl/onderwerpen/ontwikkelingssamenwerking/hervorming-ontwikkelingssamenwerking (Accessed: 1/12/2011).

—(2011b), *New Policy Letter to the Dutch House of Representatives*. The Hague: MFA. AVT11/BZ101370.

Mundy, K. (2006), 'Constructing education for development: International organizations and education for all'. *Comparative Education Review*, 50, (2), 296–8.

Mundy, K. E. (2002), 'Retrospect and prospect: education in a reforming World Bank'. *International Journal of Educational Development*, 22, (5), 483–508.

Negri, A. (2008), *Reflections on Empire*. Cambridge: Polity.

NOS nieuws (2008), 'Minder steun voor missie Afghanistan', NOS Nieuws [Online] 21 April. Available at: nos.nl/artikel/70516-minder-steun-voor-missie-afghanistan.html (Accessed: 1/12/2011).

Novelli, M. (2010), 'The New Geopolitics of Aid to Education: From Cold Wars to Holy Wars'. International Journal of Educational Development, 30, 453–9.

OECD/DAC (2005/2008), The Paris Declaration on Aid Effectiveness and the Accra Agenda for Action, [Online] Available at: www.oecd.org/dataoecd/30/63/43911948.pdf (Accessed: 1/12/2011).

—(2007), *Principles for Good International Engagement in Fragile States and Situations*, [Online] Available at: www.oecd.org/document/48/0,33 43,en_2649_33693550_35233262_1_1_1_1,00.html (Accessed: 1/12/2011).

—(2008), *Resource Flows to Fragile and Conflict-Affected States Annual Report 2008*. Paris: OECD.

Offe, C. (1984), *Contradictions of the Welfare State*. London: Hutchinson.

Reality of Aid Network (2008), *The Reality of Aid 2008: An Independent Review of Poverty Reduction and Development Assistance*. Quezon City: Ibon Books

Roberts, A. (2000), 'Humanitarian issues and agencies as triggers for international military action'. *International Review of the Red Cross*, 839, 673–98.

Robertson, S., Novelli, M., Dale, R., Tikly, L., Dachi, H. and Ndebela, A. (2007), *Education and Development in a Global Era: Ideas, Actors and Dynamics in the Global Governance of Education*. London: DFID.

Robinson, W. I. (1996), *Promoting Polyarchy: Globalization, US intervention, and Hegemony*. Cambridge: Cambridge University Press.

SAEC – Southern Aid Effectiveness Commission (2010), *Towards more effective Aid Assessing reform constraints in the North*, April 2010, facilitated by Eurodad and The Reality of Aid.

Santos, B. (2007), 'Beyond Abyssal Thinking: From Global Lines to Ecologies of Knowledges'. *Revista Crítica de Ciências Sociais, 77*.

Save the Children (2007), *Last in Line, Last in School: How Donors are Failing Children in Conflict-Affected Fragile States*. London: Save the Children.

—(2008), *Last in Line, Last in School 2008: How Donors can Support Education for Children Affected by Conflict and Emergencies*. London: Save the Children.

—(2009), 'Background paper on trends in donor policies towards conflict-affected countries', paper commissioned for the EFA Global Monitoring Report 2010 'Reaching the marginalized'. Available at: unesdoc.unesco.org/images/0018/001865/186587e.pdf (Accessed: 1/12/2011).

—(2010), *The Future is Now, Education for Children in Countries Affected by Conflict*. London: Save the Children.

Slim, H. (1996), 'Military Humanitarianism and the New Peacekeeping: An Agenda for Peace?' *IDS Bulletin*, 27, (3), 86–95.

Sogge, D. (2002), *Give and Take: What's the Matter with Foreign Aid?* London: Zed Books.

Southern Aid Effectiveness Commission (2010), *Towards more effective Aid Assessing reform constraints in the North*, [Online] Available at: www.realityofaid.org/userfiles/newsandfeatures/Southern%20Aid%20 Effectiveness%20Commission%20Report.pdf (Accessed: 1/12/2011).

Stewart, F. (2003), 'Conflict and the Millennium Development Goals'. *Journal of Human Development*, 4, (3), 326–50.

Stoddard, A., Harmer, A. and di Domenico, V. (2009), *Providing aid in insecure environments: 2009 Update Trends in violence against aid workers and the operational response*, London: ODI-HPG. HPG Policy Brief, 34.

Stoddard, A., Harmer, A. and Haver, K. (2006), *Providing aid in insecure environments: trends in policy and operations*, London: ODI-HPG. HPG Report, 23.

TNS NIPO (2007), *Meer Nederlanders tegen dan voor verlenging missie Uruzgan*, [Online] Available at: www.tns-nipo.com/tns-nipo/nieuws/van/meer-nederlanders-tegen-dan-voor-verlenging-missie/ (Accessed: 1/12/2011).

Tromp, B. (2006), 'Van afscheid van de neutraliteit tot postmoderne identiteitscrisis?' *Internationale Spectator*, 60, (11), 590–4.

UNICEF (2011), *EEPCT Programme*, [Online] Available at: www.educationandtransition.org/implementation/emergencies-countries-regional-maps/ (Accessed: 1/12/2011).

US State Department (2008), *Country Reports on Terrorism 2007*. Washington: United States Department of State Publication Office of the Coordinator for Counterterrorism.

USAID (2008), *Civilian–Military Cooperation Policy*. [pdf]. Washington: USAID.
  Available at pdf.usaid.gov/pdf_docs/PDACL777.pdf (Accessed: 1/12/2011).
Verger, A. (2009), 'The merchants of education: global politics and the uneven
  education liberalization process within the WTO'. *Comparative Education
  Review*, 53, (3), 379–401.
Wang, T. Y. (1999), 'US Foreign Aid and UN Voting: An Analysis of Important
  Issues'. *International Studies Quarterly*, 43, 199–210.
World Bank (1998), *Assessing aid: What Works, What Doesn't, and
  Why*, [Online] Available at: www-wds.worldbank.org/external/default/
  WDSContentServer/WDSP/IB/2000/02/23/000094946_99030406212262/
  Rendered/PDF/multi_page.pdf (Accessed: 1/12/2011).

CHAPTER TWELVE

The National Politics of Global Policies: Public-Private Partnerships in Indian Education

Antoni Verger and Sanne VanderKaaij

Introduction

Public Private Partnerships (PPPs) for education are perceived as a new policy solution to increase access to education and bring new resources to education systems at a time when many countries feel more and more pressure to achieve Education for All (EFA). International agencies, such as the World Bank, UNESCO and the Asian Development Bank, have become enthusiastic supporters and global carriers of the PPP idea to a range of contexts, i.e. national, regional and sub-national.

This chapter analyzes, first how the PPP idea is institutionalized in the global education agenda and by whom, and second, how it is being re-contextualized in specific education systems. The case of India provides evidence to understand the ways in which ideas about PPPs in education are translated, debated and negotiated in the landscape of national policy. India is one of the countries where the PPP debate has penetrated with most intensity in recent years (Fennell 2007; Srivastava 2010). In this paper, we will explore the processes and agents through which the new policy discourse on PPPs in India is created and the reasons why it is becoming popular at this point in time. However, we will also focus on identifying the shortcomings of the PPP proposal when it comes to stimulating a coherent and comprehensive education reform in the country.

The Indian case is especially appropriate for ascertaining the relationship between new ideas and policy change as at the time of conducting our fieldwork in the country, the debate on PPPs was very much alive. Education stakeholders provided details regarding the formation of ideas and stakeholder interaction which, as Boxenbaum *et al.* (2005) suggest, individuals tend to forget rapidly and consequently cannot be captured accurately through retrospective interviews. The data sources, aside from interviews with national and international policy entrepreneurs and other education stakeholders operating in India, include policy documents and observation of political debates on PPPs and education in New Delhi. The data were gathered between November 2009 and April 2010.

The chapter is structured in four main sections. In the first, we present the programmatic idea of PPPs for education and, through a set of theoretical and conceptual tools taken from policy analysis, we explain how it has been constructed by global agents and what the conditions are for its re-contextualization in specific education systems. In the following two sections, we develop the PPP case study in India. We present our data, first by exploring the contextual factors that promote or hinder the advancement of the PPP proposal in the education domain in India, and secondly by referring to the positions and strategies of key education stake-holders in the PPPs for education debate. In the fourth and final section, our findings shall be discussed.

PPPs for Education: The Framing of a New Global Education Policy

PPPs were first theorized and implemented in policy areas such as urban and local economic development in the US at the beginning of the 1980s. However, this idea progressively extended to other areas and to other contexts, mainly in high-income countries (Wettenhall 2003). In the 1990s, PPPs also became popular in the developing world. At that time, the international development policy discourse was shifting from a focus on macro-economic prescriptions to a focus on governance and institutional change (Fine *et al.* 2003). As a result, many aid agencies began to reflect on innovative ways of strengthening governance structures in developing countries and the role of the private sector in economic and social activities.

The World Bank, as one of the most fervent advocates of this shift in paradigm, became especially interested in exporting the PPP solution to the developing world (Miraftab 2004). This organisation has been interested in private sector development for decades, but has been trapped by a histori-cally ambiguous and somewhat paradoxical relationship with the private sector. This is due to the fact that, on the one hand, the World Bank group is sympathetic to private sector involvement in public services, but, on the other, with the exception of the International Finance Corporation (IFC)[1], the Bank can only lend to governments (or with a government guarantee), which usually implies that its loans make the public sector larger (Miller-Adams 1999). PPP programmes can become a solution to this paradox since, as we describe below, they constitute a policy instrument to make the private sector grow through state policy and state funding. This explains, to some extent, why the Bank is one of the most active promoters of public sector reform through PPPs in a range of policy sectors, including education.

PPPs for Education as a Programmatic Idea

PPPs for education have recently been incorporated into the global education agenda by a number of international aid agencies, also under the leadership of the World Bank (Verger 2011). The Bank defines them as contractual relations between governments and private providers to acquire education services of a defined quantity and quality at an agreed price for a specified period (Patrinos *et al.* 2009). From a political analysis perspective, PPPs for education can be conceived as a programmatic idea, i.e. as a technical and professional idea that specifies cause-and-effect relationships concerning the problems that need to be addressed, and prescribes a precise course of policy solutions to address such problems (Campbell 2004).

The education problems that PPPs for education aim to address are mainly related to access and quality. Partnerships are conceived as the best and most rapid solution for overcoming the challenges associated with the Millennium Development Goals (MDGs) and with the EFA framework for action. Moreover, in a context in which the expansion of education has often been accompanied by a deterioration in average learning levels, PPPs are expected to boost the quality and effectiveness of schools. The promoters of this idea consider that partnerships will bring more choice and pluralism, innovation, new knowledge and infrastructure from the private sector, as well as competition and incentives into the education system (Patrinos *et al.* 2009).

In terms of policy solutions, PPPs for education involve a contract between the public and the private sector, which, in the opinion of the experts, should be formalized and based on performance outcomes. Thus the PPP gives the state direct control over the education system. Through quality assurance and evaluation mechanisms, the state can decide whether providers reach the minimum standards to be part of partnership frame-works. Once the PPP is at work, the state can reward those private schools that are successful, and expel those that underperform. Generally speaking, state regulation and state control are crucial elements for generating an environment that is conducive to partnerships producing the expected outcomes (Fielden *et al.* 2008).

PPPs for education can cover different areas of collaboration between the private and the public sectors, but the emphasis is placed on the delivery of core education services, i.e. the management and running of schools[2]. In this respect, the private sector can be contracted under the following formats: delivery of education (as in charter schools), private operation of public schools (contract schools) and education vouchers (IFC 2001). PPPs can also vary in their level of intensity. The highest level of PPPs occurs when 100 per cent of education is provided by the private sector within a voucher framework (Patrinos *et al.* 2009, p. 16); in fact school choice and vouchers are policy instruments often associated with PPP frameworks. Moreover, a great emphasis is placed on giving schools the capacity to manage, hire and fire teachers more directly, as well as to make schools and teachers more accountable and responsive to community and family demands (IFC 2001).

From a governance perspective, PPPs for education mean the reconfiguration of the role of the state in education. They imply that the state should move away from direct education provision and focus on the planning, funding, regulation and evaluation of the education system instead. PPP promoters consider the state is not effective when it comes to delivering education because the public sector lacks the accurate incentives to operate services in a competitive way, and consequently the quality and the cost of education services are adversely affected (IFC 2001).

To conclude, PPPs are not adverse to state intervention, but they require a redefinition and, to some extent, alteration of the state functions in education. The PPP proposal appears paradoxical in this respect. On the one hand, it shows a strong belief in market solutions in education. On the other hand, state intervention is seen as crucial in generating the conditions and the incentives to make education markets work.

The Re-contextualization and Translation of Programmatic Ideas

Having described the programmatic proposal, we will now explore the conditions that mediate its promotion and adoption by local policymakers. One group of these conditions is related to the internal properties of the programmes such as clarity and consistency, familiarity, feasibility and resonation (Verger 2011).

Concerning *clarity and consistency*, the causal beliefs and causal stories behind the programmes must be coherent and convincing, and the policy prescriptions clear, concise and easily understandable by policymakers (Campbell 2004). Furthermore, beyond the real content of ideas, the manner in which they are packaged is also important. Thus the substantive simplicity and rhetorical sophistication of a certain policy discourse is a further factor that contributes to its advance (Fairclough 2000; Ball 2007).

Regarding *familiarity*, it should also be acknowledged that politicians and regulators are usually averse to risk and tend to be sceptical about the adoption of new policy ideas. Thus, to be re-contextualized successfully in particular contexts, programmes may be translated in a way that sounds familiar to local policymakers, or amalgamating the new policy idea and already existing local practices (Boxenbaum *et al.* 2005).

The *feasibility* principle implies that new policy ideas are most likely to be taken up if they are perceived as technically workable (i.e. the country has the necessary capabilities) and fit within budgetary and administrative constraints (Kingdon 1994).

Finally, *resonation* means that the way programmes are framed can make them resonate positively – at both normative and causal levels – within a range of audiences and broader contextual ideas. In this sense, programmatic ideas must fit within the prevailing policy paradigm and public sentiments in the society at the time formulation and implementation (Hay 2002; Campbell 2004). The success of PPPs in a range of policy sectors in the recent past has largely resulted from the fact they have worked as an accommodating mechanism, i.e. the proposal fits within a range of political ideologies, including social democracy, conservatism and neoliberalism (Linder 1999).

However, policy ideas do not only have effects by virtue of their inherent logic, framing qualities or argumentation strengths. Policy discourses often maintain their credibility through their repetition (Fairclough 2000; Ball 2007), or because of the resources, political clout and reliability of the organisations backing them (Hay 2002; Campbell 2004). For the analysis of the diffusion of PPPs in the educational field, it is important to consider that the main policy entrepreneurs behind the proposal are located in powerful organisations such as the World Bank or regional development banks.

The political economy of reforms should also be taken into account to understand the adoption of new policy ideas, since they might meet the support or resistance of important constituencies in the policy sector in question. This is the logical consequence of the fact that the implementation of a new programme may force certain stakeholders to make significant adjustments in their work, or challenge their power or status. For instance, PPPs have the potential to alter teachers' working conditions because they will allow contractors to hire cheaper and non-unionized labour, reward teachers according to their performance, or dismiss them if they underperform (IFC 2001; Patrinos *et al.* 2009). The World Bank is aware that this idea can generate resistance and suggests that it might be 'useful for policymakers to recruit leading figures in the politics and business communities who understand the potential benefits of PPPs and can use their influence to help to overcome any resistance' (Patrinos *et al.* 2009, p. 5).

Broader contextual factors also affect the strategies of political agents when endeavoring to advance a certain idea, as well as its selection in a given context (Steiner-Khamsi 2004). For instance, critical junctures such as periods of crisis or the increasing demand of a public good can make policymakers more open to experiment with new policy solutions (Walsh 2000). Finally, beyond the limits and scope of a concrete policy sector, broader political, normative and legal structures prevailing at the national level favour some ideas and strategies over others (Jessop 2001). To sum up, the reception and adoption of a programmatic idea may vary in different contexts and points in time due to a range of factors both intrinsic and extrinsic to the properties of the policy idea itself.

PPPs for Education in the Indian Policy Landscape

The concept of PPPs has been part of the Indian development discourse for almost two decades now (Bava 2008, p. 410). The concept has mainly been discussed and applied in fields such as infrastructure, water and solid waste management (Dhar 2008; Singh 2008). The debate on its applicability for the education sector in India is much recent.

Four contextual factors have contributed to the emergence of the policy discussion on PPPs for education in India. The first factor is the *increased demand for education*. Over the past two decades, India has seen an impressive increase in enrolment rates at the primary education level, and by now enrolment at this level has become almost universal (Kingdon 2007). At the secondary level, the gross enrolment rate remains significantly lower; in 2006, it stood at 47 per cent (Dhameja *et al.* 2008). Nevertheless, the demand for secondary education has increased significantly due to the success of education awareness campaigns, as well as due to the universalisation of education at the primary level (Mehrotra 2006). Lower enrolment rates at the secondary level should therefore be explained by a lack of supply rather than a lack of demand.

The second relevant contextual factor is the new *normative and legal framework* that has been created in India. In the past decade, India became a signatory to the MDGs, set up its own EFA programme (*Sarva Shiksha Abhiyan*), amended its Constitution to include primary education as a fundamental right and passed the Right to Education Act 2009. With this act, India newly committed itself to the goal of universal, free and compulsory education for all children from the age of 6, as well as to investing 6 per cent of its GDP in education.

Thirdly, in India, an open *discourse on the low quality of education in government institutions* prevails among the public. Moreover, there is no strong public sentiment in support of 'public education', to some extent as a result of the historically rooted elitism in Indian society (Grant 2012, forthcoming). At the same time, there is a broad consensus that government schools are usually a last resort when it comes to school choice. Parents who can afford to do so choose private schools and, increasingly, children who attend government schools are from 'families who cannot access non-state institutions, whether for reasons of cash, geographical inaccessibility, caste, community exclusionism or gender bias' (Jeffery 2005, p. 27; see also PROBE 1999; Govinda 2002). In other words, those who *have* a choice opt for non-government schools.

The final relevant contextual factor is the *long history of private players' involvement in education in India*. Two main forms are found in India: the fully private school and the private-aided school. Fully private schools are privately founded, managed and financed. Their expenses are generally covered by a combination of donations (from well-wishers and/or parents) and school fees. Although formally prohibited, some of the fully-private schools yield profits: sometimes through charging extra fees for certain courses (e.g. computer classes) or, more often, through hefty donations demanded from parents upon admission of the child.

Private-aided schools are founded and managed by private parties, but largely funded by the government through grants-in-aid. The grant-in-aid system stems from colonial times when (often faith-based) philanthropic trusts set up schools and, over time, started receiving support from the government to run them. After Independence, the right for non-government actors to set up and manage schools was enshrined in Article 30 of the Constitution[3]. Some commentators have argued that, over the years, private-aided schools have become more and more like government schools. Over time, teachers started receiving their salaries directly from the state, and were increasingly appointed by government selection committees rather than by the school (Kingdon 2007). Private-aided schools are generally put forward as the first *de facto* type of PPP model in education that India has witnessed. However, at the same time, the government argues that for the private-aided system to become a proper PPP, incentives and competitive funding formulas need to be embraced (GOI 2009).

Until the early 1990s, the number of aided schools grew as state governments turned private unaided schools into aided ones. This process slowed down when the fiscal constraints of state governments increased (Mehrotra *et al.* 2006). As with the fully private schools, most private-aided schools can be found at the secondary and higher levels of education (Kingdon 2007). However, over the past decades, the primary level, particularly in urban areas, has witnessed the greatest acceleration in the number of private schools, with the permission of the Indian government (Mehrotra *et al.* 2006). In particular, the country has witnessed an unprecedented growth of so-called *low-fee private schools*. These schools, some of them recognized and others unrecognized by the educational authorities, are mostly attended by the poor. Their main source of cost-effectiveness relies on the low salaries they pay to teachers (Härma *et al.* 2012, forthcoming).

The Politics of the PPP Debate in India

The Indian government has not yet come up with a comprehensive policy on PPPs for education. Nevertheless, there are three main documents and several speeches from which the ideas of the Indian government on PPPs can be distilled, and which have become points of reference in the debate for other stakeholders. The first document is a concept paper by the Ministry of Human Resource Development (HRD), published in September 2009 under the title *PPP in School Education* (GOI 2009). It can be read as an exploration of the possibilities for PPPs in the Indian education system. The second document is a concrete proposal presented in the *Eleventh Five-Year Plan* (2007–2012) of the Planning Commission to set up 6,000 'model schools' (or schools of excellence) in the entire country, 2,500 of which as a PPP (GOI 2009). The third document in which forms of public-private mixes are contemplated and debated is the *Right of Children to Free and Compulsory Education Act, 2009* (RTE Act 2009).

All these documents demonstrate that the current government embraces the PPP idea for education with enthusiasm. In the words of the Planning Commission: 'In the liberalised global economy, where there is a pursuit for achieving excellence, the legitimate role of private providers of quality education not only needs to be recognised, but also encouraged' (GOI 2008, p. 9). Moreover, the GOI is strongly committed to the idea of 'India evolving into an information society and knowledge economy,' and partnerships with the private sector, especially with ICT-related corporations, are key in this respect (GOI 2002, p. 64). Though the PPP idea is thus accepted and promoted by the government, there is no single definition of 'partnerships' in the abovementioned documents, nor in speeches made by government officials.

In total, we can distinguish at least four different forms of PPPs in government discourse. In the *first model (infrastructure PPP),* the private sector supplies the hardware (building, electricity, etc.) and the government retains full responsibility for all education services.

The *second form of PPP (subsidies to the private sector)* gives the private partner responsibility for education delivery, while the government provides funding on a per capita basis (Seethalakshmi 2009). Specifically, the private partner will have 'full autonomy and management control' over the education service, while the role of the government lies in (1) providing 'a capital incentive' to be released annually based on performance indicators, (2) releasing a per capita grant for 50 per cent of the student population from socio-economically disadvantaged families, and (3) providing land at concessional rates (GOI 2009, p. 11). In section 12 of the Right to Education Act 2009, it is stipulated that 25 per cent of the seats available upon admission to Class I in all private schools should be reserved for economically disadvantaged communities. State governments will reimburse the expenditure on a per capita basis.

In May 2010, the Minister of HRD, Kapil Sibal, put forward a *third model (charter-type of contracting)*, one in which government school premises can be used by the private sector for conducting evening classes on the condition that they reserve 50 per cent of the seats for students from less privileged sections. The government would pay their expenses[4].

The *fourth model (support services)* suggested by the government focusses on contracting non-core education services. They include, for example, the transfer of inspection duties from government bodies to the community, the running of school libraries or ICT services, etc. (cf. GOI 2002; Srivastava 2010).

The vouchers-type of PPP, which is the 'integral' form of PPP according to the World Bank (see Patrinos *et al.* 2009), is absent from the GOI education discourse. Even though there is an active Indian lobby pushing for vouchers under the slogan 'Fund students not schools!'[5], and the World Bank – India has suggested that 'a voucher system seems likely to be beneficial for India' (World Bank 2009, p. 93), the Indian education authorities are not considering them seriously. Kingdon (2007, p. 191) notes that, in India,

> Unlike in some other countries where there has been a vigorous debate about and experimentation with alternatives to public schools (...) the recommendations (...) have never seriously included consideration of the possibility of providing school vouchers, as a way of empowering (especially) students/parents and improving accountability of schools and teachers towards students and parents.

Finally, when it comes to defining who the private partner in the PPPs may be, the HRD Ministry seems to think mainly of private education providers and corporate partners (GOI 2009, pp. 19–20). The Planning Commission mixes 'philanthropic foundations, endowments, educational trusts and reputed private providers' in its list of possible private partners (GOI 2008, p. 17).

Education Stakeholders in the PPP Debate

Apart from the central government, we have identified six key education stakeholders in India that are active in the PPP debate, all of whom have different opinions, preferences and ideas on partnerships in education. These are the World Bank, UNESCO, the National University of Educational Planning and Administration (NUEPA), the National Coalition for Education (NCE), teacher unions and the private sector[6].

The *World Bank* made its entrance in India after 1991 when the country went bankrupt and was forced to reform its economy. The economic growth and rapid development that followed, as well as the generally perceived success of interventions, have prevented the growth of criticism and scepticism toward the Bank and its policies, characteristic of many Latin American and African countries[7]. The World Bank is currently the biggest lender in education in India. In the last decade, together with DFID (the UK aid agency) and the European Commission, the Bank has supported India's EFA programme (*Sarva Shiksha Abhiyan, SSA*) with more than US$ one billion distributed in two big projects, one approved in April 2004, and the second in March 2010 (Ward 2011).

The Bank has consistently promoted private sector development in education, and is also the main carrier of the PPP idea into India (Mehrotra *et al.* 2006). The SSA loans have promoted different types of PPPs, including quotas for disadvantaged students in private schools, and the role of non-state School Management Committees (World Bank 2008; World Bank 2010). The first SSA loan encouraged PPPs with private aided schools, but, as the Bank pointed out in the final report of the project, it was 'less well developed on partnerships with private unaided institutions, to a large extent reflecting the lack of consensus either nationally or in some states on how to move forward' (World Bank 2008, p. 26)[8]. Nonetheless, the Bank insisted that partnerships with un-aided private schools should be explored in the future (World Bank 2008). The Bank has also presented its ideas on PPPs for education in India through policy reports such as the 2009 *Secondary Education In India: Universalizing Opportunity*. There, PPPs are presented as a cost-effective means of achieving universal secondary education, but also as a way of making schools more competitive, for instance by financing them according to their achievement (World Bank 2009).

The World Bank office in India does not use one single definition of PPP. They see possibilities for PPPs 'ranging from facility services (...) to a full PPP model where the private sector partner is contracted to provide all teaching and non-teaching services (...)' (World Bank-India in IL&FS 2009, p. 24). It emphasizes that this lack of definitional clarity is a conscious strategy for India: '[G]iven the diversity among states there is no single strategy for all India in terms of secondary school management' (IL&FS 2009, p. 45). Nevertheless, in August 2011 the Bank, in collaboration with the India's HRD Ministry organized an International Conference on PPP in Secondary Education that aimed 'to discuss, debate and understand PPPs – their definition, role, types, structuring systems, key performance indicators, financial arrangements, regulatory and legal aspects and exit strategies'[9].

The second stakeholder, *UNESCO-India*, supports the PPP idea as well. In the words of our interviewee, 'we always endorse it, we always have. We are the ones pushing governments to follow' (Interview 01). However, its definition of PPP seems to be different from that used by the World Bank and other agencies. UNESCO focuses on the idea of corporate social responsibility and is inclined to think in terms of not-for-profit partners, such as NGOs. Actually, it considers PPPs in terms of multi-stakeholder partnerships, which is a type of partnership of a very different nature from the more operational partnerships. In any case, UNESCO does not perceive itself as an influential player in the Indian education debate.'World Bank is [one of] the real players in the field (…). We do not fund, so we do not have that kind of say' (Interview 03).

NUEPA, apart from undertaking research and training students, also conducts training for policymakers and practitioners. It is an important education stakeholder that often works as a think-tank and even as a policy entrepreneur in the Indian education field. In the words of one of its staff members: 'We are like the antennas of the Ministry (…) before the HRD Ministry wants to make a policy decision, they want some authentic data-based research and that is only available from us' (Interview 02). However, within NUEPA, there is no single position on the PPP debate. There are staff members who endorse the proposal and others who reject it (Interview 02).

The *NCE* is a nationwide coalition of civil society organisations and teacher unions that organizes advocacy campaigns to achieve free universal quality education for all children up to 18 years of age. The NCE, which represents India in the Global Campaign for Education, emphasizes that they are 'not being for or against PPPs in education in toto', but there is a 'need [for] proper regulation' when it comes to PPPs for education. Nevertheless, the spokesperson for the NCE is quite critical of PPP proposals, as it is feared that it 'dilutes the concept of education as a funda-mental right' (Interview 04).

The *All India Federation of Teachers' Organisations (AIFTO)*, the most important teacher union in the country, is openly critical of the PPPs proposal. It is not against all types of private participation in education, but considers that overall PPPs will promote education privatisation and the exploitation of the teaching workforce (Interview 05). It has addressed these and other concerns in written letters and statements sent to the educa-tional authorities in the country[10].

The final stakeholder identified is *Infrastructure Leasing & Financial Services (IL&FS)*. This company is one of the most active private sector participants in the PPP debate. Thus far, IL&FS has organized two National Consultative Meetings to discuss the PPP model with govern-ments, education organisations and academicians. It is an open promoter of PPPs for the education sector and uses these meetings to keep the topic on the agenda, to put forward particular models, and to urge for speedy implementation. IL&FS is also important in that it delivers 'proof' to the government of the workability of PPPs in education by pointing to the various programmes they have run in several Indian states (IL&FS 2009, p. 9). The company works with two main models of partnerships: an infrastructure model, and a model in which the private partner 'runs the whole thing' (Interview 06). Its main political aim within the debate is that for-profit providers be allowed to operate within the Indian education system.

Framing the Debate on PPPs for Education

PPP supporters deploy several meaning frames to advance their preferences. The first frame is the *budget constraint,* which the government of India uses as follows:

> There is a huge gap between the requirement and the availability of school infrastructure in the country. (...) It is not possible to provide such a large amount from the government alone in a short period of time. (...) Many state governments have stopped opening new high schools in the last decade due to acute financial constraint. (...) It does not appear feasible for the state governments to fill this gap in the short term due to constraints on budget and capacity (GOI 2009, pp. 6–11).

Private sector involvement is presented as a solution to the perceived *short-term or long-term lack of finances* (IL&FS 2009, p. 24). This argument is refuted by some critics who point to a 'lack of political will rather than of resources' (Interview 04). Interestingly, the private sector also rejects this argument. Though they think the government can definitely save money, and that this is part of the rationale for initiating PPPs, they do expect the government and not the students to pay for their services, at least in the first years of the partnership. In the words of the IL&FS: 'I would be happy charging user-fees and I think the community can take it also. But *ideologically* it doesn't go down yet. (...) It is a non-starter. (...) Maybe after five years' (Interview 05).

A second frame employed by supporters of the PPP proposal is that of *efficiency due to increased accountability.* This argument is used in two ways. First, with regard to the construction of schools, private sector involvement is expected to address 'unduly long time in the government set up' (GOI 2009, p. 12) that the founding of new schools takes. Supporters of the PPP proposal argue that 'since the private partner would be interested in getting payment as soon as the services start being made available, the speed of implementation would be much quicker.' Secondly, they think that schools managed by private parties operate more efficiently:

> [T]he private sector will be able to enhance efficiency in these areas and can bring professionalism [to] the system. (...) Because of greater efficiency and competition, the cost of operation is expected to be much lower than in [a] government set up (GOI 2009, pp. 7–12).

The World Bank agrees with the government of India when it argues that PPPs will 'allow for faster and less costly recruitment of personnel and mobilisation of teaching and non-teaching services than would be possible through a purely public system, enabling faster and cheaper expansion of access' (World Bank 2009, p. 24). The corporate sector, for its part, uses the following argument: 'In the actual market the salary range for academically qualified teachers is far below that of the existing public sector teachers.' Not only will the cost for salaries come down with PPPs, but, according to IL&FS, there will be simultaneously 'increased accountability of teachers in a private set-up' (IL&FS 2009, p. 45). Furthermore, they argue that private sector involvement will 'help to leverage limited public funds, reduce life cycle costs, develop and execute more projects on a sustainable basis' (IL&FS 2009, p. 18).

A final pro-PPP argument says that partnership frameworks will increase the *relevance* of education because closer ties between industry and education institutions will be created. In the words of IL&FS, PPPs are necessary to create 'good vocational skills education' (IL&FS 2009, p. 20).

Arguments against PPPs

The arguments *against* the PPP model by certain stakeholders are twofold. First, there are concerns over the consequences for the equity of access and quality. In particular, the possibility that PPPs for education will introduce user charges is feared (Interview 3). Critics argue that poor groups in society may not be able to assume this additional burden. Furthermore, they fear that in the absence of clear policies on 'regulatory issues relating to PPPs in education, such as protecting the public interest and the effective monitoring of non-state actors', those schools charging lower fees, and thus catering to the poor, may be of sub-standard quality, but still receive recognition from the state (cf. Srivastava 2010). In other words, PPPs may institutionalize the inequity in provision already existing in India.

Secondly, critics see PPPs as 'privatisation with public funds' (Tilak 2010). They feel that the government is 'taking this PPP stage just to hide their intention to privatize education in the future' (Interviews 01 and 05). Confronted with this criticism, partnership advocates emphasize that PPPs are different from privatisation. They do so by pointing toward the roles the government retains, and regains, in the regulation and financing of education (IL&FS 2009, p. 89, Interview 06). Moreover, the state will regain control of the private sector that is currently lacking (Interview 05), and will retain a role in providing education in underserved areas and for disadvantaged groups (GOI 2009, p. vii).

Closely related is the question of profit-making in education. Although currently a widespread phenomenon, profit-making in education is officially prohibited in India. All stakeholders, except for the corporate sector, agree that this should remain unchanged. The opponents of profit-making argue that allowing the commercialisation of education would undermine equity in education. The corporate sector is clear in its wish to make a profit when participating in PPPs but, at the same time, gives assurances that PPP schools, in the initial years at least, will work as public schools 'as long as the government pays for them' (IL&FS 2009, pp. 12, 20).

PPPs for Education in India: Lost in Translation?

On the basis of the data presented above, this section analyses the contested processes of adoption and translation of the PPPs for education idea in the Indian policy landscape.

PPP Selectivity in India

International development organisations perceive PPPs as an opportunity to rectify inefficiencies in the public delivery of education and to mobilize new resources to increase educational access and quality. These agencies, led by the World Bank, have propagated this policy idea very actively and supported its advance both discursively and materially. The political clout of the World Bank and other donor agencies, including the ADB, DFID and the European Commission, is considerable in India and national policy-makers are strongly networked with them (Ward 2011). The most fervent believers in PPPs in India are found in the education planning division of the government, which considers partnerships as a means of strengthening India's education and the country's competitiveness in a global economy. This boosts the political and moral authority of the proposal and ensures that the debate will reach broader policy networks and core political decision-makers. Moreover, it guarantees that the necessary resources are generated for PPPs to be properly debated and, at some point, implemented. In addition, the *Eleventh Five-Year Plan* is enthusiastic about PPP solutions, and several pilot experiences involving public-private mixes are being implemented in the country.

National education stakeholders recognize that the Indian education system faces important challenges. Finding a solution to the problem of access, in particular, is perceived as an urgent need by many of them, the government included. The urgency of solving this problem has grown in recent years, above all in secondary education, due to increasing educa-tional demand and the new regulatory environment in which the Right to Education must be guaranteed by the state. This urgency, in combination with a perceived lack of public funds, has made many agents consider the private sector as a potential ally to face the access challenge. Importantly, in a scenario of a growing number of unregulated schools operated by private providers, even progressive agents consider PPPs as a lesser evil. They are aware that the privatisation of education by default is taking place in the country and consider it preferable if the state steps in to introduce at least some control measures. By enabling policy entrepreneurs and policy-makers with different ideologies to agree on its implementation, the PPP proposal demonstrates its accommodationist powers (see Linder 1999).

Finally, the PPPs for education proposal resonates positively in India for at least three other reasons. First, it sounds like a familiar policy practice to national policymakers, as the country has twenty years of experience with PPPs in non-education sectors, and consequently education policymakers are less adverse to adopting it in the education field. Secondly, the PPP proposal resonates with broader changes occurring at the polity level in India. Public sector reform and new modes of service provision are very much present in the Indian political agenda, and PPPs are being adopted as a cross-cutting policy solution to address many of the problems perceived in the public sector (for instance, see Singh 2008; Dhar 2008). Thirdly, there is no strong public sentiment in support of public education in the country. This, together with the fact that more and more Indian families choose private schools, which they perceive as superior to public ones, could help PPPs to be welcomed by broad sectors of Indian society.

Missing Pieces and Hindering Factors

The GOI, together with other key education stakeholders in the country, has enthusiastically engaged with the 'global talk' on PPPs, and has even approved some concrete reforms in this area, such as grants for students attending private schools. However, this talk is not necessarily translated into corresponding policies and substantive changes. The adoption of global policy talks is usually a strategy by financially or politically weaker agents that adopt the language of the powerful in order to access resources or to legitimate their policy action (Steiner-Khamsi 2004). Of course, there are some parallels between the global and the Indian discussion on PPPs, but the translation of the programme into the local reality has been very selective and mediated by existing necessities and political interests.

The GOI is, first and foremost, using the PPPs discussion as a political device to pledge education access in a cost-effective way, above all at the secondary level. However, the quality problem that PPPs are also supposed to address has been lost in translation and, so far in the discussion in India, the quality of education rationale takes a second place. Of course, quality arguments are employed rhetorically to garner support for the PPP proposal; however, there is no evidence that, under partnership frameworks, education quality will be guaranteed via concrete policies. In fact, the PPP agenda in India seems to focus on promoting private provision with a diminished role of the state in key policy areas such as regulation and funding (Rose 2010). At least three elements of concern can be highlighted in this respect. First, the government has not presented plans to open competitive bidding processes and/or to implement an evaluation system that would allow authorities to certify education quality, or to disaffiliate or close underperforming schools. Secondly, within the PPP agenda in India, the discussion on public education financing has a low profile. It is especially significant that there is no firm commitment by the GOI to increase public education funding to the promised 6 per cent of GDP (Srivastava 2010). Thirdly, in case the government decides to establish partnerships with the so-called 'low-fee schools', the quality of education in the country could be undermined even further.

Quality is not the only element of the PPP programmatic idea that is missing in India. Policy tools such as school choice and vouchers have a low profile in the Indian discussion on partnerships in contrast to their prevalence in the global discourse. Moreover, the PPP *global* policy programme departs from the understanding that the public sector should transfer resources to the private one in exchange for the services provided by the latter, whereas the Indian government sees PPPs as an instrument for bringing more private funding and other resources to the national education system, both from parents and providers. In relation to this, it should be noticed that the global PPP proposal aims, at least rhetorically, to strengthen the power and control of the state over education by changing its functions from direct provider to funder and regulator. However, in the way the PPP idea is framed in India, the partnerships bear more resemblance to conventional privatisation and to the transfer of several education responsibilities from the public sector to the private one (Srivastava 2010) than to the introduction of an innovative managerial practice.

At the same time, the current debate on PPPs in education in India is characterized by a lack of clarity and consistency around the ideas and proposals under discussion. Reading the official discourses, it seems that any kind of public-private mix may be considered a PPP. Indeed, there is a remarkable lack of common understanding among the key education stakeholders in the country on what PPPs for education mean and imply. Their expectations and definitions of PPPs are very diverse, and even contradictory. Some maintain that for-profit education providers should be allowed, others do not; some feel PPPs entail the transfer of resources from the private to the public sector, and others that PPPs mean that the money flows precisely the other way around; some highlight that PPPs should focus on core education services, others emphasize their role in the provision of infrastructure, ICT and non-core education services; some say that PPPs are similar to corporate social responsibility, others to outsourcing services, etc. Overall, this shows that in India the PPP label is working as a 'floating signifier', i.e. a vague concept that represents an undetermined quantity of signification, but that at the same time allows 'symbolic thought to operate despite the contradiction inherent in it' (Mehlman 1972, p. 23; Burgos 2004).

Finally, important education stakeholders are against the advance of PPP reforms, although for very different reasons. This is the case, on the one hand, of teacher unions, which are a key and powerful constituency in the Indian education system. They are openly against the PPP proposal due to its similarities and conduciveness to education privatisation and commercialisation, and to teachers' deprofessionalisation. On the other hand, the private-corporate sector will not support PPPs if the prohibition on profit-making in the education system, as established in the RTE Act 2009, is not challenged by the government.

Conclusions

This research engages with broader discussions in political analysis aimed at explaining how, why and when new global policy ideas matter. In India, the national interpretative frameworks of the PPP debate are, in different ways, supranationally shaped. The adoption of PPPs for education in the country is being justified by a discourse that invokes the development of a globally competitive knowledge-based economy and the achievement of the EFA goals, which is very similar to discourses deployed to frame education reforms in many other world locations (Carney 2009). The PPP proposal fits within the current emphasis of most international organisations on focussing education reform on governance and managerial solutions. Their promoters are telling governments that they need to increase the access to and quality of education, but to do so, they need to leverage the role of the private sector, especially when it comes to education provision duties (Patrinos *et al.* 2009). Thus the PPP case reflects the extent to which globalization is changing the nature of the educational problems facing nation states, but also their capacity to respond to them (Dale 2000).

At the same time, the PPPs for education discourse resonates with the ideologies and public sentiments on education prevailing in Indian society and, at the government level, they are increasingly perceived as a policy solution to the urgent challenges that Indian education faces. Furthermore, PPPs are seen as a familiar policy solution, and are backed by a group of political actors, including international organisations that are highly profiled and influential in the country.

However, like many other global education polices, PPPs in India have undergone processes of local adaptation, modification and resistance (cf. Steiner-Khamsi 2004). In fact the governmental discourse on PPPs is far removed from the way the PPP policy stream is being defined globally and does not address serious concerns regarding the quality of the potential private partners. We have also identified a number of elements that challenge its practical implementation. Among them, the ambiguity and low consistency of the official discourse on PPPs for education and the absence of common expectations and understandings among the key education stakeholders in the country stand out. The different meanings prevailing within the PPP discourse in India are, to a great extent, the consequence of different education agents pushing for their particular agendas and interests. As Mitchell-Weaver and Manning (1991, pp. 47–8) observed:

> Like many public policy concepts, public-private partnerships have become mired in a muddle of conceptual ambiguities. To some extent, this is attributable to the way in which new policy doctrines come into good currency (Starling 1988). Everyone at various stages of the policy-making process tries to fit conventional activities into the new mould.

As our study reflects, many agents in India, including the GOI, consider that identifying their policy priorities and interests with the popular idea of PPPs is strategic. In this sense, the 'global PPP idea', beyond being considered an external imposition, works as an instrumental frame – a floating signifier – for local actors to settle national and sub-national education agendas, and legitimate and push for their pre-established preferences in the educational field. Summing up, India is not a passive adopter of the global PPP discourse. PPPs are penetrating the Indian policy landscape as the result of the interaction between global ideas, political and economic conditions prevailing at the national level, and the interests and strategies of key international and local education stakeholders operating in the country.

At the time of conducting this research, the PPP debate was still ongoing in India. Though we have shown the contested re-contextualization and uneven translation of the 'PPP in education' talk at the national level, conducting more research is necessary to understand the actual implications of its adoption. PPPs in education have become a global experiment with unexpected outcomes. Even their advocates recognize that evidence on the benefits or drawbacks of PPPs in education is not conclusive (Patrinos *et al.* 2009). Future research should pay attention to the manner in which PPPs alter the governance, effectiveness and equity of education systems and, thus, feed a policy debate that, as the Indian case shows, is highly speculative and ambiguous.

Notes

1 The IFC is the Bank's agency specialized in lending to the private sector.

2 Other areas are the building of schools or the delivery of non-core services (books, school transport and meals).

3 The purpose of this Constitutional provision was to protect the interests of minorities.

4 See 'Play A Role in Inclusive Education, Sibal Tells Private Sector'. India-Forums. 18 May 2010. (www.india-forums.com/news/education/249164-play-a-role-in-inclusive-education-sibal-tells-private-sector.htm).

5   See schoolchoice.in/

6   Although the Asian Development Bank (ADB) is an important international organisation for India in many sectors, it does not currently have projects in education. For the present discussion, it is only important to mention that the ADB does endorse the concept of PPP in different sectors, and had a role in introducing this policy idea in India (Dhar 2008, p. 422).

7   Indeed, in the 1990s, India increased its reliance on market forces, but their policies remained far from the Washington Consensus dogma, with high levels of trade protection, lack of privatisation, extensive industrial policies, and lax fiscal and financial policies (Rodrik 2006).

8   Interestingly enough, the same document reflects that some stakeholders problematized the fact that the World Bank reporting team had 'a pronounced favour for private schooling systems without convincing evidence in India' (World Bank 2008, p. 65).

9   See go.worldbank.org/AVVY7BNFJ0

10 See, for instance, the letter 'PPP in School Education – Some Observations' [manuscript].

References

Ball, S. J. (2007), *Education Plc: Understanding Private Sector Participation in Public Sector Education*. New York: Routledge.

Bava, N. (2008), 'Public Private Partnerships in Public Service and Development: A Conceptual & Empirical Framework'. *The Indian Journal of Public Administration*, July–Sept., 395–416.

Boxenbaum, E. and Battilana, J. (2005), 'Importation as Innovation: Transposing Managerial Practices across Fields'. *Strategic Organization*, 3, (4), 355–83.

Burgos, R. B. (2004), 'Partnership as a floating and empty signifier within educational policies: the Mexican case', in M. F. Barry, M. N. Bloch and T. Popkewitz (eds), *Educational Partnerships and the State: The Paradoxes of Governing Schools, Children, and Families*. New York: Palgrave Macmillan, pp. 55–82.

Campbell, J. L. (2004), *Institutional Change and Globalization*. Princeton: Princeton University Press.

Carney, S. (2009), 'Negotiating Policy in an Age of Globalization: Exploring Educational 'Policyscapes' in Denmark, Nepal, and China'. *Comparative Education Review*, 53, (1): 63–88.

Dale, R. (2000), 'Globalization and Education: Demonstrating a 'common world educational culture' or 'locating a "globally structured educational agenda"?'. *Educational Theory*, 50, (4): 427–48.

Dhameja, N. and Gupta, R. (2008), 'Public Private Partnership for Elementary Education'. *The Indian Journal of Public Administration*, LIV, (3), 455–69.

Dhar, T. N. (2008), 'Public Private Partnerships in India (Policy, Strategies and Operationalisation Issues)'. *The Indian Journal of Public Administration*, LIV, (3), 417–30.

Fairclough, N. (2000), *New Labour, New Language?* New York: Routledge.

Fennell, S. (2007), *Tilting at Windmills: Public Private Partnerships in Indian Education Today*, Cambridge: University of Cambridge. Working Paper, 5/2007.

Fielden, J. and LaRocque, N. (2008), *The Evolving Regulatory Context for Private Education in Emerging Economies*. Washington DC: The World Bank.

Fine, B., Lapavitsas, C. and Pincus, J. (2003), *Development Policy in the Twenty-First Century: Beyond the Post-Washington Consensus*. New York: Routledge.

Goel, S. L. (2008), 'Editorial Special Number on A Policy Framework on Public Private Partnership'. *The Indian Journal of Public Administration*, LIV, (3), V.

GOI (2002), *India Vision 2020*. New Delhi: Planning Commission.

—(2008), *Eleventh Five Year Plan 2007–2012 Volume II. Social Sector*. New Delhi: Planning Commission.

—(2009), *PPPs in School Education*, unpublished discussion paper. New Delhi: Ministry of HRD.

Govinda, R. (2002), *India Education Report. A Profile of Basic Education*. New Delhi, Oxford: Oxford University Press.

Grant, L. (2012, forthcoming), 'Transnational Advocacy for "Sarva Shiksha Abhiyan"', in A. Verger and M. Novelli (eds) 2012, *Campaigning for EFA: Histories, Strategies and Outcomes of Transnational Social Movements in Education*. Rotterdam: Sense.

Härma, J. and Rose, P. (2012, forthcoming), 'Averting human crisis via low-fee private schooling?', in S. A. Robertson, A. Verger, K. Mundy, and F. Menashy (eds), *Public–Private Partnerships and the Global Governance of Education*. London: Edward Elgar.

Hay, C. (2002), *Political Analysis. A Critical Introduction*. New York: Palgrave.

IFC (2001), Handbook on PPPs and Education, [Online] Available at: www.ifc.org/ifcext/edinvest.nsf/Content/PublicPrivatePartnerships (Accessed: 23/11/09).

IL&FS. (2009), *Second National Consultative Meet on Public-Private Partnerships in Education*. New Delhi: IL&FS.

Jeffery, P. (2005), 'Introduction: Hearts, Minds and Pockets', in R. Chopra and P. Jeffery (eds), *Educational Regimes in Contemporary India*. New Delhi: Sage. pp. 13–39.

Jessop, B. (2001), 'Institutional (Re)turns and the Strategic-Relational Approach'. *Environment and Planning A*, 33, 1213–35.

Kingdon, G. (2007), 'The Progress of School Education in India'. *Oxford Review of Economic Policy*, 23, (2), 168–95.

Kingdon, J. W. (1994), *Agendas, Alternatives, and Public Policies*. New York: Pearson Longman.

Larocque, N. (2008), *PPPs in Basic Education. An International Review*. London: CFBT.

Linder, S. H. (1999), 'Coming to Terms with the Public-Private Partnership: A Grammar of Multiple Meanings'. *American Behavioral Scientist*, 43, (1), 35–51.

Mehlman, J. (1972), 'The "Floating Signifier": From Lévi-Strauss to Lacan'. *Yale French Studies*, 48, 10–37.

Mehrotra, S. (2006), 'Reforming Elementary Education in India: A Menu of Options'. *International Journal of Educational Development*, 26, 261–77.

Mehrotra, S. and Panchamukhi, P. R. (2006), 'Private Provision of Elementary

Education in India: Findings of A Survey in Eight States', *Compare*, 36, (4), 421–42.

Miller-Adams, M. (1999), *The World Bank: New Agendas in a Changing World*. London: Routledge.

Miraftab, F. (2004), 'Public-Private Partnerships: The Trojan Horse of Neoliberal Development?'. *Journal of Planning Education and Research*, 24, (1), 89–101.

Mitchell-Weaver, C. and Manning, B. (1991), 'Public-private partnerships in third world development: A conceptual overview'. *Studies in Comparative International Development*, 26, (4), 45–67.

Patrinos, H., Barrera-Osorio, F. and Guáqueta, J. (2009), *The Role and Impact of PPPs in Education*. Washington DC: World Bank.

Pratham (2007), *ASER 2006 – Annual Status of Education Report*. New Delhi: Pratham.

PROBE (1999), *Public Report on Basic Education in India*. Oxford and New Delhi: Oxford University Press.

Rodrik, D. (2006), 'Goodbye Washington Consensus, Hello Washington Confusion? A Review of the World Bank's Economic Growth in the 1990s: Learning from a Decade of Reform'. *Journal of Economic Literature*, 44, (4), 973–87.

Rose, P. (2010), 'Achieving Education For All Through Public–Private Partnerships?'. *Development in Practice*, 20, (4–5), 473–83.

Seethalakshmi, S. (2009), 'PPP Model in Govt School, A Panacea?'. *Times of India*, 8 October, p. 17.

Singh, B. D. (2008), 'Policy Framework for Public Private Partnership in Human Development'. *The Indian Journal of Public Administration*, LIV, (3), 572–86.

Srivastava, P. (2010), 'Public-Private Partnership or Privatization? Questioning the State's Role in Education in India'. *Development in Practice*, 20, (4–5), 540–53.

Steiner-Khamsi, G. (2004), *The Global Politics of Educational Borrowing and Lending*. New York: Teachers' College Press.

Tilak, J. B. G. (2010), *Public Private Partnership in Education*, [Online] Available at: www.hindu.com/2010/05/25/stories/2010052551031200.htm (Accessed: 25 May 2011).

Verger, A. (2012), 'Framing and selling global education policy: the promotion of PPPs in education in low-income countries'. *Journal of Education Policy*, 27, (1), 109–30

Walsh, J. I. (2000), 'When Do Ideas Matter? Explaining the Successes and Failures of Thatcherite Ideas'. *Comparative Political Studies*, 33, (4), 483–516.

Ward, M. (2011), 'Aid to education: the case of Sarva Shiksha Abhiyan in India and the role of development partners'. *Journal of Education Policy*, 26, 543–56.

Wettenhall, R. (2003), 'The Rhetoric and Reality of Public-Private Partnerships'. *Public Organization Review*, 3, (1), 77–107.

World Bank (2008), *Implementation Completion And Results Report: Elementary Education project (IDA-38820)*. New Delhi: World Bank. Report ICR0000193/2008.

—(2009), *Secondary Education In India: Universalizing Opportunity*. New Delhi: World Bank.

—(2010), *Project Paper on a Proposed Additional Financing Credit to the Republic of India for the Second Elementary Education Project*. New Delhi: World Bank. Report 53021–IN.

PART THREE

Conclusions

CHAPTER THIRTEEN

Measuring and Interpreting Re-Contextualization: A Commentary

Gita Steiner-Khamsi

The re-contexualisation of global education policy is a recurrent theme in this book. Several authors draw on studies in El Salvador, India, Kenya, Nicaragua, South Africa, Turkey, Uganda or Zimbabwe to make a case that global education policy means different things to different actors, is embraced by these actors for different reasons, and is, depending on context, implemented differently. In my commentary on this inspiring book, I scratch at the surface of such statements that at first sight appear to be commonsensical but at closer examination lend themselves as a starting point for developing novel approaches to measuring and understanding policy change. My commentary offers a methodological thought and a few theoretical observations on the challenges and the gains associated with the study of re-contextualization.

How to Trace Global Education Policy Methodologically

How does one measure global education policy? Is it sufficient to provide evidence that the reform resembles – in design or in rhetoric – policies in other countries or, even more telling, in the majority of countries of this world? Is the occurrence of a traveling reform, which surfaces in different corners of the globe, indicative of a global policy? These types of methodo-logical questions are key concerns in globalization studies. They are hardly new, and three of the most common replies are briefly sketched in the following: neo-institutionalist theory, diffusion/social network analysis, and policy-borrowing/lending research.

Scholars with a neo-institutionalist worldview tend to draw on a large number of cases, countries or institutions, over a long time period (50–150 years), but only a few variables, to draw conclusions that there is nowadays a shared global understanding of particular beliefs such as social justice and equity. Decision-makers align the national with the educational and promote educational practices that are in line with these shared beliefs and global standards. This is a bird's-eye view on social development, in that similarities are observed and recorded at a supra-national or cross-national level. From such a distance, re-contextualization does exist but has little conceptual relevance. In fact, loose coupling is a metaphor that is frequently used by scholars in institutional theory and organisational sociology to denote the discrepancies between the various levels or activities of an organisational field. Gili Drori, John Meyer, Francisco Ramirez and Evan Schofer (2003), for example, apply the concept to demonstrate that despite the [universal] 'belief that science is a tool for achieving development' (Drori *et al.* 2003, p. 159), international organisations have developed a variety of 'solutions.'

According to the authors, the solutions vary from IMF-type to UNESCO-type solutions; the first promoting technology parks and the latter school science education programmes for young children. Similar to discrepancies between attitude and behavior, intention and action, policy and practice, loose coupling is, depending on the author, seen as irrational, idiosyncratic or particularistic and therefore yields few insights for understanding bigger, long-term changes at societal level. In comparative and international education, Francisco Ramirez (2003) and David Baker and LeTendre (2005) revert to loose coupling as an explanation whenever they encounter profound differences between a universal standard (e.g., student-centered teaching, gender awareness, etc.) and its local manifestation. For example, Baker and LeTendre (2005, p. 177) insist that the 'classroom in Seoul, Paris, Santiago, Cleveland or Tunis will be remarkably similar' and add, drawing on the argument of loose coupling, '[w]hat differences remain will be mostly across schools within nations for intentional reasons and some idiosyncratic variation introduced by teachers.'

The second method of inquiry emphasizes and measures transnational interaction. Diffusion of Innovation studies date back to the 1920s, were revived in the 1970s (see Rogers 1995, first 1962), and refined in the new millennium as part of social network analysis (Watts 2003). The quintessential question of diffusion/social network analysis is best illustrated in the classic example of the spread of the stone axe (see Rogers 1995): is the fact that the stone axe was discovered in different locations at about the same time an expression of maturation (trial and error) or an expression of interaction (borrowing from others)? More than three thousand years later, only a few researchers wonder whether conditional transfer programmes (CCT), implemented in over forty countries, represents a 'best practice' that matured over time, based on trial-and-error methods for attracting and retaining children from poor families in school. The majority of researchers assumes transnational interaction and acknowledges that CCT programmes, actively propagated, funded and disseminated by development banks, have been transferred from one context to another, and were subsequently re-contextualized.

Finally, borrowing/lending research is genuinely interested in understanding the disjunctures that occur between global education policy and local re-contextualization. I share this critical, contextual or culturalist perspective with many authors of this book. Indeed, it is the social, political, and economic conflicts, the power differentials and the legitimacy issues within a particular context, country or case that facilitate the circulation of global education policy. Unsurprisingly, one of the key questions is: why does a global education policy resonate in a particular context? The analytical unit of policy borrowing/lending researchers is the local policy context. Concretely, references to other countries, other sub-systems within a country (notably the economy), or more broadly to 'globalization,' 'international standards' or 'best practices' are interpreted as political maneuvers to build policy coalitions in situations of protracted policy conflict. In line with the theory of self-referential systems (Luhmann 1990, Schriewer 1990), a group of us argues that externalisation provides, literally translated, 'additional meaning' (German: *Zusatzsinn*).

Without going into too much depth here about the Advocacy Coalition Framework in policy studies (see Steiner-Khamsi 2010), 'additional meaning' is actually exactly what it takes to make adverse interest groups come together in unison or at least temporarily build a coalition to bring about change. Precisely because the act of externalisation takes a best practice or a lesson learnt from other countries out of context, it is amenable to adoption by groups with divergent policy agendas. Indicator research and statistical measurements help neutralize and provide a stamp of scientific rationality on policies that in reality are politically charged. The different local actors selectively borrow aspects or rhetoric of a global education policy that best fits their own political agenda. The theory explains why liberal and progressive groups selectively borrow certain aspects of CCT (conditional cash transfer), PPP (public-private partnerships), NPM (new public management) and other neoliberal reforms. The de-contextualized best practices, lessons learned from others or international standards present themselves (or more accurately are actively promoted) as neutral, and thereby allow for all kinds of projections, speculations and ultimately broad support (see Takayama 2010, Waldow 2010, 2012).

Having briefly sketched the main features of three widely referenced theories on globalization in education, it is now possible to situate the contributions made in this book. With the exception of Anja Jakobi (in this volume), none of the authors takes on a neo-institutionalist research agenda: nobody in this book assumes that global education policy spreads because it represents a 'best practice' or because it fits into a universally shared understanding of what constitutes 'good education.' To put it politely, the theory is of limited value for understanding re-contextualization because for neo-institutionalist theory loose coupling *is* the explanation (Latin: *explanans*) rather than the issue that begs for an explanation *(explanandum)*.

Without any doubt, the contributions in this book help advance theories in diffusion/social network analysis and in policy borrowing/lending research. The place allocated for this commentary is too short to get caught up in the narcissism of petty differences. The distinctive feature between the two related yet distinctive interpretive frameworks is the act of externalisation. For researchers of borrowing/lending it matters a great deal whether an explicit reference to another educational system, to another sector or to an international standard has been made. The emphasis is on agency and on agenda-driven policy borrowing and lending and not on diffusion alone. Thus it is not sufficient to state the resemblances between various policies and interpret them *a posteriori* as a case of policy borrowing. This said, many studies in this book are about diffusion and fewer about policy borrowing/lending.

Arguably there is a reason why there are more studies on diffusion than on policy borrowing/lending. Peter Hall's distinction between three types of policy learning helps to explain the methodological differences between diffusion/social network analysis and policy borrowing/lending research. Hall (1993) differentiates between first-order policy change (incremental change), second-order policy change (policy goals are maintained but the instruments are changed) and third-order policy change (policy goals and instruments are changed). He applies the classification to explain why the emergence of the monetarist, neoliberal thought in the 1980s and 1990s represented a Kuhnian-type paradigm shift or a third-order change in the United Kingdom. Incremental or first-order changes constitute the most common type of policy learning, but naturally most scholars are more interested in understanding bigger changes in the form of second-order and third-order changes. Most chapters in this book deal with third-order policy change (see Hall 1993) and document radical or fundamental policy alterations in the direction of neoliberalism (privatisation, school-based management, decentralisation) or individualism (student-centred teaching, life-long learning, human rights). Several chapter authors observe the diffusion of these traveling reforms in two or more countries and analyse how they were locally adapted.

It would be wrong to assume that this book is only about diffusion and translation. It is also to some extent about reception, resonance and cross-national policy attraction, all issues that are prototypical for policy borrowing/lending research. The co-editors of this volume have reframed the issue in the following fascinating research question: 'Why do policy-makers *buy* global education policy?' (Verger, Novelli and Altinyelken, chapter

1 of this volume). For example, Antoni Verger and Sanne VanderKaaij examine in this volume why the global education policy PPP (public-private partnerships) resonated in the Indian policy context and, in effect, made the private sector in India grow through state policy and state funding. They highlight the 'accommodationist mechanism,' designed by the World Bank and implemented by the Government of India, which made the PPP proposal fit 'in a range of political ideologies, including social-democracy, conservatism and neoliberalism' (Verger and VanderKaaij, in this volume). In other words, externalisation to a particular global education policy – in this case PPP – enabled the temporary building of a policy advocacy coalition between actors that are normally at war with each other.

As well as scrutinising in great detail the interaction between local and global actors and the timing of externalisation, several studies identify the economic and political reasons why local decision-makers buy into global education policy (see also Verger 2011). Besides political gains – coalition building – there are, in particular in the interaction between global donors and recipient governments, economic benefits. Economically, the 'purchase' of a particular reform programme is closely associated with the 'terms of agreement' (programmatic conditionality) for receiving a loan or a grant from a global player. For the donor, in turn, lending a portfolio of (their own) 'best practices' presumably reduces transfer cost, makes it managerially easier for them to monitor and evaluate expected outcomes, and helps them to strengthen their visibility and ascertain their position vis-à-vis competing donors.

Re-Contextualization: So What?

Not all studies on re-contextualization contribute to theory building. The great bulk of re-contextualization studies document in minute detail – sometimes across vertical levels, multiple sites and spatial scales – how the same global education policy plays out differently in two or more contexts. Such case studies or vertical ethnographies are 'thick' in description but 'thin' with regard to generalisations. The question becomes: What does the act of re-contextualization tell us about the policy process and, in particular, about policy change in an era of globalization?

Brent Edwards and Stephen Klees (in this volume) examine the inflationary usage of 'participation' in development and, drawing from reforms in El Salvador, convincingly show that the same label served not only diverse but also opposing political agendas. They compare in particular the neoliberal agenda (manifested in EDUCO), the liberal programme (exemplified in Plan 2021) and the progressive programme (illustrated in Popular Education in Santa Marta). The neoliberal proponents and free-market believers, represented by USAID and the World Bank, were enamored with the concept because individual participation in the market and community participation in school councils fitted their larger agenda of parental choice and school-based management. The liberal spin on participation also included civil society organisations and advanced, among others, participatory poverty assessments. The progressive approach to participation finally used a far-reaching definition that implied transformative change and change in power relations. According to Edwards and Klees, 'EDUCO schools reflect neoliberalism's preoccupation with a narrow version of efficiency and effectiveness through community-based accountability relations' (Edwards and Klees, in this volume). At the heart of an EDUCO school is the Community Education Association (ACE, in Spanish) which is in charge of hiring, firing and managing teachers.

There is no doubt that EDUCO, similar to CCT, PPP, NPM, life-long learning and a host of other programmes discussed in this book, qualifies as a global education policy or a traveling reform. The study by Edwards and Klees is so compelling because only a few scholars shed light on the origins of a global education policy. Most studies deal with re-contextualization and compare how early versus late adopters of a global education policy, years later, re-define or modify the imported reform. Let me explain why it is important to differentiate between the initiators, early adopters, and late adopters of a global education policy. The study of initiators, as presented by Edwards and Klees, helps us to understand that there always exist several competing policy options, some backed with massive financial capital and strong government support, and others only supported by civil society organisations or smaller advocacy groups. In El Salvador, the new government, with backing from USAID and then the World Bank, introduced EDUCO as a means to regain control over schools. The neat distinction that Edwards and Klees make in their case, whereby one political group promotes one particular reform, however, evaporates at a later stage of a global education policy. It disappears when we deal with global policy borrowing. Once a policy goes global – in this case EDUCO – the policy takes on different meanings and therefore resonates with different political groups for different reasons. EDUCO ceases to be associated only with neoliberal groups and is, for reasons utterly unrelated to its original context, selectively adopted by different political camps.

The study of early or late adopters of EDUCO in Central America and in other continents (see Poppema in this volume) shows little similarity with the initial context for a particular reason: every reform program, including EDUCO is, figuratively speaking, an octopus with several arms. For neoliberal groups, the social accountability arm might have been appealing because it helps to improve financial management at school levels, whereas for progressive groups parental involvement and community participation were – to lean on Verger's great metaphor – the 'selling point.'

The ambition to interpret the findings on the various re-contextualization studies for a larger theory on policy change makes it necessary to lay bare the theoretical assumptions underlying one's work. One of the assumptions that I invoked in the previous paragraph relates to the lifespan of a global education policy. As discussed in other publications (e.g. Steiner-Khamsi 2010), I find it important to acknowledge the continuous deterritorialisation and decontextualization process that accompanies a global education policy over the course of its lifespan. A global education policy ends up becoming nobody's and everyone's policy within a short period of time, making its import or adoption increasingly likely. I therefore suggested that we distinguish between the designers, early adopters, and late adopters of a global education policy. In social network analysis, the three distinctive phases are labeled slow growth, exponential growth and burn-out. They are typically illustrated in the shape of a lazy S-curve (see Steiner-Khamsi 2010). There is nothing more practical than having a theory: for example, the assumption of a policy lifespan helps us to differentiate between the various time periods of a global education policy and explain why local policy-makers at some point – typically during the exponential growth phase – refer to a particular global education policy as a 'best practice' or 'international standards.' The example of the lifespan of a policy only served as an appeal for making one's theoretical assumption transparent.

Naturally, many attempts have been made to label various assumptions and categorize them into a larger framework. This book presents one of the most persuasive frameworks that I have read to date. Susan Robertson's brilliant synopsis, published in this volume, categorizes different strands of thought that attempt to locate the 'global' in education policy. The following list reiterates Robertson's categorisation (presented in italics) and adds kin constructs used by others in globalization and education research. The term 'global' captures a wide range of social phenomena including a

- *condition of the world*, labeled by most authors as globalization

- *discourse*, also known as 'semantics of globalisation' (Jürgen Schriewer)

- *project*, popularized with the term 'globalisation optique' (Stephen Carney)

- *scale*, typically addressed with terms such as global players/actors

- *reach*, in this book referred to as global education policy.

Robertson's thoughtful categorisation enables us to dig deeper into the question of how re-contextualization studies help advance theories on globalization and the policy process. It helps us to identify the areas under scrutiny. For example, several of us have made it a vocation to challenge the current nationalistic and parochial theories on policy change. The conviction has to do with our particular angle: we see a global map underlying national policy agendas. This particular *globalization optique* makes us interpret national or local education police in a particular manner. For us, 'globalisation' is – to use Robertson's terminology – a 'project' that helps us to see and interpret local education policy in its larger context. Globalization is the relatively new terrain of reforms or, as Verger, Novelli and Altinyelken (in this volume), phrased it, the 'context of contexts' of education policy.

Robertson's categorisation of how scholars localize the 'global' is multi-dimensional, relational and, without any doubt, the opposite of flat. The relational feature of critical globalization research is pointed out by many (see, for example, dos Santos and Soeterik in this volume), yet rarely empirically investigated. I find in particular the notions of 'positionality' and 'audience' key for understanding the relational nature of global education policy. In my earlier work on global education policy in Mongolia, I noticed that government officials frequently engage in double-talk. One talk is directed towards donors ('global speak') and is instrumental for securing external funding, and another, printed in party action programmes, funded from the national education budget, and distributed over the media, is addressed to a Mongolian audience ('local speak'). The first one is published in English and recycled in technical reports, education sector reviews and strategies that are funded by international donors. In contrast, the local speak is in Mongolian and is barely accessible to international consultants and researchers, leading donors to perpetuate the myth that the only reform projects that the Government of Mongolia is carrying out are the ones funded by international donors. It was in this context that I suggested that we examine policy bilingualism, that is, the two different scales or 'spaces' from which one and the same policy actor or state institution speaks or operates.

In his research, Tavis Jules takes the distinction a step further and analyses the different audiences that one and the same Caribbean government addresses in different policy documents (Jules 2012). He finds that the same government addresses different reform priorities and strategies, depending on whether the audience is a national, regional or international entity. His work on policy triangulism represents a fascinating study on the spatial or scalar dimension of globalization studies.

Theoretical debates on policy bilingualism, multi-scalarity or multi-spatiality of policy actors are crucial for abandoning the frequently made distinction between global (out there) and local (in here). It appears that the twin notions of 'positionality' and 'audience' helps to soften the dichotomy between external and internal that has afflicted globalization research. The twin notion first surfaced in the era of postmodern theories in the 1990s and nowadays also holds a prominent place in post-colonial and post-development studies.

The relational nature between the global, regional and local is not to be underestimated. The most dazzling phenomenon is that local politicians periodically invoke globalization, as a discourse, and present the condition of globalization toward their local audience as a quasi-external force for the sole purpose of generating reform pressure in their local context. The fact that a series of similar global education policies circumvent the globe is often taken as proof that national educational systems are converging toward the same reform package or global education policy. Note the circularity of the argument: local politicians first create the phantom of (vaguely defined) international standards to generate reform pressure; then they use the existence of such (self produced) standards as proof that all educational systems, including their own, must be aligned with them. To put it differently, 'globalisation' is a reality but also a phantom that is periodically mobilized for political and economic purposes. Robertson's distinction between globalization as a condition (real) and a discourse (imagined) comes to mind here (see Steiner-Khamsi 2004).

For all the reasons listed in this commentary, it is important to study re-contextualization and interpret why particular features of a global education policy have resonated in a particular policy context. Our interest does not lie with describing the global education policy (often reduced to a meaningless label when analysed comparatively) but rather with understanding the re-contextualized versions of the policy. It is the re-contextualized versions of one and the same global education policy that tells us something about context but also about the policy process and change.

References

Baker, D. P. and LeTendre, G. K. (2005), *National differences, global similarities. World culture and the future of schooling.* Stanford: Stanford University Press.

Drori, G. S., Meyer, J. W., Ramirez, F. O. and Schofer, E. (2003), *Science in the modern world polity. Institutionalization and globalization.* Stanford: Stanford University Press.

Hall, P. A. (1993), 'Policy paradigms, social learning, and the State: the case of economic policymaking in Britain', *Comparative Politics*, 25, (3), 275–96.

Jules, T. D. (2012), *Neither world polity nor local or national societies: Regionalization in the Global South – the Caribbean Community.* Berlin: Peter Lang.

Luhmann, N. (1990), *Essays on self-reference.* New York: Columbia University Press.

Rogers, E. M. (1995), *Diffusion of Innovations*, 4th edn. New York: Free Press.

Ramirez, F. O. (2003), 'The global model and national legacies', in K. Anderson-Levitt ed., *Local meanings, global schooling.* New York: Palgrave Macmillan, pp. 239–55.

Schriewer, J. (1990), 'The method of comparison and the need for externalization: Methodological criteria and sociological concepts', in J. Schriewer and Holmes ed., *Theories and methods in comparative education.* Frankfurt-am-Main: Peter Lang, pp. 25–83.

Steiner-Khamsi, G. (2004), 'Globalization in Education: Real or Imagined?', in G. Steiner-Khamsi ed., *The Global Politics of Educational Borrowing and Lending*. New York: Teachers College Press, p. 1–11.

—(2010), 'The Politics and Economics of Comparison'. *Comparative Education Review*, 54, (3), 323–42.

Takayama, K. (2010), 'Politics of externalization in reflexive times: Reinventing Japanese education reform discourses through 'Finnish success''. *Comparative Education Review*, 54, (1), 51–75.

Verger, A. (2011), 'Framing and selling global education policy: the promotion of public-private partnerships for education in low-income contexts'. *Journal of Education Policy*, doi: 10.1080/02680939.2011.623242.

Watts, D. J. (2003), *Six degrees: the science of a connected age*. New York: Norton.

Waldow, F. (2010), 'Der Traum vom "skandinavisch schlau Werden" – Drei Thesen zur Rolle Finnlands als Projektionsfläche in der gegenwärtigen Bildungsdebatte'. *Zeitschrift für Pädagogik*, 56, (4), 497–511.

—(2012), 'Standardisation and legitimacy: two concentral concepts in research on educational borrowing and lending', in G. Steiner-Khamsi and F. Waldow (eds), *Policy Borrowing and Lending*. London and New York: Routledge, pp. 411–27.

CHAPTER FOURTEEN

Global Education Policy: Creating Different Constituencies of Interest and Different Modes of Valorization

Roger Dale

From the opening page of the Introduction, the central unifying role of the idea of Global Education Policy (GEP) and development in the volume is very evident. All authors seem comfortable to operate under its auspices. The very wide range of instances and foci that make up the volume instantiates the potential reach most effectively. This is indeed an impressive range of studies that can make a serious claim to represent the state of the art.

What is also striking is the fact that despite the very wide range of cases, locations, objectives, sponsors, partnership models, levels of education, academic approaches and so on, the most consistent conclusion to be drawn from the separate projects and cases, and collectively across the projects and cases, is that most if not all of them appear to fail. Looking across the fascinating range of the projects and the varied and important detail reported in the various chapters it is evident that what they have in common, besides involving 'outside' 'interventions', in typically national education systems, is that little if any net gain or successful achievement of objectives is reported.

Equally notable are the similarities in the accounts of the very diverse range of projects and examples contained in the volume. On the one hand, there is a recurring account of what is seen as 'technical' failure, including inadequacy of conceptualisation of the problem, ineffectiveness or inappropriateness of implementation mechanisms, lack of capacity, insufficient funding, etc. On the other hand, we find discourses of cultural disjunction, which are especially clearly and effectively reported in chapters that contrast two or more examples of the implementation of the same programme (Jakobi, Poppema, Altinyelken, Deventer-Wells and Sayed, for instance).

What is also notable about these accounts is not just that they undoubtedly shed light on the difficulties of 'doing development,' but that we would not have been surprised to read similar accounts of doing development at almost any point in the last three decades and more. Over that period, perhaps the dominant accounts of the shortcomings of educational aid have been (largely from the right, e.g. Easterly 2006) that it is inefficient, ineffective and counter-productive, and from the left that it is a form of perpetuating colonial relationships between the West and the rest (Amin 2011). Now while there are more criteria for appraising and evaluating educational aid from the richer parts of the world to the poorer than are apparent in the simple conception of success implied by these accounts, and more dimensions to understanding the political relationships involved than are captured in 'colonialism' discourses, nevertheless that apparent continuity does – properly and importantly – generate the questions: 1) why does it persist in these forms?; 2) what is different about GEP?; and above all, 3) why do we keep doing it?

In terms of the first of these questions it is clear from the wider critical literature around the topic that the aid relationship does generate a complex range of associations and affiliations between the multiple stakeholders and interests that it brings into being, which may be quite distinct from the formal goals of projects. And we might accept that it does satisfy some needs for all or most of the parties involved, even though these needs may not be directly related to the aims of the project or intervention itself. For donors, it is a means of demonstrating commitment. For recipients, aid provides means of accessing goods and services that would not otherwise be available, irrespective of their relationship to the aims of the project. However, the second question, about the difference that globalization makes, is the core concern of this volume, and I will try to unpick a little in this brief contribution. Finally, addressing the third question a little obliquely may enable us to take a small step toward understanding it.

The editors recognize the importance of the question of the difference GEP makes, and they address it head on in their Introduction. Quite rightly, and productively, they see it as what Jamie Peck and Nik Theodore (2010, p. 172) refer to as the 'context of context', the macro institutional patternings, ... scalar architectures, (and) broad-gauge regulatory variegation', in other words, the broader structures and conditions that frame and give meaning to new forms of the discursive and material power of national and international institutions. They proceed to catalogue what they refer to (perhaps somewhat infelicitously) as 'impact dimensions' of globalization in education policy, pointing to the multiple ways that policy is affected; that it generates new problems for education policy; alters the capacity of welfare states; implies the deterritorialisation of the education policy process; revitalizes the role of international (sic) players and brings new ones in; benefits from ICT; transforms the legal framework of transnational education; creates a private transnational education market; as neoliberalism, frames education policy ideas; and finally, and more positively, fosters the development of transnational social justice movements.

One useful way of putting this kind of list to work is to employ Bob Jessop 2002's categories of structural and strategic selectivity. Put very simply, structural selectivity might be seen to represent the 'context of context' through which the various cases of the 'impact' of GEP are framed: why is this kind of 'development' occurring at this time, in these places, in these forms? Major elements of the 'context of context' are common to all the cases elaborated in the text, most importantly, though very broadly, elements of what is known as neoliberalism. Strategic selectivity relates, equally broadly, to the perceived options open to the actors involved in the specific circumstances of a particular development relationship. What possible courses of action seem to be available to them, under what circumstances and with what likely outcomes? The value of such an approach is that it provides us with a means of drawing back somewhat from the particular cases, and potentially enables us to examine them in a comparative way, so as to be able to explain the differences between them. These differences are quite evident in the cases described in the text, but we do not have a means of comparing them, or bringing them into productive conjunction with each other. This is a theoretical as well as a methodological issue. It assumes that there may be explanations for the similarities and differences between the cases. For such comparison to be able to lead to explanation (of the different forms and roles of a hypothesized GEP), we would need to go beyond the restrictions of juxtaposition of cases, to look more closely at their constitution; this is not a matter of the number of cases; juxtaposing more cases does not take us closer to understanding what, if anything, makes them comparable. This entails a double analytic shift – from concrete to abstract, and from simple to complex.

One simple basis for doing this is to use what I have referred to as the 'Education Questions' (see Dale 2000, 2005), which, very briefly, shift from the observed practices of education, to the socio-political conditions that enabled (but did not require) them – the level of strategic selectivity – to the level referred to here as the context of context, or structural selectivity, where the broad conditions framing the possibilities of education policies are laid down.

The other main component of the context of context is what might be called the discursive context, and recent work in critical geography (e.g. Sheppard et al. 2010; Silvey et al. 2011) has shed valuable light on this through the changing nature of what might be called the 'development paradigm.' Sheppard and Leitner point to what they see as a 'continuous socio-spatial imagery' underlying all conceptions of development: 'one that presents capitalism as capable in principle of bringing development and prosperity to all.... It has repeatedly legitimized discourses of first world expertise even as the policies based in this expertise repeatedly fail' (186, 192). It is based on: (1) a Rostovian conception of a single trajectory of development, 'that has the effect of presenting places with no choices about what development means, and of ranking (them) on a (single) scale of development' which has settler colonies at the top; (2) 'an imaginary of globalisation and capitalist development as process that is flattening out the world, creating a level playing field that equalises opportunities everywhere' (192), but which (3) does not mean a homogeneous world 'so much as one where differences need not be sources of inequality,' and where 'cultural differences are recognised and valorised in terms of how they can be utilised in the market, ... (but) where social and cultural differences that are not regarded as commodifiable are dismissed as barriers to development, in need of modernisation' (ibid.). One of the key accompaniments of these changes in the post Washington Consensus has been the 'governance turn,' the shift away from one-size-fits-all approaches to one that recognizes the importance of local institutions. The key point here, of course, is that this shift does not signal or represent a shift away from neoliberalism, but an intensification of it; the move to governance essentially means eroding differences between state and market, as states themselves are led to operate according to market principles.

This is crucial to the understanding of the nature of the GEP and of the explanation of the differences between the cases presented in this book. For what they crucially point to is an assumption of sufficient similarity of condition for all cases to be subjected to the same 'treatment.' Key to the basis of the exceptions identified in the paradigm is the nature of the cultural and social differences, and whether, how far and in what ways they may be seen as commodifiable, or as obstacles to commodification that are to be overcome through modernisation. We see here a broad but fundamental distinction between the logic of intervention to be employed in different cases. At one end are those countries whose cultural differences (from the West, let it be remembered) are such that they can be valorized – classic cases here, of course, are the 'Asian tigers' (a term that sounds oddly old-fashioned, as the possibilities of using them as a model for countries with other, less commodifiable differences, recedes). The problem here is how to valorize the differences. At the opposite end of the scale, the problem is how to remove, ignore or neutralize the differences in countries whose cultural patterns are not so supportive of capitalist marketisation. This is a problematisation to which the governance turn is a clear response, and creates a project in which education is effectively handed a dual role, as a process and as an outcome.

What we see here is the consistent application of a strategy – imposing western capitalism as the model for all – which remains valid, but calls for different tactics as the relative commodification possibilities themselves are changed by changing global regional and local relations.

However, even this approach contains some extremely important potential lacunae. It tends to see 'commodification' as the only relevant outcome, and thus to see the donors, 'the West', as the definers of and the (thwarted) beneficiaries from local cultural and social differences. In addition, where they do not have the desired effects on 'local' situations, western interventions are seen to have no (relevant) consequences for local social and cultural differences. This leads to consequences in the form of interventions being recognized only through a cost-effectiveness lens, and the assumption that the particular modes of intervention create, or recognize, only particular forms and beneficiaries of valorization.

The crucial point here is that as well as threats to existing groups, development projects necessarily generate new constituencies of interest, and produce a range of different opportunities for different groups – and not only for those designated as beneficiaries. What this means is that the balance sheet of development effects cannot be confined to that stated in the prospectus (and it is this that lies at the heart of the response to the question: why do they keep doing it?) In a nutshell, the answer is that education development/GEP interventions produce a range of groups, constituencies, organisations, etc., with a powerful interest in maintaining those interests through the medium of the development paradigm as implemented in the 'traditional way'. These groups run from national governments to village stores. The interventions also, of course, create new 'disadvantaged' groups and intensify the disadvantage of others, as well as creating new groups of beneficiaries. And a major consequence of this is that this uneven distribution of opportunities and beneficiaries itself changes the 'local' social and cultural differences and challenges in ways significant for the 'reception' of the next wave of interventions, with new commodifiable interests and barriers to development.

One example of this is the creation of comprador groups of intermediaries and go-betweens at national and local levels who facilitate and in many cases enable processes of international intervention. A good account – mutatis mutandis – of the nature and work of comprador groups can be found in the case of their role in making possible the transformation of former Communist countries in Eastern Europe.

'The international environment in which transition and post-transition policy-making took place had indeed a crucial role in explaining final outcomes. But there is a missing link. The pressures of the transnational environment had first to be translated, embodied and expressed by key actors in the state – the comprador service sector. Domestic politics plays a crucial role in this process. Domestic politics, however, cannot be understood as completely internally determined. It must be treated as an instantiation of locally materialising transnational processes. Transnationally constituted domestic politics explains both the initial inward-oriented outcomes and later shifts toward the competition state. The emergence of externally oriented competition states has been conditioned upon the unfolding hegemonic role of ... the comprador service sector. This created a field of force that allowed this sector to come to the forefront as its interests become increasingly 'universal'. The role and agency of this sector, however, do not explain the policy as such. They work as a linking factor that influences when, in which way, and in what form such a shift toward the competition state takes place. The comprador service sector helped to translate the structural power of transnational capital into tactical forms of power that enabled agential power to work in sync with the interests of the multinationals' (Drahokoupil 2008, p. 176).

Though this example of the 'transnational constitution of domestic politics' is drawn from a quite specific time and place, the role of the 'transnational in the domestic' is clearly crucial in creating the chances of success of the transnational project. That project does not contain the conditions of its own success; it is dependent on the involvement of key domestic interests. It shows very clearly the need for local spaces to be opened up in which transnational projects can flourish, and which can be occupied and valorized by different social groups. We can see examples of this in several chapters in this volume (and note that this piece focusses on the chapters not discussed in Gita Steiner Khamsi's response), and I will refer to them very briefly now.

Though these points are not fully developed in the contributions, one 'big message' that characterizes the studies in the book is that local recipients of GEP are not passive, but active 'strategic selectors' from what is offered. We might say the preferred account of the nature and influence of the GEP in the volume is the 'mediating, recontextualising, even undermining or openly resisting' (Altinyelken) reception given by different groups to manifestations of the GEP within recipient countries. However, one element of these forms of response is that they tend to be reactive rather than responsive; that is, they might be seen to adjust to the existence of the GEP, rather than seeking to alter it more fundamentally. 'Recontextualization' may be seen as an exception to that claim, though it might be noted that for a concept that is asked to carry a considerable burden in this volume, it is used rather loosely and imprecisely at times. More broadly, there is a tendency for the studies to concentrate their focus quite narrowly on matters that are obviously – and self-identifyingly – associated with education, sometimes quite narrowly conceived as schooling; they tend to be 'strategic *sectoral* selectors'. There can be no objection to the focus on the relationship between GEP and schooling, but this should not occur at the expense of recognising the wider implications of education policy. It is interesting that in studying educational development, we tend to concentrate much more on things that are obviously directly related to access to schooling, for instance, rather than on the deeper solution relations with which access, for instance, is implicated, with rather less attention paid to the kinds of issues addressed in the sociology of western education.

So we do find in the book a range of interesting and very different examples of forms of local brokering of opportunities. Stenvoll-Wells and Sayed, for instance, show how education decentralisation, a significant plank of GEP, was appropriated in the rather different cases of South Africa and Zimbabwe, as a reaction to colonial rule, where educational decisions that concerned whole populations were taken by minority white governments. They also record that, in practice, groups with the 'necessary cultural capital' dominated the supposedly participatory school governance. This might be seen as a classic instance of the valorization of parts of the reform policy by particular groups for their own interests (and it should be noted that such valorization need not take only the form of seizing educational advantage, as we discuss in the section on the comprador groups.)

Altinyelken also shows how the same reform of pedagogical approaches in the rather different cases of Uganda and Turkey allowed – possibly encouraged –the emergence of a distinct group of 'modern and progressive' teachers, a group likely to be identified as future educational leaders, while Unterhalter notes a similar phenomenon in her case study. A further example of particular groups retaining power in the face of policies intended – at least formally – to democratize education governance with a rhetoric of local participation is offered by Poppema, through the example of the use of school-based management to advance the project of 'Partnership for Educational Revitalisation in the Americas' (PREAL). These were hugely instrumental schemes, aimed at undermining 'politically dangerous' civil society organisations in El Salvador and Nicaragua, and at the depoliticisation of socio-economic organisations and the building of new forms of socio-economic coexistence at local level.

Unterhalter's chapter on gender equality aspects of the MDGs and EFAs produces valuable evidence of the different levels of penetration – and perhaps immediate relevance of discourses of poverty, human rights and gender equality, with the more 'metropolitan' staff involved embracing such aspirations fully, but 'district education officers, primary school teachers and rural NGO staff' seeing poverty, rights, gender equality discourses as 'other people' projects. Jakobi's chapter addresses the most 'global' of the discourses broached in the volume, that of Lifelong Learning, in what might be seen as a classic case of 'policy alignment without policy implementation.' Her focus is on Africa, and in particular Nigeria and South Africa, but she finds neither country implementing the reform fully. However, this is an important and interesting example of how GEP might be seen to work. While neither country, and especially Nigeria, is fully engaged with Lifelong Learning in practice, both have made at least symbolic shifts of policy to be seen to align with it, South Africa though the development of a qualifications framework, and Nigeria with a concept of basic education. Of particular significance here is that this major GEP effectively involves a major break with the philosophy, and especially the patterns, of education worldwide, from an activity spanning a number of years to one covering a lifetime.

This has, of course, been well recognized by students of education and development, but may now be entering a quite new phase, with the explicit creation of what amounts to comprador bourgeoisies in the traditional sense, of local representatives of international or global capital, in the form of public-private partnerships in education, discussed in Verger and VanderKaaij's chapter. Rather than valorization of development education through other forms of capital, which is made possible because it is involved with both sides of the partnership – cultural, social, political, etc. – the privatisation/commercialisation of education, which is being very actively pursued by the World Bank – opens up opportunities for direct financial comprador operation in education. This is itself a very significant outcome of the governance turn, and one that opens up a wide range of possible consequences, outside the specific consequences for access, quality and control of education itself.

Conclusion

As the editors make very clear, GEP raises serious conceptual issues. The volume itself underpins and illustrates the sense that 'global' talk entails recognition that that involves not just a quantitative increase in the diffusion of similar policies, but fundamental reappraisals of what is meant by 'global' 'education' and 'policy', that recognize and respond to qualitative political, economic and cultural changes that the GEP concept at its best and most rigorous summarizes and represents. So, for instance, 'good governance' is not 'a form of government by any other name', but a quite distinct phenomenon, a way of framing and constituting new and distinct problems, and of creating 'solutions' that go with rather than against the grain of the dominant neoliberalism, and of assembling new forms of education strategies, tactics and mechanisms. It has done this through a rich collection of closely observed case studies.

This brief contribution has aimed to suggest that it is not only through the framing and attempted implementation of its goals that GEP has effects beyond as well as within the education sector, but that it also has significant consequences, through the opportunities it offers to various kinds of groups to develop new modes of valorization, beyond as well as within the education sector.

References

Amin, S. (2011), *Maldevelopment: Anatomy of a Global Failure*, 2nd edn. Oxford: Pambazuka Press.

Dale, R. (2000), 'Globalisation and Education: Demonstrating 'A Common World Educational Culture' or Locating 'A Globally Structured Educational Agenda'?'. *Educational Theory,* 50, (4), 427–49.

—(2005), 'Globalisation, knowledge economy and comparative education'. *Comparative Education,* 41, (2), 117–49.

Drahokoupil, J. (2008), 'The rise of the comprador service sector: The politics of state transformation in Central and Eastern Europe'. *Polish Sociological Review,* 57, (2), 175–89.

Easterly, W. (2006), *The White Man's Burden.* New York: Penguin.

Jessop, B. (2002), *The Future of the Capitalist State.* Cambridge: Polity.

Peck, J. and Theodore, N. (2010), 'Mobilising Policy: Models, Methods and Mutations'. *Geoforum,* 41, (2), 169–74.

Sheppard, E. and Leitner, H. (2010), 'Quo vadis neoliberalism? The remaking of global capitalist governance after the Washington Consensus'. *Geoforum,* 41, 185–94.

Silvey, R. and Rankin, K. (2011), 'Development geography: Critical development studies and political geographic imaginaries'. *Progress in Human Geography,* 35 (5), 696–704.

INDEX